REALITY

REALITY

Pon Spillers
August 03, 2013

PETER KINGSLEY

First published in the United States in 2003 by
The Golden Sufi Center
P.O. Box 456, Point Reyes, California 94956-0456
info@goldensufi.org
www.goldensufi.org

Fourth Printing 2010.

Printed and bound by Thomson-Shore

Kingsley, Peter.
    Reality / Peter Kingsley.
        p. cm.
    Includes bibliographical references.
    ISBN 1-890350-08-7 (alk. paper) -- ISBN 1-890350-09-5 (pbk. : alk.paper)
    1. Parmenides--Miscellanea. 2. Empedocles--Miscellanea. 3. Reality--Miscellanea.
I. Title.

B235.P24K57 2003
182--dc21   2003051436

ISBN 10: 1-890350-09-5
ISBN 13: 978-1-890350-09-3

CONTENTS

I

THE FINAL JOURNEY

ONE

I will make a road in the wilderness,
rivers in the desert

Isaiah

1

I had better write these things down before they are lost for another two thousand years.

Please don't get me wrong. What I have to say is everywhere: in the air we breathe, each falling leaf, in every single object we see. But to make it conscious, to snap out of the fairytale spell we live under—that's another matter.

This will make a strange story: strange, because it's the story behind the story of our lives. If it was about anything else, if it was simply about things that once might have happened long ago, then we would be free to go on forgetting. But it's not, so it won't leave you alone or give you any peace.

So often we try to convince ourselves we are living a full, contented life. But there is always something pulling at our heart; ambition, restlessness, are just its shadows. And it will go on tearing at our hearts until we start to acknowledge what is missing.

Perhaps this is a story you will be tempted to believe. Let me warn you gently though that, if you do, you will find yourself losing a hold on your other beliefs. The stakes are high.

You might feel inclined to suppose there is some kind of halfway house where you can have things both ways. But believe me, I can tell you from experience: there is none. If you want to keep a grip on what you think you already know, you will have to dismiss what I say.

Either way, it makes no real difference to me. My job is just to tell the tale—that's all. And besides: there are some things that, once they are said, there is no unsaying them.

They are written in stone.

And the writing on the stone is about you. And you are the stone.

Towards the end of the sixth century before Christ, someone called Parmenides was born.

His home: a small city called Velia in the south of Italy. But if we want to understand Parmenides' background, simply focusing on southern Italy is not enough—not nearly enough.

The city of Velia was created and built just a few years before Parmenides was born. The people who founded it were Greeks, and they happened to be known as Phocaeans because they came from Phocaea: a town hundreds of miles away from Velia towards the east, on the coast of what now is western Turkey. It was about 540 BC when they were forced out of their old hometown by Persians and made to wander in the Mediterranean sea, back and forward, up and down, looking for a new place to settle and live.

The story of their wanderings—of heroes in search of lost heroes, of men and women along with children staking their lives on whether or not they could find the answer to a riddling oracle of Apollo—is such a romance that historians have sometimes wanted to dismiss it as a piece of fiction. But all kinds of discoveries made here and there in recent years have shown how much truth it contains.

And besides: when dealing with Phocaeans, bit by bit we have to open our minds. For people like them, fiction was a fact and what we delight in referring to as facts were a fiction that had not yet been invented.

In all of the drama leading up to their final arrival at Velia, just those few brief years before Parmenides was born, one particular point needs bearing in mind.

This is that the Phocaeans were a very, very conservative people. After they moved out to the west they kept their ancient Anatolian customs unchanged and intact for centuries—close to a thousand years. Even in their nightmare situation, with the Persian army waiting at the gates and not a moment left to waste or spare, they made a priority of rescuing every single object they could that would help them keep the thread of their religious traditions unbroken wherever they managed to go.

It could seem a small point, not worth much attention. But for our story it's quite crucial.

The Phocaeans could seem a small people, worth forgetting. But appearances can be deceptive.

3

You may wonder why I trouble myself, and you, with these details.

It all has to do with Parmenides.

This man Parmenides played an extraordinary, almost inconceivable, role in the West: in shaping the world and the culture we live in.

The chances are good that you have never even heard of him, and there is a reason for that. People have always had a strange tendency to keep him just behind the scenes—even when writing about him. There is something about Parmenides that falls outside all the familiar frames of our understanding.

For a long time now he has been recognized among specialists and historians as the founder of logic; as the father of rationalism. And as you can see from this last expression, it's not just a matter of his special significance for people studying the past. It's not even a matter of his importance in laying the foundations for philosophy and science, for the whole process of modern learning and education. What really is at stake here is even more basic than that.

It's the origins of our western culture, of how we think and reason. And this is something that intimately affects us all.

Talking about reason and logic is easy enough. But to understand what they are, to catch a glimpse of what lies behind them, is a very different affair. For the fact is that what we have ended up calling logic and reason are just frauds, posing as what they are not.

Reason is one of those things—like common sense—that everyone is assumed to know the meaning of. Already as children we are told to be reasonable, which essentially means doing what others want us to do. We are all supposed to have a clear idea of what reason is. But there is no one who does.

The closer you look at it the vaguer it becomes. And the closer you look at people who claim to be most rational, the more irrational they turn out to be. We live in a world of shadows without even realizing it, or understanding what has happened.

As for logic, this too is not what it seems—or what it once was. Originally it had nothing to do with complicated formulas, fancy calculations. Its purpose was to awaken: to touch and transform every aspect of a human being.

What we refer to nowadays as logic is like a baby girl shuffling around self-importantly in her mother's shoes. With our endless learned debates over the last two thousand years about religion and reason, logic and science, we have lost any grip on reality and been behaving like little children. It's time we started growing up.

The people I will be talking about in this book are not imaginary. And they come not from Central America or India or some exotic far-eastern world but from the roots of our western civilization. They are the roots of our western civilization; they are where this culture of ours comes from. Slowly, gradually, they have been misunderstood. And, as a part of that process, we have misunderstood ourselves.

This is a story we are all a part of: a book in which we are the pages.

The implications of this misunderstanding are not ordinary or mediocre. They are so huge, so all-embracing, that we can hardly grasp them any more. Perhaps the simplest way of describing the situation would be to say that, two and a half thousand years ago in the West, we were given a gift—and in our childishness we threw away the instructions for how to use it. We felt we knew what we were playing with. And, as a result, western civilization may soon be nothing but an experiment that failed.

The writings of Parmenides, and other people like him, survive in fragments. Scholars have played all sorts of games with them. For centuries they have experimented with distorting them and torturing them until they seem to yield a sense exactly the opposite of their original meaning. Then they argue about their significance and put them on show like exhibits in a museum.

And no one understands quite how important they are. Even though they only survive in bits and pieces, they are far less fragmentary than we are. And they are much more than dead words. They are like the mythological treasure—the invaluable object that has been lost and misused and has to be rediscovered at all costs.

But this is not mythology, or fiction. It's reality. Fiction is like sitting on a goldmine and dreaming about gold; it's everything that happens when you forget this.

There is absolutely nothing mystical in what I am saying. It's very simple, completely down-to-earth and practical. We tend to imagine we have our feet on the ground when we are dealing with facts. And yet facts are of absolutely no significance in themselves: it's just as easy to get lost in facts as it is to get lost in fictions.

They have their value, and we have to use them—but use them to go beyond them. Facts on their own are like sitting on top of a goldmine and scratching at the dust around our feet with a little stick.

All our facts, like all our reasoning, are just a façade. This book is about what they have covered over, about the reality that lies behind. It's about the buried treasure that is our birthright, our heritage; and about what we have to be prepared for if we want to reclaim it.

4

The closer we move back towards Parmenides, the stranger everything becomes.

The trouble is that we lost the ability to learn from strangenesses a long time ago. They frighten us, question our assumptions—and the more deeply they affect us, the more threatened we feel. So it has become far easier to create a safe, substitute world instead; see only what we want to see and ignore the rest.

Most modern translations of what Parmenides said bear little real relation to the meaning of his original Greek. Pages and pages are published about him every year—interpreting him in the light of contemporary interests and issues, splitting endless hairs. But what is most essential is left completely untouched.

There is some basic ground that has to be covered, some essential points that there is no escaping. We have absolutely no choice. As a culture and civilization we may think we are progressing. But in spite of our love for creative and destructive toys, we are going nowhere.

We are just like someone who has caught a strap on a door handle. The only way forward is to start by going back—is to detach ourselves from the misunderstandings about our past and about what we are.

Parmenides' reputation as the inventor of logic rests on a poem he wrote. And already here we encounter something strange. There was no need for him to write poetry. He could just as easily have used dry prose instead.

It's quite true that for a long time he has been dismissed as a bad poet. But this is a judgement based on pure prejudice. It goes back to the old belief, first formulated with any clarity by Aristotle, that logic and poetry have nothing in common— and that if someone concerned with finding the truth even thinks of becoming a poet then the result will be a disaster.

The fact is that Parmenides' poem is not a disaster. A few modern scholars who have tried to approach his writings with fresh eyes have realized he created some of the most beautiful and subtle lines of poetry ever written in any language, not just Greek. And besides: this dismissal of Parmenides as a poet stems from an assumption that the basic aim of poetry is to entertain. As we will gradually see, Parmenides' poem served a very different purpose.

And then, apart from the question of how he chose to express himself, there is the question of what it is that he said.

Certainly he wrote about logic—but only in the central section of his poem, in the second of three parts. Somehow, it has become the done thing to slide over the first part and quickly forget about the last. You may have noticed that one important aspect of learning to reason involves mastering the ability to focus on a fraction of the whole and overlook everything else.

Parmenides explains in detail how he came to know what he knows. He gives gentle hints on how we need to prepare ourselves if we want to come close to an understanding of the things he says. He offers clear warnings about the traps, the problems that stand in the way.

But no one nowadays has the humility or patience to take these indications and warnings seriously. People rush straight to what he says about logic, and are so confident in their ability to ignore instructions that they never even notice how hopelessly entangled they have become.

Ours has become a culture of convenience; but learning about ourselves is rather inconvenient because it turns the world we live in upside down.

And with someone like Parmenides there are no shortcuts. We simply have to start at the beginning.

5

And for Parmenides it all starts not with thinking, or scratching
our heads, but like this:

The mares that carry me as far as longing can reach
rode on, once they had come and fetched me onto the legendary
road of the divinity that carries the man who knows
through the vast and dark unknown. And on I was carried
as the mares, aware just where to go, kept carrying me
straining at the chariot; and young women led the way.
And the axle in the hubs let out the sound of a pipe
blazing from the pressure of the two well-rounded wheels
at either side, as they rapidly led on: young women, girls,
daughters of the Sun who had left the Mansions of Night
for the light and pushed back the veils from their faces
with their hands.
There are the gates on the pathways of Night and Day,
held fast in place between the lintel above and a threshold of stone.
They reach right up into the heavens, filled with gigantic doors.
And the keys—that now open, now lock—are held fast by
Justice: she who always demands exact returns. And with
soft seductive words the girls cunningly persuaded her to
push back immediately, just for them, the bar that bolts
the gates. And as the doors flew open, making the bronze
axles with their pegs and nails spin—now one, now the other—
in their pipes, they created a gaping chasm. Straight through and
on the girls held fast their course for the chariot and horses,
straight down the road.

And the goddess welcomed me kindly, and took
my right hand in hers and spoke these words as she addressed me:
"Welcome young man, partnered by immortal charioteers,
reaching our home with the mares that carry you. For it was
no hard fate that sent you travelling this road—so far away
from the beaten track of humans—but Rightness, and Justice.
And what's needed is for you to learn all things: both the unshaken
heart of persuasive Truth and the opinions of mortals
in which there is nothing that can truthfully be trusted at all.
But even so, this too you will learn—how beliefs based on
appearance ought to be believable as they travel all through
all there is."

And the clue to the whole poem lies already in the first line.

The one crucial factor in this strange affair that for Parmenides influences everything—that determines just how far on this journey he can actually go—is longing.

The Greek word he uses is *thumos*, and *thumos* means the energy of life itself. It's the raw presence in us that senses and feels; the massed power of our emotional being. Above all it's the energy of passion, appetite, yearning, longing.

Since the time of Parmenides we have learned so well to hedge it in, dominate it, punish and control it. But with him it's what comes first, right at the beginning. And there is a profound significance in this, because what he is saying is that—left to itself—longing makes it possible for us to go all the way to where we really need to go.

There is no reasoning with passion and longing, although we like to deceive ourselves by believing there is. All we ever do is reason with ourselves about the form our longing will take. We reason that if we find a better job we will be content, but we never are. We reason that if we go somewhere special we will be happy; but when we get there we start wanting to go somewhere else. We reason that if we were to sleep with the lover of our dreams we would be fulfilled. And yet even if we were to manage that, it would still not be enough.

What we call human nature means being pulled by the nose in a hundred different directions and ending up going nowhere very fast.

But although there is no reasoning with our passion, it has a tremendous intelligence of its own. The only trouble is that we keep interfering; keep breaking it up into tiny pieces, scattering it everywhere. Our minds always trick us into focusing on the little things we think we want—rather than on the energy of wanting itself.

If we can bear to face our longing instead of finding endless ways to keep satisfying it and trying to escape it, it begins to show us a glimpse of what lies behind the scenes. It opens up a devastating perspective where everything is turned on its head: where fulfilment becomes a limitation, accomplishment turns into a trap. And it does this with an intensity that scrambles our thoughts and forces us straight into the present.

Parmenides' poem is not for academics. There is nothing scholarly here at all. The word "scholar" means, literally, a woman or man of leisure. Scholars are people with time on their hands, even when they are busy: time to waste, time to kill. But to understand Parmenides is a serious matter. It demands the same intensity and urgency he talks about— the urgency of our own being.

And for that, there is no time at all to spare.

6

In this strange world of myth and mythical beings evoked by Parmenides there seems, at first, absolutely nothing familiar to hold on to.

What he is describing is a journey to end all journeys: way beyond any ordinary human experience, "far away from the beaten track of humans." But it's only natural to want to reduce something so unusual to more comfortably familiar terms.

And basically what has happened is that a tremendous amount of energy has been put into explaining the journey away.

It has been put aside as nothing but a rhetorical device, an allegory; as just a vague poetic attempt at describing how the philosopher leaves confusion behind for clarity, darkness for enlightenment.

Of course we are free to use whatever devices we choose to dispose of Parmenides' journey. But before we do that, it can be a good idea to look at what he has to say.

And the fact is that really there is nothing vague in it at all. Even when it seems vague, this is because the vagueness serves a very specific purpose. Each image plays its part in a completely coherent whole. Every single detail has its own particular place.

Parmenides is guided on his journey by young girls, Daughters of the Sun. They have come from the Mansions of Night which were well known in Greek myth as the depths of darkness at the furthest edges of existence, beside the great chasm called Tartarus, where earth and heaven have their roots. This is the place where the world above meets the world below; where all the opposites we feel and experience while alive come together and join.

And this is where the sun goes back to rest at home with his family every night.

As for those gates that Parmenides is brought to on the pathways of Night and Day, they are the gates opening into the underworld—separating this familiar world of ours from the vast chasm just behind.

And Justice, who guards the gates, is a familiar figure too. She is the goddess who watches over the underworld: the ruthless source of order, origin of all laws.

As for the nameless goddess who greets Parmenides, it's not time to say anything about her yet.

In short, the Daughters of the Sun have come along to fetch him from the world of the living and take him right back to where they belong. This is no journey from confusion to clarity; from darkness into light. On the contrary, the journey Parmenides is describing is exactly the opposite. He is travelling straight into the ultimate night that no human being could possibly survive without divine protection. He is being taken to the heart of the underworld, the world of the dead.

But then there is a question that has to be asked: a very basic question.

What did it mean for a real flesh-and-blood person in ancient Greece—not some mythical or legendary figure—to make a journey consciously, deliberately, knowingly into another world?

And in particular: how could such a person go down or claim to go down to the world of death while still alive, touch the powers that live there, learn from them, and then come back to the world of the living?

The answer is extremely simple.

There was a specific and established technique among various groups of people for making the journey to the world of the dead; for dying before you died.

It involved isolating yourself in a dark place, lying down in complete stillness, staying motionless for hours or days. First the body would go silent, then eventually the mind. And this stillness is what gave access to another world, a world of utter paradox; to a totally different state of awareness. Sometimes the state was described as a kind of dream. Sometimes it was referred to as like a dream but not a dream, as really a third type of consciousness quite different from either waking or sleeping.

There used to be a whole technical language associated with the procedure; an entire mythical geography. And there was a name that the Greeks, and then the Romans, gave to this technique.

They called it incubation.

As soon as you come to this basic connection between Parmenides' journey and the practice of incubation, things start falling into place.

For example when Parmenides meets the goddess who is going to teach him everything he will go on to formulate with such care in the rest of his poem, she addresses him straightaway as *kouros*: a word that means "young man," "boy."

Scholars have often asked why, and come up with the most extraordinary solutions. But the answer is very straightforward, and at the same time extremely subtle.

In fact it has been known for a long time that the Greek term *kouros* didn't just refer to physical age. It pointed to vastly complex traditions and rituals associated with bravery, manhood, initiation—and, in particular, with the initiatory journey into another world.

That other world is the world of the gods where the *kouros* finds a source of nourishment and guidance that nothing in the ordinary world of humans can ever give him; where if he is lucky, divinely protected, he can encounter the divinity who will become his immortal parent and teacher and guide.

And there is one other Greek worth mentioning here alongside Parmenides.

His name was Epimenides and he came from Crete, an island in the eastern Mediterranean not very far from the coast of Turkey. He, too, wrote poetry; gave accounts of what he learned in the underworld. And it has often been noticed how—just like Parmenides—he made a point of describing his direct encounters in another world with the mythical figures of Justice and Truth.

The stories about him go on to say that after these encounters he became famous for his role in making laws: well known as an executor of justice in his own right. It's no coincidence at all that Parmenides, according to the best of sources, also became a famous lawgiver for his own city. On the contrary, in time we will see what an important detail that is.

And on the island of Crete the people addressed Epimenides, in their own dialect, as a *kouros*. This, too, is far more than a coincidence. For we happen to know that the ancient *kouros* traditions on Crete had the closest of links with *kouros* traditions at one other place in particular.

That was Phocaea—the home of Parmenides' ancestors before they sailed out west to settle at Velia.

But there is more to all of this than justice or lawgiving or the title *kouros*.

Epimenides also had a huge reputation as a successful healer and prophet. We are even told that he recited his poetry for the sake of healing. The laws he helped to create came to him through prophecy: through his ability to see how justice is carried out in another world. And the purpose of those laws was to heal cities as well as people.

There was a word that Greeks in general tended to use for describing someone like Epimenides. It was Iatromantis, a name that simply means "healer–prophet."

And tradition describes how Epimenides became a Iatromantis after sleeping for years in a cave and being carried, while he lay there quite motionless, into the strange world of Justice and Truth.

In other words: he was taught everything he knew through the practice of incubation.

Iatromantis figures were a breed apart among the ancient Greeks.

They were specialists at invoking other states of awareness, in themselves and in others.

And apart from being famous because of their poetry, one particular technique they were well known for was the incantatory device of repeating and repeating the same words.

This point has a very real significance. You may have noticed that at the start of his poem Parmenides keeps on repeating the same words over and over again.

One of the more obvious examples comes right at the beginning, where he repeats the word for "carry" no less than four times in quick succession. This repetition is so striking, in the original Greek as well as in English, that it's almost unbelievable how virtually no one has even noticed it.

Of all the scholars who have studied Parmenides, only two have bothered to say much about it. And in line with the belief that he was a hopeless poet they totally dismiss the phenomenon as "naive" and "amateurish," as an "awkward and pointless repetition of the same word," as a classic example of "carelessness" and "expressive failure."

However, they are wrong. A careless poet might possibly repeat a word once by accident. But this repetition of the same word four times right at the start of a poem is neither careless nor accidental: it's deliberate. And if you look at the kind of systematic repetition of words found in Greek poetry, right through from the earliest hymns to the latest magical texts that were written down centuries after Parmenides, you will see it was used for a very particular purpose—either as a technique of magical, incantatory healing or as a way of evoking another state of consciousness.

It's no accident, either, that shamans are famous for singing poetry in which they keep repeating the words for "journeying" and being "carried." And they do this not just to describe the ecstatic journeys they make into another world but as a way of invoking them: of bringing them about.

That, too, is no coincidence. The Iatromantis healers in Greece and shamans in Siberia, or Central Asia, are part of one and the same phenomenon. Modern historians have tried hard to create all kinds of divisions between them—in language and culture, space and time. But the only barriers that exist are the barriers in our understanding.

Iatromantis figures always, in one way or another, have their origins on the far eastern fringes of the Greek world. The earliest among them left accounts of journeys into Central Asia, or even came from there themselves. And they introduced the Greeks to traditions and legends shared by people living in the regions not just of Central Asia but of Mongolia, India, Tibet.

For Greeks, the god of the far north and the distant northeast was Apollo. And Apollo happened to be the god, the divine model, of the Iatromantis—of wandering healers and prophets who were known for covering huge distances on foot but also for travelling into other worlds while their bodies stayed completely still.

"Taken by Apollo" was one of the more simple expressions used by Greeks to convey the state of these poets and travellers into worlds ordinary people shuddered even to think about, let alone dared to go. And especially in Anatolia, where the Greek world met the East, Apollo was notorious for inspiring strange hypnotic words in his prophets that seemed just like poetry but were very different from usual poetry—and that no one could quite understand.

In Parmenides' own poem, the emphasis he gives to being carried is only the beginning: only the start to a whole series of peculiar devices and deliberate repetitions. His poetry seems oddly to limp and falter, until you realize that this rhythmic effect is chosen because it mirrors the sense of what he is saying. There is no poor craftsmanship here; on the contrary. At each step he breaks any ordinary sense of continuity and creates a space of utter stillness and simplicity instead, keeps drawing the listener out from the details of the narrative rather than into them.

And the repeated repetitions that he uses soon start to show he is not just describing a journey into another world. He is actually reproducing the effects of the transition.

Everything begins spinning, moving in circles. The movement of the chariot wheels mirrors the movement of the gates and the other way around. And everywhere he sees the shape of pipes, hears the sound of piping.

Here, too, there is nothing accidental.

The standard Greek texts that discuss the practice of incubation consistently describe what happens when you start to enter another state of consciousness. Everything begins spinning, moving in a circle; and you hear a piping, hissing sound just like the hissing of a snake.

People familiar with the process of entering other states of awareness often used to recognize this particular sound as the first sign indicating the presence of Asclepius—the divine son of Apollo who, like Apollo himself, was one of the great gods of incubation.

But it had a far deeper significance as well. This piping or hissing was known as the sound of silence, the sound behind the whole of creation. Above all, it was the sound always being made by the sun as it moves through the sky.

And there was one god, more than any other, to whom the sound was sacred. That god was Apollo.

All of this ought to have been noticed and taken seriously a long time ago.

But nothing has been made of it because of the modern insistence on treating Parmenides as just a rationalist, a man of reason; as the first logician. It's so easy not to see what we have no wish to see.

And this was the situation until—only a few years ago now, but already in a century that has passed—some discoveries were made. I am at a loss to say what is more extraordinary: the significance of the discoveries themselves or the blanket of silence that has surrounded them, as if they had never been made.

It was the 1950s and Claudio Pellegrino Sestieri was director of excavations at Parmenides' hometown of Velia in southern Italy.

There, towards the end of 1958, he came across some marble inscriptions along with the remains of a few statues in the ruins of a large old building down by what once had been the harbor. Then more inscriptions were found in 1960, and again in 1962.

Each of them was only a few words in length. But together they speak volumes.

On one inscription, plainly intended as a public offering of thanks, the traces of three words could be made out. The second of them is Iatromantis. The third is Apollo.

Finding these two words mentioned together is nothing surprising in itself. The direct connection between the title Iatromantis and the god Apollo had already been known about for a long time. In fact it was a title traditionally applied either to Apollo or to someone considered his deputy, his "son."

What's so important, though, about the wording on this little piece of marble is that it shows the presence of Iatromantis figures not just at the eastern edges of the Greek world but right here in southern Italy—in Parmenides' hometown. Here at Velia there used to be people who worked through ecstasy, through inducing other states of perception and entering other worlds so they could directly receive divine guidance and revelations, and who worked in particular through the technique of incubation.

That leaves the first of those three words on the inscription.

It was Ouliadês. A name given to certain people in the ancient Greek world, it comes from the word Oulios which used to be one of the formal titles reserved most specifically for the god Apollo. Apollo Oulios meant "Apollo the destroyer" but—with an ambiguity typical of the god himself—could also be understood as "Apollo the healer," "Apollo who makes whole."

As for that name Ouliadês, literally it meant someone who is a son of Apollo Oulios: son of Apollo the healer, of the god who destroys but also makes whole.

And yet this word, Ouliadês, not only had a very particular meaning. It also had a very particular origin.

It came, just like the practices and traditions associated with Apollo Oulios himself, from Anatolia: from the western coastal regions of what now is Turkey. To be more precise, it had its main home in an area a little to the south of Phocaea that the Phocaeans had a great deal to do with before they were forced to leave Anatolia for the west. The area was called Caria.

And this was not the only inscription discovered at Velia that mentions the title Ouliadês.

It was a couple of years before the other one was found, alongside a statue of Apollo's son Asclepius that showed him with a hissing snake climbing up the side of his robe.

This second time, though, the wording on the marble applied the name to someone extremely familiar—to Parmenides.

The fact that the Parmenides mentioned on the inscription and Parmenides the philosopher, the founder of logic, are one and the same person is beyond the slightest doubt. But what the fact means deserves a little emphasis. It means that here, recorded in the ruins at Velia, we have the ancient confirmation of exactly those features already implicit in his own account of a journey to another world.

We are being shown Parmenides as a son of the god Apollo, allied to mysterious Iatromantis figures who were experts in the use of incantatory poetry and at making journeys into other worlds.

There is no need to say a great deal about the other inscriptions.

Bit by bit they revealed the existence of a whole tradition of priests dedicated to the service of Apollo Oulios. Each piece of evidence fitted together into a picture of these healer–priests forming a line of succession that stretched back, over a period of five hundred years, to Parmenides as its founder.

And one particular aspect of this picture is more than interesting. It's also highly symbolic.

Needless to say, the standard literature in the West about Parmenides contains hardly a hint of him having anything to do with traditions of healers. All the emphasis has been put on making him a pure logician; a dry, abstract thinker.

But it just so happens that Arabic and Persian literature managed to preserve the trace of something quite different: of Parmenides as the legendary founder of a medical tradition who had healers for his successors. You can even find it stated that the healing techniques these successors used included magical incantations. In the East, unlike the West, there was room for such things to be remembered.

And there is one other point worth mentioning about the line of healers recorded on those fragments of marble at Velia.

Each priest is given a ritual title so extraordinary that it seems almost to defy explanation. The Greek word is Phôlarchos— which means "someone in charge of a lair," "lord of the lair." Few things could sound more mysterious. Even so, we can still see exactly what the title means.

All we have to do is look to the east, to Anatolia and above all to that region so important for the worship of Apollo Oulios which was called Caria.

There Apollo was known, precisely, as the god of lairs; as the divine protector of those who lie down in lairs. And the reason is simple. In those regions it was quite normal to draw the obvious parallel between places of incubation and an animal's lair. Anyone who was sick or who needed guidance would come and do nothing else except lie down in utter stillness—the most common Greek word for this stillness was *hêsychia*—without moving, hardly breathing, for hours or even days at a time, just like animals hibernating in their lair.

As for the priests at these places, they were totally in charge: the lords of the lair. It was their responsibility to decide whom to allow in, whom to turn away. It was up to them to settle people down, make sure they were safe. And afterwards it was their job to teach them how to decipher the dreams or visions they had had in the darkness and stillness; to guide them and, when appropriate, introduce them to the mysteries of the god they served.

And those who came needed protecting because, later if not sooner, they left all hope behind. They had tried everything and, somewhere in themselves, realized they were helpless: that there was absolutely nothing they could do.

You can only hope for so long when you are lying utterly still in total darkness. Eventually even the hope of being helped, even the hope that brought you in the first place, is taken away. All the wanting, even wanting something to happen, starts to go. Incubation is not for unripe fruit bobbing around here and there in the breeze.

It's for the fruit that has fallen to the ground and has no idea any more if it will be picked up or left to be trampled.

As for the god Apollo: just like Parmenides the man, he has been converted into what he was not. He has been made into the god of reason, all brightness and straightforwardness and clarity and light. To be sure, he was very closely connected in Greek myth with the sun and the chariot of the sun—and especially with the Daughters of the Sun who were so important for Parmenides.

But we can still see just why.

It was because Apollo's home, like the place called home by the Daughters of the Sun, is at the furthest edges of existence: in the most distant north where east and west are one, near where the heavens plunge into the underworld and the sun sinks into the depths of night.

Particularly in Anatolia and southern Italy he was well known for his links with incubation and darkness, with the middle of the night, with the underworld and the caves that lead there. And he had the most intimate and mysterious of ties with the goddess of the underworld and queen of death whose home is guarded by Justice where it stands, just beyond the gates on the paths of Night and Day, right next to the chasm of Tartarus and the Mansions of Night: Persephone.

She is the goddess who greets initiates when they manage to make their way down to her by warmly reaching out to them with her right hand; who accepts them, welcomes them to her home, with a kindness that defies all human logic; who was often referred to with the most deliberate vagueness as "the goddess" whom it's best not to name.

And Apollo himself was the god of a clarity only found buried deep in riddles, in ambiguous oracles, impossible enigmas—a clarity so elusive but so precious that it was something people had to be prepared to risk their lives for.

11

Long before the inscriptions started coming to light at Velia, something was known about Parmenides' teacher.

It was not much—only a few words about him left behind in an ancient Greek book. And from what they tell us he was not much, either: poor, obscure, without any apparent influence. But the greatest of people are often like that.

Historians who have taken the trouble to look at these words are always struck by the obvious note of authenticity in the details they provide. At the same time they find themselves having to shy away from the main detail, or somehow try to modify its meaning. For what we are told is that the one thing Parmenides' teacher and guide introduced him to was stillness: *hêsychia*.

Sometimes it can be good to stand back for a moment or two and look at things from a distance.

To be told that the father of western rationalism, the founder of logic, was introduced to extraordinary methods of reasoning by his teacher: this would be easy enough to understand. To be told that he was taught great metaphysical truths would be quite believable, too. But to be asked to accept that the one thing his real teacher taught him was stillness—this should come as something of a shock.

Shocks are often healthy. They help point out the gap between how things are and how we assume things should be. We can keep wandering around in the dull, gray limbo of our assumptions if we want. Or we can take the other way.

In this particular case the implication of that word *hêsychia*, or "stillness," is simply waiting to be discovered.

As a matter of fact, the details left behind in that brief report about Parmenides' teacher provide all the background we need for understanding what was involved. They situate the term in a very recognizable context of people who practised incubation for the sake of the experiences and visions it gave access to—a context where, as one fine scholar already pointed out back in the 1920s, the mention of stillness formed part of a precise technical vocabulary which was used to describe the state achieved "during deep meditation, ecstasies or dreams."

So those lords of the lair at Velia, the priests who were linked with Parmenides by a particular affiliation and even in a line of succession, belonged to a tradition that had one decisive characteristic: the practice of incubation in *hêsychia* or stillness. And the fundamental characteristic of the stillness that Parmenides was introduced to by his teacher was also the practice of incubation.

The pattern should be clear. Parmenides is surrounded on either side by stillness.

As for where we want to go from here, that's a question of courage; of whether we are willing to follow things through to their simple conclusion.

To be prepared to admit that Parmenides' predecessor, and successors, were somehow involved in the practice of incubation but to want to exclude Parmenides himself from any such involvement—that would hardly be logical. And besides: the report about his teacher makes it clear that this teaching of stillness was the essence of what he passed on to Parmenides.

But of course even that is not all, because an incubatory context is exactly what happens to be implied by the strange account of a journey into another world placed right at the start of his poem by Parmenides himself.

There are those who love to argue. Like expert lawyers they will spend their time skillfully refuting the obvious, proving the absurd. And there are sure to be people who would want to claim that the practice of stillness might well have been a matter of concern for Parmenides' predecessor, and for successors of his at Velia, and even for Parmenides himself—but that of course this has no bearing at all on the main part of his poem with its immensely influential teaching about logic.

And yet an argument like that would not just be unreasonable. Realistically, it would be impossible to maintain. For the fundamental characteristic of reality that Parmenides will go on to demonstrate, time and time again, in the main part of his poem is its utter stillness: its complete lack of change or movement.

As a matter of fact Plato and the other Greek philosophers who used to put so much effort into trying to make sense of Parmenides' teachings liked using one particular word to sum up his understanding of reality.

That word was *hêsychia*, stillness.

There are no coincidences here. We have gone far beyond the level of coincidence; and the implication of all this evidence is quite straightforward. For Parmenides it's through stillness that we come to stillness. Through stillness we come to understand stillness. Through the practice of stillness we come to experience a reality that exists beyond this world of the senses.

12

And the moment you accept that this may be the case, you are already trapped.

The evidence all points to these conclusions. But for reasoning to accept them would be for it to accept its own destruction—because reasoning is based on thought and stillness is the end of thought.

In the central part of his poem Parmenides talks about the nature of reality and the nature of thought.

For over two thousand years now, people have thought and thought about what Parmenides says about thinking; have written the most persuasive and learned books, all of them disagreeing with the others. But trying to think about thinking is utterly futile. There is only one way to understand and discover the nature of thinking—by arriving at the standpoint of stillness that lies beyond thought.

It's fascinating to see how thinking struggles to understand itself, keeps being drawn to what lies beyond it like moths to a flame. But in over two thousand years, arguing has got no one anywhere. As soon as it manages to clarify something, it promptly covers it over again. And if scholars were to go on arguing about what Parmenides is saying for another thousand years they would still get absolutely nowhere. Argument serves no purpose at all except when used as an instrument, by someone who has already arrived at stillness, for showing the way to others.

The stillness surrounding Parmenides on every side is like a noose around the neck of every single theory about what his teaching might have meant. For what he taught has nothing to do with theory. It's a simple matter of experience: the experience of reality.

But somehow, with all our foolish intelligence, we have managed to cheat ourselves of that reality. We dismiss it out of hand without the slightest understanding of what we are dismissing. And even if we happen to think about it sympathetically, it becomes just food for thought.

Parmenides' teaching has been turned into something utterly dry; quite dead. But it's about life, life itself. And it's not about something we can afford to interest ourselves in if we wish—or afford not to. It's about something that has to be understood if we want to understand anything else.

Learning about anything at all is time wasted unless it includes learning about this. We are faced with opportunities to be seized or opportunities lost, because all our thinking is nothing but the longing for this.

TWO

Once you have
touched it
there is no
division; no tearing
your heart away.
For it knows
no separation.

ORACLE OF APOLLO FROM ANATOLIA

1

With Parmenides there is no turning back. On the route he is made to follow there is no stopping halfway.

His poem has no breaks. Really it has no parts: it's one seamless whole. And we are sewn up inside it—our present, our future, our past.

Right at the beginning he evokes the journey he made, with the Daughters of the Sun, to the underworld and the home of the nameless goddess; then he goes straight on to mention the warm welcome she gave him, along with her opening summary of the things she is about to teach.

And after that comes the teaching itself.

Here, as before, every detail is significant. When we feel tempted to run on ahead to somewhere just over the horizon, towards what we imagine will be really important, that's when we need to slow down: it's right at our feet. And where everyone gets sidetracked by pointless arguments, that's where we have to keep on going.

After the greetings and introductory formalities, the goddess comes straight to the point. The very first statement she makes as she launches into the main part of her teaching is usually translated, without too much attention to detail, as "I will tell you, and you take my words to heart once you have heard them ..."; or as "I will tell you, and you pay attention to what I say once you have heard it ..."

And yet there is not a single word in the original Greek about paying attention or taking anything to heart. What it does contain is the passing suggestion that Parmenides needs to take good care of the goddess' words, look after them—although for their sake, not his. But the basic meaning of the Greek here goes further than that; and the main sense of her instructions is clear beyond any doubt.

What Parmenides is being told is to take away her teaching: to carry it with him.

> *I will do the talking; and it's up to you*
> *to carry away my words once you have heard them.*

Of course that raises the question of where Parmenides needs to take her words. But the question answers itself as soon as we remember where he already happens to be.

His journey took him to the underworld, and this is where he still is. All she is telling him is to take her teaching back with him from the world of the dead to the world of the living.

In other words, Parmenides is simply to be her messenger.

2

As a messenger—this is how Parmenides presents himself but how no one cares to see him. It's purely a matter of taking him at his word.

There is one particular name that well describes the kind of messenger Parmenides finds himself becoming: prophet. The real meaning of the word "prophet" has nothing to do with being able to look into the future. In origin it just meant someone whose job is to speak on behalf of a greater power, of someone or something else.

As for being invested with the role of messenger from the underworld, this was once a very specific function. In ancient Greece, much the same as in neighboring regions further to the east, it was a main characteristic of someone who had the knowledge of a shaman—who was able to travel to the world of the dead and back again not for any personal gain but for the sake of the living as well as the sake of the dead.

And there are other issues here, also, that are just as important as noting the place Parmenides' message comes from or where he has to take it.

The implications of being a messenger like this are extremely precise. It's up to one party—the goddess—to do the talking. It's up to the other—Parmenides—to do the listening and then carry the message away. The task of the messenger is not to interfere in any way, not to change the message or try to improve it, not to add the slightest detail or leave anything out: is simply to report.

And this is where we are brought back, once again, to the fact that Parmenides used to be well known not only as a philosopher or poet but as a lawgiver.

Certainly it's already a step in the right direction to notice how much he shared with Epimenides—the healer and prophet who became legendary for his knowledge of how to give laws after the encounters he had with Justice while sleeping for years in a cave.

But there used to be other people too, especially in southern Italy, who became famous as lawgivers after being given their laws by a god or goddess during a vision or a dream. And these people had one hallmark. This was the solemn assurance they gave that nothing in the laws they were presenting was their own creation; that they reported them just as they received them, without changing or tampering even with the smallest detail.

Of course that's completely preposterous nowadays. We have forgotten about these things: have a hundred sensible reasons for dismissing them as nonsense, as fraud. All we have become able to see is the messenger, not where the message comes from. And we have learned to assume without a moment's doubt or hesitation that the messenger is simply the inventor. It's so natural to project our own egoism onto the few people in whom this egoism is quite absent.

There is a great wonder here—but one we only dare to make room for in children's stories. As for believing this is how things once could have been for the people who seeded and shaped and formed our western culture: that seems inconceivable. But the result is that we end up doing something even more preposterous ourselves. We learn to read people like Parmenides, if we ever happen to bother with them at all, without really reading them; become so used to overlooking or changing what they say that we no longer even notice what we are doing.

Most of us think the greatest possible achievement is to come up with everything ourselves, to invent and be creative, put our stamp on the world. But there are those who consider that the greatest achievement is to listen, to change this world by bringing into it what no one else is able to hear. Into the humdrum and ordinary they bring something extraordinary, a magic: not the fabricated type of magic that we invent to try and escape from the tedium of existence but a totally different kind, far more mysterious and infinitely more real.

And this magic always has a sign it can be recognized by—in the same kind of way that an orange with its stalk and leaves still attached can be a gentle reminder of how it has been brought to us from somewhere else.

That sign is its freshness: a strange sense of wholeness so alarming and out of place in this fragmented, upside-down world of ours that we feel a desperate need to complete it. But however hard we try to change it, interpret it, force it to make sense, we can never persuade it to fit in.

This is because we are what needs completing—not it. And the only way we can understand it is when we learn to judge and assess ourselves in its light; not it in the imagined light of ourselves.

Messengers like Parmenides are like fishers bringing back their catch from the ocean. If we have ever been near the sea ourselves, then we know when fish are fresh because of the way they smell of the sea. And even if we have never been to the sea we are still able to recognize the smell by its strangeness.

This book is all about the smell of the sea. But so far we have only been walking down to the shoreline.

Now it's time we were heading out into the ocean.

3

I will do the talking; and it's up to you
to carry away my words once you have heard them.
What I will tell you is which roads of inquiry,
and which roads alone, exist for thinking.
The one route, that is, *and is not possible not to be,*
is the way of Persuasion; for Persuasion is
Truth's attendant. And as for the other,
that is not, *and is necessary not to be:*
this, I can tell you, is a path from which no news
returns. For there is no way you can recognize
what is not—there is no travelling that path—
or tell anything about it.

Any sensible person who was to read this and be told that it's a foundational text for the western science of logic would have every good reason to die of laughter. Everything about it is absurd.

It's absurd in what it says, absurd in its vagueness and obscurity; and its careful, measured tone creates an illusory impression of reasonableness that makes everything about it even more nonsensically obscure.

Nonsense is what it sounds like. And nonsense is what this is, because there is nothing here to do with our familiar world of the senses. What Parmenides is saying comes from another world.

Specialists and experts in the fields of logic and philosophy have brought their heaviest equipment to bear on the task of explaining his words. The problem they are faced with seems a huge one, and they apply themselves to it with great industry. They use mysterious logical symbols—strange characters taken from foreign languages; ordinary letters of the alphabet turned upside-down—to try and clarify Parmenides' meaning. But of course this only plunges everything into further obscurity. They argue endlessly over whether his use of the word "is" should be explained as copulative in meaning or existential, introduce all sorts of other complicated terms. And disputes keep on raging over what the subject of this verb "is" could possibly be: is he talking about being, or reality, or inquiry, or paths, or the universe, or something else?

The work goes on, just like it has for hundreds of years. And behind all the ceaseless labor there is one fundamental assumption—that Parmenides, as a philosopher and logician, was dedicated to making his meaning as straightforward and plain as possible.

It's the old, old story of seeing only what we expect to see and looking for what we assumed at the beginning we would find.

But if it were possible to stop being so busy for just one moment and look instead at what we have right in front of us, something would become apparent straightaway. This is that Parmenides is not being clear at all—and is not making the slightest attempt to be clear.

These lines are pure mystery, sheer obscurity. In their form of expression, their language, in what they manage to convey without seeming to say anything specific at all, they are a classic example of a riddle.

And the greatest mystery is how anyone could ever have imagined Parmenides would speak any differently.

There is a strange idea among historians that philosophy arose in Greece out of the desire to make things clear. But the simple fact is that other early philosophers, living in or around the time of Parmenides, also introduced their writings with mystifying riddles as confusing to anyone then as they are now.

As for the legendary Epimenides, a figure so closely related to Parmenides, he was famous not just for his healing powers or his role in the making of laws but also for expressing himself in riddles.

And then, of course, there are Parmenides' more immediate affiliations.

The discovery of those inscriptions at Velia has opened up a whole new perspective that shows him linked in his own hometown with Iatromantis figures—whose chosen form of expression was the language of riddles—and with the god Apollo, who happened to be notorious among the Greeks for his riddling oracles. The riddles he spoke in were blessings, because they contained hidden inside them the destinies of women and men. But they were also a curse because if you missed their real meaning, interpreted them wrongly or superficially, then your life became not worth living.

And there is something else: one other little point that needs to be mentioned.

From the very beginning of his poem Parmenides presents himself as an initiate. He refers to himself immediately, using a standard initiatory expression, as "the man who knows." His descent while alive into the underworld was a journey that only an initiate would dare, or be able, to make. All the signs, that only a fool would choose to miss, are that this is a text for initiates.

But among ancient Greeks the language of initiation was, above all, the language of riddles. For them, initiation and mysteries and riddles went hand in hand. The formal process of initiation was often structured around riddles that were deliberately used for testing people, for putting off those who are easily discouraged, misleading those who are happy to be misled.

So when the goddess starts talking to Parmenides straight-away in the form of a riddle, one thing should be quite plain. This poem is not just for initiates, is not a text that only speaks to those who already know.

It is, in itself, an initiation—the starting-point for stepping into another world.

4

In everything Parmenides says as he introduces the two paths of inquiry, one particular detail is even stranger than the others. This is the way he describes the second route as "a path from which no news returns."

And here is where we have to start understanding some basic facts about how he managed to communicate far more than he seems at first glance to be saying.

For people in his time, as well as in the centuries that were still to come, there were some old Greek poems that almost had the status of bibles; and this was especially true of the ones said to have been written by Homer. The main characters in these poems were so well known they became models for how to behave and not behave. The words and imagery that the poetry contained were engraved in people's memories, were used as a common language for expressing feelings—and, by writers like Parmenides, as a continual point of reference in their own poems.

What this meant was, in practice, as simple as it was important.

Just by picking an unusual phrase that echoed a very similar expression already used somewhere by one of the great old poets, Parmenides could automatically evoke the whole context of the phrase in the original poem together with all its subtle and not-so-subtle associations. He was able to hint at meanings beyond any obvious meaning, trigger entire sequences of ideas, awaken the memory of vivid scenes through only one or two well-chosen words.

There is nothing open-ended here. The method is as much a precise science as an art. And as scholars have often noted, even without always understanding the full implications, it was a technique that Parmenides excelled at.

As for this mention of "a path from which no news returns," it will have meant something very specific to any intelligent Greek. In those days, to hear news about someone was considered proof that the person was alive. Silence spelled death; and in the poetry of Homer anyone about whom "no news returns" was simply somebody who was assumed to be dead.

So according to the conventions of ancient poetic language, Parmenides' road of "is not" from which no news returns is the road leading to the silence of non-existence and death. All we need to do now is add that for Greeks, just as for us, "not to be" was a veiled but self-evident way of referring to death— and the picture is almost complete.

It doesn't need much thought to see how significant this is. To reach the goddess, Parmenides has travelled the legendary road into the underworld: the road of death. He happens to be standing, right beside her, in the world of the dead. In the last place where anyone would expect to receive a warm welcome, that is precisely what he receives.

And everything there is a paradox, a riddle.

From the one place from where no knowledge returns, he is about to bring back the ultimate knowledge contained in his famous poem. Parmenides, the messenger, is coming back to the world of the living while still alive with news from where no news is ever supposed to come.

But there is also something else.

The fact of Parmenides being faced, here in the underworld, with a choice between two different paths is far from accidental. We happen to know some details about initiation among ancient Greeks—particularly among the Greeks in southern Italy. And perhaps the most famous detail of all is that after initiates, "those who know," made their journey into the underworld they were confronted with a choice between two paths. To be more precise, they arrived at a famous fork in the road where the major decision was waiting to be made as to which way they would be allowed to go.

One of them is the path that only the initiate is able to follow: the path that leads to life, real life.

The other is the path of forgetfulness and death, of slipping into silence, of utter non-existence.

Knowledge about these paths was traditionally kept a mystery. The details were hidden in the riddles of initiation. But we are already in a position to see that Parmenides is suggesting nothing is what it seems. He is hinting at a reality very different from the one we take for granted—which is not much of a surprise considering he has so little respect for any reasonable values or distinctions that he gladly, wholeheartedly, lets himself be taken on a journey straight to the one place any sane person would do everything in the world to avoid.

And we are also in a position where we can start to see that if this poem of his has given rise to western logic and philosophy and inquiry, then things have gone very seriously wrong somewhere along the way.

The choice he is being faced with has come to be explained and interpreted as some kind of intellectual game. But, quite literally, it's a matter of life and death.

It's no coincidence that Parmenides finds himself being taken on his journey into the depths of darkness and the Mansions of Night. Initiatory riddles were routinely compared by Greek writers "with darkness and night."

The secret of riddles like this is that nobody will ever solve them through struggling or trying to work them out. But if we are patient enough, they start to solve themselves. The trick is not to rush in gripping our bright lights and tools but to leave all that behind and learn to get used to the darkness.

Initiatory riddles, like oracular riddles, are a tricky affair. Interpreting them rightly and misinterpreting them are a world apart. But they have rules.

The first is that if something immediately strikes you as the right solution, then it's the wrong one. They are highly deceptive—not because they deceive us but because they create the opportunity for self-deception. They play on our weaknesses; flatter our desire to come up with quick answers; bring out the worst in us as well as the best.

Just like mirrors, they offer us a glimpse of ourselves. If we are prepared to see in them nothing except what we want to see, this is exactly what we will be shown. But if we are ready to look at ourselves in ways we have never looked before, then we will start to notice what was always waiting in the shadows—longing to be seen.

In those lines spoken by the goddess about the two paths of inquiry, there is not the slightest explanation of what she is talking about when she says "is not" or "is." The subject of the verbs is left in the dark. And yet there is a very good reason for that.

This lack of clarity is the core of Parmenides' logic. His logic is not about symbols and formulas, but about us. This is an initiatory logic that, if we allow it, will draw us into the shadows of ourselves—right to the edges of our experience, beyond the limits of everything we dreamed we were.

If we want to understand the way it works then all we have to do is learn to watch in stillness as, stage by stage, the poem unfolds. And if we can bear to keep on looking without yet knowing what we are looking at, eventually we will be shown what it is that the goddess wants us to see.

There is no rush to find any answers, because we are the answer; no hurry to go anywhere, because there is absolutely nowhere to go.

6

Sometimes things become worse before they get any better. And the riddle about the two paths that "exist for thinking" is only the start of Parmenides' enigmas.

The mysterious choice he presents us with between two even more mysterious paths is already obscure enough—between the route of "is, and is not possible not to be" and the other route that the goddess dismisses as no real path at all because there can be no thinking about what is not, no talking about it, no recognizing it.

This is nothing, though, compared with the enigma about to come.

With any other writer, it would be amazing how such a short statement could cause so many misunderstandings. But with Parmenides nothing is impossible. Some of the greatest philosophers in the ancient world took it without any hesitation as meaning that he identified thinking with existence; and this identification even came to be viewed as a kind of trademark for his teaching. Most modern scholars, as well, are only too happy to interpret and translate it in exactly the same way: "For thinking and being are one and the same."

The difficulties surrounding this translation on every side are overwhelming. Not the least of them is the fact that, later on in his poem, Parmenides plainly denies thinking and being are the same. To be sure, he explains in detail how one is related to the other—but identical they definitely are not.

The trouble is that this way of translating Parmenides' words is natural enough. In fact it happens to be the simplest and most obvious way of interpreting his statement, which is why so many people have assumed it has to be correct.

And they have fallen straight into the trap.

We come back to that one thing which tends to be quite certain when dealing with initiatory language and riddles. The easy choice will lead you astray. The obvious and simple meaning, the one that seems so clearly right, is the wrong one: just a red herring, a dead end. For those who are willing to look, to watch how everything hangs together, to resist the quick solution, there will always be another meaning waiting to be seen. And, in this case, Parmenides has left all the signs we need to discover what it is.

First words are often the most important ones; but it can be easy to miss how, right at the start of her announcement about the existence of two different paths, the goddess introduces them as the only roads that "exist for thinking." This expression, "exist for thinking," is a striking one in the original Greek. Translated literally, Parmenides' particular choice of words would mean these are the only two paths that "are to think." For the words to mean "exist for thinking": that was perfectly acceptable in the Greek language of his time. But, even so, it was a rather special way of choosing to express oneself.

And the same kind of wording occurs here yet again, just as it will keep on appearing at key points in the poem. All we have to do is take Parmenides' hint and give it the same meaning in this second passage that it certainly has in the first. Then everything falls straight into place:

For what exists for thinking, and being, are one and the same.

What exists for thinking is whatever you are able to think about. So, in other words, Parmenides is saying that anything you can think about has to exist for you to think about it. And thanks to the strange logic only found in the realms of nonsense, this immediately makes perfect sense when set alongside what the goddess has already said.

To state that thinking and being are the same would be to say something about the existence of the thinker. But to bring up the question of what exists for thinking is very different: is to say something instead about the existence of what can be thought, of what can be pondered or recognized or considered. And, as we already know, this is the goddess' fundamental concern. For as soon as she introduces the two paths of inquiry she dismisses the second one straightaway because

there is no way you can recognize
what is not—there is no travelling that path—
or tell anything about it.

Non-existence is unrecognizable, unmentionable, unthinkable. Whatever you think about must exist simply because it exists for you to think about. And of course this is totally absurd. It means unicorns would have to exist just because we can think about them or imagine one. But if we want to understand Parmenides then the worst thing we can do is dismiss the absurd. On the contrary, we have to hold on to it as tight as possible.

And this is where we have to remember, again, the place Parmenides happens to find himself in as he hears these words from the goddess.

He is "far away from the beaten track of humans" in the world of the gods. And, for Greeks, the world of the gods had one very particular feature. This is that simply to think something is to make it exist: is to make it real.

Parmenides is bringing back a message from the realm of goddesses and divine beings to people in the world of the living—or at least to the world of those who imagine they are living. To be more precise, he is returning with a revelation about the laws of divine reality and about the laws of human existence. The human law is that you will spend the greater part of your life desperately thinking of ways to make the things you want exist and the things you fear not exist.

As for the divine law: the very fact of thinking something is the assurance that it already is.

7

To say that anything we think has to exist: this may not sound the most practical of statements to make. So we need to see what it really means.

We have built a wall between thinking and reality.

All our waking lives we measure our thoughts against what appears to be the realness of the external world. We decide to call them ineffective, pointless, imaginative, unrealistic; or appropriate, fruitful, constructive, realizable.

With Parmenides all these distinctions come tumbling down.

For him any thought is about something that exists: is just as real, as perfect a part of reality, as any other. Its criterion of rightness lies not in its relation to some solid, concrete, objective external world—but in itself.

Every thought is its own validation. It needs no confirmation outside it. Whatever we are able to think is true.

And the fascinating thing is to see how people react to this. Scholars rush like lemmings to qualify what Parmenides says. They claim that when he talks about thinking he is not just talking about any kind of thought but about right thinking, good thinking, true thinking—about thoughts that have a genuine relationship to reality.

But this is not what he is saying at all. He is not talking about any particular kind of thinking: he is referring to each and every thought we happen to have.

Absolutely everything is included. And this is why the goddess' message is so difficult to understand. It would be very comfortable for our minds if she were to discriminate; to distinguish between right thought and wrong, helpful and unhelpful, good and bad. But there is nothing like that.

The goddess herself is utterly ruthless in her generosity. Whatever you think exists.

It's so important to see how much we depend on discrimination—how much we need it emotionally, intellectually, spiritually—and how Parmenides destroys it. Here is the founder of logic, the one man to whom anyone could hope to turn for clear distinctions: for formal processes of exclusion and rejection.

But he gives none. All he rejects is what doesn't exist, and nothing doesn't exist.

In our own, very private ways each of us is always looking out for guidance; for instructions on how to think and what not to think. But with Parmenides we are faced with everything— with direction that will take us beyond any direction. We are forced along a path that leads everywhere. And there are no answers, no clarifications.

To be guided, truly, by what he says is to discover that there is nothing at all except what is: is to follow him into what to our discriminating minds are oceans of confusion, waves of bewilderment. At first you might think that with the solid help of his words you can touch dry land. But the more you try, the more it keeps receding just beyond your grasp. The desert of reasoning becomes a mirage inside the oasis of unthinkable meaning.

And there is a trick here, a great irony that can only be appreciated if you really take the goddess at her word.

The trick is that, the moment you accept every single thought as equally true and also see the truth of this, then all thinking fades into unimportance. It's simply a reaction of fear to try pretending that Parmenides is concerned about right thought, good or accurate thought, because this at least gives us a goal to keep thinking our way towards. The irony is that by accepting every thought he is actually taking us beyond thought: showing us it doesn't matter, helping us to leave it all behind.

By saying that everything we can think is true, by refusing to discriminate between thought and thought, the goddess is indicating that ultimately she is not concerned with thoughts at all.

There is no understanding this by trying to think it through or work it out, because anything whatsoever that you happen to think about it will be true. There is no thinking about thinking, because that way you fall straight into the world of thought you are trying to define. There is no arguing, because you are only arguing with yourself.

The only possible way to understand is by standing back in the stillness that lies underneath thinking and sees things as they really are. It's like watching hundreds of colors, each of them trying to persuade you it happens to be the most important one—then stepping back and seeing they all form a single rainbow. Thoughts in themselves are always leading to division and separation. But all thoughts, together, are a single whole.

We are our own enemy. Everything is one. And there is no need to struggle for anything at all because whatever we think already exists: nothing to fulfil, nothing to fear.

Thinking is the realm of all that we know, or think we know. And this end to discrimination is the end of all wisdom, the end of philosophy—as well as its beginning. It's where everything we work for or try to work out by ourselves becomes useless.

And it's where the prophet steps in, bringing impossible news from another world.

Naturally people who study Parmenides want to bring him back from the brink of such an abyss; to make his teaching reasonable, thinkable, acceptable; to dismiss his initiatory language as nothing more significant than empty figures of speech. But this is how logic once used to be before it was corrupted into reason.

8

If you are wondering why it is that Parmenides focuses so exclusively on thinking, the answer is quite simple. He doesn't.

From the moment he brings up the subject of thought—when he introduces the riddle about the two different paths that "exist for thinking"—he uses one particular word for it in Greek. The word is *noein*, which was a whirlpool of subtleties.

Certainly in Parmenides' time it had the sense of thinking. But there was a great deal more to it than that. This one word referred as much to the act of perceiving as to the act of thinking: to direct, intuitive perception as well as perception through and with our senses. And, beyond even that, it described exactly what nowadays we would refer to as consciousness or awareness.

Such a vast spread of meanings can be infuriating to our modern minds. But we have to remember that all these various senses only seem different or separate to us—and that it would be a big mistake to believe Parmenides was referring with this one particular word to nothing but the little thoughts spinning around in our heads.

He was using it to cover the whole spectrum of our existence as aware, sensing, intelligent beings. And the path being gradually laid out for us, the one we are expected to follow, is an absolutely unbending line of one-hundred-per-cent acceptance: whatever we are aware of is, whatever we perceive or notice is, whatever we think of is.

But just as important as this endorsement, this total acceptance, is the fact that Parmenides is also saying something else when he formally identifies existence with what exists for perceiving or thinking.

There is nothing that exists except what can be thought or perceived. In other words, the world is not at all what we think it is; or rather it's exactly what we think it is but only because we think it. And whatever we think it's not, that is what it is as well.

We are not some tiny, insignificant specks lost somewhere at the edge of a vast, impersonal universe—unless we want to believe we are. Ultimately the world is just where we happen to be. Everything else is our imagination. Wherever it seems that you are, in some bleak corridor or watching trees outside the window, this is the center of reality and your thoughts are its edges.

The situation is one of utter simplicity: far too simple for our thinking minds to understand. Existence is not anywhere else, is not somewhere separate from us. But really to understand this means having to take a tremendous responsibility for what we are.

And as soon as one glimpses it, any sense of isolation from anything at all dissolves. The moment you understand that the only criterion of reality is thinking and perception, that there is nothing that is not, then everything is suddenly together—linked to itself in a perfect continuum.

There is nothing but fullness, utter fullness. The whole of existence is one complete, unbroken whole.

We may seem to have drifted far away from ordinary human experience—but this is just an appearance. All that happens is that ordinary experience drifts far away from this.

The goddess stays, as usual, focused on the essential with fine precision:

> *See how it is that things far away are firmly*
> *present to your mind. For however much you want to,*
> *there is no way you will manage to cut being off*
> *from clinging fast to being.*

Her words are so direct that, as always, they evoke incredible confusion. But all she is describing, the one thing she is concerned with, is the abolition of separation.

If you think about something out of sight, hundreds or even thousands of miles away, then your mind knows no distance: whatever you are thinking is directly present in your awareness. And if you look at mountains or buildings on the distant horizon, the sight of them is absolutely present to your mind.

There is no distance at all between yourself and what you are imagining or seeing. We can only entertain any sense of separation because our consciousness is completely free of separation. The appearance of discontinuity is impossible without a perfect continuity; the illusion of absence is created by what is always present.

Wherever we look, the very act of looking means that separation simply doesn't exist. And this absence of separation is not some intellectual or mystical ideal, something reserved for spirits or angels. It's the reality of the everyday world that we live in.

Until we realize this we are always endlessly wandering from place to place. Once it has been realized, there is no longer anywhere to go. Our consciousness is no longer something lost, somewhere, inside a world that hems it in on every side—but the other way around.

Wherever it seems that you go, or come, everything happens in your consciousness. And that consciousness never moves, is always the same.

But even so, there are a hundred thousand ways to lose ourselves inside it; to get trapped by our own magic. And one of the easiest ones is to imagine that it really matters what we think.

If everything we think about exists, then it sounds very reasonable that we should choose our thoughts with care: only think good things. But this is just to discriminate all over again. To choose good thoughts is to reject the bad ones—and to reject something is to entertain it, is to make it exist. The moment of choosing creates the momentum of denial which only leads to more and more problems further down the road.

There is one real choice that we have. This is to see that, as we are, we have no choice at all because our thoughts are not ours; never have been. They are simply reality thinking itself. Trying to think good thoughts creates a good illusion, which happens to be the most seductive illusion there is because it sends us even further asleep.

And this is the story of our lives. Our thinking is always separating us from ourselves, darting away into the future or the past. Even our thoughts about the past and future are in the present—but we are too busy to see this because we keep on running after little things, snatching at small pieces of reality because we are too greedy to settle for the whole.

Thought never stops choosing and tearing things apart, then trying to gather bits of existence together and hoard them like a squirrel. But if instead of running towards what we want and away from what we are afraid of we just stay in the present, then even pain is not a cause for fear. Sometimes pain is all we have: is what makes us real and gives us existence, is the earth and soil of our being, is what makes us human and offers us the eternal dignity of being a human being.

Most of the pain we experience is only the result of running away from pain. Pain, itself, is intense sensation—and sensation is nothing but reality perceiving itself.

The strange thing is that, if we are able even for a moment to let pain be, it tends to start finding its own solution as a part of the present; a part of the whole. The more we isolate it, the more it becomes a problem, and it's only when we try to escape from pain that we are weak. When we face everything in the moment, as a whole, then we are invincible.

This has nothing to do with theory. On the contrary, at the level of theory it makes no sense at all. The only way it makes any sense is when we start to experience it. What Parmenides is pointing to—the oneness, the fullness, the absence of separation—is a reality we are living without even realizing it. And the idea of approaching his poem as nothing but clever speculation is a total abuse of what he is saying.

The journey he describes himself as making, into another reality, is not some matter of theory. The evidence for him as a practising priest of Apollo has everything to do with practice; nothing with theory. The same applies to the mention in ancient Greek literature of something that all modern writers about Parmenides, with their basic assumption that his teaching was just a matter of theorizing and argument, are completely at a loss to understand: the existence, thousands of years ago, of a "Parmenidean way of life."

And the same is even truer of one report about how Parmenides' successor and chief disciple, a man called Zeno, finally died.

It says that he was caught helping some people who lived between Italy and Sicily to protect themselves against invaders, and was tortured. But in spite of the pain he stayed silent; refused to give in or betray his friends. And, we are told, through his suffering "he tested Parmenides' words in fire like gold that's pure and true."

10

Parmenides has made the preparations: shaped up the canvas, primed it, sketched in the background. And now he is about to fill in the details of what happens to be more familiar to us than anything else—but which is the last thing we are willing to see.

He starts off by emphasizing once again how futile it is to try following the second path, the path of what is not.

> *What exists for saying and for thinking must be.*
> *For it exists for it to be; but nothing does not exist.*
> *You ponder that!*
> *This is the first road of inquiry that I hold you back from.*
> *But then I hold you back as well from the one that*
> *mortals fabricate, twin-heads, knowing nothing.*
> *For helplessness in their chests is what steers their*
> *wandering minds as they are carried along in a daze, .*
> *deaf and blind at the same time: indistinguishable,*
> *undistinguishing crowds who reckon that being and*
> *non-being are the same but not the same. And, for*
> *all of them, the route they follow is a path that keeps turning*
> *backwards on itself.*

To begin with, he uses exactly the same language as before. There is the same oddly characteristic phrase, "what exists for thinking." And there is the same defiant riddle about the non-existence of what is not; the same total disrespect for all our reasonably normal gestures of discrimination. Whatever we can think or talk about must be.

This time, though, he puts a little extra salt on the wound by adding "You ponder that!"

It's interesting to see how these words are invariably understood. The expression is interpreted without any thought as the clearest of signs that we are all being invited to participate in a feast for the intellect by using our faculty of reason—that we are being encouraged to join in and help think matters through.

But there is nothing accidental about the painful statistic that those who study Parmenides and struggle with his words have managed, in spite of all their reasoning, to understand as little about his meaning now as they ever have done. The way we are, we are not in a position to help anyone with anything. One day we might be able to help the goddess; but not yet.

And, here, what people have failed to notice is that this "You ponder that!" is not the language of intellectual debate. Instead, it just so happens to be the standard formula spoken in ancient Greek by givers of oracles after they have said something particularly obscure: is their way of rubbing in the fact that the apparently innocent statement they have just made is a riddle as dark and black as night.

This is no time for chickens to be running around. It's the hour of the wolves.

And there is no reasoning with what Parmenides is saying for the simple reason that it undermines the basis of our reasoning. There is nothing here that can be politely discussed and resolved in an hour or two, even in a year. You have to take it home with you instead; take it to bed. You can never let it out of your sight until one day or night you find it staring straight back at you—eye to eye.

Then comes the surprise. Just when we might have expected at least to be about to catch a scent of Parmenides' real meaning, we are confronted instead with the one factor we would never have dreamed of encountering: ourselves.

To begin with, there were only two paths and no more. Suddenly there are three. The goddess had seemed to be presenting a straightforward choice between just two alternatives. Either there is the path of existence and absolutely no non-existence or there is the other path, of non-existence and no trace of existence. That appeared to be all.

But now Parmenides is being warned away from another route as well—a middle path combining existence and non-existence. First there was the great yes to everything, then the great no. And now we are being shown a picture of people who mix up the two paths and create a fantastic third one, who dabble in existence while still holding an option in non-existence, who spend their lives saying both yes and no.

And as always happens when someone tries to say yes and no at the same time, the result is chaos.

Scholars have agonized for generation after generation over the question of who these people could possibly be. They have written hundreds of pages on the subject; have searched high and low, looked in all the most unlikely places. And, well over a century ago, one particular expert had a stroke of genius.

He decided that this mention of ignorant "mortals" must be Parmenides' highly generalized way of referring to another Greek philosopher, called Heraclitus, who very wisely described everything in existence as both containing and moving towards its opposite: that it must be a cutting criticism of his ideas.

The solution required a fair amount of manipulating of Parmenides' text, not to mention of the other evidence. Even so, it quickly caught on. In fact it proved almost irresistible to anyone looking to the past for a tidily packaged, self-enclosed story about the origins of philosophy. And one of the more remarkable results has been that a whole, crucial chapter in the history of western ideas has come to be written purely on the basis of this presumed attack by Parmenides on Heraclitus.

But there were a few other scholars who had a little more respect for what Parmenides actually says. They saw the craziness of this supposed solution and realized there is not the slightest reason for doubting that, when the goddess mentions "mortals," she means exactly what she says she is referring to: humanity as a whole. They even went on to define these mortals with the finest eloquence as "all who are unacquainted with the divine"; "who unconsciously get confused into contradictions because they take the changeable world for true reality"; "who only see their daily surroundings but cannot see through them."

And this is the furthest anyone has ventured to go.

All the elements of the equation are there. The figures are waiting to be added up. But nobody has wanted to see the result—which is that Parmenides is not describing some theoretical abstraction, some sample cross-section of humanity, any more than he is pointing the finger at one isolated figure in the past.

He is describing us.

And the strangest thing is that we are not able to recognize our own reflection in a mirror even when it's pointed out to us—although until we are able to do this nothing else is possible.

We are offered an insight into our own existence that, if we are very lucky, will be given to us once in a lifetime; and we throw it away by assuming it refers to someone else.

But even this is only a part of the matter.

What's most laughable of all about the situation, as well as so sad, is not just that we completely miss Parmenides' point by looking everywhere except at ourselves. It's the way he virtually predicted we would miss the point. Talking in such a critical way about humanity as a whole can sound a terrible thing—and yet the fact is that his image of mortals lost in a daze, bewildered, deaf and blind, perfectly anticipates how people have reacted to what he says.

We miss the obvious; know nothing about ourselves; are so confused we don't even recognize the description of our confusion.

Learning doesn't help in the least. In fact it only gets in the way: the more learned we are, the worse things become. But nothing could be more wrong than to think this is a problem reserved for academics or the world of scholarship. Scholars are simply people; and we are all afraid of looking at ourselves. Each of us has a scholar living inside us, every day and every night.

To watch how these particular lines of Parmenides have been interpreted in the past is like taking a very private look down the corridors of insanity linking the halls of learning. Historians have automatically deflected attention away from themselves by claiming he was criticizing someone else, any-one else—Heraclitus in particular. But the irony is that it was this same Heraclitus who with grim resignation, right at the start of what he wrote, noted how whether people in his time listened to him or not made not the tiniest bit of difference. They were so deaf, so hopelessly absent from themselves, that they understood just as little of what he was saying after they had heard him as before.

And nothing has changed. The situation is precisely the same now, for those who study the fragments of what he wrote, as it was then.

With Parmenides the story is no different, no less absurd or insane. People listen and hear nothing; read but still refuse to understand. And there is something quite eerie about the way he could accurately portray how things would be twenty-five hundred years later—but no one would even notice.

12

Considering that we are not even able to recognize ourselves in what he says, it would be surprising if we were able to notice very much about Parmenides. And so we make do with myths instead.

Perhaps the strangest as well as the strongest of those myths is that he was a very serious man—stiff and rigid, his logic congealed like ice. Somehow we manage to miss the sight of him dancing in rings all around us, let ourselves get tangled unawares in the net of his playfulness.

The insight he offers into our human condition is sharper than a knife; at the same time, though, he understood there is no gentler way of cutting to the quick than with the help of humor. And the laughter starts in earnest with the description he gives of our lostness.

His fondness for jokes should already be obvious from the main image he uses to convey how mortals live their lives: "helplessness in their chests is what steers their wandering minds." But to make the humor even clearer, it will help to note that the Greek word here for "steers" has the basic sense of steering straight—of guiding straight, keeping skillfully to a precise and accurate course without deviating to left or right.

To steer and to wander: these are straightforward opposites. Steering wandering minds is a blatantly ridiculous image, a poignantly funny contradiction in terms.

And then we come to the even more sensitive part—our helplessness.

Helplessness is what does the steering because it gives us the illusion that we are really in control even though we lost any sense of direction long ago. The plainest sign that people are badly disorientated is when they start orientating themselves by their disorientation. Then they become so confused that they believe everything is perfectly in order; proceeding just fine. They are so helplessly lost they forget they are lost, even if they happen to be reminded. And this, Parmenides is softly saying, is the case with us.

Of course his choice of travel imagery is no accident. The goddess has presented us with a crucial decision to be made between two routes, and to follow the one we decide on means steering a path straight down it. But just like drunkards, who have the most peculiar ideas of what it means to walk straight ahead, this is the last thing we know how to do. We are all on self-correcting courses going nowhere.

And yet there is more to these images of paths and travel than that—much more.

All of the key expressions that Parmenides is using to evoke our state of lostness belong to a very specific vocabulary. And the essence of this vocabulary can be summed up in one single word: *mêtis*.

Mêtis was the Greek term for cunning, skillfulness, practical intelligence; and especially for trickery. It was what could make humans, at the most basic and down-to-earth level, equal to the gods. *Mêtis* might sound like just another concept. But really it was the opposite of everything we understand by concepts. It meant a particular quality of intense awareness that always manages to stay focused on the whole: on the lookout for hints, however subtle, for guidance in whatever form it happens to take, for signs of the route to follow however quickly they might appear or disappear.

And in the world of *mêtis* there is no neutral ground, no second chance. The more you let yourself become a part of it the more you begin to discover that absolutely everything, including the fabric of reality itself, is trickery and illusion. Either you learn to stay alert or you will be led astray. There is no pause for rest, or hesitating, in between.

Parmenides chooses the word "helplessness," rather than any other, to evoke the human condition. In Greek the word is *amêchania*—which literally means "without a ruse." It was used to describe people who have been tricked and trapped, outwitted, who are deprived of any resources in a hopeless situation.

And it was the one word used to define, to perfection, the result of a total lack of *mêtis*.

Then comes Parmenides' reference to "steering." As any Greek knew, the only way of steering horses or a chariot—or a ship across the ocean—was through *mêtis*. To be able to steer one had to know all the tricks of the road or the sea, to be watching, completely in the moment. Allowing one's mind to wander was not allowed.

Always it was a matter of keeping both eyes on the path ahead; looking out for warnings and, above all, for anything that could serve as a signpost or sign. But it was also a matter of listening, of being fully alert in every sense. Even a minute of deafness or blindness and one was lost.

There is a good reason why the imagery of journeying is so important for the language of *mêtis*. It's because of the speed involved. There is the absolute need to keep focused in spite of the way everything is constantly changing, or appearing to change. *Mêtis* has nothing to do with argument or careful reasoning, because there is not even the time to think. There are no moments for leisure, because everything happens far too quickly.

The demands on one's awareness are enormous. And the fact that Parmenides happens to use this language of *mêtis*, rather than anything else, to define the human condition can be viewed as a promise or as a threat.

We can see it either as a hope of rediscovering something we have lost or as a warning sign on the horizon—whichever we wish.

13

Parmenides' teaching is focused, in all its turnings and un-
foldings, on the reality of utter stillness and oneness and lack
of separation. And right from the start people have preferred
to go off down other paths of their own.

Ever since Greek thinkers in Athens laid hands on his teaching thousands of years ago, the assumption has been that he
was turning a deaf ear and a blind eye to the world of the senses
with all its changes and movement: that he was simply denying
it, escaping into a world of pure thought instead.

The assumption has been a tempting one to make. And it
seems reasonable enough—provided you pay no attention to
what Parmenides says.

From the very first moment that the goddess brings up
the issue of oneness she looks for a demonstration of it, as we
have seen, straight to the world of the senses.

How she could ever deny the senses is really quite inconceivable. Her way, the way that she says is the only one, denies
absolutely nothing. Whatever we can perceive or think of is. And
then, the minute she turns to describe the human condition,
she starts to define it as the lack of *mêtis*: a very particular
quality of awareness firmly and squarely rooted in the ever-
shifting world of the senses.

To be sure, Parmenides received his wisdom through incubation; through making the journey into another world. But
one of the most striking aspects of his journey is the importance
he attaches to describing what he sees along the way and what
he hears—especially the strange sound of hissing that was so

significant in the practice of incubation because it lies behind all the sounds of existence.

As for the place he arrived at, this was not some remote and far-off heaven. On the contrary: it was the roots, the source-point of everything that exists. As for what he discovered there, it's a teaching that embraces everything; from which nothing is excluded. And as for the teaching itself, that he is ordered to take back with him, this is not some intellectual parlor game.

Just like the knowledge of law-giving brought back by Epimenides from the underworld, it happens to be immensely practical.

Mêtis is so governed by its own inner logic that it destroys any expectations, shatters all the normal molds. Whatever *mêtis* touches is graced with such precision that it very rarely seems neat and tidy. Following the reasonable and sensible route, turning away from the risks of deception, is not its style.

It looks for certainty in the realm of uncertainty, not any-where else; is always heading straight into the heart of danger.

And the reality that the goddess is pointing us to is not some safe haven from the senses. She is showing us how to steer our way through the ocean of existence, how to navigate a world riddled with cunning and deception—how to find stillness in the middle of movement, the proof of oneness in apparent separation, the evidence of something beyond our senses through the use of reading and hearing.

As for Parmenides, he can pass on her guidelines and re-minders. But they are just signposts; and the only way to check their accuracy is by travelling. If we refuse to keep our eyes and ears alert and follow the signs, this is no fault of his or hers.

It's because we prefer to stay the way they described us well over two thousand years ago: very deaf and completely blind.

14

Lofty ideas send us to sleep. This is why *mêtis* is always stooping to meet the details scattered at our feet.

One of the most precious details in what the goddess has to say comes with her description of people as "indistinguishable, undistinguishing crowds."

In Parmenides' Greek this is just two words: *akrita phula*. The basic meaning of *akrita* is "without distinction," "incapable of discriminating." Here, the sense is perfectly—and very deliberately—ambiguous.

It means of course that the crowds are so enormous there is no real way of telling individuals apart. And the fact is that we live such collective and unconscious lives we all form a single, undifferentiated mass: following the same crazy path as everyone else, going through exactly the same basic motions with the same unquestioned habits and beliefs. Even the desire for individuality is just a mass movement of the whole. There is nothing quite as anonymous as the search to find fulfilment and self-expression.

But for the goddess there is an even more fundamental sense to this total absence of differentiation, distinction, discrimination.

The whole of Parmenides' poem is built around the need to distinguish clearly between those two paths she has pointed out—around the urgency for a conscious choice or decision. And failure to distinguish clearly, to choose, to decide, is an essential meaning of the word *akrita*.

Seen through her eyes, our problem is just this: we fail to decide. But at the same time it goes far deeper than that, because no one is even aware of any choice waiting to be made.

The fact that Parmenides plainly lays out the alternatives makes no difference. There is something eternally fascinating and intriguing about what he says; but no one would suspect he is being serious when it turns out that the choice we are being offered is between a ridiculously unreasonable route of sheer being and a totally inconceivable route of utter non-existence.

So instead we stay with the sensible middle course, twisting backwards and forwards from path to path, drifting around blindly across the no-man's-land in between.

And Parmenides manages to sum this all up—our own inability to differentiate, the impossibility of differentiating between us as we are carried along in the steadily shuffling crowds—with just one word. But, as always, there is more to what he is saying than at first meets the eye.

The sound of the two words *akrita phula* would immediately have reminded any intelligent Greek of a rather striking expression already used by Homer: *akritophullon,* which means "with countless leaves." In fact *akrita phula,* "indistinguishable crowds," sounds more or less identical to *akrita phulla,* "indistinguishable leaves." Again there is the dance of meaning, the ingenuity in evoking Homer's poems: the subtle play that makes it seem as if Parmenides was using a musical instrument rather than a simple word or two.

And nothing here is random or out of place. There is nothing arbitrary at all about the image he so artfully conjures up of humanity not just as crowds but also as leaves. For Greeks considered it quite normal—almost a commonplace—to compare mortals with leaves. As Homer had stated repeatedly, well before the time of Parmenides, the human race is as short-lived as leaves that now are growing on a tree and a moment later have been blown away in swirls by the wind.

This is the eternal perspective, the divine wisdom that Greek poets at their best were able to touch and convey: in reality all our wonderful experiences and great ordeals amount to nothing.

And from the divine point of view all our intelligent decisions are nothing but indecision. Every choice we ever make stems from the lack of any true ability to discriminate. What for us is discrimination is the exact opposite for Parmenides; is what keeps us spinning around in a daze. And what Parmenides means by discrimination is total madness to us.

The difference in perspectives could hardly reach deeper, or be more paradoxical. And yet it's very easy to understand. The decisions we make, the only type of decision we are familiar with, are always between one thing and another; between something and something else. But the decision that the goddess is facing us with is between everything and nothing—which is a completely different matter.

It makes no sense at all to our usual restless thinking, to what Parmenides calls our "wandering minds." But one thing should be quite clear: there is nothing even remotely rational about this decision, this choice between two paths.

Rationality is the first thing to go out of the window, because the choice we are being asked to make involves saying yes to absolutely everything we see or think or hear. It demands a state of total alertness, complete acceptance. There is no time to discriminate, no room to be reasonable.

And there is not the slightest reason to go along with this choice that the goddess is urging us to make. Having divine logic on her side has never been enough for her to convince anyone, because only one single factor will ever persuade us.

This is the silent awareness, nurtured in stillness, of how all our careful decisions are nothing but avoidance of that one crucial decision the gods have been waiting and waiting to see us make for thousands of years.

15

Then there is the detail I have left for last. It can seem so insignificant; and this is why it matters so much.

Parmenides' description of mortals as "twin-heads" appears almost to make sense—but not quite. So either it's passed over as quickly as possible or else it gives rise to the usual flurry of learned misinterpretations: the predictable comedy of errors. In fact, though, we have every clue we need for understanding what it means.

And, as always, the answer is so very simple.

All we have to do is look the word up in the best dictionary of old Greek terms—it was put together, in Greek, over fifteen hundred years ago—that has survived from the ancient world. And this is what it says. "'Twin-heads': forks in a road. The expression is to be understood as describing a route that has a single starting-point but then splits off into two."

Of course nothing could be more relevant to what Parmenides is saying than this particular configuration of forks in a road. It fits perfectly with all his imagery of routes and travel. And, even more than that, a fork in the road happens to be exactly where he is. The point he has come to on the route that brought him to the underworld, to the goddess, is the point where it splits in two—one fork leading off to being, the other disappearing into utter non-existence.

But that still leaves the question as to why he would have wanted to call humans "twin-heads" when the name would seem to belong more naturally to the paths themselves than to the people who travel them.

For an answer we just have to turn back to that expression used by the dictionary writer, "forks in a road." In the original Greek this is only one word—*trihodos*, which literally means "three-ways." Wherever this word *trihodos* crops up in ancient texts you will usually find it translated into English as "crossroads," but that's not right at all. Modern crossroads are shaped like an "X": two roads intersecting. And yet the ancient Greek "three-ways" were shaped like a "Y": one single road splitting off into two.

These forks in the road used to have very special properties. They were mysteriously magical; were places of power. In particular, they happened to be notorious as meeting places for the ghosts of the dead. And they were gathering places, too, for certain specific groups of people while they were still alive—people who came to be named after the places where they spent so much of their time.

"Three-wayers" was the collective name for street-walkers, cheats, third-rate tricksters and magicians, for people whom it was a good idea to steer well clear of because of their abusive and vulgar language, for the lowest of the low; in short, for the dregs of humanity.

When Parmenides describes humans as "twin-heads," there is of course the obvious humor involved—the grotesque image of people wandering around with twin heads, their consciousness split in two. But with this joking expression he is also implying much more. He is hinting that humans as a whole are just like the people who hang around at forks in a road; that in spite of our professions and all the clothes we wear, we are only bums and prostitutes and cheap tricksters who end up tricking ourselves more than anyone else.

And there was one other kind of person associated by Greeks with forks in a road. To stand at a three-ways, to be at a three-ways: these were common expressions for describing someone who is not just faced with a choice but incapable of making it, who is confronted with an impossible quandary and quite unable to decide. Parmenides' "twin-heads" are this too—people at a meeting of three ways, crowds hovering around at the point where the road divides without a clue which fork to follow.

Now we can understand precisely what this third route is that humans have fabricated for themselves. And we can understand what has confused and bewildered commentators for hundreds of years—the reason why Parmenides describes this third route as "a path that keeps turning backwards on itself."

In our indecision we go from one route to the other, then back again: take a step down one path, turn around and start to set off down the other instead. We are stuck every moment of every day at the fork in a road, going nowhere. And our famous path, our trajectory through life, consists of nothing but shuffling backwards and forwards at the point of intersection.

All the time, with Parmenides, there is the push from somewhere beyond our awareness to remind us that things are never the way they seem. Our apparent singleness of purpose is only fragmentedness and forgetfulness. Our longing for harmony is just a deep division. Our apparent clarity and decisiveness are nothing but confusion and indecision.

And this push is coming from a very particular source: not from some exotic teacher or eastern mystic but from the father of logic, from the man who helped perhaps more than anyone else to lay the foundations of our western world.

16

But, as always with Parmenides, this is not all. There is something else here as well.

He has come down to the underworld and been met by the goddess who confronts him with a forking road. He is faced with a choice as to which route to follow—either the path leading to being or the other path that leads off to annihilation and non-existence. And this vision of a forking road in the underworld, of a place where two paths meet, will have been very familiar to his audience. For traditionally, and especially to people in southern Italy, the underworld was known as the place where we come to the great fork in the road: to a *trihodos* or "three-ways" where the fateful decision is waiting to be made between life and death, between lasting existence or utter non-existence.

Then, gradually, skillfully, he conjures up the image of us humans as stuck at this place where the road divides—unable to decide between the two paths, incapable even of seeing what the choice involves, just dithering in the space in between.

And what that means is something we need to understand very clearly. We humans are already in the underworld. We are already dead.

This could seem amazing: that Parmenides would leave his fellow humans behind only to be faced with them again as soon as he arrives in the underworld. But this is simply the nature of the initiatory journey.

Initiation is never what it seems. If it were, it wouldn't be initiation. And initiatory journeys are never just a matter of travelling from one physical place to another. At the end, there is always the understanding that the point of arrival is the same as the point from which one started.

The initiatory journey leads "far away from the beaten track of humans," into what can sometimes seem unbearable darkness and isolation. But the journey eventually brings us back to exactly where we began. Nothing new is found that wasn't already present all along. And it's not a matter of leaving any physical place behind: the only thing we leave behind is our old terms of reference, every idea we have about ourselves.

There used to be other people—particularly in southern Italy, and in circles very closely linked with Parmenides—who said we are already dead, already in the underworld. Historians tie themselves in all sorts of knots trying to understand them. They argue that if these people said we are already dead then there would have been no conceivable motive for them to make, or even think of making, a journey into the underworld.

The reasoning seems quite logical, faultless. But it's totally wrong because it leaves out the one most crucial factor: consciousness.

The journey to the underworld is needed for us to realize we are already dead, for us to encounter in full consciousness the truth about ourselves as we are. Whether someone makes subtle jokes about our failure to understand this truth or laughs out loud at its devastating obviousness, hints at it very discreetly or talks about it quite openly, makes no real difference—because these are all so many alternative ways for trying to jolt us, to help us glimpse the reality of it in our own lives.

Everyone we see or know is a ghost. We are all dead. There is nothing to be afraid of because our worst fears have already been realized.

The whole of our complicated, intricate existence is just an endless limbo: a mis-step, a foot placed wrong, one shuffling movement backwards and forwards in the world of the dead.

17

For someone to say people in general know nothing, are deaf, blind, live their whole lives in a daze is bad enough. To say we are all dead and in some kind of living purgatory is even worse.

There is hardly a scenario that could seem bleaker. And quite apart from the bleakness, for anyone to say such things could seem an extraordinary arrogance.

But perhaps this is to misread the situation completely. Maybe the only real arrogance is ours—the collective arrogance of insisting that life in the way we seem to live it is all there is to existence, then accusing anyone who knows otherwise of being arrogant.

And if we start to look more closely at the bleakness in this picture Parmenides presents, we will begin to notice that the utter futility he is confronting us with is just something we have to accept as a part of his bitter gift. The gift is bitter because it means having to acknowledge some unpleasant truths about ourselves. And yet it's a gift because of the mysterious promise it contains: the promise of far more than we could ever conceive or imagine.

Eventually a time comes when there is no alternative to laying all the cards on the table and being quite honest. We have to face the situation as it is, admit its hopelessness, because only then is there any possibility of being able to move beyond it.

That we know nothing about ourselves, that all our imagined knowledge only tends to blind us even more, is demonstrably true. As for our being dead: this is not just a poetic metaphor, or the expression of a personal opinion. It's the simple statement of a truth we can all discover for ourselves at one time or another—not a question of guesswork or theory but a matter of knowledge and experience.

And its gloominess is only an appearance. Of course we all have our moments of beauty and wonder and joy; but it's no pessimism to say these passing moments are nothing but the fragmented reflection, viewed in a distorting mirror, of a reality that's far richer and vaster. All our longing is secretly focused on that vastness, waiting for it, expecting it, breathing for something that's already available to us but so untouchable because we keep reaching out for other things instead—always settling for the little things, for second best.

The greatest possible pessimism is the one each of us shares when we take at face value this ridiculous world we have managed to construct for ourselves; is when we imagine that soon we are going to die and that is that.

We can cite as many reasoned arguments as we want. But in our hearts none of us believes we only live for thirty or fifty or eighty years, because we all know there is more to us without even understanding how we know. And this is the knowledge Parmenides was working to bring to life, in our minds as well as hearts.

Without it, all the beauty and the wonder that we are able to experience are nothing. They are just a film being shown to prisoners, hovering between existence and non-existence, as they wait to be executed on death row.

18

The third way, the one that tries to patch existence and non-existence together, is what gives rise to this strange world we live in. And it has also created the most terrible complications for commentators.

It can be exquisite fun to watch the most learned men and women play hide-and-seek with each other, make obscure mysteries out of themselves, keep colliding in the dark.

One group of scholars exists that is absolutely confident Parmenides believed in three separate routes. But there is another school of experts who claim he never mentioned a third route at all. They point out that the goddess plainly introduces only two possible roads of inquiry to begin with, not three, so there is no room for a third; then they do whatever they feel is needed to erase any trace of a third way from the rest of Parmenides' poem.

And the battle rages. But no one, not a single scholar, has stopped to notice that this dispute over whether a third route exists or doesn't exist is a perfect reflection of the route itself as Parmenides portrays it: completely self-contradictory, a path on which things exist and yet at the same time don't exist.

Just as the soundness of the goddess' observation that humans are deaf and blind is confirmed by people's failure to see or understand that she is referring to them, so this fighting over whether a third route exists or not is the best possible confirmation of the terms in which Parmenides describes it. There is no need to try either validating or disproving the accuracy of what he says. We, in all our unconsciousness, are its living validation.

Certainly there are some fundamental things that can be said about this highly-disputed third route.

To begin with: Parmenides goes out of his way to emphasize its difference from the other two. He states quite plainly in the original Greek—although most scholars manage somehow to mistranslate his words—that people have fabricated this route, imagined it, invented it. In other words, this is no authentic route in the sense that the other two are. And we are already in a position to see why.

The third way is just a dizzying confusion at the fork in the road where the other two meet; a laughable to-and-fro backwards and forwards between the start of one and the beginning of the other. We can believe this is a real route if we want, call it what we like, even turn it into our whole lives. But that makes no difference. As a genuine third route, in the very basic sense of a path that leads somewhere, it simply doesn't exist.

So there would seem to be no problem in saying that really only two paths exist: not three. And yet this, too, is not right.

Parmenides makes it clear that the second of his paths, the route of non-existence, is also no real path at all. When he says there is no travelling it he means that whatever journey you might try to make on it would never take you anywhere. You might think you could start off along this route, but there would be no arriving.

It can't be travelled for the simple reason that this happens to be the route of non-existence—and non-existence doesn't exist. As a path, it's like the hand inside an empty glove. Life is generous; is supremely happy to offer us the alternative of non-existence at every moment of our existence, wherever we happen to be. But it also loves paradoxes. Because everything exists, the route of non-existence is the one thing that doesn't exist.

That leaves us with just a single route: no second, no third. And at least it would seem we can say that this one, the first of the goddess' routes, exists.

But even this is not true.

The whole point of a route is to take us from one place to another that's distinct and separate from it. And yet in reality there is no such distinction: no separating one thing from anything else. Neither, according to the goddess herself, is there any movement—so there is no room or possibility for travel. Everything is already together.

So we are being faced with three apparent alternatives. There is a path that turns back on itself and goes nowhere. There is a path that doesn't exist. And there is a path that finishes where it begins.

We can insist that the goddess has three routes, or two, or one or none. In fact it makes no difference what we say.

The only important thing is to understand that in talking to us about paths and routes she is simply using the familiar terms of our ordinary experience; is giving us some images to hold on to for as long as we need them. Our minds always try to force us into believing there is somewhere to go—somewhere else. All our apparent experience is based on movement and change. But at the heart of Parmenides' message is the need to break away from everything we are familiar with, to discover another kind of experience altogether.

Reality is trackless and pathless. We could talk, if we really wanted, of a path leading to reality: this would be the route that has already brought Parmenides, as an initiate, face to face with the goddess in the underworld. But the initiatory journey is the last we ever make. It unravels the illusion of distance, of movement. And there is no avoiding it, no shortcut, because it has to be made so we can realize there is nowhere to go.

All of the goddess' paths are just a trick. The second is an illusion, the third a joke. And as soon as you put one foot on the first, it stops you in your tracks.

You have already arrived at the end, are exactly where you always longed to be.

THREE

Think of nothing
except the creator of thought

RUMI

Our minds are like a dog's bladder. Dogs pee on things that catch their interest so they can leave their mark on them, so they can put a claim on what they imagine is somehow theirs. When anything catches our interest, we think about it and overwhelm it with the smell of our thoughts.

Just by thinking matters over we bring them onto our own level, make them a part of our world—without even realizing what we are doing.

The art of knowing how not to impose ourselves on the things we see or hear or read is a hard one to discover. We are not aware that there are secret ways of allowing them to penetrate and change us, rather than us always changing them. For this one, essential art no schools or colleges exist to teach us. Learning it takes either a long and lonely training—or just a few intense moments of searing honesty and sheer disgust with oneself.

I could take you straight to the pure gold in what Parmenides says. But if I were to do that you would give it some thought, have a pee and walk away.

So I will show you instead what has been done to the gold; the dirt it has been buried in; how what he said has been changed over the hundreds and thousands of years, altered beyond recognition. Then you might feel enough regret and remorse for what has been done that you will manage to catch yourself in the act of doing the same thing—and stop yourself in your tracks.

For there is nothing at all to be learned from Parmenides by thinking over what he says. That way you will only change it. And yet there is a way, if you approach it with alertness and the greatest stillness, of allowing it to change you.

The goddess has already managed, for someone who knows there is no separating anything from anything, to cover a fair amount of ground: has arrived at the point of exposing the horrific condition of humanity, dazed and lost on its comically illusory path.

But no one is particularly shaken or disturbed to hear about this, which is a good cause for concern. In fact scholars stay supremely unperturbed, and set about translating what she goes on to tell Parmenides next about this imaginary path without a care in the world:

"Don't let much-experienced habit force you along this way, so that you exercise an unseeing eye and echoing ear and tongue, but judge by reason the highly contentious argument put forward by me."

The results of this basic translation—there is a tendency for individual translators to vary a word here or there, but the sense they give is always the same—are as simple as they are stunning.

On his great search for truth Parmenides is being told to reject everything he experiences and rely on reasoning instead: to follow the path of rational analysis, not empirical inquiry.

And he is also being confronted with the momentous discovery of a formal distinction between the path of reason and the way of the senses. Pure thought can get us to reality—provided we turn away from this messy world of sense perception, abandon it, leave everything we see or hear or touch or smell behind.

So the goddess is against experience, an enemy of the senses; rejects them both out of hand. As for Parmenides, he is hailed as the intellectual ascetic who stripped the world of all its colors and left nothing behind except for dry argument: the tasteless food of philosophers, the logic and hair-splitting taught in schools.

But this has nothing to do with what he said. That's not the message he came back with from the underworld.

The Greek words he used have been distorted, twisted; forced into yielding a sense he never gave them and never could have given them. The result, as any sound scholar should be able to appreciate straightaway, is sheer fabrication—an imaginary invention. And what you will detect here, in these modern versions of Parmenides, is not the scent of reality: the lingering perfume of another world.

It's the smell of our own pee.

2

With a steadiness and clarity that only come from centuries of practice, Parmenides' goddess takes matters firmly in hand. She has already steered him away from the path that can't be talked about, can't even be conceived of—the one that leads to total annihilation and non-being. That was fairly simple.

And now she does much the same thing again. She steers him away as well from the path of chaos invented by humans: the one that mixes everything up, confuses existence with non-existence, manages to give things existence and then say they don't exist.

From this path of inquiry hold your mind away.
And don't let much-experienced habit force you to
guide your sightless eye and echoing ear and
tongue along this way ...

It's really important not to play around with these words. Their meaning is much too profound and serious and true. This is not just a question of getting the grammar right, of not adding commas where they don't belong. Whole lives are involved here; entire lifetimes. If one simply wants to be clever, it would be better to solve some crossword puzzles or change the tires on one's car.

There is no "path of the senses" in what the goddess is saying here, any more than there is a "path of the mind." Things are far more subtle and intricate than that. This third way gives us every opportunity for misusing our minds, our awareness, our intelligence through complicated thinking—just as it offers us every opportunity for allowing ourselves to be dragged into a world of perceptions that we are not able to make any real sense of.

And all she is asking is that we watch how we do both.

Each of us is aware of those moments when we catch ourselves staring blankly with our eyes and seeing nothing; hearing vague sounds without really hearing a thing. But the reason why we keep falling into this state is not because the senses themselves are misleading. It's because we see and hear in a daze, because we don't know how to look or listen.

Our problem is not that we see and hear. It's that we don't.

As long as we are thinking, drifting away from the present moment into daydreams about the future and past, of course there is no way we will notice what's right in front of our eyes or be able to make out the sounds coming from around us. Our eyes will be sightless, our ears dully echoing with a mass of background noise like the roaring of waves as they crash against the shore.

And this is just what happens.

The goddess has already pointed us not away from the senses, but towards them—to a state of alertness. We are so blind and deaf that we don't even notice. She is saying it's in the world of what we see and hear that oneness and lack of separation are to be found. But unless we see consciously, until we notice how everything holds together in our awareness, we are just sightless and blind.

It would be very convenient if Parmenides was telling us not to use our senses, because then there would be no need to face the fact of our blindness and deafness. We wouldn't have to confront the challenge of learning to see and listen and touch not only with our eyes and ears and fingers, but with our conscious awareness as well. For consciousness is the goal, ever-present, that the goddess is pointing us towards. And to recognize it we have to become conscious.

She would seem to be barring us from certain paths. But really she is not barring us from anything. There is nothing at all that needs to be denied or given up, except what doesn't exist. And that's nothing.

Her apparent barring is her divinely unique way of being generous. There is generosity even in the ironical humor of her laughing comment about us carefully "guiding" our sightless eyes—in just the same way that there had been laughter in her contradictory image of people steering their wandering minds.

She is simply trying to wake us up.

But we go on drifting through life, as dazed as ever, hardly aware of the reality around us. In our rush to get nowhere we just glimpse it in tiny shreds and shards, misunderstanding whatever we see or hear.

She is only trying to show us the way things are. But we turn even her message into grist for the unconscious mill. And what she says is misunderstood with a clockwork predictability, century after century: exactly the same mistakes repeating themselves time and time again as if they are being dictated by a habitual, hidden hand.

3

The basic terms of Parmenides' warning are very plain. He is telling us that the danger, with this third way, is not of our casually deciding one day to go out on it for a stroll. The real danger is that we are being forced along it right now, pushed down it by "much-experienced habit."

His mention here of much experience has been seen as the clearest possible proof that we are being warned away from giving any credence, attaching any importance, to our experience. But once again this is to get everything back to front—and completely miss Parmenides' sense of humor.

In Greek, even more than in English, the word "much-experienced" has all the overtones of vast and rich experience: of an unusual breadth and variety of experiences together with the benefits in knowledge and wisdom that they bring. And there is something nearly unbelievable about the way no one has ever noticed that this mention of "much-experienced habit" is a blatant contradiction in terms.

Habit, in all its narrow repetition of the same actions, is precisely what holds us back from breadth and fullness of experience. There happen to be other Greek texts, quite apart from this passage in Parmenides, that show as elegantly as one could hope what a joke this "much-experienced habit" is—just as much a self-contradiction as the third way itself, or as the idea of "steering" our wandering minds or skillfully guiding our sightless eyes.

To talk of much-experienced habit is like talking about a generous miser. Parmenides' point is not that we get distracted from truth by the vast wealth of our experience; it's that the broad scale of our imagined experiences is nothing but a grandiose illusion.

As for how anyone could have conceived, from Parmenides' own words, that he simply would have wanted to reject experience: this is almost unimaginable. Here is a man who, by his own account, has just had the experience of a lifetime. He has gone far beyond the limits of ordinary human experience—has made the journey while still alive into the world of the dead, come face to face with a goddess. And, in the light of this encounter with reality, our little human experiences are no real experience at all.

They are just the result of going through the same motions over and over again in our tiny sector of reality as we spend our entire lives oscillating backwards and forwards at a single fork in a road.

"Much-experienced habit" is Parmenides' gently mocking reference to the utter poverty of our existence—so gentle that, if we are genuinely proud of our corner of experience, we will even be spared the awareness that he is mocking us.

For he is not against experience. He is all in favor of it. The only problem is that the reality of experience he is pointing us towards begins where our experience ends: is far beyond anything we are used to or equipped for, almost beyond the range of our comprehension. The possibility of that experience is waiting. But it's closed to us until we start to realize how completely bound by habit we are.

And this is where the trouble lies.

The habit Parmenides is referring to is the sum total of all our little habits, and much more. It runs far deeper than the habitual behavior of having the same food for breakfast or taking the same route to work. He is talking about the habit responsible for creating this whole world we perceive and move around in; is referring to the grooves we are caught in that convince us the lives we are living are really worthwhile.

But even understanding this is not what matters most. More important than the immensity of habit that keeps us trapped is something else—the sheer difficulty of escaping. Commentators have done everything in their power to interpret these lines of Parmenides as offering a clear, rational choice between a world of the senses and a world of pure thought. And yet there is one detail in what he says that they have overlooked: the "forcing."

We are already being pushed and dragged along this way by the force of habit, violated by it. There is no simple conscious decision to be made here, at least in the sense that we usually understand decisions. This is not a choice to be made calmly in an armchair. Before any decisions can be made we first have to become aware of the forces that operate in the world to keep us exactly the way we are—that are making us stay unconscious, in a daze, deaf and blind.

The pressures ranged against anyone who wants to wake up are enormous. And there is only one power stronger than this force: greater than this pressure of habit, able to overcome it.

We will soon find out what it is.

And so we are brought face to face with the most famous statement Parmenides is ever supposed to have made. Thrown all over the place by the goddess' overturnings of everything we value or hold dear, suddenly we are confronted with something quite different—with something truly reassuring, calmingly familiar. Finally, and none too soon, Parmenides the initiate starts talking to us in a language we can appreciate and understand: "Judge by reason."

It's not easy to shake off the impression that no one has really been able to make head or tail of anything Parmenides says, with the exception of this one little statement. For thousands of years people have been blaming him for not expressing himself more clearly, for not writing in a way they could understand; have been fighting over what he meant.

But this single comment makes up for everything else, sets everybody's minds at rest.

Not only has it become Parmenides' most famous, most quotable remark. It has been presented as the jewel in the crown—the first truly great achievement in western intellectual history. Everyone from the most specialized of experts in ancient Greek philosophy through to the most popular of historical writers is unanimous in celebrating the profound significance of that one, tremendous moment when Parmenides first announces "the autonomy and superiority of the human reason as judge of reality."

And to be sure, such a moving statement would have been profoundly significant if he had ever said anything like it.

One would have thought, even might have hoped, that after what he has said so far such a statement would be glaring in its absurdity. For this would be a wonder of wonders, if the goddess were really to be telling us to judge her words by reason—we helpless humans who are incapable of judging or deciding anything by anything, not to mention by reasoning.

Then there is the possibility that the goddess could be telling Parmenides in particular, as one of the very few "men who know," to judge by reason. But this would be just as absurd. All the goddess has done so far is bewilder him with outlandish paradoxes and riddles that strip away any resemblance of reason, that at every stage keep pulling the carpet even further from under his feet.

The logic she is using is something infinitely elusive and exquisitely divine; boggling to the human mind. On this road that goes nowhere she keeps slipping forward at a lightning pace, always managing to keep one step ahead. The best he can do is listen and follow. To believe in all seriousness that here she could be telling him to judge with the help of his reason, one would have to have been fast asleep—completely unaware of what has been going on between them ever since the first moment of his arrival.

She might just as well be telling a man who is in danger of being shipwrecked far out on the high seas that all he needs to do is keep a firm grip on dry land.

But such considerations have little force for the writers of history. All of Parmenides' unclarities are a small price to pay for his single, marvellous clarity. These simple words, "Judge by reason," have become one of the greatest milestones in our past: the marker of mile zero, where reason was invented and rationality began. Everything can confidently be measured from here.

They have been made into the foundation for the whole edifice of reasoned thought on which Plato and his great successor Aristotle, followed by later philosophers, were all able to build. But no one has dared to ask if the building work was carried out in the right place—or if the foundation is really solid, let alone still standing.

They have been turned into a castle, a last line of defence against the waves of doubts that in spite of everything keep crashing in from time to time: doubts that maybe Parmenides was a mystic after all, an ecstatic, a shaman. As soon as anyone has the courage to suggest that his famous journey into another world indicates he was more than a rigid logician, the objection is immediately crushed with the reminder of the goddess' unmystical words: judge by reason.

But it has occurred to no one to suspect that this final line of defence is the ultimate fantasy, a collective piece of wishful thinking. There has been no rush to look behind the scenes and discover just how much irrationality is needed to keep defending the bastion of rationality.

For years now, scholars here and there have quietly pointed out that the goddess could never have said "Judge by reason"; that there is no possible way the word Parmenides uses could have meant "reason" in his time.

But the problems have been kept out of sight, under lock and key. The difficulties have been pushed away, the implications not been followed up.

It's just like the story of the emperor out on parade, wearing no clothes. Everyone is much too polite to point the matter out. And not one person has been willing to think things through to their logical conclusion—and admit that this whole idea of Parmenides saying we should judge by reason is another very human invention, just another fabrication.

5

The original Greek words translated into English as "judge by reason" are *krinai logôi*. Generation after generation of very reasonable scholars has worked hard to make it seem likely that *logôi*, here in Parmenides' poem, could mean "by reason." They have even tried to make this look perfectly unproblematic; not worth a second thought.

And they succeeded, at least for a while.

There is just one problem. The translation happens to be wrong. "Reason," in the sense of the faculty that appears to make us rational beings, is a particular sense this word *logos* only came to have a long while after Parmenides was dead.

The first time it starts to mean anything like "reasoning," or come anywhere close to our modern ideas about "logic," is with Plato. But that was a whole century after Parmenides. And just as significant as the gap in years is the fact that, even then, this meaning doesn't suddenly burst on the scene fully grown. On the contrary: we can watch it evolving gradually in Plato's writings, step by step, out of a strange idea he took over from his teacher Socrates and then started developing along his own lines.

This was the idea—so mysterious, people are still trying to justify it over two thousand years later—that the way to arrive at the truth is through careful discussion, by debating matters patiently, talking them through. The beginnings of all our notions and beliefs about logic lie in the spoken word.

And so we come to the original meaning of the word *logos*, as it was used from the earliest of Greek writers onwards.

That meaning was not thought or reason, or anything quite so abstract. It was talk, discussion; words said.

As for Parmenides, he uses the word more than once in his poem. And each time, just as we should have been able to guess, he gives it this same straightforward sense of words spoken or things said.

There is one point, right at the end of her teaching about the true nature of reality, where the goddess refers to what she has told him as a *logos*. And she emphasizes very tellingly that this *logos* of hers—the message she is passing on to him in words—is "trustworthy," "reliable."

The detail is important. We have become so intoxicated with what we optimistically think of as the powers of logic, so confident of our ability to distinguish true from false and tell right from wrong, that we have tended to forget one humble fact about the origins of *logos*.

Not only did it mean words spoken. It also had the strong connotation of words spoken deceitfully. In Parmenides' time there was still a very healthy assumption that if someone claimed with great seriousness to be telling the truth about how things really are, the chances were it was all a trick.

People had much more respect in those days for the magical power of the spoken word—for its ability to charm and bewitch. They were far less naive than we are: were more aware that those who know most and are most articulate are the ones most likely to deceive.

And there is another place as well, much earlier on in his poem, where Parmenides uses the word *logos*. This is the point where he describes how the Daughters of the Sun "cunningly persuaded" Justice "with soft seductive words" to open—just for them—the gates giving access to the home of the goddess who is given no name.

Some scholars have been so anxious to make anything not completely rational in Parmenides' poem disappear that they have gone to extraordinary lengths to overlook the obvious. With the greatest seriousness they have claimed that these words being spoken here by the Daughters of the Sun, these *logoi*, were logical arguments aimed at convincing Justice to let them through. But this is to mess everything up and miss the point entirely.

Soft words, cunning, seductive persuasion were all trademarks of humans or divinities who are experts in *mêtis*: who know exactly how to turn a difficult situation to their advantage, twist those who are more rigid and less flexible around their little finger, find their weak spot, who know how to charm them in every sense of the word.

These are the irresistible tools of those who use magic, who make use of *mêtis*, to get their way.

Hardly anyone has noticed that the chosen method for getting Parmenides to the goddess who will teach him is trickery, cunning, deception. And even the few who have noticed have been shocked—with good reason. But the only real shock should be our blissful unawareness of what Parmenides is actually saying.

As soon as we look behind the scenes of his supposed "reasoning" we start coming across something totally different: a world with a mysterious life and rhythm all of its own, governed by *mêtis*, where things are never quite what they seem. And we are just dancing around on a little stage in front of a non-existent audience, not able to hear anything apart from the pounding of our feet.

6

There is one simple way of assessing how specific writers use a particular word. That's by looking at how they use it. Often the most effective methods are the most straightforward.

Parmenides uses *logos* for referring to the words spoken by the Daughters of the Sun—or by the goddess herself. And this is exactly how we should expect anyone would have used the term in his time. So if we come to a place where the goddess seems to be telling him to judge the things she says by *logos*, we have to suppose she means he should judge her words by words; her talk by talk.

The only question, in this suspiciously complicated situation of his words being piled on hers, is whom he is supposed to do the talking to. And there are three alternatives: no more.

The first is that perhaps she could mean he needs to judge what she has said by talking things over with himself—in other words, by thinking. Greeks were very aware that thoughts are just an internal dialogue; and so it's no surprise that this word *logos* often crops up in expressions like "I gave myself a talking to," "I had a discussion with myself."

But there is one crucial point here that we have to bear in mind, because the moment we lose sight of it we will be floating off into the clouds. Language is something we can only get a real sense for if we stay rooted, down-to-earth; if we understand and respect the most fundamental rules of communication.

In Greek as it was spoken around Parmenides' time, if you wanted to use the word *logos* to indicate the process of thinking then somehow or other you had to make the matter clear.

Just like in English, dialogue only becomes internal dialogue when we are told that's what it is. Simply to say "I talked" or "I had a discussion" was not good enough, then any more than it is now. For the basic sake of communication, which is all that language is, you had to add the extra detail "to myself" or "with myself."

And here there is no such qualification: none whatsoever. If the goddess really is telling Parmenides to talk, one thing we can be sure of is that she is not telling him to talk to himself.

Then there is the second possibility—that he is being told to discuss what he has heard from her with other human beings after he returns to their world. But this, too, is no real possibility at all. Some plain indication, at least some hint from the goddess that those are the people she wants him to talk to, would be needed; and there is none.

And that's the least of the problems.

We might find it flattering to imagine he is being told that the way to arrive at an informed decision about her teaching will be by talking it over with other people. But that would be to forget one very forgettable detail: to the goddess, humanity is totally deluded. For her men and women are *akrita phula*, undistinguishing crowds who are unable to judge or decide correctly about anything. For Parmenides to discuss her teaching with people in general could be a good way of discovering how accurate her portrayal of the human condition really happens to be—except this is not what she is saying here.

And even that is not the main problem.

At this particular point Parmenides is being told to pass judgement, *krinai*. But only a few lines later he will suddenly be told *kekritai d' oun*: "But it has already been decided," "Judgement has already been passed." For the goddess, the whole matter is already settled. There is only being, no non-being or anything in between. There is no possible way she could be telling him here to "judge through discussion." There is no time for talking with anyone, simply no chance for consultation or informed debate.

In the goddess' eyes the judgement, the decision, has already been made. The clock is ticking away in the background. The time is up.

So we are left with just one possibility—no more. This is that she is telling him to judge what she has said by going over and discussing the details with her.

But again, there is no time.

In a minute the goddess is going to be reminding Parmenides that the decision has already been made; judgement passed. It's all over. She is not concerned in the least with any problems or objections he might have. There are no pauses in her teaching for intelligent conversation over a cup of tea. She is not the kind of goddess who has much interest in chatting.

And the fact is that she has made the situation very clear from the start. As she stated right at the beginning, she will do the talking and it's up to Parmenides just to carry away the things she says. She stuns him with brilliant riddles, tells him exactly what to do, holds him back from thinking this or that. There is no room for talk.

For centuries scholars have tried every trick to give Parmenides what they consider a more positive role. They have done what they could to make him participate in the only way that they know how to—by arguing, thinking, reasoning. But the time for all that has run out. Every possible alternative has led to a dead end. The famous announcement, *krinai logôi*, can mean neither "Judge by reason" nor anything else. Parmenides could simply never have said this. The Greek text as it has been handed down to us is wrong.

All those words he uses for describing decision or the lack of it—*krinai, akrita, kekritai*—lie behind our modern terms "critical" and "crisis." And when every single option runs out, that's the critical moment: the moment of crisis.

It's the moment of panic when there is no room left for working things out, no more time to talk or think. However hard we try to buy more time, when we look in our pockets we will find there is no money left. The delusion that we can sit down and argue in comfort for a few thousand years about what the goddess might possibly mean is over.

This is nightmare time. Parmenides' rushed ride, with the Daughters of the Sun, away from our familiar world into another reality: this is only the beginning of his journey. Travelling along the path pointed out by the goddess is a matter of tremendous speed. She has already moved off, and there is not a minute to wait or think. You are either with her or you are not.

Either you follow the signs on this path—or you will be left behind, again, with the ghosts at the fork in the road.

7

When things are not right and the situation is quite hopeless, it's best to accept they are not right. Otherwise we can spend forever trying to adapt to what is wrong. And then, after a time, nothing at all is right.

In this particular case there was no lack of opportunities for things to go wrong.

Almost every single text that has percolated down to us from ancient Greece has been filtered through a whole series of monks who acted as scribes, copying out old manuscripts as well as they could.

But they became hungry while they were working. They got bored. They were too hot, too cold; would feel tired, and they would make mistakes. Often they read the words on the old manuscript out to themselves to make the job of copying easier. But sometimes they would mishear what they said as their minds wandered, and end up putting down words that sounded like the original ones even though they meant something very different. It's also difficult to avoid the impression that now and then, unconsciously, they changed the text they were copying just for the sake of a little variety: to bring a bit of fun into their lives.

But in the case of this passage where Parmenides is supposed to have talked about the senses, and about judging by reason, things had already gone wrong long before those monks even started their quietly repetitious work through the Middle Ages.

Back in the ancient world itself there were Greeks and Romans who became experts at rewriting the past. They specialized in taking the texts of well-known older authors like Parmenides and tweaking them to give an up-to-date, clear-cut, more acceptable and respectable meaning.

They were quite open about the matter: even gave the practice high-sounding names. One group of philosophers who were known as Stoics coined the term "accommodation" to describe it—the systematic practice of adapting the past to fit the present.

And they did what they did for the noblest of causes, with the best of possible intentions. Aristotle had already laid down the ground rules for this specific game by stating that all the philosophers before him had just been making stammering, ineffective attempts to explain what he could say far more intelligently and clearly. So to update the older texts, make them more fashionably rational, was to do everyone a favor.

People like the Stoics would take statements made by ancient writers and stretch their sense as far as they could to make them yield the meaning they wanted. And if they couldn't bend them as much as they liked, then they did the next best thing.

They just changed a word or part of a word here or there; altered the text; made the older authors say what they knew they had intended to say all along.

And, as you may have guessed, our only source for what Parmenides once said about the senses and about judging was a work written by a Stoic. Everything we know about this passage in Parmenides' poem, all our quotations from it, goes back to that one work.

The man who wrote it lived not long before the time of Christ: he was well-read, highly intelligent, very genteel in his learning. And in it he quoted philosopher after philosopher, subtly forcing them to say what he reckoned they ought to have said, wrapping their statements in a cocoon of rationality like a spider after it pounces on its prey.

It was one of the many killing grounds for the life once put into words by the ancient Greek teachers of wisdom.

Even before starting to quote these particular lines from Parmenides, he carefully explained what they are saying: that we need to reject the senses and judge instead by *logos*, which of course by then had come to mean the faculty of reason.

None of the details in the explanation that he offers is any surprise. The governing theme and whole point of this work he wrote—his name is Posidonius—was very simple. It was to show how all the older philosophers had been arguing consistently, century after century, that instead of our senses or anything else we have to use *logos* as the main criterion for judging what is real and deciding what is not.

But the problem is that this same statement about the need for judging by reason doesn't just crop up in Posidonius' helpful commentary on the text of Parmenides.

It crops up again in the text itself. And yet those words, supposedly spoken by Parmenides, are something that Parmenides could never have said. They are simply what a good philosopher living hundreds of years later would have wanted him to say.

In other words, by Posidonius' time Parmenides had been well and truly accommodated; his message almost perfectly transformed. But as always happens with near-perfect transformations, the stitches and telltale signs of what has been done still stay visible—for anyone who cares to look.

That leaves us with the question of what was said before the transformation. And the answer could hardly be simpler. It's contained in the text itself.

Parmenides' goddess has already made the initial presentation of her case: explained in the most basic terms why, as they are, people are not able to understand the nature of reality. And now, she is telling him, the crucial moment has come. He has to decide about her presentation of the truth—about the demonstration "as spoken by me," *ex emethen rhêthenta*.

Very pointedly, very firmly, she is steering him back to her own words; to what she has just been saying.

But *logos* in Parmenides' time meant exactly that—words said. To be more specific, it's a term he himself happens to use later on in his poem when referring to the spoken teaching he is offered by the goddess. And as for the word *logos* that occurs right here: to give it back from Parmenides, who has nothing to say and not even a moment to say it, to the goddess is as easy as jumping into water.

There is a little mistake that it was quite natural to make when copying out ancient Greek texts, especially if one wanted to. That was the mistake of changing *logou* to *logôi*. We can even see examples of this very simple alteration being made elsewhere. And if we return the word *logôi* here that happened to be so important for Posidonius to *logou*, the resulting sense could hardly be more perfect—or less difficult to find exact parallels for in the literature of the period when Parmenides was writing.

All the goddess is saying is that the moment has come for passing judgement, one way or another, about "the demonstration of the truth contained in these words as spoken by me."

But there is one final piece to this puzzle.

Parmenides' word for "judge," *krinai*, had certainly come to mean just that by the period of the Stoics: to weigh something up impartially, make an objective decision, pass judgement in a neutral and balanced way. And yet when Parmenides himself was writing, centuries earlier, it was open to being understood in a subtly different sense.

Then it still had a meaning which is very common in the oldest surviving Greek literature—the preferential sense of choosing, opting for, selecting one alternative rather than another, of siding with someone, deciding in somebody's favor.

And as soon as we give the word in Parmenides this sense, that was so natural for his time, we at last have him not saying what other people hundreds or thousands of years later wanted him to say.

Instead we have him talking very simply about the blind alley often referred to as the human condition, and about the alternative to it, in his own voice; in the language and the poetry of his own time.

> And don't let much-experienced habit force you to
> guide your sightless eye and echoing ear and
> tongue along this way, but judge in favor of the
> highly contentious demonstration of the truth
> contained in these words as spoken by me.

140

The goddess is telling Parmenides to pass judgement but she is not going to wait for his decision. For her, it's all a foregone conclusion. And now we can begin to see why.

She is expecting him to be persuaded: is simply assuming he will give her his vote, side with her.

She is not just hoping he will be persuaded. With divine confidence she is taking his agreement for granted. And that, of course, is persuasion at its most persuasive.

We ought to have known this was coming; should have smelled it in the air. We have already been warned more than once.

Even the Daughters of the Sun who guide Parmenides into the underworld had to use persuasion to trick their way past Justice and bring him to the unnamed goddess. And there, from the moment she opens her mouth to speak, she makes it clear that her prime concern will be to introduce him to "the heart of persuasive Truth." Then, again, as soon as she presents him with the first path—the one she expects him to choose—she describes it quite frankly as "the way of Persuasion."

Now there is only one small difference from before. In telling him to accept the truth as she has presented it and go along with what she has said, she is not just talking about persuasion. She is doing it.

And she absolutely has to. She has no choice.

For her to appeal instead to our faculty of calm and balanced reasoning would be out of the question because we have no such faculty. Our objective serenity is self-deception.

We are unable to see straight, hear clearly, think intelligently or pass judgement on anything at all; are helpless, swept along by forces completely outside our control. And we are going to need something very powerful to pull us free from the "forcing" that keeps us trapped but tricks us into believing we are free already.

So it is that we are brought face to face with one of the most fascinating themes in ancient literature: the conflict between persuasion and force.

When Parmenides' goddess pits her powers of persuasion against the force of habit that drags us relentlessly along a route heading nowhere, when she draws us with her words onto another path instead, she is testifying to the old belief in something even more powerful than the violence of brute force.

For Greeks Persuasion was, herself, a goddess—the archetypal power of the female at its most erotically alluring and seductive, a being of tremendous magic who is able to overcome all the force in the world.

It's so easy to forget that Parmenides was not sitting around in a circle chatting with men. He has been rushed off into a strange reality by girls who are his "partners": to whom he is very intimately related, with whom he has a mysterious and inseparable bond. The fact that the word describing this bond is always mistranslated is significant in itself—but was only to be expected. And as for the goddess who will teach him about the mysteries of reality, she is not the straight-faced or impartial being she has been made out to be. That's just a caricature invented by people who are terrified, even at a distance, of her power.

She is not the kind of goddess who is going to leave it to you to make such an important decision about whether you stay in your little world of this-and-that or choose everything instead. She knows very well you can't possibly make the decision on your own. If you were to try, you would only make another mess of it—turn it into one more this-or-that choice when she simply wants you to have everything.

And at the same time she wants everything that you think you already have: your cleverness, your imagined ability to decide and argue and choose. She wants you.

She absolutely insists that you follow her wherever she will lead. There is no alternative; no other way. We were dragged into this illusion by a force far greater than ourselves. Something even stronger has to drag us out.

That's what logic is.

To begin with, her words can seem so fragile: so easy to ignore or contradict, argue with or argue away. They are just a haunting, unfathomable voice coming through faintly from another world with an absurd message that spells death to everything we believe. We are influenced so deeply by the force of habit that the choice she is presenting us with can seem nonsense, impossible; quite inconceivable in terms of our daily experience. But if we manage to stay with her words, steadily listen to what she is saying, then little by little things start to change. What had looked hopelessly ridiculous turns into the only hope. The choice that had seemed impossible becomes the only possible one left to make.

It's like slipping into another stream—a stream of seduction that at first seems subtle and weak but then becomes stronger than anything we have known. Before, we were being swept along like everybody else in one direction. Now we are being swept along in the other. All our little necessities fade into the background and suddenly we are brought into the presence of the one necessity that lies behind every need: the truth behind the illusion, the hidden powerhouse behind every force.

Behind the scenes of this world we have fabricated for ourselves, there is a power just waiting patiently. It speaks with a female voice that talks, in silence, through every woman who has ever lived.

And this is what logic once used to be. It was a fine, fine thread connecting us with another world: a gift from the gods, a magical lure drawing us into oneness.

But that was before it was transformed into reason and used to tie us in knots; before it was forced to operate, distorted and disfigured, in the world it had been designed to undermine; before the goddess was violated, discarded like a piece of rococo junk.

It was before people learned how to use reasoning as a mask to disguise their terror of logic.

10

Learning to see in the underworld is not so easy, to begin with. But as our eyes gradually start adapting to the darkness we find ourselves confronted with an extraordinary scene. Parmenides' goddess is presenting her case as if she is in a court of law, and he is being instructed to pass judgement.

It can seem just like a scene out of Alice's adventures in wonderland—bizarre images that come and go. Scholars wisely decide to look away; and certainly it's very strange. But there is a profound logic to it as well.

According to ancient tradition the underworld was a famous place of judgement: where fates are decided, futures sealed. And the particular place in the underworld where the road suddenly forks and branches off into two happened to be a classic site for choosing or being chosen, judging and being judged.

Parmenides' case is no exception. You have to laugh, though, at the judgement scene as he describes it. Instead of the goddess judging him, she seems to be asking him to pass judgement on her. But you also have to appreciate how true to form this is. For he loves frustrating expectations, turning normal perceptions upside down: that's a part of his job. And this is only one of the places where his almost devilish sense of humor shows through—as it often happens to do when he touches on matters of law.

But at the same time it's seriously important that we see what's going on.

The underworld, for certain Greeks, was the source of law. And these certain Greeks happened to be precisely the people Parmenides had the strongest of ties with.

In southern Italy itself there were groups of men and women—sometimes they are referred to as Pythagoreans, sometimes they preferred presenting themselves as followers of the prophet and magical enchanter Orpheus—who were closely linked with Parmenides. Just like him, they were familiar with the goddess Justice who stands guard in the underworld and watches over the realms of night. And they said it was possible to meet her, along with other divine beings in the world of the dead, through the practice of incubation.

They explained as well that the father of Justice was a god called Nomos, or "Law"; also that she had a sister keeping watch beside her whose own job was not just to make sure the divine laws are respected but to create them, to be lawgiver for the universe, to provide the laws for gods as well as humans.

And then there are those legends about Epimenides. They state that he got his knowledge through incubation, like Parmenides; that he was brought face to face with the goddesses Justice and Truth, just like Parmenides; that he learned about matters of law and legal judgement in the underworld and, because he had seen how justice is conducted there, was able to help in upholding justice and creating laws after he came back to the world of the living.

This is not all, though.

According to an old and long-standing tradition Parmenides, too, was a lawgiver. Specialists in the history of philosophy feel perfectly free to reject or accept this tradition as they choose, convinced it could have no possible bearing on our understanding of his poem. But, as usual, they fail to notice the obvious. For when we look at the poem itself we are presented with a picture of him being brought to the goddess Justice in another world, then being made the key player in an extraordinary court of law. And as we will soon see, in fact there is an entire legal dimension to his poem that takes us right to the heart of its message.

We have to understand that none of this, not the slightest aspect of Parmenides' underworld adventure, is for him alone. He makes it clear that he wasn't taken there for his own pleasure or entertainment—not even for his own information or instruction.

"Rightness and Justice" are what sent him; and the whole point of the journey is for him to observe, take note, then carry back to the world of human beings the knowledge of what he has experienced.

He is simply to be a messenger, a prophet, bringing back to his fellow men and women the laws revealed to him in another reality. And even the fact that he was selected for the journey is a part of the divine justice.

We tend to imagine the Greeks as tidy rationalists, altogether separate from the revelatory traditions of the Near East. But that's all nonsense.

It's still possible to trace in detail how the transmission of revealed teaching and inspired healing that was kept alive, for the Greeks, by Parmenides and others like him was directly related to the greatest traditions of prophecy in the ancient East. And the connections lived on.

In the Islamic world during the centuries after Muhammad there were people who explained that we would literally not be able to survive without the teachings revealed to prophets, because they are the only thread connecting us with reality. We can criticize them, manipulate them to suit our purposes, imagine we know more than the messengers who brought them;

but without those teachings we are nothing. And these people knew what they were saying when they traced the thread of revelation back to some of the earliest Greek philosophers—who for them were not impractical theorists or intellectuals but prophets and lawgivers, links in an initiatory chain, teachers of an esoteric wisdom appropriate to their own particular time.

But of course bringers of a new law, creators of a new religion, will always be misrepresented. Their teaching is bound to be hopelessly distorted. This, too, is a law.

There were a few who understood the real significance of Parmenides' teaching and kept it alive, for a while, at Velia. Then they allowed it to go underground while aspects of it were transmitted through to Egypt and into the Islamic world. Others followed the inevitable route of taking what they imagined he had taught and turning it to their own uses. Then they transformed it into what was to become that extremely successful religion—the cult of reason.

Nowadays we like to think of rationality as completely distinct from mysticism, of science as something utterly separate from the knowledge of another reality. But that's just an optical illusion.

Really there can only be one kind of knowledge. And rationality is simply mysticism misunderstood.

"Highly contentious" seems an appropriate enough way for the goddess to describe what she refers to as her demonstration of the truth. It's perfectly normal to talk about contentious theories; statements; ideas. And the one thing that Parmenides' poem has generated is an enormous amount of contention.

But there is contentiousness and there is contentiousness.

The Greek word that he uses here means much more than what we normally imply by contentious. It has the basic sense of battle, of strife. Imagining that his goddess is all smiles and charm would be as wide of the mark as taking her for poker-faced and humorless.

She means war.

She has also made it clear what the war is about. It's not about intellectual theories and ideas. Parmenides hasn't been taken all the way to the underworld just to listen to some interesting arguments. On this battleground between brute force and persuasion, the war is about our lives—about the most basic values that we stand for.

She is demolishing our whole view of the world, undermining our deepest assumptions; has just been saying that we know nothing and are lost. If we try to pretend she is talking about someone else, we can go off and win an imaginary battle or two. But we will be fighting the wrong war.

The real issue is not what we decide to think when we are reading Parmenides. It's what we do all the rest of the time.

Everything is on the line.

And so we come to the term used by Parmenides for "demonstration of the truth." In Greek it's just one word, *elenchos*. Scholars have come up with a brilliant display of colorful translations—"challenge," "argument," "testing," "proof," "refutation." And, in their own way, each of these translations has a certain validity. But the key in such a situation is to find the one, core meaning of the word from which all the others derive. That needs a steady hand and a steady mind.

This particular word, *elenchos*, always refers to a process: the process of demonstrating the truth about a matter, of exposing the truth, of getting to what's real at all costs. And just as with the word "exposing" in English, sometimes the focus is on uncovering the truth but often it's on revealing the deception or fraud. To get to the truth you have to unveil whatever is false; remove what stands in the way.

As for Parmenides' goddess, she has already pushed through to the essential truth about being and absence of separation. But to do that she has had to unmask one particular illusion: everything we confidently refer to as the human condition.

This is her *elenchos*, her bewildering but flawless logic which is flawless for the simple reason that it points straight towards the truth. And this is the process that, as Parmenides well understood, you will only allow yourself to submit to if you have let yourself be bewitched; seduced. Otherwise, as so many people have done already, you will discover ways to escape from what he says and find illusory battles to fight somewhere else—anywhere else.

There happens to be another man who became very famous in the ancient world for his use of *elenchos*. I am referring to Socrates.

Socrates went around Athens talking to people. His talk, his *logos*, was the immediate ancestor of what we have come to describe and know so well as the process of reasoning. But we haven't the least idea any more of what his talking meant.

He would start up discussions with powerful politicians or simple craftsmen; lure them into conversation about themselves; make them contradict themselves; show them how, in spite of their belief that they knew things, they knew nothing.

And what's most difficult to understand is that for him there was nothing at all intellectual about this procedure.

His one concern was with exposing the reality about people's lives—not just their ideas. He was quite charming in his *elenchos*, bewitchingly so, but ruthless in his desire to get to the truth at all costs. And after a while the Athenians got so sick of being exposed as idiots that they killed him.

Now, of course, we romanticize the whole thing. Students learn in schools and colleges about the Golden Age of Reason, and Socrates at Athens is held up as the perfect example. But no one dares to be too specific about when exactly this golden age was: whether it was before the Athenians killed Socrates, or after he had been put to death, or perhaps right at the moment of his execution.

The one thing we can be sure of is that if Socrates were to come into a modern classroom he wouldn't last for long. His questions might be tolerated for a couple of minutes. But after that he would be thrown out. There is no more room for him in our institutions than there was in ancient Athens, with the exception of our mental institutions.

And we are left in the unenviable position of thinking we know all there is to be known about reason but somehow forgetting what it is; of feeling very comfortable believing we are rational beings, and irrationally afraid of what that really means. Socrates' *elenchos* is something we have every reason to be proud of, when looking back at it from the safe distance of a few thousand years.

But it would most definitely not be welcome here.

12

The fact that Parmenides and Socrates both attached such importance to the process of *elenchos* is rather significant—considering they are often viewed as the two great fathers of philosophy. And it could seem surprising that this similarity is never looked into. But on closer examination we can see why there are few who would want to do that.

The practice of *elenchos* was not a matter of personal choice or satisfaction for Socrates. The accounts agree that he did what he did because of a divine command: he had been ordered by the gods to do it. As for Parmenides, he explains that the process of *elenchos* was revealed to him by a divine being. He, too, had no choice at all in the matter. He was given a divine command to take back what he had been shown in another world to the world of the living; and that's precisely what he did. The two founding fathers of supposedly "rational" philosophy were both carrying out a mission on behalf of the gods.

For the whole of his life Socrates went on receiving the divine guidance that had brought him to the practice of *elenchos* in the first place. It came to him through oracles, but especially through dreams. As for Parmenides: the evidence connects him with a line of priests who were experts at incubation, at invoking divine guidance through dreams. And the poem exposing his teaching on *elenchos* is the direct result of an incubation experience that brought him face to face with a goddess. We happen to find the same basic process repeating itself, centuries later, with the so-called Hermetic writers in Egypt—who left texts recording the divine knowledge that they were given in incubation and then were instructed to make available for other human beings.

To turn to the essentials: the core of the *elenchos* process as shown to Parmenides by the goddess was that men and women "know nothing." The heart of Socrates' message, the unwavering purpose of his *elenchos*, was to show people that they "know nothing." For both of them, there was no hope of real knowledge without first accepting and understanding this.

Socrates' *elenchos* took the very particular form of making the people he talked to contradict themselves: of revealing that, in spite of their apparent knowledge, they were completely at odds with themselves. For Parmenides, exposing the human condition for what it is meant showing that we are totally at odds with ourselves—living, walking self-contradictions—and that all our intelligence and best intentions only make matters worse.

For both of them, arriving at the knowledge of knowing nothing meant confronting utter helplessness. It involved having your whole being turned upside down until you no longer knew if you were coming or going. Socrates used to talk about *aporia* or "pathlessness," about watching every familiar sense of direction vanish. But later philosophers managed, gradually and very cleverly, to shift this word *aporia* away from any sense of personal vulnerability or helplessness so that it ended up becoming a technical term for the formal practice of proposing specific solutions to particular problems.

All that was at stake now was how smart one was. One's fundamental intelligence was never open to doubt. One's being was no longer on the line.

Ironically, the only signs of the *elenchos* process being kept alive in its intensity and terrible reality come not from Greece but from Egypt—from the Hermetic groups who lived there.

The two founding fathers of philosophy had offered something incalculably valuable: the chance for self-transformation. But in the West people just threw the opportunity to the dogs.

As for Parmenides, he went gladly and willingly to the world of the dead. The whole setting of his poem is meant to explain that we will never get this knowledge unless we are prepared to die before we die. Socrates, too, was well known for welcoming death with gladness. And we are told that he defined philosophy, very specifically, as the practice of learning to die before we die.

What makes Parmenides' journey "far away from the beaten track of humans" possible is longing; and he is taught through a process of divine seduction. Socrates' whole teaching was based on love and seduction. He evoked the strangest emotions in the people he met, the most overwhelming longing, and described philosophy as a love affair where lovers just have to let themselves be taken far away from their trivial attachments to wherever they are led.

Parmenides uses incantatory language to describe how he was drawn through a mysteriously magical process into reality. As for Socrates' *elenchos*, it didn't have the expected effect of making people think more clearly. It numbed them instead, paralyzed their thoughts, made them feel bewitched—and Socrates liked to describe himself as a magician, an enchanter, an expert in incantations.

Now, of course, this is all dismissed as pure irony on Socrates' part while Parmenides' incantatory language is ignored. But the loss is only ours.

The essence of what Parmenides learned from his teacher was stillness. He got his knowledge through the total stillness experienced for hours, or even days, in incubation. And he happened to be a priest of Apollo—a god who was famous for inducing extraordinary states of stillness. Socrates said the god he was most closely linked to was Apollo, and he was notorious for his extraordinary states of stillness: for staying utterly motionless, rooted to the spot, for hours or even a whole day at a time. Nowadays scholars think that all he was doing was busily thinking problems through. And of course they are free to do so.

But the fact is that a busy mind makes a busy body. When the mind is restless and starts wandering it makes the body wander, too. Constant thinkers are very fidgety people.

It seems good enough for us to say that Parmenides and Socrates were philosophers. Then our skins are saved, everything is safe. Everything is understood.

And yet there is no secret about the fact that originally the word "philosophy" meant love of wisdom. Now it has just come to mean the love of endlessly talking and arguing about the love of wisdom—which is a complete waste of time. Philosophy is a travesty of what it once was, no longer a path to wisdom but a defence against it.

There is only one way to wisdom: by facing the fact that we know nothing and letting our reasoning be torn apart. Then reality is what is left behind.

13

There is only one tale of a path left to tell …

Perhaps you haven't noticed it. But the moment for choosing has come—and gone. There are no options left any more.

The path of non-existence never had the makings of a story, good or bad: there is nothing whatsoever to say. And the story about the human predicament was a good joke, for a while. But then it's time to be moving on.

There is no question about where the goddess is leading us. That we already know. The only question is whether we are really able to follow. For we have come to the great divide.

When she talks about the one remaining "tale of a path," the word that she uses for "tale" is *muthos*—the distant origin of our "myth." And this isn't the only place where she uses the same word to refer to her teaching. The detail is rather eloquent.

Historians have invented an entire schedule to help us understand the marvellous progress of the ancient Greeks and make sense of our western culture as a whole: a grandly ordered process of transition from *muthos* to *logos*, from myth to reason. But Parmenides' goddess is supremely unaware of any such sequence. She uses *muthos* just as much as *logos* for describing what she has to say. And, even though you might think this insignificant, it's not hard to see the ultimate reason why.

We distinguish between myth and reason on the same basis that we distinguish between fiction and fact: some things are real, others are not. But for the goddess everything, including her teaching, is what we now would call a myth. She is a myth. Everybody is a myth. You are a myth. And this is the truth.

It can be astonishing to watch how serious people are in insisting that Parmenides' teaching about the reality beyond illusion should fit into the framework of their illusion. They are perfectly sure that for Parmenides we are real and unicorns are not. In spite of all the evidence to the contrary, they are confident that for him some things exist and others don't; then they judge on this basis what he could or could not have said.

But they are not with him at all. They are back at the fork in the road—which is a good enough place to be. There are many other ghosts to keep one company. Everything keeps coming and going, living and dying. We can feel terribly lonely; but there is enough to worry about to make us forget our loneliness. And of course science performs great wonders there. It has set up telephone booths at the place where the road forks, and keeps inventing new forms of communication. But if you are happy to stay there, at this mythical place in the underworld, you can't possibly follow Parmenides where he goes.

These words of his, saying there is only one path left to talk about, mark the beginning of what is by far the most discussed and studied passage in his poem: the passage where he introduces us to reality. It has become known by the title "Fragment Eight," and this is where people turn to for the nuts and bolts of his teaching. This is what they focus all their effort on; what they argue about most extensively.

What they don't realize is that Fragment Eight can never be understood, or even approached, without the necessary preparations. Until we have focused on the earlier part of Parmenides' poem and absorbed what he has to say, reading it or studying it is useless. The fragments of his poem come together not on a drawing board, or in a book, but in ourselves.

More pages have been written about this Fragment Eight than about anything else Parmenides cared to mention. The irony is that this is precisely the section of his poem about which the least can be said.

Things have to be said about the sections that come before, because we need to understand as well as we can exactly what's involved. But once the point is reached where there is only one path left, very little in the way of explanations is really possible because this is not a path that can be trodden with someone else.

You simply have to follow the signs.

So I will just draw attention to a couple of things here and there: that's all. I will offer a few points of orientation, because the signs have become rusty and covered over through lack of use. But you will have to make the journey on your own.

And that's the beauty of it. It exists for you alone.

14

There is only one tale of a path
left to tell: that is. And along this way there are many,
many signs that as well as being birthless it's also deathless
and whole and of a single kind and unmoving—and neither
is it incomplete.

This is how the famous Fragment Eight begins. The goddess is already at work, weaving her web of logic. But although we can see quite clearly how she starts, we can only guess how it's going to end.

Defining logic is very easy. It's the expression of a reality which is utterly impersonal, which is governed by an absolute necessity that has nothing to do with our ideas or beliefs. And it gives us more than we could ever hope for, but also much less.

These few brief lines provide the basis, the foundation, for what the goddess will go on to say. The structure that she will begin to create around them is extraordinarily detailed and intricate—as she turns to explain and justify and build on each of these points in turn. But in spite of the elegant precision she puts into her work, there is one factor that makes all this preciseness infuriating and downright absurd.

We really don't have the faintest idea what she is talking about. Instead, we are just faced with the signs in the middle of darkness and the riddles at the heart of clarity that we ought to expect from a goddess at home in the underworld.

As to exactly what it is in what she says that "is," this remains a mystery in spite of all the learned theories and possible solutions that philosophers have come up with over the past two thousand years. The arguments for birthlessness and deathlessness, wholeness, completion, are added by her one after another; meticulously interwoven. But she leaves us none the wiser about precisely what it is that her arguments relate to. We are not given a single direct pointer to the identity of the "it" that is all these things—not yet.

It's as though someone were to start building a house across the road from you. Or rather, you only guess it will be a house; and you have no idea what it will look like once it's finished. You have no way of knowing, either, who is going to live there. And it would be strange if, at last, you were to find out that the house is being built for you.

The goddess' work is to show us we are living in an illusion. But the only way for her to do this is by entering the illusion and creating an illusory structure in it that will help us to realize we are surrounded by illusion. If we listen to what she is saying, follow her in what she is doing, we will gradually start to find ourselves inside that structure she has built—able to look out at the world we used to live in from the perspective of this structure rather than looking on at what she is creating and desperately trying to understand it from our old, familiar point of view.

But she can't tell us what the building is because we have to discover that for ourselves. All she can do is build it and invite us in. And to accept her invitation we have to pay attention to her signs.

The fact that the one and only path pointed out by the goddess with approval should be so full of "many, many signs" was of course to be expected. Signs are needed for guidance. They are invaluable for finding a way out from pathlessness and helplessness, for discovering one's bearings; are essential if one is going to use the help of *mêtis*, of cunning and watchful alertness, to escape from an impossible situation.

But "signs" for the Greeks were associated not just with the path-finding abilities of *mêtis*.

They were also associated intimately with the gods—with the type of guidance revealed by them that can only be described as divine. And every one of the goddess' signs is like a thunderbolt shooting into this world of ours, devastating in its ability to destroy our whole perception of existence.

They are signs pointing to oneness, stillness, completeness. And if you dare to look, you will see them lighting up the whole night landscape so that you don't have to rely on a little flashlight any more. Everything looks practically the same, nearly ordinary; almost familiar.

But if you manage to keep going, you will find yourself walking in another world.

15

When the first signs start coming, one after another, they are all pointers to something birthless and deathless. And they come fast. They appear so quickly that unless you are very alert they will begin to blur; to seem nothing but words.

It never was
and never will be because it is now, all together,
one, holding to itself. For what possible birth of it
will you look for? In what way could it have grown?
From what? To say or think "from what is not"
is something I won't allow you, because there
is no saying or thinking that is not. And, besides:
if it started out from nothing, what could have
made it come into being later rather than sooner?
So it must either be, completely, or not be.
Neither will the strength of persuasive proof ever permit
anything to come into being out of non-being
alongside it. And this is why Justice has not allowed
freedom for creation or destruction by relaxing her
constraining grip. Instead, she holds fast.
And the decision in these matters comes down to
this—is or is not. But it has already been decided:
the judgement has already been passed as necessary
that the second of these paths is to be dismissed
as unthinkable and unnameable because it's no true way
while the other is to be allowed to be, and really
be. And how could it be that being could be at some

later time? How could it come into being?
For if it came to be, it is not; and if at some point it
intends to be, then again it is not. So it is that creation
has been extinguished, and of destruction there is
not a word to be heard.

To understand what the goddess is saying you have to keep a firm grip on yourself, not allow your mind to wander. And to learn this can take years.

But one thing that's hard not to notice very quickly is the way she wastes no time.

In a few brief words, almost before you can blink an eye, she has got rid of the past and the future. And now is the only thing left: all that exists is now.

Philosophers have gone into shock. Most of them have decided she is a fool who has no understanding of time; and the general consensus nowadays is that, even though she has taken away the past and future, there can't possibly be anything time-less about her now. "Now," as they argue very reasonably, is our standard way of referring to a point in time different from the future or the past—and so the fact that she chooses this particular word shows she is talking not about anything time-less but about simply one point in time.

And those who talk this way betray another fact: that they have never consciously experienced what it means to exist now. The goddess' words are a hundred-per-cent correct. There is only now, always the same as itself in its present and timeless fullness; and whatever seems to happen, happens now.

Pondering the future, pondering the past, even pondering the nature of future and past and now, occurs now. Everything is now, all together, without the slightest gap or absence. Nothing at all is missing that could create any separation. Even the thought of something missing is only a sign of wholeness. Even the feeling of separation is simply a proof of oneness.

But to realize this our minds have to be very, very still.

The goddess is doing her absolute best to get through to us in a way we can understand. And yet there is only so much that even a goddess can do.

We, too, have to do our part. The trouble is that even to analyze her message with the greatest attention to detail is not enough, because there can be no real scrutinizing of the details without scrutinizing the whole. And we are that whole. Unless we realize this, it's just as if we were to receive a hand-written message warning us our lives are in danger—and were to spend all the time that's left to us arguing over the color of the ink.

This may sound rather serious. And that's because it is. But the goddess' job also has one other aspect: to make sure we never get lost in being too serious about our seriousness.

Right at the end of her "signs" about birthlessness and deathlessness, she makes the comment that "of destruction there is not a word to be heard." The remark sounds so casual that it hardly seems worth stopping to notice.

And yet it contains a tremendous joke.

Her word for "destruction" was a standard term, especially with Greek poets, for death. And—as Greek poets liked to say—this destruction, this death, is what silences us so that when we have disappeared or died "there is not a word" about us "to be heard."

But here, instead of death silencing us, death itself has been silenced. With a grand, magnificent gesture the goddess has destroyed destruction; put death to death.

Her humor here is of the very particular kind that belongs only to gods or magicians. It springs naturally from an awareness of total freedom: the freedom of being able to turn the tables on all those apparent realities that haunt us and seem to govern our lives.

By extinguishing creation and destruction, destroying death, the goddess is magically twisting our perception so that what had seemed unquestionable has vanished and only what had been unthinkable remains. But it's not that, in doing this, she is rewriting history. There is no history to rewrite. It's not a matter of changing what has happened, because nothing at all has happened.

And that's what it means to exist now.

16

The goddess' announcement that destruction has been silenced looks, at first sight, just like an authoritative statement about the way things already are. It can seem infinitely tempting to suppose she is doing no more than describing the laws of existence laid down in the distant past. But that would be to forget one rather important detail.

In terms of reality there is no past.

You may think I am joking. But this is perfectly serious; and it calls for a little explaining.

With her sweeping statement about the extinguishing of creation and the silencing of destruction—or the extinguishing of birth and the silencing of death, because in Greek her words for "destruction" and "creation" also meant "death" and "birth"—the goddess is pointing back directly to the announcement she made just a moment before about the great decision that has been arrived at. This was the decision to abolish any form of non-existence as "unthinkable and unnameable," as so impossible to think or talk about that it no longer even has a name.

And yet we know more than a little, already, about that crucial judgement she has just announced: about how exactly she was able to say *kekritai*, "it has been decided." The particular decision she has in mind had been made only a minute or so earlier, with the help of a great deal of encouragement and persuasion on her part—by Parmenides.

With all her talk about solemn judgements, so far-reaching that they are responsible for the rearranging of reality itself, the goddess is referring to decisions made not at some earlier point in history but at a slightly earlier point in Parmenides' poem.

In other words, we are being allowed to watch and listen to her demonstrate her powers as a goddess: are in the extraordinary situation of being able to observe her as she exerts the peculiar divine authority which guarantees that, the moment something is decided, it becomes reality in the same instant. Simply to say that something is the case is, for a goddess, quite enough to make it happen.

She is not just offering us some unique insider's perspective on the cosmic scheme, providing an accurate description of the laws of reality. Her teaching and her message—which is Parmenides' poem—turn out to be far more than some inspired account of the ways things already happen to be. They are a magic spell, and his record of them a magical text, that through their own power determine how things are to be.

The cosmic order is being established at the only possible moment it ever can be: right now.

But even to say this is just to tell a fraction of the story.

If Parmenides were simply being allowed to watch her shape reality and lay down the laws of existence, that would be extraordinary enough. And yet the fact is that he is not only standing by, watching and listening. He has already been sucked into the process, drawn into becoming a party to the final judgement. It was never the goddess' intention that he should wait there passively preserving her divine decision for generations to come. She can encourage him, use all her powers to persuade him. But the decision, however necessary, has to be his—just as the decision, now, is ours.

I already explained why this decision Parmenides is faced with, this choice, has nothing to do with intellectual dilemmas or matters of theoretical interest. It's a question of life and death; is what will decide his fate and destiny. All the choices and decisions we are faced with in our lives are make-believe. But to make this decision demands a very specific quality of consciousness, as well as a tremendous sense of responsibility.

Now, though, we can start to see that it's not just a matter of him taking responsibility for his own destiny. It's a question of being asked to become responsible for something even vaster, and almost inconceivable: the destiny of everything, the fate of reality.

Through being drawn into the legal process that determines what is and is not to be, Parmenides is being invited to participate actively and consciously in the origins of the universe. The place he has come to, in this strange court of law at the heart of reality and the roots of all existence, is where everything has already been decided—but still is being decided, because the origin of the universe is now.

We can have no idea of what it means even to touch the edge of that consciousness, that responsibility, until we are able to experience what it means to exist now. Without any knowledge of the stillness that allows us to do this, Parmenides' message will always be just complicated words.

And yet what's so amusing, and so amazing, is that there is no escaping from this responsibility: not even for a moment.

Reality has no middle ground. It offers no neutral territory that we can safely retire to, where we can ponder things at leisure and put aside what's important for another day. The laws of reality are ruthless. Somehow or other, we have to contribute; in one way or another we are bound to participate.

Even our failure to understand that there is a decision waiting to be made is already our decision. We are responsible even for our irresponsibility.

And if we love trapping ourselves, if we enjoy being swept away into an imaginary existence of our own, that's a decision we are totally at liberty to make. We are free to play the role of slaves, and we are free at every moment to be free.

17

After the signs of birthlessness and deathlessness come the others. They follow in close sequence: signs of wholeness, signs about being of a single kind, unmoving. And then, last of all, there will be the pointers to completeness.

> And also: there is no dividing it
> because it's all alike. There is nothing more here
> that could stop it from holding together with itself
> or less there. But all of it is full of being. So it is that
> everything is continuous with everything because
> being draws near to being.
> And what's more: motionless
> in the bonds of great fetters it has no beginning or end
> because creation and destruction have wandered far
> far away. And true and persuasive evidence is what has
> driven them out. It stays just the same in the same
> unaltered state, lies by itself on its own and so remains
> constantly where it is. For mighty Necessity holds it
> fast in the fetters of a bond that shuts it in from all
> around; and this is why it's not right for it to be
> incomplete. For there is nothing that it wants or lacks—but
> non-being would lack everything.

None of the goddess' main points here should, in themselves, be surprising. The particular awareness of completeness that contains no sense at all of any need, of the slightest lack, was something Greeks associated very closely with the divine;

with matters of religion. And it's no secret, even though there are those who have tried to keep it a secret, that the language she uses for describing reality has an intimate connection with the language of religious hymns.

As for the reality that always remains the same, "in the same unaltered state," it's still waiting to be discovered now— just as it was in Parmenides' time.

What's so peculiar , though, is the images she has chosen to use.

The imagery of bonds and fetters is impressive. And in fact it's far more than simply striking. As we'll see later, it contains the final clue to understanding Parmenides' poem.

But just as impressive, in its strangeness, is the imagery of creation and destruction being made to wander far away. The goddess has just got rid of them both: nothing would be more natural than to assume we have heard the last of them. And yet here they are again. What's more, her picture of them being driven out and forced to wander far away makes no sense at all in terms of the reality she is describing—where no separation can exist, where everything is motionless and holds together with itself.

There is a puzzle here as to why these images are so important she would want to include them. And the puzzle has its answer.

Parmenides is very clear about the decisive factor responsible for having creation and destruction driven out. He calls it "true *pistis*." And this word, *pistis*, had a great deal to do with persuasiveness or the act of being persuaded. It could mean the special trust and confidence built up as a result of being won over, having all one's doubts dispelled. Or in certain circumstances it could mean the things that help create this trust in the first place.

Parmenides' "true *pistis*" is usually translated as "true trust." But here this makes no real sense at all; is far too vague. And the other translations that have been offered along the same lines are just as hollow, as inappropriate.

And yet there is also another meaning that *pistis* could have.

This was the true evidence presented to a court of law. In a legal context it became the technical term often used for describing evidence that would allow a final judgement to be based not on gossip or unreliable rumors but on a persuasive, convincing demonstration of the truth. And of course a legal context is precisely what Parmenides has been evoking, with such patience, through his imagery and language.

He has been drawn by the goddess into participating, at the roots of all existence where there is no past and no future, in a court of law that happens to be the origin of every court of law—which is not exactly irrelevant or inappropriate for someone known to have been a famous lawgiver himself.

It was almost a hundred years ago now that an American scholar saw what Parmenides' powerful image of driving out and wandering away naturally implied. He realized that "true *pistis*" here means the persuasive legal evidence or proof presented to a court, explained that "Parmenides clearly has in mind an action at law" and that with the driving out of creation and destruction he was describing something quite specific: a formal act of banishment.

But, as so often happens in such cases, later writers quickly pushed his observations aside. We tend to have the fond idea that scholarship is always marching forwards in its evolutionary stride, constantly progressing. The reality is that it's like a tide—sweeping in and out with the waves of fashion, throwing up beautiful shells on the beach along with garbage and then sucking them back into the ocean.

As for the American scholar: what he saw was perfectly true. And yet he didn't go far enough.

18

People have often noticed how generous Parmenides is with his use of the words "for," "because." It would be difficult not to. But what's not so often noticed is the fact that these same words played an important role in the language of religious hymns: being able to throw a little light on the mysteries of divine existence has always been a crucial aspect of religious life.

With Parmenides, the "for" and the "because" help to create a unique impression of disciplined logicality. The further we follow him on his journey, and the stranger the signs that appear, the more reassuring this impression of logicality becomes—until with a little luck we will start to realize, even if we didn't notice before, that his understanding of logic has nothing to do with ours.

He adores giving explanations. We adore him for it. There can be an immense security and sense of satisfaction in having things explained, and Parmenides loves to play with our expectations. He is so accommodating of our desire for clarity: so considerate in his willingness to make things plainer for us even when his explanations turn out to be jokes, even when they are more mystifying than anything he set out to explain and end up drawing us still deeper into a world impenetrable by our reasoning mind.

And here, where he has come to the point of explaining that the reality he is concerned with never moves or stirs or ends and we might be expecting some impressively reasoned argument for why this should be the case, he confuses and disappoints us by offering nothing of the kind.

Instead, all he gives is a vivid image: that's the way things are "because" creation and destruction have been banished by persuasive evidence, driven out.

This peculiar explanation needs, itself, some explanation. First, though, we have to see what it is that Parmenides felt needed to be explained.

For a cosmic order or divine reality to be immovable, unchangeable, unending, sounds natural enough to us. But to Greek poets and audiences in Parmenides' time it would have seemed anything but natural, or normal. In those days it was still taken for granted that changes in the cosmic order are a rule. The universe was based on the very same laws of creation and destruction, of birth and death, that Parmenides has banished. Everything depended on the principle of succession as children among the gods tried to inherit and take over from their parents—usually with a great deal of violence. Only extreme measures could ensure that things would stay just the way they are without another round of patricide, another killing of another father.

And extreme measures are exactly what Parmenides is describing.

Precise details of legal practice used to vary from city to city. But there was one form of banishment that dated back to the ancient Near East, and the terms chosen to describe it changed very little over thousands of years. It was so severe in its consequences that historians have called it perhaps the most solemn single public act known to Greek law. This was the formal act of *apokêruxis*: of disowning and banishing children from the land where they once had lived.

Its general purpose and design made it an almost perfect reverse image of adoption. In place of acceptance or inclusion, it spelled ultimate rejection. And because the punishment meant being banished not only from one's home but from one's country, we find the same word being used for referring to it that Parmenides uses here—*apôthein*, to "drive out" or "push away."

Disowning a child meant disrupting not just the family but the family's whole lifeline; meant breaking its basic cycle of death and birth. This process of disinheritance was considered so serious that outside of Athens it tended, as a rule, to need submitting to a court of law. Over time a whole industry of persuasion and artful rhetoric grew up around it as people tried their best to convince those who were going to decide each individual issue that they should pass judgement in one way rather than another. Sometimes, to make the case on behalf of the father as strong as possible, the child would openly be accused of intending the most unthinkable of crimes: the crime of patricide.

And apart from the simple fact of banishment this punishment undid the children completely, had the power to make them nobodies in the eyes of the law. It even undid the birth ceremony—when people are given their name in the first place—by taking the name away. In being made nameless it was as if even the reality of their birth had been cancelled.

Now we can start to see how everything Parmenides says hangs together.

The basics of legal language used to be very straightforward. *Pistis*, the persuasive evidence presented in a court of law, is what leads to *krisis*: the critical final judgement. With the goddess' new announcement about the verdict already arrived at on the basis of persuasive evidence, she is pointing straight back to her other announcement a little earlier about the judgement already passed thanks to all the persuasive pleading on her part. Her statement, here, that creation and destruction

177

have been driven far away is inseparable from her statement, there, that creation and destruction have been abolished—and that anything apart from unchanging being is to be rejected as not just unthinkable but "unnameable."

Or to use her exact word there, from this moment onwards it's *anônumos*: "without a name."

In both places she is summarizing one and the same decision. A single legal process is being described with the help of different phrases and terms. Her words hold together with a simplicity that illustrates, to perfection, what she says about the utter singleness of reality; about how it all holds together with itself.

And just as the spinning of the chariot wheels in Parmenides' initial account of his journey imitates exactly the spinning motion of the opening doors, so the closer we come to this oneness the more clearly everything becomes one.

The joking remains constant, too. The goddess' crazy, delightful, grand sense of humor stays as true to form as ever. What has been banished is not just one, or two, individual successors but the principle of succession itself: not just a child by birth but the entire process of birth and death.

And what's left behind is all alone—without any future to look forward to although without the slightest sense of any lack, because it already knows the perfect fullness and completion that we always long for but are also terrified we might one day be able to find.

19

And so we come at last to the mystery at the heart of Fragment Eight. There has been the sense so far of always following a path, making the effort to keep up. But sometimes the hardest thing of all after travelling a long way is to acknowledge that one has finally arrived.

It was only to be expected that here, in the climactic part of Parmenides' poem, a riddle would be waiting to be solved. What was perhaps not so predictable was how utterly simple the solution would be.

The goddess' final signs are, appropriately enough, signs of completion. You may have noticed her slip into introducing them when she started to explain why "it's not right" for existence to be incomplete—because "the fetters of a bond" shut it in "from all around." And, now, she is about to seal her whole description of reality by rounding it off with the same language and the same ideas:

> *Because there is an ultimate*
> *binding limit, this means it's perfectly complete—*
> *just like the bulk of a sphere neatly rounded off*
> *from each direction, equally matched from the middle*
> *on every side.*

The agreement between her earlier words about enclosing fetters and what she will end up saying in this final passage is perfect. Here, too, there is the same emphasis on existence as complete because it happens to be held fast in a circular bond.

And if that was all there was to the matter, there would hardly be a problem. But it's not.

After she has already introduced the signs of completeness with her comments on the surrounding "fetters of a bond," and before she comes to this closing passage about binding circularity, the goddess speaks a few additional lines. That's the riddle—not just to understand what these extra words really mean but to discover why she should have chosen to speak them at, of all places, this particular point in her teaching.

Here is how those additional lines begin.

> *And what exists for thinking is the same*
> *as the cause of thought. For you won't find thinking*
> *without the being in which it has been uttered.*
> *For there is nothing else and will be nothing else*
> *apart from being, because Fate has bound it to be*
> *whole; unmoving.*

The goddess' logic moves forward, as always, with the sure-footed "for" and "because" that will only make you giddy if you start looking to the left or off to the right. But if you make a point of remembering what she has already said, and stay close to her at every step, nothing could be more straightforward.

20

First of all Parmenides repeats the old familiar expression, "what exists for thinking." That, by now, should need no more explaining. But next he mentions something quite new—that what exists for thinking is the same as the cause of thought.

This does need some explaining. And an explanation is exactly what we are offered.

By describing the act of thinking as something which is uttered "in" being, he is telling us to begin with that there is no question of thought and existence being identical. They are the most basic aspects of reality, as intimately intertwined as anything can be. But they are not the same.

Then there is his choice of words when he states that thinking is "uttered" in being. This is a reminder that the Greeks naturally considered thought an internal form of speech. But here, where we have been brought to the point of seeing that reality consists of nothing apart from existence and what thinks or perceives it, there is no longer any question of inner or outer. Whatever we consider outside us is really inside, and anything we view as internal is right out there—just as much a part of the existence all around us as anything else.

And what Parmenides is also saying is that being is the indispensable, inescapable medium for consciousness. You won't find thought or perception without existence because existence is what makes it possible for them to be expressed: is the medium that nourishes them, the ocean that consciousness occurs in.

But this little word, "in," used to mean more to the Greeks than it does for us.

As well as having the obvious sense of indicating where something could be found, they also used it to indicate what that thing depends on. For example they would tend to talk about someone's fate being "in" something where we would talk about it being "in the hands" of that power or thing.

This is why, when the Greek bible makes the famous statement "In Him we live and move and have our being," in fact we are being told that the divine reality is not only the medium of our existence but the cause of our existence as well: what makes it possible to begin with. And this is the reason, too, why Greek philosophers after the time of Parmenides liked to emphasize now and then that to be "in" actually means to be "caused by."

So we can see just what it is that the goddess is explaining, and how she is choosing to do so.

She has already explained that whatever exists for thinking—the object of all our thoughts and perceptions—is being. But now we are being told something else: that the initial cause of thought, what gave rise to it in the first place, is also being.

In other words we are being shown that the object of our thinking or perceiving, the end-point and result of the process, its final focus, is identical to its point of origin. The beginning and the end are the same.

For Greeks, to imply that the beginning and end of something are one and the same was to conjure up immediately the image of a circle. And the circle, for them, was the perfect symbol of completion; of finishing what already has been started; of creating the magical bond that links the end back to the beginning.

To say that the cause and object of thinking are the same is to point to the utter completeness of thought. And this could only belong precisely where we find it stated: among the signs of completion.

But that's not all. To say this is also to evoke the image of thought or perception as a process that sweeps around from its starting-point right back to it again, just like the circumference of a circle. Thought itself is a circle. And by surrounding her final account of it, on both sides, with the imagery of circular bonds the goddess is not only emphasizing its perfect circularity. She is demonstrating it at the same time through her own words—completeness within completeness, circle held fast inside of circle and bond inside of bond, perfection surrounded by perfection.

And from this perfect reality that she describes, there is no escape.

21

In reality, the cause and the object of perception are one and the same. They have to be, because there is only being. And yet, in our awareness, they almost never are.

We are constantly being bombarded by thoughts and perceptions. Whatever we see or hear, every idea that enters our minds, sends us off into a maze of thoughts about the past and future. Our whole lives are an incoherently coherent picture of reeling from one impulse to another, of always struggling for the completeness no one quite manages to find. We try to discover it by making plans that will lead to fulfilment in some future; but the greater the effort, the further it slips away.

For the only completeness is now.

Real completeness is a nightmare. If we are ever lucky, or unlucky, enough to touch it for a moment it will never stop haunting us. Nothing will ever be enough. We can wander backwards and forwards forever trying to relive it; but even our endless circlings are only a parody and mockery of a circle, because we have no idea of how to bring the beginning together with the end.

With the goddess, things are very different. Naturally they are different, because she is a goddess.

Her words are spoken not out of restlessness and searching but out of completeness. And this is why they keep exerting such an uncanny attraction: because we long for that completeness even while trying to analyze or tear it apart. Her awareness, itself, is complete. She starts from being and ends exactly where she began—with being in all its perfection and completion.

And this is just how things have to be, because in reality we never find out more or discover anything with time.

Everything is already present in the beginning.

Reality is perfect, complete. But we are lost in its perfection, trapped in its completeness while imagining we are free. And there is nothing we can do to change it—to make it less perfect, or more—except by making one decision. The only choice we have, our single real freedom, is to decide whether to participate in it consciously or be at its mercy; whether to help complete the circle through our own awareness or just stay lost inside it.

Reality is our problem and also our answer. For, as always, the answer to the problem lies not in running away from it—there is simply nowhere to run to—but in turning to face it.

The one option we have is to turn around and face, head-on, all the impulses that keep bombarding us and pushing us in every direction. By turning each impulse back on itself, we are returning thought and perception consciously to their source. For every thought and perception comes from being, and in returning them to being we complete the circle: make them perfect.

Then, instead of being caught somewhere along the circle like an animal in a cage, we stop being a victim of reality and become the cage.

Whatever thought or perception comes at us, all we have to do is turn our attention back onto it. Instead of seeing without really seeing, we can stop to look. Instead of half-hearing sounds that irritate or please us, that either make some sense or just seem to be noise, we can listen to them all but at the same time be aware of listening to them.

This is simply a matter of letting nothing go unperceived, because every single thought and sensation and perception is waiting to be returned by us consciously to its source. Their aggressiveness and gentleness, their violence and impatience and their sweetness, are their way of urging us to do what we have to do.

Of course to our usual, wandering minds—that can only focus at the very best on one thing at a time—to do this is not just difficult. It's unimaginable. But there is another state of awareness we all have access to; and, for that, nothing could be more natural.

This is the awareness known to Greeks as *mêtis*.

Mêtis is the particular quality of intense alertness that can be effortlessly aware of everything at once. While our wandering minds go off on their endless journeys, it always stays at home. And its home is everywhere. *Mêtis* feels, listens, watches; can even be aware at the same time, if left to itself, of every thought drifting into and out of our consciousness. It misses nothing.

This is how the circle begins.

When we really become aware of the sights and sounds and other impressions coming from all around us, after a while there is no longer the sense of just hearing and seeing this or that: instead, there is the awareness of everything as forming a single whole. Everything is exactly what it is, and always has been—but as a continuity now, all together, without any separation or division. And in this wholeness even the past and future start to merge until they are no longer separate. For they are both included in the now.

Then even the sense of any motion disappears. *Mêtis* is so fast in its response, so rapid in its alertness to the moment, that any movement is only perceived as stillness. But, by now, instead of just perceiving a tree or a chair you have become aware that you are perceiving one single being: whole, unmoving, quite still.

And eventually, if you look, you will discover that instead of you perceiving reality what in fact is happening is that reality is perceiving itself through you.

This is how the circle ends.

And you may not be surprised that one of the symbols of *mêtis* is a circle. *Mêtis* is the encircler; the completer of the circle; the awareness that allows us at any moment, in spite of the raging torrent of appearances, to connect the beginning to the end.

I can say these things. But really there is nothing at all to understand. For even to try to understand something is to step out of the one reality surrounding you in every direction and to separate yourself from it. These words are no different from any other shapes and sounds around you, with only one exception.

They are different in reminding you they are no different.

22

There is a strange idea that esoteric teachings are something hidden far away. In fact they have been placed in such a way that they are staring us in the face. But because we forgot a long time ago how to recognize what's right in front of our eyes, they are concealed much better than if they were locked up at the furthest ends of the earth.

The best way to hide an esoteric truth is to leave it in the marketplace. Mostly it will be ignored. A few people will stop and fiddle with it for a while; try to adapt it to fulfil what they consider a useful purpose. Then they will pee on it and go away.

There are four words, tucked away here in Parmenides' poem along with the final signs about completeness, that happen to be the core of his whole teaching.

Philosophers have pored over them for centuries; have struggled to unlock their secret as if they were written in some mysterious, undeciphered code. They have investigated every apparent possibility for understanding them, followed every clue, tried what they imagined was every conceivable permutation. They play their usual game of stretching and distorting the meaning of the words he uses in defiance of all the most basic rules of grammar and language and communication— just for the sake of, hopefully, extracting some acceptable sense.

And many are still trying. But what's so remarkable, and at first can seem almost incredible, is that those four words spoken here by Parmenides can have only one possible meaning in the Greek language. And this meaning is so utterly simple, so totally obvious, no one has even noticed it.

There is a principle involved here that can take a long time to grasp because it's a little too straightforward for us to appreciate. This is that true simplicity is the most potent form of magic. It acts just like a cloak of invisibility: makes what it conceals completely imperceptible to our complicated minds.

Some particularly powerful magicians know not only how to hide their meaning in this way but also how to entrance people at the same time—how to fascinate, how to seduce and intrigue us with the possibility of being able to grasp what in fact we will do everything we can not to grasp.

They know how to use words, just like Parmenides' four words here, in a way that will bewitch grown men and women; leave them spellbound; make them act in the most bizarre and irrational ways. For, as these magicians are aware, most people would never want to understand what they say because if they were to do so that would upset everything.

As for those four words I am referring to: Parmenides mentions them just after the comments he makes about the object and cause of perception being one and the same. In Greek the words are *tôi pant' onom' estai.*

Onom', or *onoma*, means "name." Everyone is agreed on the undeniable fact that he is offering some kind of statement here about ordinary human names—the names we use for all the things we experience at every moment of every day—and about their relationship to the reality he has been describing. And the unquestioned assumption is that these names have been given wrongly, in total ignorance of the true nature of reality which is unchanging and unmoving and one.

This assumption is partly right. But, at the same time, it's altogether wrong.

The words *tôi pant' onom' estai* are identical in form and structure and meaning to a very familiar expression that was perfectly standard in ancient Greek literature. This identity would have been as unmistakable to any Greek of around Parmenides' time as the identity in structure between the statements "he loves you" and "she loves you" would be self-evident to us.

In just the same way that the words *tôi Odusseus onom' estai* meant "his name shall be Odysseus," *tôi pant' onom' estai* meant "its name shall be everything."

What we are being given here is not, as for so long has been supposed, simply some details about the mistakes and errors that people make with the names they use. In fact we are being shown something entirely different.

We are being confronted with the goddess, herself, in the act of naming reality.

I can offer a few pointers for understanding what she is doing. I can also offer some explanations for why she is doing it just here—right in the middle of the signs about completion—rather than anywhere else.

But ultimately this is something you will have to discover for yourself. And you will only do that by learning to breathe the words, live them, make them a part of yourself until you become a part of them.

> *And what exists for thinking is the same*
> *as the cause of thought. For you won't find thinking*
> *without the being in which it has been uttered.*
> *For there is nothing else and will be nothing else*
> *apart from being, because Fate has bound it to be*
> *whole; unmoving. Its name shall be everything—*

every single name that mortals have invented
convinced they all are true: birth and death,
existence, non-existence, change of place, alteration
of bright color.

23

Logic is, to our minds, an impossibility. It has laws but no fixed rules. Rules exist to trap us, but logic exists to set us free.

This is why those who know logic love to laugh. You have to be careful with them, though, because when they are telling the most outrageous jokes is often when they are being most serious. Just when at last you think you are grasping their meaning, they are likely to contradict themselves completely and undo everything they had seemed to be working so hard to achieve—only to show you that you never really understood them at all.

There is such an enormous disproportion, such a total discrepancy, between the goddess' world and ours that laughter can be the only way to bridge the gap. Her humor is a doorway for what has no other point of access. And to miss it—to scratch our heads, insist on looking extremely reasonable and serious, get upset when things seem not to be going our way—is not just to miss a good joke. It's to lose yet another opportunity.

In the ancient Greek world, to make an announcement that so-and-so's "name shall be ..." was to perform a very significant and solemn act. This was the act of giving a newborn baby, or a child who has not yet even been born, the name to be used in future by everyone from that day on.

And by gauging the solemnity of this act you will be able, once again, to appreciate the goddess' outrageous sense of humor. For here, with the same light-hearted laughter that has dogged us ever since she demolished all our pretensions by portraying us as idiots who are very clever about knowing nothing, she is performing a mock ceremony over the one thing that has never been born and never will be because it knows no change and has no past or future. She is performing a naming ceremony for reality.

And this is the least of it.

She has been working so hard, so consistently, patiently, to get rid of creation and destruction and birth and death and movement and change and every possible shade and form of non-existence or non-reality. And just when we were feeling quite sure that we understood her intentions, that we saw where it all was leading, she suddenly hauls back in whatever she had thrown out.

Every illusion she had wrenched away and banished, de-molished, all those names and expressions we were convinced we had seen the back of: here they are again. This is not what we had come to expect.

But, crazy as her behavior might seem, the one thing it most definitely is not is self-contradictory. Quite to the contrary, her unpredictable humor and extravagant outrageousness fit into place alongside what she has already said with the type of precision one could only ever hope to expect from a goddess.

The act of naming a child and the act of disinheriting were exact polar opposites; inverted mirror images of each other. Before, with all due formality, the goddess had banished every form of unreality and stripped it of its names. Now, just as formally, she is giving each of its names back—to reality.

In banishing creation and destruction, birth and death, she had left non-existence nameless. And now, with supreme logic, she is transferring every one of its titles to existence instead.

There is a perfect symmetry here between the two acts of taking names away and then reassigning them. But it's not just a matter of symmetry. You might have supposed, very understandably, that to strip non-existence of all its names was the beginning and end of the goddess' job. In fact it was only the first half of her task. By returning to reality the names she took away from unreality, she has finally accomplished what she started.

The names had a certain application to begin with. Then they had none at all. And now, at the end, they are valid again. The transfer is over: she has completed the circle, right here in the middle of her culminating words about circularity and completeness.

As you can see, the goddess loves our human dramas and ceremonies. She waves and gestures, takes this away from here, adds it there—and at the end of the day you are bound to end up wondering what the fuss is all about. With her shuffling and sleight of hand she produces one effect and then the opposite, undoes whatever she had done in a way that makes you wonder if she is being unbelievably clumsy or incredibly skillful. And, with the completing of the circle, it could seem that from every possible angle nothing in the least has changed.

But although it looks like we are back exactly where we started, we are not.

From the point of view of reality, nothing at all has changed: it never can. And from the point of view of this strange un-reality that we move around in, again nothing has changed. We still walk down the same stairs; see the same faces; lie in the same bed at night.

And yet, from the point of view of the individual who has witnessed the goddess' performance, it's a very different story. For there is nothing quite as capable of changing a human being as the experience of utter changelessness. When you go down to the underworld and then come back, nothing has changed at all—but everything is different because instead of waiting to die you know you are already dead.

The future and past that were taken away from you are given back. But they are no longer the independent realities they once had seemed to be: they are only inseparable parts of now. Every name you had used for referring to this or that is perfectly usable all over again, except that instead of applying to any number of separate objects they only apply to one single thing.

For anyone else, the difference could seem smaller than a hair's breadth. But in actual fact it's a work of magic—as complete as it happens to be subtle. Suddenly, instead of seeing and hearing a thousand things you only see or hear one. And if you have a particular fondness for giving to what you experience one of those names that mortals have invented: everything is divine.

24

The best mystery stories always have their crucial moments of unveiling; their dramas of recognition. And Parmenides' poem has them, too. But there is just one catch.

This is no work of fiction. There are no imaginary characters here to do the unveiling for us while we sit back and read. We have to do it ourselves.

The situation is very simple. If we fail to recognize what needs to be recognized, there will be no recognition. Everything will stay exactly the same.

You could say this doesn't matter; that there are enough small compensations, anyway. And in a sense there are. Even the obvious lengths that learned people have gone to just to keep the unveilings veiled, cover up the tracks and conceal the signs, hinder the magical moments of recognition, make a fascinating story in themselves. But that would hardly be the kind of tale worth bringing back from another world.

In the best mystery stories, those strange little unexplained details that had bothered you while reading finally make sense at the end. And, in precisely the same way, now we can understand at last why the reality that the goddess has been describing had no name: why it was so mysteriously anonymous.

It had no name for the very simple reason that it had not yet been named.

Looking back, it's easy to see that she had been dropping plain hints about its identity all along. And yet until the final naming ceremony there was no identifying it with complete certainty. Without her taking this last step, there would have been room for us to go on guessing and arguing and then guessing some more. But now the identity of what she had been talking about is literally staring us in the face. What you see all around you: that's it.

We have gone through so much, have had to travel so far, just to arrive at this point of being shown that reality is everything. It was there to begin with. There is no coming to it or leaving it, because there is nothing that it's not.

Everything we see or hear is reality, but the only problem is that we have not yet learned to see it or hear it. Every movement we are aware of is simply the imperfect perception of something quite motionless and still—motionless not because it's static and lifeless but because it contains all movement inside it. Every desire, every sense of any lack, is nothing but the experience of a reality too whole for us, with our fragmented minds, to hold together; too powerful and too full for us to bear.

We look everywhere for the ultimate reality, have a tremendous investment in the idea that there is a more real reality waiting for us somewhere else just around the corner. This keeps us busy; gives our crazy lives a sense of purpose. And the idea is so totally enthralling.

But there is no other reality to escape to and no unreality to leave behind. For this apparent unreality is also reality—the one and only reality there is.

Parmenides' great recognition scenes, you may have noticed, come at intervals. There was the one about those unnamed "mortals": the ones who know nothing at all. Specialists went looking and searching for them, came up with the most ingenious identifications. But there was no need to guess or go looking.

Those mortals are right here. They are us.

And the same basic situation is repeating itself now with the goddess' famous, unnamed "it." There is no need to go anywhere else looking for it; no point in speculation. If you want to see what she is referring to, all you have to do is look at everything around you.

But just as there was no way people were simply going to admit that they are lost and helpless fools, there was no way they were going to accept that the ultimate reality is whatever they see around them. That would be far too amazing: much too simple, too immediate and straightforward. And so Parmenides' second great recognition scene, like the first, has gone unnoticed. Instead, philosophers have worked their hardest for more than two thousand years to make his "it" some kind of logical abstraction that exists somewhere else—on another level of reality. And they were bound to want to play around a little with his words; fudge their meaning here and there; do some careful mistranslating.

It was perfectly reasonable of them to do so. But what they forgot to take into account is that goddesses have never been famous for their reasonableness. We are always wanting to exclude, separate, divide: this is real, this is not. And yet Parmenides' goddess, with her feminine logic, excludes nothing. She takes away unreality because we have been making fools of ourselves with it, then folds it up and hands it back to us as a gift. Separation, as they say, is not the name of her game.

The idea that reality itself has no name because every single name we ever use is only a name for it—this is as outrageously paradoxical as it also happens to be beautiful. But I would be wrong if I were to imply that the understanding behind this idea died out with Parmenides.

The same tradition reappeared in Egypt, among the members of Hermetic and Gnostic circles. We can still read their statements about how the divine reality "has no name, and all names refer to it" because there is absolutely nothing that it's not. Then, from Egypt, it was taken back to the East.

But these traditions never go away for good: never just vanish or disappear. And even goddesses, at the edge of time where past and future have no real existence, eventually run out of patience with all the games we play while their message stays unnoticed.

To say it once again, Parmenides' poem is a sacred text. And if we want to glimpse the extraordinary reality he is pointing us to, all we have to do is this.

Go to the window and look outside. Look at the sky and the trees; and listen. All the intellectual and mystical journeys end here, where they began. For in spite of our blindness and deafness we are surrounded at every moment by completeness.

FOUR

As one coming suddenly out of darkness,
I perceived the full meaning of the doctrine of immutability
and said: "Now I can believe that fundamentally all things
neither come nor go." I got up from my meditation bed,
prostrated myself before the Buddha shrine
and did not have the perception of anything in motion.
I lifted the blind and stood in front of the stone steps.
Suddenly the wind blew through the trees in the courtyard,
and the air was filled with flying leaves which,
however, looked motionless. I said to myself:
"This is the whirlwind that will destroy Mount Sumeru
and which is permanently still." When I went to the back yard
to make water, the urine seemed not to be running.
I said: "That is why the river pours but does not flow."
Thereafter, all my doubts about birth and death vanished.

HAN SHAN

And that would seem to be that. Completion, after all, is completion—and you might well suppose there is no more to be said.

But if you were to think that, you would be wrong. For when all our quests and searching finally come to an end, this doesn't mean the story is over. On the contrary: it has only just started.

The deception is about to begin.

Even reality, so perfectly still, has its tides. Just when you might believe you are at last on the point of touching solid ground, you find yourself instead being swept once again out into the ocean. In this teaching, as soon as you arrive somewhere secure you have to leave it behind; the moment you understand something clearly you have to let the understanding of it go. There are no little corners for memory or safety because there is only room for being.

The goddess has led us, exactly as she said she would, to the motionless heart of reality. And to get there we had to keep following her through thick and thin as, bit by bit, she ripped our familiar existence to shreds; had to trust her implicitly and without hesitation as she lured us, along a path that there was not the slightest chance we could travel on our own, into oneness.

But now, as soon as this has been done, she turns around and quite calmly states that the time for trusting her is over. Here—she explains—is the point where my reliable and trustworthy account of reality comes to an end,

and from this point on
learn the opinions of mortals by listening to the
deceptive ordering of my words.

And, from here on, we are totally on our own.

Philosophers and scholars have already had more than their fair share of problems in trying to come so far. But then for them to be told by the goddess in such a matter-of-fact fashion that she is about to deceive us—this is the problem of problems, is to take things just a bit too far. For deceptiveness was a very particular, and extremely potent, force in the minds of Greeks: the force of illusion, of trickery, of passing something off for what it really is not. So the problem that those commentators find themselves faced with is the dilemma of either having to claim she somehow doesn't mean what she says here, or needing to explain what possible reason she could have for wanting to deceive us.

There is one, little thread of hope that it seems almost possible to cling on to.

This is the reassuring belief that in the end it doesn't matter too much if we find a solution or not because the problem is so strictly localized. After all: it only affects the very last part of the poem where, for reasons best known to Parmenides himself, he decides to start mimicking our ordinary human opinions. And besides, this final section is not just the most eccentric part. It's also, as people like to suppose, the most uninteresting one; the most easily put to one side and left alone.

But even that thin thread snaps as soon as anyone tries to snatch it.

We should know well enough by now that one thing the goddess will never do is accommodate our desire for neat divisions: for segregated parts and isolated halves. She is the famous, nameless queen of death—notorious for stripping everything away. And yet there is also another side to her, only known to those who dare to die before they die.

This is that she is waiting to give absolutely everything in return. Her generosity makes her constitutionally incapable of holding back, of isolating things from each other, of ever stopping half-way. And if she chooses to talk in terms of our own deceptive, fragmented opinions after revealing the true nature of reality this can only be for one reason: because she feels that even completeness is somehow not complete without incompleteness, that reality is not quite real enough without the inclusion of illusion.

Then there is the specific riddle we are faced with here. Of course we can prefer to imagine there is no riddle; but that doesn't make it go away.

By announcing her intention to talk deceptively, the goddess is declaring something very significant. She is presenting herself as one of those divine or human beings who are either masters or mistresses of *mêtis*, of trickery: who as a direct result of their insight into the nature of reality have the power to tell the truth but, also, to produce deceptions that only have a plausible appearance of being the truth.

And there is one, essential feature that all these gods or people have in common. This is their ambiguity.

They are the alert ones; always a step ahead of anyone else; wide awake even when they seem to be sleeping; so subtle they are impossible to pin down. You can never be completely sure when they are deceiving you or when they are telling the truth—unless, that is, your cunning happens to be even greater than theirs. But when they claim you can trust them, and rely on what they say, then you can be fairly certain they are tricking you.

And when they do decide to deceive you, they are not just going to advertise the fact. So when the goddess announces that now she is going to deceive us, there is far more to this seemingly innocent statement than meets the eye. It happens to be a perfect double bind, a superb example of *mêtis* always outdoing itself: yet another of her subtle twists, an extra turn of the screw, one more spanner in the works of our helpless minds.

We have just been introduced to the honest deceiver.

2

There is enough ambiguity already lying hidden here, in this deceptively honest statement about deception, to confuse anyone. But Parmenides' goddess, to say the least, does nothing by halves.

To her, even that ambiguity is not quite enough. So for good measure she has thrown in another.

When she says that now we need to listen to "the deceptive ordering" of her words, her term for "ordering" is *kosmos*. This was the Greek word for a clever piece of work, a pretty arrangement, a charmingly seductive decoration—among other things. For it was also becoming the standard word used to describe our whole world, the universe, the cosmic order.

And here she is laughingly tantalizing us into taking it both ways. Whatever she is about to describe, all those moving and colorful objects that make up what we humans consider the real world, will be a deceptively pretty ornament. Everything she is going to talk about—the stars, planets, the sun and moon, this earth—is a few flashy jewels around her neck. But, at the same time, we should not let her language mislead us. These deceptive words of hers are about to conjure up a complete illusory universe: a very familiar universe, because it happens to be the one we imagine we live in.

Lurking in the shadow of her smile, in the troubling obscurity of her riddling ambiguity, is the dark reminder that we are listening not to a philosopher but to a goddess; to a divine being at the source of all existence whose magic is ultimately responsible for this world around us.

The Greeks understood that there is nothing quite as terrifying or disorientating as the encounter with a divinity. And now that we are confronted with a self-declared goddess of deception, our whole attitude has to change very quickly. We can't reason with her. Whatever anyone might have believed, we never could. But now we can't even trust her any more—in anything. For with a being so powerful nothing is what it seems.

When she says she is deceiving us she well may be, in a way. And yet you can be sure that on a deeper level she won't be deceiving us at all. On the contrary: she will be undeceiving us by showing how we deceive ourselves. And while doing that, she will be offering us the most precious truths if we are able to catch them.

For there will be more truth in her deception than in all our honesty put together. The irony, though, is that we will only be able to spot those truths when we allow ourselves to be deceived.

As to her earlier assurance in her teaching about reality that she was being trustworthy, dependable, you can be certain that without our even noticing it she was taking us for a ride. And, to be quite truthful, the signs were there all along. The warnings were just waiting to be noticed. Right at the start there were the Daughters of the Sun who, very tellingly, used trickery and cunning to bring Parmenides to the goddess. Then there were those references to the persuasion—such a notoriously ambiguous, deceptive power—that the goddess told him would be so indispensable for luring him down the right path.

And there is also the fact that all her "paths," every single one of them, turn out to be illusions; imaginary routes that, each in its own different way, go nowhere. And then there are all those people Parmenides had to leave behind in the world of humans, helplessly trapped and tricked by the very same illusion she is about to plunge him back into.

In fact, whichever way we look, we are surrounded by trickery. And as we will see when the time comes round, all the parts of Parmenides' poem are bound to each other as tightly as possible: there is deception at the heart of reality, and the other way around.

Faced as we are with the impossible situation of not knowing what we can trust or believe, there is only one wise thing to do. This is to accept the impossibility and admit we are helpless. For the real problem has nothing to do with whether the goddess is deceiving us or telling the truth. We could argue about that for ever but it would just be an entertaining distraction.

The real trouble is this: every single idea we have about what truth is, is itself a deception.

All our attempts to discriminate between reality and deception or between truth and illusion are exactly what keeps on tricking us, because the things we take for reality happen to be the greatest illusion.

And as so often is the case in hopeless situations, the most intelligent course of action is the one that can seem the most idiotic. For now that we know we can no longer trust her without reservation, this is when we have to trust the goddess completely—and allow ourselves to be deceived.

3

Hardly anything is left from Parmenides' account of the great deception. All that survives is a few scattered words, quoted here or there, along with some passing references by later writers to ideas it once contained.

And no one cares too much. People's main focus has always been on his famous logic: on the extraordinary things he said about reality. There has also been a deep-rooted assumption for a long time that his account of our familiar world was never meant to be any more than some kind of stopgap, a filler, a feeble sequence of second-rate thoughts.

Aristotle already put the matter in a nutshell when he noted that from a factual, practical point of view Parmenides' crucial description of reality is "close to madness"—so close it would only be natural to suppose he must have got cold feet at the last moment and decided, towards the end of his poem, to throw in a few unoriginal ideas about the world we all know so well just for the sake of convincing everyone he was not completely crazy.

But as a down-to-earth assessment of the facts, this could hardly be less accurate.

Even the tiny traces that remain of what Parmenides once said about the deception we happen to live in give no hint at all of feebleness or unoriginality. On the contrary, they evoke with exquisite artistry a world of haunting beauty: a world of dark and light, day and night, death and life, where everything is a transparent veil thinly masking but also revealing its polar opposite. The world he presents is one of sweetly agonizing self-contradiction where there is nothing real enough to be touched, let alone held on to. And the fine ambiguities he uses, his subtle play of sounds and senses of words, are meant to indicate this meaningless fall and flow of meaning.

We have what has sometimes been called one of the most beautiful lines of poetry ever written in his description of the moon as a

nightbright earth-roaming foreign light—

"nightbright" to convey how the opposites of light and dark are nothing without each other, "earth-roaming" as a joking transference to the moon of an expression that would naturally apply to some banished vagrant, and the last two words as another delightful word-play. For Parmenides is taking full advantage here of the fact, which was to become so significant in later esoteric literature, that the Greek word for "light" is spelled just like the word for "human being." And with this apparently simple "foreign light" he is imitating almost to perfection a standard phrase in Homer's poems that used to mean something quite different: "a foreign man."

But, as is always the case with Parmenides, there is also something else. For behind this poetic dance—in case you were to think there is no more to what he says—lies a serious pointer to the fact that the moon has no light of its own, that it just borrows it from a foreign source.

As a piece of practical knowledge this was extraordinary enough in Parmenides' time, quite remarkable. And, as you will see, knowledge for him is wrapped in humor; science in beauty.

4

This quality of elusive beauty in the world Parmenides describes, as well as in the way he describes it, should come as no surprise. For there is one very particular divine being whom he presented as ruling our visible universe.

That's the goddess Aphrodite, queen of infinitely tempting beauty and love and charm.

But there is something else we need to know about Aphrodite apart from her famous association with love and beauty, something extremely important. And the fact that its relevance to the second half of Parmenides' poem has never been noticed is a clear enough sign of how little real attention has been paid to his teaching as an integrated whole.

Aphrodite was not just a divinity of beauty. She was also the supreme goddess of deception and illusion.

She is the great charmer who loves seducing gods, as well as humans, through the glitter of appearance; through desire and attraction and love. As for her sweet shimmer and the delicate magic of her sheer charm, they are precisely what gives her deceptions their ruthless power. Greeks understood very well that underneath the beautiful surface she is a superb hunter, expert at trapping and cunningly binding her prey.

And the one term that best summed up the effects of her deceptions on her victims is a word we should already be familiar with: *amêchania*, "helplessness."

There is the same, strangely fascinating scenario here that we have encountered before. The only way to explain how scholars have kept failing for centuries to notice the connection between humanity's fate, helpless and dazed in an illusory world, and the notorious ability of Aphrodite, ruler of the illusory world, to make her victims helpless and dazed must be that they are dazed in exactly the same way Parmenides is describing. After all, the best trick for keeping people helpless is also the oldest one: deceive them into thinking they know what they are doing, into imagining they are anything but helpless.

Hide from them the horrifying reality of their situation for so long that, even when eventually they are told how things are, most of them will never believe it.

Parmenides' portrayal of humans as dazed and deaf and blind and governed by helplessness or *amêchania* was inseparable, you may remember, from his crucial image of them as incapable of steering a straight course; as unable to keep on a steady path. But this is only one half of the picture.

The other is the remarkable description that we know he happened to give of Aphrodite as a helmsman: a description of her as the accomplished navigator who "steers everything" in this deceptive universe straight and true by guiding female and male unfailingly together, by keeping all the opposites in tow on their perfectly illusory course.

And the missing link that holds the whole picture together, as you may have guessed, is *mêtis*.

Mêtis is the one essential quality navigators need if they are going to keep to a straight course instead of drifting, wandering, travelling aimlessly backwards and forwards, being led astray. At the same time, though, it's the one fundamental factor that according to Parmenides' teaching humans lack: the factor that simply through its unnoticed absence leaves us helpless, lost and trapped.

So we could almost have been able to predict how, as an invaluable little fragment of evidence tells us, Parmenides portrayed Aphrodite creating and establishing and organizing this illusory world of attraction and desire "through *mêtis*."

Of course *mêtis* itself is not only the particular quality of cunning and practical skill, combined with intense alertness, that navigators need if they are going to avoid being swept away at sea. It sums up as well, in one single word, the skill of those who are experts in the arts of trickery and deception.

And just as *mêtis* is the factor that—when missing—leaves us deceived and tricked, it also happens to be what allowed Aphrodite to create this beautiful trick in the first place.

5

Now that we know a little about the goddess responsible for
the world of reflections and illusions we live in, the next step
should be obvious. We have to see how she is related to the
goddess encountered by Parmenides in the underworld, who
teaches him not just about the illusions but about reality as
well.

This is no small matter. In fact by understanding how
the two goddesses are related to each other we are also going
to understand, effortlessly, automatically, the nature of the
relationship between the two halves of Parmenides' poem.

Philosophers have looked high and low for some explanation of how, if at all, what he says about reality is connected
to his account of this deceptive world. But it's the same story
as usual. The answer was waiting, all the time, in the one place
where they were unwilling to look.

The two central goddesses in his poem are not the lifeless,
philosophical abstractions they have been turned into by century after century of thinkers. They are real potencies: Persephone,
queen of the dead whose home Parmenides has come to in the
underworld but who is happiest not being named, and Aphrodite
who rules over the realm of the living.

And these goddesses have strikingly similar roles at the
heart of their own respective worlds. Even from the little that
survives of what he wrote towards the end of his poem, we can
still see how the language he used in referring now to one of
them and then to the other was pointedly similar as well. In fact
the various similarities are so strong that it can be more than

a little tempting to want to suppose the two goddesses are one and the same.

But Parmenides' teacher is not just describing herself when she talks, quite objectively and matter-of-factly, about a divinity manipulating the universe of illusion. The two great beings, all-powerful in their two contrasting realms, are different from each other even though mysteriously similar; almost the same and yet not identical.

The queen of death in the world of reality and the queen of life in the world of illusion: they make a striking combination. But what gives the combination its deeper significance is the fact that these two particular goddesses—Persephone, Aphrodite—had a remarkably close and mysterious relationship to each other.

In the framework of Greek religion as a whole they formed a perfect polarity: life and death. But there was also the profound, lingering awareness of a hidden complicity behind the opposition. And in one part of the Greek world, more than anywhere else, the dynamics of this relationship were viewed as extremely meaningful. That was southern Italy.

There the worship of Persephone and the worship of Aphrodite came to be intimately connected, and this very special juxtaposition even led to the merging of their attributes— to the paradoxical shaping of a dual divinity, Persephone– Aphrodite, who virtually became a single goddess. Combining diametrically opposite features and qualities, belonging to diametrically opposite worlds, Persephone and Aphrodite in the Greek West came to be associated and even identified just because the opposition between them was so fundamental. One and different, reflected mirror images of each other, they blended into a single figure and yet at the same time also managed to stay distinct.

The two halves of Parmenides' poem are the two faces of a dual goddess: life in death, death in life. The solution to that great, central problem which has baffled scholars for so long is right here—in mythology, in the person of the divine being they have tried so hard to argue away and reason out of existence.

And now we can see why that particular quality known as *mêtis* has been so important right from the very beginning of his message. The cunning and trickery of *mêtis* are woven into the fabric of the universe. Everything around us is an elaborate trick; and we can either go on letting ourselves be deceived or learn to trick our way in and through and out.

To start with we are all quite helpless—dazed and confused, trapped by Aphrodite. And that, for most people, is the end of the matter. It's how they live; how they die.

But there is also a possibility, ever so remote, of being drawn out from the illusion by a mysterious power behind love that happens to be even greater than love. This is the secret most people never know.

And this is why the hidden goddess offers so kindly, with an austere tenderness so different from all the superficial glamour and charm we are familiar with, to lead the initiate who reaches her out of the illusion into reality. For behind the force that drags us into the illusion in the first place is the power that can set us free.

Or to be more precise, the one being who seduces us into believing in her grand deception can then decide to seduce us out of it.

And yet to leave things there, to remain simply disabused, would be impossible. It would be to deny a half of what she is; to turn our back on her deceptive face; to stop half-way. In other words, it would be just as one-sided to stay in reality as it is for most people to stay caught in the illusion.

So we have to give the deception its due—plunge back into it, but now with the knowledge imprinted consciously on our heart of the oneness always present in the heart of reality.

One face of the goddess is movement; the other, utter stillness. But just as we had to learn while approaching reality how all movement is held in stillness, we now have to be able to watch as the stillness dissolves again into apparent motion.

And just as the one thing we needed to guide us along that non-existent path to reality was the presence and continuous alertness of *mêtis*, so *mêtis* is what we are going to need now more than ever to carry us right through the deception.

6

Parmenides' goddess happens to offer a very clear and explicit reason for why she is going to the trouble of describing this illusory world. All we have to do is discover what she is really saying underneath the cloak of her explicitness and clarity.

You may wonder why we need to bother—why we have to keep following her down little alleys and byways, why we should even care. The answer is so that she can bring us to what matters for her, not just to what we think matters for us. It can be surprising what unfamiliar worlds are opened up by simply one word; or two; or three. And we may find at the end that what matters most for her is what matters most for us, as well.

The explanation she offers Parmenides for plunging him back into the realm of human opinions all over again certainly seems specific enough. And, for once, instead of just translating her Greek I am going to transcribe it word for word:

hôs ou mê poté tis se brotôn gnômêi parelassêi

so that nobody among mortals will ever manage,
in practical judgement, to ride on past you.

But we are faced here, straightaway, with a strange problem. For the image of nobody being allowed to ride on ahead of Parmenides is peculiar precisely because of the way it happens to be so specific. As a matter of fact the particular Greek expression, *parelassêi* or "ride on past," is quite unusual; and when it does occur in early poetry it most often refers to the situation of one horse-driven chariot being ridden on ahead of another.

As for why Parmenides should want to evoke such an image of chariots and charioteers, this is where scholars have traditionally drawn a blank. Of course there is the chariot right at the start of his poem that takes him to the goddess. But here seems a rather unlikely place for a chariot race.

And yet the question we need to be asking is the one we always have to bear in mind when reading Parmenides. That's the question not just of what a word or image means according to the dictionary but of what meanings and associations it carried with it for the people of his time, what images and scenes it naturally evoked inside their minds. This, after all, is the way he liked to write: using one single word to trigger memories of whole scenes, especially scenes from Homer, along with all their vivid details.

Here we don't have far to look for the answer to our question.

As commentators on Parmenides have often noticed, all the known examples of this word *parelassêi* or "ride on past" being used to describe charioteers racing with each other come from one and the same scene in Homer.

It's a long and famous passage, right towards the end of the *Iliad*, about a dramatic chariot race between heroes. And it was to stick in people's minds, century after century, for a very good reason.

It was one of the two most perfect illustrations, in all Greek literature, of *mêtis*.

The passage reads like a classic exposition of *mêtis* in its various subtleties and shapes and forms. It even contains a little hymn of praise to *mêtis*—to the mysterious, indefinable factor that relies on presence of mind to achieve what could seem impossible. For *mêtis* is what allows a charioteer in the toughest race, regardless of any apparent limitation or disadvantage and in spite of all the odds, to get ahead and win.

There is the supreme *mêtis* that outstrips everybody through skill and pure alertness, elegantly making the right move at just the right moment, always aware of the whole without excluding anything. And yet there is another type of *mêtis*, too: far more spectacular as a rule and much easier to acquire the habit for but also much more immature because it's light, superficial, heady, caught up in the appearances it so badly needs to master. It focuses on the immediate challenge to the exclusion of everything else, imagines that to be in the moment is simply a matter of thrills and adrenalin and the giddy excitement of living for the day.

This, in Homer's story, is the *mêtis* used by the apparent winner to ride on ahead and push his competitor out of the chariot race along a narrow stretch of road through a sheer test of nerves—forcing him to pull over to avoid what could be a fatal accident if the two riders collided while both driving their horses and chariots at full speed ahead.

But the last joke will be on him.

The trouble is that, just like an impatient child, he fondly imagines he is the winner only to end up the victim of his cleverness; is trapped by his own trick and stripped, at the last moment, of his victory and glory.

For a brief minute or two he really believed he had got ahead. In reality he had outstripped nobody at all.

With just a single word Parmenides' goddess manages to convey what I have had to say in several hundred. By using the rare expression *parelassêi* or "ride on past" to tell him that no one will be able to ride on ahead of him and win, she is explaining in her own delicately understated way what the purpose is for all the knowledge she is going to offer him about the universe.

The knowledge she is about to give him will be a supreme exercise in *mêtis* presented by the ultimate source and origin of all *mêtis*: a teaching to make sure that no illusory person with any illusory tricks in this illusory world will ever manage to outwit or get the better of him.

At one point it might have seemed easy to suppose that the purpose of the goddess' teaching was to leave Parmenides stranded blissfully all alone on some mountaintop, immersed in the fullness of being. But this was never a part of her plan.

There is one single factor that holds the illusion of reality and the reality of illusion together, that knows how to stay ever-present and watchful not just at the heart of stillness but also in the middle of deception—*mêtis*. And now that Parmenides has travelled the non-existent path to reality, there is a second challenge he has to accept.

He has to run an illusory race against illusory competitors in an illusory cosmos. And he most definitely has to win.

But even this is not quite the end to what the goddess has in mind with that comment of hers about no one being able to ride on ahead of Parmenides. And here is where we come to the reason why a little while ago I transcribed what she said word for word: *hôs ou mê poté tis …*, "so that nobody …"

There is a second passage, just as famous as the classic action scene at the end of the *Iliad*, that demonstrates to perfection the nature of *mêtis* with its intricacies and subtleties. It comes in Homer's other great poem, the *Odyssey*, at the point where Odysseus has been trapped inside a cave along with his men by the great monster Polyphemus.

He has to use every ounce of cunning and ingenuity to find some way out. And he does. But what makes the passage such a superb piece of entertainment and humor and hidden irony is that instead of offering Polyphemus his real name he gives himself a similar-sounding name—with a twist to it. In front of the monster he introduces himself as *Outis*: "Nobody."

The laughter starts when he manages to blind him by tricking him in his own cave. The monster yells for help until all the other monsters gather round outside to see what's wrong. With the kind of concern that monsters reserve for each other, they ask if he is all right and say: surely nobody, *mê tis*, is stealing from you or trying to kill you by cunning or force? So when Polyphemus screams out that Nobody, *Outis*, is killing him they assume things are not too bad and make their way back to bed.

This is the point where the real jokes begin—as Homer draws out through word-play after word-play all the ambiguities stretching from Outis through *ou tis* and *mê tis*, which in Greek are alternative forms for "nobody," to *mêtis*.

As Odysseus laughingly comments about the episode, well after the events have taken place, it was his *mêtis* that allowed him to blind the monster because it allowed him to be nobody: *ou tis*, *mê tis*. By modern standards the subtlety, as well as the sheer extent, of this play on words in the *Odyssey* is so extraordinary it has often defied belief on the part of scholars who fail to appreciate how important a manifestation of *mêtis* this kind of linguistic skillfulness used to be. But the fact is that, from the time of the *Odyssey* onwards, *mêtis* would always be associated in the minds of Greeks with this particular episode; with this notorious play on the words *ou tis* and *mê tis*.

So you will be able to see how it's no accident that, at the exact moment when she introduces her hint about nobody being able to outdo Parmenides in *mêtis*, the goddess expresses herself with the help of a pointedly emphatic double negative— *ou mê poté tis*, nobody at all, absolutely nobody.

Here are the *ou tis* and the *mê tis* very blatantly placed right together, in the context of a cunning reference to *mêtis*, just waiting to be recognized.

And so we come back to that delightful myth about the founding fathers of western philosophy trying as hard as they were able, struggling to their limit, to write clearly and plainly; going out of their way to liberate themselves from the veiled language of mythology by being as explicit and straightforward as they possibly could. For if there is one thing Parmenides could not have cared less about, explicitness is it.

Nobody in the whole history of modern scholarship has noticed his subtly understated play here on *ou tis* and *mê tis* and *mêtis*. And if you are quite determined not to notice it, even now you will refuse to see it—which will be just fine.

What's more striking than anything is the way Parmenides is so supremely indifferent; so completely unconcerned. Far from being anxious to get his point across and be understood, there is a relaxedness in his attitude. There is even a little laziness. He knew that perhaps a few people might catch the hint. He also knew very well that most never would, and would never even want to.

This joke is a rather personal affair. Subtlety, concealment, even trickery, are sometimes the greater part of communication; and what one says openly is only the least part of what could be said. So Parmenides did all that he felt was necessary—no more.

He just left the almost invisible play on words behind in this line as his own private signature for those who would be able to read it.

8

There is one point in Homer's notorious story about Polyphemus where Odysseus makes a rather significant remark. It sums up the whole episode, captures its essence, in just a few words.

He has been caught up in a tragedy; has not escaped from the cave yet. The monster has eaten some of his closest friends and is bent, even without being able to see, on butchering everyone. But Odysseus' spirit and sense of humor are still strong as—to repeat what he would say later on when describing the scene to others—

> my dear heart laughed at the utter deception
> created by my name and faultless *mêtis*.

Here is one more pointer to the unbreakable link, sometimes invisible but always strong, between *mêtis* and deception. And it's no coincidence that this term, "utter deception," comes from the very same word used by the goddess in Parmenides' poem when she announces her "deceptive ordering of words."

You could say that, with her account of this world we live in, deception has simply become the order of the day. Just as *mêtis* is the one thing needed for explaining or understanding or getting by in a universe created and sustained through *mêtis*, the same thing applies to deception. In a place of deceptions, deception is called for. In a world governed by trickery, it's not only telling the truth that counts. What matters just as much is being able to play the best tricks.

And then there is Odysseus' mention of the role played in this deceiving by the all-important "name." That, too, should be a reminder of something else.

Commentators on Parmenides have tried, with commendable earnestness, to find some ultimate justification for the names we use: to give the act of naming some genuine place in his teaching about reality, some true validity. But Parmenides makes it as clear as he can that the root of all our problems, the basic cause of our being so confused, is the very serious obsession we have with naming—with separating things off from each other and then starting to imagine our intellectual distinctions are real.

Our continual naming is what deceives us. And from the first fatal moment that the goddess allows mortal names back into the utter stillness and oneness of existence, her deceiving has really begun.

Even more important, though, than Odysseus' mention of his *mêtis* or his famous name is the other factor that he refers to: his hearty laughter. For Parmenides laughs too—at his own clever trickery with words, at his subtle evocation of the chariot race in the *Iliad*, but above all at the *mêtis* he uses with his *ou tis* and *mê tis* to demonstrate and simultaneously conceal his own *mêtis*.

And yet if you were to think Parmenides is only laughing at some clever little game of words, this would end up being the greatest joke of all. For when the goddess promises him the knowledge and ability to outstrip everyone else through *mêtis*, she is thinking about a great deal more than excellence in verbal trickery. After all, it hardly makes sense that she would go to the trouble of teaching him about deception just so he could play around with a few words in a way no one would even notice.

In fact she has something vastly more significant in mind, something infinitely and incomparably more serious.

As for what that is, and as for what she really meant by claiming he would be able to outdistance anybody in *mêtis*, this is not so difficult to discover. All we have to do is take just one example of her teaching about this illusion we live in and keep following it right through to the end.

It will only be one illustration. That's all. But it will be enough to convey an idea of exactly how far her *mêtis*, and Parmenides', was able to reach.

I should warn you, though, that you will need to follow very closely on this journey through deception. If you stop to think, or even to look around too long, you will be lost all over again: trapped in the illusion.

For however familiar some of the scenery will seem, it's utterly unreal.

9

We all know the earth is round. We have seen the photos.

Once, centuries ago, it used to be a matter for argument and dispute. Now there is not the slightest room for doubt. A spherical earth is the symbol and reality of our dawning global culture—the central axis around which the whole modern world revolves.

Judging by how fundamental the reality of a spherical earth has become, it would seem natural to suppose there was nothing mysterious or strange about the process of its discovery. But appearances can be deceptive. Nothing is quite what it seems. The greatest strangenesses of all have to do with the things right here: in front of our eyes, at our feet. And the greatest mystery is how we ever managed to imagine otherwise.

The discovery that this earth of ours is a sphere has been traced back to the famous philosopher Plato. And yet things are not so simple. Plato is certainly a stop along the way; but he is not the end of the trail.

A long time ago now, he wrote an imaginary dialogue. It paints a picture of his teacher, Socrates, talking with the disciples who came to visit him in the last few hours before he was put to death.

What Plato wrote is not just a work of fiction. It's a work of art. There, close to the very end, he includes a beautiful myth. And in the myth you will find it mentioned that the earth is round.

According to our familiar ways of calculating time, Plato finished writing this dialogue—it's known as the *Phaedo*—early in the fourth century before Christ. It's the oldest continuous, unbroken text still surviving that contains the idea of the earth as a sphere. And Plato points out that what he has to say about the shape and nature of the earth is altogether different from the usual Greek accounts: startlingly different. But he is also careful to note that the question of whether the earth is flat or round had already become a serious subject of debate among intelligent people in his day.

And he goes out of his way to explain that the ideas he is presenting are not his own invention—or Socrates'. Instead, they have been handed down by others. And we can say who those others are.

All the ideas here in this myth at the end of the *Phaedo* belong together. They form an extraordinary but perfectly coherent set of explanations: a fantastic series of interlinking statements about the earth we live on that Plato heard from the people he met and stayed with while travelling in southern Italy, then took back with him to Athens when he went home and started writing his story about Socrates' death.

But there is still further that we have to go. For another piece of evidence also exists. And it points back well before the time of Socrates or Plato or those Italians, often known as Pythagoreans, whom he happened to be friends with.

One ancient writer—he is among the oldest and most reliable of sources on such matters—offers a name for the first philosopher who ever stated that the earth is round. The man he mentions came from Velia, in southern Italy, and was a Phocaean: a direct descendant of the people who were forced to leave their original home of Phocaea for the west.

His name was Parmenides.

Considering that Parmenides was born towards the end of
the sixth century BC, he would have been saying the earth is a
globe around a hundred years or so before the situation Plato
was wanting to describe—when the idea was still a hard one
for someone at Athens to accept or take seriously. But this is
no problem.

On the contrary: to expect everyone would have wanted
to believe Parmenides' theory straightaway would be completely
unrealistic.

The fact is that another generation after Plato, in the time
of his successor Aristotle, the idea was still being argued about;
being elegantly tossed backwards and forwards. And for centuries after that there were Greek and Roman philosophers
who kept on mocking at the notion for being so ridiculous even
though, by then, exact figures for the diameter of the earth had
become readily available.

As for the time when the giants of early Christianity would
decide that to doubt the earth is flat is outright heresy: this lay
even further in the future.

The problem in accepting that Parmenides was the first
philosopher who said what, to us now, is so totally self-evident
has nothing at all to do with how long ago he lived. It has to
do with what he was.

We are told that, as the founder of logic and the father
of rationalism, he was a man with no interest in the world of
the senses. He was a pure intellectual, totally unconcerned with
tangible realities. At least so we are told. And to suppose such

a man, who dismissed the world around him as an illusion, could somehow have been implicated in the discovery that our earth is a sphere verges on the edges of the absurd.

As a well-known expert on the Greeks nervously decided a while ago to describe the situation: it's "a strange freak of history that so fundamental a discovery should have been made by one for whom the whole physical world was an unreal show."

The situation has every appearance of being an awkward one. The authority for our information that Parmenides was the first philosopher who said this earth of ours is a sphere is good—too good to reject. And so historians have done what anyone normally tends to do when faced with some "strange freak" of an event.

Rather than struggle to get to the bottom of it and find out what lies behind, we try to explain it away.

In the case of Parmenides and the earth, one easy enough explanation seemed ready to hand. This is that he had a particular liking for round objects. After all, he was so fond of curves that he even described reality as being circular—and so it was only logical that he would want to present the earth as a sphere.

In other words it was a sheer guess on Parmenides' part: a very lucky guess.

This is how things stand, and have stood for years. But, even at first glance, the explanation looks just a little too convenient to be real. And when we care to look a little further we can start to piece together what has gone wrong.

11

One other fragment of evidence about Parmenides has managed to survive, tucked away in the folds of the past. And it, too, has to do with the earth.

It states that he was the first person who formally divided the earth into five zones—a hot equatorial zone, the two extremes of intense cold at the poles, and two temperate regions in between. And, from what we are told, it would seem he paid special attention to the size and extent of the zone at the equator.

To accept that someone in Parmenides' time could already have had such a detailed understanding of the earth's general shape and nature is not easy. And there was a time when historians used every strategy they could to undermine the report, deny its accuracy. But none of the strategies worked: as scholars have started to realize, the evidence stands strong. We have no reason at all to doubt it.

And this is the end of the road.

It marks the absolute limit to how far anyone has wanted, or dared, to go. The reports about Parmenides have been left scattered around in small pieces—dry and lifeless—as if out of an instinctive dread that if they were put back together they would create something disturbingly real. The "strange freak of history" seems best left well alone, in case it opens the way to even greater strangenesses.

But in fact all it would take is one single minute to see where the evidence about Parmenides and the earth is pointing.

Portrayal of the earth as a sphere, division of it into five zones: these are far from isolated, unrelated ideas. On the contrary, they have everything to do with each other. The scheme of two cold poles, a hot equator, two warm regions in between only makes sense if you are thinking in terms of a globe; and this is why the theory of zones and the theory of a spherical earth keep being mentioned together in later texts about geography or exploration.

But there is more to the matter than that.

It's not just that the two theories belong together. What lies behind both of them is also one and the same—and takes us far beyond the realm of lucky guesses.

Division of the earth into different zones depends on familiarity with weather conditions well outside the little world of the Mediterranean. Knowledge about regions to the east or west would have been useless; in fact it would have been worse than useless. All that matters is the knowledge of regions to the south and to the north.

As for the earth being round: people in the centuries after Parmenides who started agreeing it has to be that shape offered all kinds of reasons why. Some of their arguments were theoretical. Others were based on observation.

Some of them—like reasoning from the shape of the shadow seen during eclipses of the moon, or from how ships seem to appear and disappear at the horizon—will have helped in their own way towards arriving at the conclusion that the earth is completely round. And some of them are the kind of arguments thought up after the event to confirm a discovery that has already been made.

But the most fundamental and decisive one, the argument that keeps cropping up right through from the earliest discussions into and beyond the Middle Ages, is based on what happens when you travel to the south and to the north.

It's not just a question of travelling northwards or southwards in the Mediterranean. The distances are too small; and if you did that, you would only notice anything significant provided you already knew exactly what to look for.

But when you travel further to the north, and to the south, the stars that seem to rise and set are no longer the same. The stars that stay visible, or invisible, change. The sun behaves differently, rises to different heights. The length of the daytime varies.

And eventually, if you are prepared to observe them well enough with care and an open mind, all these phenomena lead to one conclusion—that the earth is a sphere.

But in the whole literature that has grown up around Parmenides over the last century or more, there is not so much as a hint of any of this. Instead, everything said about him nowadays is like a rusty gate: very noisy, a barrier, difficult to open or get through.

And yet as soon as we do, things start changing. They become real; alive.

It's utterly useless to sit and watch the evidence as if we are on the banks of a river. That will get us nowhere. We just have to throw ourselves into the river and let it take us wherever it leads.

12

For Greeks in general everything was fairly straightforward. Most of the time we have our limits—even though it always seems easier to see other people's limits than our own—and they had theirs.

The greatest of their heroes, Heracles, had laid down clear boundaries for what was possible. The rocks at either side of the Straits of Gibraltar were known as the pillars of Heracles: his boundary stones. Beyond them, to the west, was utter mystery—no place for mortals to go, or even dream of trying to go.

Beyond was the realm of Plato's fantastic Atlantis; of silver-rooted rivers shooting up out of the earth. It was another world.

Physical realities turned into a vast symbol. To dream of sailing out past Gibraltar, beyond the pillars, became the embodiment of overweening arrogance: of a pride that knows no bounds. In the words chosen to describe the situation by a famous poet, one of the most exquisite songbirds among the Greeks,

> What lies beyond is inaccessible for wise and
> unwise.
> You will not see me chasing off in
> that direction:
> I would be an empty fool!

And the Phocaeans could hardly have cared less for any of this.

Among the other Greek people they were almost like a race apart, especially after they started moving out to the West from their original home on what now is the coast of Turkey. Of course they made their contacts; their alliances. But Romans as well as Greeks never really knew what to make of them, ended up seeing them as absurdly brave and grotesquely effeminate, impossibly moral, hopelessly decadent.

In the middle of their activities and interactions they managed to stay strangely isolated, elusive, private. Wherever they settled, they always liked building their cities the same way: in the harshest of places, ostensibly austere, hardly any land, focused intensely on the sea. And when—in around the year 600, over a generation before the beginnings of Velia—they sailed all the way westwards from Phocaea to found a city called Massalia at the base of France, one thing is clear. They built it as a stepping stone for travelling further.

Being a Phocaean used to mean certain things. In fact even the name, Phocaea, had a significance all of its own.

It meant City of Seals. The Phocaeans were fully aware of the fact, used the seal as their symbol. And that could not have been more appropriate.

Seals, for the Greeks who thousands of years ago lived around the Mediterranean, were the ideal amphibian: dwellers in two worlds, able to survive on the earth and also out in the ocean. But although they were very comfortable in the hard and rocky areas where sea meets land, they tended to spend most of their time in the water itself—in the depths where they belonged.

Simply through being what they were they gave a sense of joining what has been separated for so long; of merging the elements of water and earth and air back into the common source they come from; of belonging to the primordial powers that date from a stage of creation far older than the beginnings of our carefully ordered cosmos. For Greeks they had the deepest of affinities with furthest edges and limits, with outermost boundaries and the ultimate reaches of nature, with the roots of existence as they plunge into the great beyond known as Tartarus.

Close and yet so distant, unfamiliar but somehow very familiar, they were a living enigma. Almost human at times in their behavior as well as their appearance, they could seem threatening just because of the way they kept undermining all the normal distinctions between human and inhuman.

They were assumed to be magical beings with mysterious powers—in particular the power that holds the keys to the ocean, that opens and closes the seas, that shows the way but then covers it over again so rapidly you could be left wondering if you have not just been dreaming all along. For their magic included the power of changing shape, of transformation. You could never be quite sure with them whom, or what, you were dealing with.

So it should be no surprise that they were viewed as the archetype of the slippery customer: as the embodiment of elusiveness and cunning, disguise and deception. And neither should it be a surprise that in the eyes of Greeks they were a perfect incarnation of *mêtis*—always twisting and slipping and sliding off into deep water—or that the Phocaeans themselves were notorious throughout their history as superb tricksters, supreme deceivers.

13

Exactly how far back their journeys go we no longer know. But the Phocaeans were already making their way out into the Atlantic in the seventh century before Christ.

And it's during the next century, the sixth, that the first identifiable details start emerging out of the haze. At a time when Parmenides would have been no older than a young boy, a Phocaean called Euthymenes headed out from Massalia through the Straits of Gibraltar and turned left. Then he sailed southwards past what now is the Sahara and headed down the coast towards equatorial Africa.

He got at least as far as Senegal; and to have got that far was extraordinary enough. The Phocaeans had plenty of practical wisdom, cleverness, experience. But even so, the risks involved in their journeys were enormous. As one writer has calmly noted, by any reasonable standards their behavior was not brave. It was mad.

And just as striking as the distance Euthymenes travelled is the scrupulousness of the observations he brought back. At the mouth of one particularly large river he noticed how the ocean loses its saltiness when the river's waters mix with the waters of the sea. And he reported on the animals—crocodiles, hippopotami—that he saw along the river itself.

This one little set of observations is everything that happens to survive from the record of his journey. How much even further to the south he might have managed to go: that, too, is something we no longer know.

And then, in the same period, we hear about journeys not just to the south but in the opposite direction as well.

The battered remains have been recovered of old Phocaean accounts from the sixth century BC, describing journeys up the coast of Spain. Brittany is mentioned, at the northern tip of France. And here, where most scholars are unwilling even to look, we find the oldest known references to Albion or England; and to Hierne, the sacred island of Ireland.

But this in itself was nothing. We also hear of a Phocaean called Pytheas who, everyone is agreed, seems to have been the greatest Greek explorer who ever lived.

He made his way from Massalia out into the Atlantic and headed north—all the way north. He went up as far as Britain and Ireland, left them behind. He passed the northern tip of Scotland. And he kept on going until, eventually, he came to what he called "the solid sea." People have thrown up their hands in despair; have thought it impossible to accept that he could have got as far as he must have got; have done everything in their power to dilute the obvious significance of what he says. And yet the implications are quite clear.

Pytheas went as far north as the Arctic Circle. But even stranger than the sheer distance he managed to cover is what he did along the way. And just as strange is the way no one has noticed, even suspected, that the account he gave of his journey lies behind the intricate myth put into Socrates' mouth at the end of Plato's *Phaedo*.

In other words, the ultimate source for the oldest surviving continuous text to describe the earth as a sphere is the ancient literature—so abused, fragmented, forgotten—of the Phocaeans.

14

You can sometimes come across the peculiar romantic idea that Greeks used to be lovers of the sea. In fact as a rule even the Mediterranean terrified them.

Short journeys were a major ordeal: they would cling to the coastline. Open sea for them, any sea, was a manifestation of chaos. There were no signposts or fixed markers. The water was pathless, trackless; always shifting, changing, never the same.

Pytheas on his journey up through the north Atlantic was like a living observatory. In a world of utter chaos—a world where human life to the early Greeks was physically inconceivable, mythologically impossible—he used special instruments to watch and mark and measure. He measured the sky: measured the movements of the stars and sun and moon. He measured the earth, measured the water.

Tides tend hardly to exist in the Mediterranean. While most Greeks would not even have recognized one if they saw one, Pytheas was carefully measuring them out in the Atlantic; noting everything, even the height of the tidal swells that can reach up to over a hundred feet around the islands north of Scotland. But he did much more than just measure the tides.

He also understood how they are linked with the moon and the phases of the moon.

He measured out the distances he travelled by land, calculated the size of Britain. And wherever he went he meticulously measured the maximum heights of the sun and the longest times of daylight right up to the regions of the midnight sun.

However far he travelled from anywhere he could have hoped to call home—watching everything familiar fall away and keep falling away, learning to understand and speak the strange words of the native people—he never forgot for long the absolute functionality of measuring and keeping on measuring.

Centuries later the greatest astronomers in the ancient world came across the records of his measurements. They discovered them tucked away in the famous library at Alexandria; and they realized the treasure they had found. The observations had been made and preserved in such detail that they were able to use them to calculate exact lines of latitude with no real error at all. And they used them for mapping out the world.

These were the astronomers who managed, thousands of years ago, to measure the diameter of the earth with extraordinary precision. People before them had made guesses that were wildly wrong. People after them would insist on continuing to make other guesses—which were just as wrong. But that's the way things often are.

And as you may have guessed, Pytheas made his measurements on the journey up north and back home to demonstrate in detail that this earth of ours is a sphere.

15

There is no point in making a song and dance about the obvious. So I will just say a few words.

How it ever happened that Parmenides, along with what he wrote about the earth, came to be separated off from the courageous Phocaean explorers: this is quite a mystery.

It has been known for a long time that their journeys were crucial in shaping the earliest of theories about the earth's zones. Here—among the people who were carefully exploring the regions down towards the equator, who were confirming at first hand that the earth is a sphere while other Greeks for the next few centuries would go on throwing the idea in the air and trying to decide what they ought to believe—is where the things Parmenides said about the form and nature of the earth make perfect sense. Here is where they belong; are completely at home.

And then, of course, there is that other matter. Parmenides, himself, was a Phocaean.

We can talk quite justifiably about the element of elusiveness that could make the Phocaeans seem somehow more distant from other Greeks than usual. But what can be a little harder to appreciate is that this quality of remoteness, just like everything else, also had its other side.

Even by ancient standards, the ties binding Phocaeans to Phocaeans were astonishingly close. Between one colony and another an extraordinary cohesiveness existed, century after century. The threads connecting the western settlements back to their founder-city of Phocaea, or to what remained of it after the Persians took over, stayed unbroken as well.

And yet the closest connection of all was between two places in particular.

One was Parmenides' hometown of Velia. The other was Velia's sister colony of Massalia, or Marseilles: the home of Euthymenes and Pytheas.

Even on the level of doctrine, of pure theory and ideas, Parmenides' links with those Phocaean explorers should be clear enough. But this is the least of it. His links with them are grounded in far more than some similarity of interests or concerns. They are rooted in the realities of a single world, of a shared culture; of his home and theirs.

A while ago one of the very few specialists in Phocaean culture pointed out what a peculiar riddle it is that our modern notions of Parmenides as an otherworldly philosopher fit so poorly with everything we know about the Phocaeans. He noted how intensely practical they were as a people: shrewd, cunning, experienced, their feet on the ground, worldly-wise and wily just like Homer's Odysseus.

But the discrepancy is simply of our own making. It exists not between the Phocaeans and Parmenides as he was—only between them and the monumentally distorted image we have erected of him as an abstract thinker untouched by the world around him.

To misinterpret his teaching about reality as some denial of experience and then ignore the trail of hints left behind about the rest of his poem: this is no way of doing justice to someone who was so consciously influential in shaping the culture we live among the ruins of. The Phocaeans have been described with good reason as considering themselves, once they had moved out to the West, a people in exile.

There is no point at all in exiling Parmenides even from his exile.

16

Certainly the Phocaeans were worldly-wise—in ways most people have been at a loss to fathom. Just like seals, they were at home in a world far vaster than the regions familiar to other Greeks.

And of course that created problems for all those who wanted to keep a tight grip on the little knowledge they thought they had.

This is why apart from a few brief comments of his, and even they quickly became garbled, about that river he had come to, any record of Euthymenes' journey was wiped out and lost. But the silence was the least of it.

He was mocked as a teller of tales, an inventor of stories. And we can still see how over a period of seven hundred years he kept being dismissed as a cheat and liar: as a trickster who tried in vain to contaminate the body of Greek knowledge with his cheap deceptions. His ridiculous accounts of hippopotami and fresh water in the ocean were denounced as nothing but fantasies, as absurd fictions only fit to be made into nursery rhymes for sending children off to sleep.

As for Pytheas and his travels to the north, it's difficult even to know where to begin. But we may as well start with Dicaearchus.

He was one of the most open-minded thinkers in the school of Aristotle, and is also the oldest writer we still happen to know about who took it into his head to consider Pytheas' findings from what could be called a scientific point of view.

And all we hear is one single statement. "Not even Dicaearchus believed."

Of course, you will say, there were the astronomers. At least they recognized the pure gold in what Pytheas had left behind: grasped at the astronomical facts. But even with them things became a little complicated.

The most influential of those astronomers was a man called Eratosthenes. In his time he was head of the library at Alexandria; and Pytheas caused him no end of anxiety. Faced with the evidence, we are told by a later writer, Eratosthenes found himself "totally at a loss."

All those observations and measurements made perfect sense—astronomically. They were almost too good to be true. But as for the way Pytheas claimed he had got his information, as for the circumstances and details of his journey, this was just too incredible. Eratosthenes wanted desperately to believe and had no idea how much he could: knew he had to believe, but had no knowledge of where to draw the line. It was all too much like a fairy story.

That expression, "totally at a loss," used to describe Eratosthenes' predicament happens to be a significant one. For it introduces us once again to a theme that, much the same as the song of the birds which threads its music through our days, we will keep on being drawn back to.

The expression is built around exactly the same word used to describe the state into which Socrates plunged the people he spoke with: *aporia* or "pathlessness." *Aporia*, just like *amêchania*, is the state of utter helplessness. It describes the nightmare of finding yourself in the impossible situation where no path leads to where you are and no path leads from it. All of a sudden you are lost, trapped. No conceivable plan or trick will help. You see no way out of this routelessness.

It's like trying to cross an untraversable, uncrossable space. However hard you try, however far you travel, in this state you are never able to get from one place to another. You may believe you are arriving somewhere; all the appearances can convince you this is the case. But you are getting nowhere.

For Greeks it was a word that—just the same as *amêchania*—touched the essence of confusion, the chaos of self-contradiction where you no longer know where to turn. It was used to describe the paralysis of indecision, of thinking you can think things through but not being able, of having all the questions but no answers, of having all the answers but not the understanding of how to apply them.

In other words, it expresses everything you would rather not think about. Of course according to our conscious minds this is a weakness we are no longer affected by. Someone like Socrates could hardly disturb people like us. But the reality is quite a different matter.

And there is a special poignancy, a particular suitability, in this word *aporia* being applied to Eratosthenes with his worries about Pytheas. For one of the most common images that the word evoked in the minds of Greeks was the vivid scene of navigators unable to find their bearings: the chaos of sailors hopelessly lost out in the ocean, "all at sea."

In short, Pytheas had managed to find his way to where he was going and back home again. Eratosthenes had not. For he had thought he could do something that, with a Phocaean, no one can do and get away with. He tried to discriminate; to distinguish the fact and the fiction. He wanted what Pytheas had but didn't want everything he had to offer. And *aporia* is what happens when you take something said by a Phocaean, then try to translate it into terms suitable for you.

After Eratosthenes the problems went on. At around the time of Christ the most famous of ancient geographers, a man called Strabo, came to pass verdict on Pytheas' fantastic eyewitness accounts of mysterious inhabited places. And this is what he said: unbelievable, imposture and quackery, fabrications, deceptions, a pack of lies, out-and-out tricks, a downright fraud, transparent charade, the spinning of myths. He has led many astray. He made it all up.

Needless to say, no intelligent Greek was going to make the slightest effort to check out at first hand what the situation in the far distant north really was.

For the Phocaeans were always off ahead, over the other side of the horizon, leaving everyone else standing. And perhaps it will be easier now to appreciate just how extraordinary a situation Parmenides was involved in when he managed to formulate the theories about our cosmos that he included at the end of his poem.

By describing the spherical shape of the earth, along with its zones, his goddess was fulfilling to the letter her promise that he would be able to outstrip anyone and everyone in his knowledge of the world. Her assurance had been no poetic exaggeration: no empty rhetoric, no trick. Packed away in the final part of his poem, where not too many people would be tempted to take it too seriously, lay the knowledge that was way ahead of its time.

17

And we could stop here, call it a day, congratulate ourselves on coming so far. But then we would have understood nothing.

That Parmenides was so much in advance of his time with the knowledge he had of the world is remarkable enough. But this, in itself, is the very least of it. For at the same time as presenting his knowledge he is telling us something else—that the knowledge is all a deception.

Whether we spend just half a minute contemplating what that means or the rest of our lives will make no difference. The only thing that does matter is whether we can grasp its implications.

The issue here is not one of how much more we can get of what we already have, or of how much we can start to get of what we would like to have a share of. The point is that we can realize our dreams, make greater discoveries than anyone else, achieve everything we always wanted and far more, go to the edges of the unknown and then beyond—and it's all just an appearance, unreal. You can do everything humanly possible and it's nothing.

We need to appreciate that this is not some hillbilly talking: some eccentric mystic. Parmenides is someone who knew. He was right at the forefront, the cutting edge, of the knowledge of his times; way ahead. And he said it was an illusion.

To hold the most advanced information in the palm of one's hand and describe it like that is not a scenario we are too used to.

Then again, though, we have to remember we are not dealing with an ordinary person but with someone who was a superb expert in *mêtis*. And as a rule such people are not just one step ahead of anyone else, but two. They are not simply outstripping everybody in knowledge but not even considering that important. For they have their own ideas about what is and is not important.

As for ourselves: we have become so caught up in the wonders of thinking, all the dreams of science, the miracles of seeming progress, that we have lost sight of the role played by Parmenides and other people like him in seeding this whole culture we are now little specks of.

They were the people who deliberately, consciously, laid the ground for our lives as we live them and for existence as we know it; who shaped our world, structured the ways we think and operate at a far deeper level than we are even aware of.

And when we anxiously try to categorize Parmenides' achievements as some "strange freak" of history because he happened to know far more than others but at the same time considered this superior knowledge an illusion, that's only a sign of how estranged we have become from our roots. For in spite of everything we suppose we know, we have forgotten the one thing we needed to remember.

Today we can think of Parmenides, or others who used to be like him, as strangely primitive intellectuals; as fascinating infants in the grand unfolding of western ideas, mere children in the evolutionary scheme.

But they are not the children.

Well over two thousand years ago, science as we know it was offered to the West with a warning tag attached to it:

Use this, but don't be tricked by it. And of course, impatient little children that we are, we tore off the tag and ignored the warning.

Still we play around with our imagined knowledge and don't realize it's a deception—honestly believe it's a great achievement to be able to differentiate between true and false with such apparent accuracy but aren't aware, except in our most private moments of helplessness, that even our truths are false.

We pride ourselves on being able to separate fact from fiction, science from myth, but don't see that our science itself is what it always has been: a fragile mythology of the moment.

And so we come back to the fact that in Plato's *Phaedo*—the first complete text still surviving to say the earth is a sphere—the idea of a spherical earth is presented to us fairly and squarely as a myth. For this is no coincidence. It's not the result of some bizarre accident; of some strange freak of history or nature. It's because Plato's friends had taught him well.

18

There is nothing accidental about the way that Parmenides' goddess starts off her teaching with ultimate reality in all its completeness and, only then, goes on to the illusion. First things have to be attended to first.

Her sequence could seem counter-intuitive, illogical, anti-climactic; back to front. But it's quite normal, when one has become accustomed to seeing everything back to front, for anything presented in the right order to appear wrong. And as for this sequence of hers, it has its very specific justification.

Until we have the direct experience of reality we are, as she says, totally helpless. We can't understand a thing: can't even begin to orientate ourselves. Without the prior awareness that everything is one, whole, motionless, all our science and knowledge are going nowhere.

We have the fond idea that as philosophers or scientists or mystics we can start off from the confusion we are in and gradually, steadily, work our way closer towards the truth. But there are no ladders, no stages, to reality.

The situation is perfectly simple. Either we are trapped in the illusion or we are not. And there is no way for us to extricate ourselves from the illusion, none at all—only the illusion that there is.

Certainly there are methods that reality can use to work its own way into our illusion and start to draw us out. But that's quite another matter. The point is that there are no quick, or gradual, methods for those who are caught in the deception to draw themselves out of it: only quick or gradual deceptions.

Philosophers tend to worry a great deal over the deceptive part of Parmenides' teaching because they want to know in what particular sense it could be deceptive. They feel the need somehow to qualify his statement about its deceptiveness, quantify it, categorize it, give the deception he is talking about some specific status. And it's just the same with our lives. We may be prepared at times to admit there is something illusory about them, something badly missing. But then we feel we have to justify them all over again. We assume there has to be a let-out clause: reckon there must be relative degrees of deception, a kind of hierarchy to it all.

But there are no relative degrees. There is only deception.

It can be so tempting to believe that somehow our present illusion is acceptable because it happens to be truer than other possible illusions; is better than the way things used to be. But that's all just an illusion. We may hope we are managing in various ways to work ourselves closer to reality. And yet there is no closeness to reality, or farness, because there is nothing separate from reality. There is only the illusion that there is.

The closer to reality we think we are, the more we are deceived. A good deception is not any better than any other deception: it's simply a good deception. And the best deception of all is the one that manages to make itself transparent, gossamer-thin, by showing us it's only a deception.

In fact every step we try to take out of the illusion is a step further into it. And there is not the slightest hope, not the tiniest possibility, of understanding the illusion while we are caught in it—which is precisely the reason why the goddess offers her teaching about reality first.

Understanding of the illusion only comes after the understanding of reality, not before. The knowledge of many things, of absolutely anything, comes after the knowledge of the one and only thing: not the other way around. Until we have the experience of reality, in all its stillness, we are still lost.

So we have to go straight to the reality first. This is the only science. Otherwise we are just lost in the endlessly illusory knowledge of an endless myth that keeps twisting and stretching itself and receding further into the distance to accommodate our endless expectations.

And this is why the system presented by Parmenides over two thousand years ago, at the dawn of our civilization, is so extraordinary. For it offers us completeness first: not later or at the end, not at some distant point in the future.

The completion, the perfection, comes right at the start. And that's how things have to be, because unless the end were present at the beginning we would never be able to get there.

But there is just one problem with the need for taking reality, in all its completeness, as our starting-point. This is that we can't even get there. The one thing we need is completely out of our grasp because by starting from the deception we will never arrive at the reality.

From every conceivable angle we are helpless.

We can never make our way to the truth. That would be out of the question. Like Parmenides, we have to be taken there instead; all we can do is wait. And it's only when we finally are taken that we can begin to see just how impossible it would have been to work our way out of the illusion towards the truth, out of some deception into reality.

For there is no difference between the two—no way of getting from one to the other or leaving one behind for the other because they are one and the same, quite integral to each other. There is no deception apart from reality, and no reality apart from deception. The deception is what is real.

This is why Parmenides needed to mention the things he included at the end of his poem. And this is why he took more care of his illusions than we do of our so-called reality. For we are always dividing our imagined realities; splitting them up into desirable and undesirable, fragmenting them into true and untrue, acceptable or not. But as for Parmenides, he knew that by embracing the illusion he was only embracing reality in all its perfect stillness and fullness.

Here is the ultimate absurdity, which is so absurd because it happens to be true. By totally embracing the deception we experience reality—but if we try to avoid it, run away from it, we end up deceived.

To dismiss the illusion as just an illusion is, itself, just an illusion. For ultimately it's all we have. And every illusion we have of some greater reality—that, too, is only a part of the illusion.

So we have to get by in it; do well. In fact it's crucial that we do the best we possibly can. For when we live the illusion to the full, to its furthest limits, we are nothing but reality fulfilling its own longing. In spite of the appearances, regardless of all our seeming limitations, we are simply reality completing itself.

FIVE

*The deluded are bound by chains
and find pleasure in them, saying
that all is ultimately real. Yet with
certainty must all things be viewed
as if they were a magic spell.*

SARAHA

Once upon a time the Phocaeans with their journeys were quite a thorn in people's flesh.

Today they are a problem no longer. Thanks to the guiding hand of progress, that's all in the past. Needless to say, historians still like to disagree over points of detail. They would be at a loss without finding something to argue about. But the fundamentals have been very neatly sewn up; the ancient wrongs been righted.

The real process of rehabilitation started during the sixteenth century, following in the wake of the great new explorers like Columbus. Faced with so much fresh information, men of learning saw it was best to swallow their pride and admit the Phocaeans had been telling the truth all along.

In other words it took a mere two thousand years to arrive at the general conclusion that they were not deceivers.

Since then full amends and reparations have been made. The reputation of Pytheas, in particular, has been restored untarnished; his entitlement to a place in history renegotiated; compensation freely offered for the abuse and also for the silence. Countries keep competing at making him into a national and cultural hero.

But what has gone unnoticed in the flurry and excitement, in the middle of all the acceptances and delayed congratulations, is that the essence has slipped away. Instead of holding onto a reality, we are just left clutching at a clumsily carved souvenir.

In the old days most people were quite open about rejecting the Phocaeans out of hand. And yet, as the North American Indians have come to know only too well, acceptance is what tends to conceal the bitterest end.

It was simply to be expected that, as soon as their achievements started being acknowledged, we would want to establish fixed boundaries and lay down the clearest of terms for understanding what they did. And this is just what happened. A kind of unspoken decision was arrived at that Pytheas could have had only two possible reasons for his journey—business, or pure science. The fighting still goes on over whether a scientific or commercial motive was uppermost in his mind; but no one pauses for too long to wonder if the battle has been pitched in the right place, or whether there is anything worth fighting over at all.

We forget so easily that no such thing as our notion of science existed in those days. Then, what we like to call science and what we think of as religion had hardly even started drifting apart and wandering off on their lonely ways. They still lived together in a union that baffles us, befuddles our wits.

When Pytheas set off on his journey to the "solid sea," he followed well-worn Celtic trade routes up to the centers of tin mining at the southern tip of England. But that was not, as people have often assumed, his goal. For after he had arrived there he kept moving on. His sights were on other things.

He carried on up through Britain, and we are told he covered enormous distances on foot. This is a detail historians nowadays find as peculiar as ever and try to push aside— preferring just to speculate about how quick Pytheas' fellow citizens must have been to deck him out with a fine ship all of his own, or perhaps an entire fleet of ships, for such a rewarding venture.

But even this strange detail is significant.

The whole history of the Phocaeans was intimately bound up with heroes: heroes like Heracles or those people who were able to imitate his example and his mythical achievements through their lives, heroes in the original sense of beings who manage to push back the limits of the possible and link the human to the divine. It turns out that Parmenides himself was treated as a hero at Velia after he died. So was the teacher of his who had introduced him to stillness.

And the Phocaeans' journeys, too, were closely tied up with heroes: with Heracles in particular. For Heracles was not just the greatest Greek hero. He was also the archetype of the colonist and explorer, the model for those who came after him. And it used to be said that the best of all his achievements from the human point of view were his journeys of discovery. He was famous not only because of those boundary markers he left at Gibraltar to indicate the furthest limits for safe sailing, but because of the way he had made the entire area of the Mediterranean accessible—something he had done both by clearing routes through the sea and by exploring the earth.

He had "searched out" the waters. And he had "made the land known."

The imitation of Heracles used, once, to be something as deeply meaningful as the imitation of Christ would become centuries later. And by travelling such huge distances beyond the Pillars of Heracles on foot, as well as by sea, Pytheas was imitating to perfection the most perfect of Greek heroes.

Or to be more precise, he was outstripping him; outdistancing him in a way that only a true Phocaean would dare to do.

2

Pytheas headed not just due north and south on his journey but eastwards as well, in a circle.

He came to the regions where the North Sea meets up with the Baltic around Scandinavia. And he mentioned one particular island that was a center for the other great northern trade apart from tin.

To the local Germanic people it was an island surrounded by taboos: a place of mythical kings, field of immortality, land of the dead. And it was a major source of amber.

The word used by Greeks for amber meant "the shining one." To them it was the substance of the sun. And this solar substance was carried down to them from the Baltic by tribe after tribe along an overland route that was known as the sacred way—sacred to Apollo.

The amber, too, was sacred to Apollo because it came from his home in the far distant north: from Hyperborea, his own world hidden behind the north wind. To any ordinary Greek the instructions for getting to this land of Apollo would have been very simple. First, travel as far north as you possibly can. Then, once you have done that, just keep travelling north again.

Here in Hyperborea is where the sun comes every evening in its chariot. And this mythical place also happened to be linked very specifically to some figures we already should be quite familiar with: the Daughters of the Sun.

Amber itself was said by Greeks to be the tears that the Daughters of the Sun shed for their dead brother—here in the land of Apollo where the greatest heroes and kings were brought, after they died, in a chariot which could be either Apollo's or the sun's. For it was here, in the far distant north, that Apollo's close and ancient connections with the sun were even more obvious than anywhere else.

Pytheas happened to mention the name given by the local people to this amber island in the northern sea.

It was Avalon.

A long while after Pytheas and his journey, well over a thousand years later, this name Avalon was eventually transferred to Glastonbury in the south of England: was made famous as the place where King Arthur had been taken when he died.

But even the name Glastonbury, itself, still stands as a poignant reminder—to anyone who cares to notice—of where this Arthurian mythology once came from. For "glas," or *glez* in the ancient Scandinavian languages, means "the shining one."

And, well before it ever started being used for what we now call glass, it was the word for amber.

3

As for Pytheas: Phocaean that he was, he had also carried on even further to the north than Avalon.

He described being taken by guides and shown the place where the sun goes to sleep every night—a perplexing enough detail for most commentators nowadays. But it was only to be expected.

For past Apollo's Hyperborean world according to Greek tradition, just beyond the land of amber that had such intimate ties with the Daughters of the Sun, were the realms of Night where the sun goes home to sleep.

Greeks referred to this legendary place as the point on the far side of the ocean where the cosmos comes to an end, where existence as we know it merges into the underworld. And it should be easy now to see how naturally, how inevitably, Apollo as well as the Daughters of the Sun came to be linked with the underworld and with the Mansions of Night. For here was the place at the edge of the universe where all the opposites of night and day, brilliance and darkness, life and death, start collapsing into each other and becoming one.

And Pytheas offered his personal, eye-witness account of just this.

He described arriving at a place that seemed like the lung of the sea—where everything heaved as if it was breathing, where water and mist and any hint of solid ground all merged into each other without any distinct or recognizable form. There was nothing but a primal chaos of elements still mixed together because they had not been separated out, yet, to form the carefully ordered cosmos as we know it. And he pointed out that the region he had come to was "neither walkable nor sailable," which is accurate enough as a way of evoking the impossible conditions of mist and confusion often created where sea meets solid pack ice.

But there happens to be more to this expression than meets the eye. For Greeks, to come to a place that was simultaneously unwalkable and unsailable implied arriving at the final limit of human existence; at the last barrier dividing our sailable and walkable world from the world beyond.

And he also mentioned something else. He stated that he had come at last to the *desmos* of everything, to the *peirata* of existence—to the fetter and bonds of all there is.

Of course this suggests he had reached the outermost limit and boundary of his journey: in Greek the word for "bond" and "boundary" was one and the same, as it almost is in English. But he clearly meant much more, as well, which is why those who insist on seeing in him either a pure scientist or a hard-nosed businessman are left quite clueless as to what he was talking about.

And yet, once we view his statement in terms of the language and mythology of his times, the explanation could hardly be easier.

Pytheas had touched the bonds and fetters of all existence which, according to Greek tradition, are its beginning as well as its end; its ultimate point of origin; the roots and the well-spring of our entire world. They are the primordial limits, beside the Mansions of Night, where each distinct element merges with the others and disappears into the great beyond—into the chasm of Tartarus.

You could try forever to describe this place at the edge of place, these mysterious bonds, these fetters and boundaries of existence. But only the greatest and the bravest of heroes was able even to come near them. And the essential fact about them, for Greeks, was extremely simple. "They are beyond man's ken."

There is one single man, though, known to us from the historical records of the ancient world who managed to reach them and see them with his eyes and have them in his ken: Pytheas.

Perhaps you are beginning to get the sense of coming home.

It's no longer just a matter any more of the ending to Parmenides' poem: of the things he said there about the earth, its shape, its zones. Now we are being drawn back to the start—back again to all the initial details of his journey to meet the goddess in the first place.

The fixed tradition nowadays is to split his poem into three. The first part is poor myth; the second is philosophy; the last is poor science at the very best. And of course the general inclination is to focus on the philosophy, forget about the science and skip as quickly as possible over the mythology.

You might find an occasional commentator on the poem who generously draws attention, in passing, to the Daughters of the Sun: to their close connections with Apollo's land of amber and the depths of Night that lie beyond. But in scholarship's ruthless drive towards dismissing Parmenides' journey as just an allegory, as only a fanciful way of representing the philosophical process, any comments like these are soon left behind.

The Daughters of the Sun, we are told with dazzling confidence, are nothing at all but symbols of his own "illuminating thoughts" and "clear understanding." Or as one great authority once summed up everything there was to be said about Parmenides' mention of them: "here in the allegory, purely logical in its conception and intention, any residue of mythology has evaporated."

Here is the perfect logic, the faultless consistency, of an approach that strips his poem of its mythology and then says that to do so is only what Parmenides intended. As for other details—like the insistent sound of piping he describes hearing on his chariot journey, and the fact that this sound had the strongest of associations both with Apollo and with the sun— naturally nobody would notice. And no one would even take the trouble to note that this specific piping sound happened to be associated very particularly with Apollo's land of amber.

As for the archaeological evidence, known for years now, that indicates Parmenides himself was a priest of Apollo: it's simply too real not to be ignored.

But every one of these details, inside as well as outside the poem, has its place and its significance. The myth, the philosophy, the science are all one; always have been.

This is the reason why what began as an investigation into the very end of Parmenides' poem has ended up bringing us back right to the beginning. For the poem as a whole is not only a sequence. It's also a circle, as we already should have come to expect.

Everything holds perfectly together. What's so sad about the approach that focuses on a single point along the circumference and then manages to get trapped in pointless theories and meaningless abstractions is not its utter poverty. It's the fact that people have become so satisfied with such poverty.

Parmenides' itinerary on his journey with the Daughters of the Sun is, just like its intricate details, a very particular one: to the place where the sun itself goes home every day, to the Mansions of Night, to the vast chasm falling away into Tartarus, to the final limits where existence as we know it comes to an end. And it also happens to be the same basic itinerary as the one followed by Pytheas—which is hardly a coincidence, considering they both were Phocaeans.

But there is a fundamental difference between their journeys as well.

Pytheas' itinerary is an outer one. He travels physically. In the case of Parmenides, the journey is an inner one. He travels without any physical effort, without ever moving visibly. And yet the importance even of this distinction fades away when we remember that, to him, there is no inner as opposed to outer. For one, essential characteristic of reality as Parmenides describes it is that they both are one. What seems to us outside is really inside. What appears to be inside is also outside.

In fact there is no distinguishing between the two because existence as a whole is seamless, outside and inside at the same time.

Pytheas made his way up to the bonds of existence, by sea and on foot. That was the limit, though, to how far he could go. He had travelled physically as far as any human being could reach. But Parmenides, in Velia, went even further—by going nowhere, by staying physically quite still.

And this is perfectly possible. You can be walking down a street in the evening and suddenly be taken further than any human has travelled. You can keep on walking as you had been before, or find somewhere to sit down: open your eyes or close them. It makes no difference. Regardless of what you seem to do physically, of whether you stay outdoors or go in, the journey goes on until you reach your destination.

And the experience can be so real that you wonder if you will survive. And you carry the marks of it for the rest of your life.

If you were to ask whether this isn't only an illusion, the answer would be that of course it is—but no more than anything else. For the illusion is everywhere: inside as well as outside. And yet the one thing that matters is to travel all the way through it until, regardless of the cost, we reach its source.

Otherwise the lives we live will be passed in the shadow of our failure to set out on this one journey we all have the opportunity to make, or of our decision to give up somewhere along the way.

5

Now that we are coming full circle there is one other matter we need to attend to.

Like Parmenides' opening reference to the Daughters of the Sun, it has to do with something he says right at the beginning of his poem. But it, too, has a significance that reaches out through the poem as a whole.

As soon as he arrives in the underworld, meets the goddess, receives her welcome and greeting, she sums up for him in just a few words everything she is going to teach him. She starts off by explaining that

> *what's needed is for you to learn all things: both the unshaken*
> *heart of persuasive Truth and the opinions of mortals*
> *in which there is nothing that can truthfully be trusted at all.*

But of course her own words here, simple as they may seem, make no sense at all by themselves. For there is no conceivable reason why, in addition to teaching him the truth, she should want him to learn something so untruthful and useless.

So, as a way of justifying why she should bother even for a moment with human opinions if they are not to be trusted, she goes on to present him with one of her more famous riddles.

> *But even so, this too you will learn—how beliefs based on*
> *appearance ought to be believable as they travel all through*
> *all there is.*

These last words about travelling bear all the marks, as usual with Parmenides, of oddness. They are not just odd, though. The amount of problems and sheer uncertainty they have given rise to is hard to believe; they have even been described as "the most controversial text" in the entire poem.

But as you will have gathered by now, scholarly controversy about Parmenides tends to be a rather elaborate game of passing the time of day by tying one's mind in knots over absolutely nothing. And if this particular passage happens to be among the most controversial of all, that must be because its meaning is transparent and straightforward beyond any reasonable doubt.

As a matter of fact that's exactly the way things are.

All kinds of attempts have been made over the past few hundred years at giving Parmenides' text here a sense that the most elementary knowledge of Greek would recognize to be quite impossible. For there is nothing even slightly ambiguous or uncertain about what it means. What the goddess is telling him is that as a rule beliefs are worthless and utterly unreliable—but that she is going to explain how, paradoxically, they can come to possess a certain reliability if they meet one specific condition.

This condition is that they have to be able to travel through all there is, all the way through everything, right to the end.

Parmenides' word here for "travelling" is *perân*; and it has very particular connotations. It happens to be related to another word we have encountered already—*peirata*, "bonds" or "limits"—and you can judge its sense accordingly.

Perân means to cross right over, to travel all the way through something until you come to the other side, to keep going as far as you can without letting up until you arrive at the furthest limits. And Parmenides simply draws out the fullest implications of this word by adding "all the way through all there is."

What he is saying is that human opinions can possess a certain validity provided they reach all the way through this world of appearances to its furthest limit; as long as they touch its *peirata*, the ultimate boundaries of existence.

That may not mean much to us, now. But for Greeks of his time things were very different. In their minds it would have conjured up a whole chain of associations: would automatically have suggested something quite precise. For this word, *perân*, was used time and time again by the earliest Greek poets to describe the act of travelling right across the great ocean to the *peirata* of the universe—the ultimate boundaries of existence. That was the job of the hero who manages to touch the borderline between the human and divine; to reach the realm of Persephone. Most typically of all, though, it described the daily route followed by the sun as it makes its way to the other side of the ocean surrounding the known world and arrives in the Mansions of Night.

To cross all existence and reach its furthest limit, to go the whole way: this is the mark of a true Phocaean. Pytheas described doing it. So does Parmenides.

But in his case the situation is rather special; a little unique.

You could say that his goddess has something of an ulterior motive when she tells him that human opinions and beliefs will only become trustworthy, believable, if they are able to reach as far as the ultimate limits of existence. For those limits are exactly where she is. They are where her home is: are where the Daughters of the Sun have brought Parmenides to meet her.

She is describing to him the journey he himself has just made.

With her words she is pointing to the distant place he already has arrived at. Once again her teaching forms a perfect circle—stretching out beyond imagination to return, effortlessly, to its starting-point and complete itself.

And here too, as soon as she opens her mouth to speak, she reveals her fondness for jokes: for turning everything on its head. The normal Greek standpoint was that human beliefs are quite trustworthy when they deal with matters close to home but become completely unbelievable when they try to convey anything definite about the fantastic limits of the universe. And yet the goddess, with her exquisite humor, reverses the entire situation.

To her, ordinary human opinions are utterly unbelievable in themselves and only become trustworthy when they reach the furthest limit of existence.

From the human perspective nothing could seem more frankly bewildering; more destructive of common sense; more of a temptation to get all tangled up in knots by. But in terms of the divine reality that Parmenides has been selected to express, her message could hardly be more immediate or direct.

Unless every journey we make brings us face to face with her, we are going nowhere. Our existence is beyond belief. And in the last resort unless we encounter the goddess of death with every step we take, we are totally lost.

6

The action of *perân*, of travelling right through a particular space and all the way to the end, traditionally demanded far more than determination or perseverance.

Greeks understood that it also tends to require one very specific quality or faculty—*mêtis*. It calls for alertness and cunning, for competence in navigation, confidence in finding one's way. Above all it depends on the ability to notice and follow the subtle signs that others might be inclined to misinterpret, or simply overlook.

And it needs a tremendous focus, a particular energy or intensity of one-pointedness that resists the temptation to stop and rest half-way.

What matters is being able to stay on course, regardless. For the word *perân*, like *peirata*, was linked directly to another word that happens to express its exact opposite: *aporia* or pathlessness. *Aporia* is the result of pausing when one shouldn't, of hesitating in mid-stream, of looking around for a reflection of one's lostness instead of for guidance, of doubting halfheartedly instead of having the courage to doubt one's doubt, of wondering whether it really could be possible to go the whole way when the only chance of finding out is by going the whole way.

But with Parmenides the situation is special in more respects than just one. In fact Pytheas' journey to the Arctic Circle was child's play compared with what he is asking us to do. Pytheas travelled further than any other historical Greek we know about, to the limits of the cosmos. Parmenides is talking in similar terms about something apparently rather similar and yet really quite different.

He is expecting us to travel into and across an illusion—and the whole way through it, right to the end.

We need to appreciate a little of what that means. It means, very simply, that we have to drink this deception we live in to the dregs. As with everything that the goddess teaches him, there is no stopping half-way.

Grasping the fact that this world of ours is an illusion is not enough. Realizing it's a deception and then wobbling on the edge of it or trying to turn away from it in the hope of finding reality somewhere else: this is the coward's way. That's the path followed by people who become more and more complicated with every step they think they are taking away from illusion—who create dualities and conflicts all around them because they are aware, in spite of themselves, that by walking away from the illusion they are running away from the reality.

To go the whole way through what one knows to be an illusion and not get caught in it is extremely tricky.

Plenty of *mêtis* is needed, more than a human could ever find by herself or himself. And the greatest trap of all is the risk of mistaking one's beliefs for knowledge. For when Parmenides talks about the need to travel to the furthest limit that human opinions are able to reach, he is referring to something very different from any idea we might have about pushing back the boundaries of knowledge.

We have become remarkably efficient over the last two thousand years at extending the limits of what we call knowledge. And yet, in doing so, all we have managed to do is expand the illusion that we live in. We have ended up with vast amounts of information about planets and galaxies and space; but none of this is real. It's just imagination, a web of beliefs that shifts and gradually changes shape as our illusion expands.

To keep pushing back the boundaries of knowledge is quite the opposite of getting to the edges of knowledge. In fact it's simply a way of extending the hangman's rope. What we need is to be able to reach so far we can touch the noose that binds us, and what Parmenides is talking about is just that—the urgent need to get to the furthest limits of everything we think we know without ending up trapped inside it.

This is not at all abstract. On the contrary, it could hardly be more real. Even to compare Parmenides with somebody else, with something you have heard or read or thought about, is to get caught in what you know. But this need to get to the limit of whatever we know is also so subtle that it keeps eluding our rational understanding, because as soon as we try to make sense of it we immediately drag it inside the boundaries of our imagined knowledge.

And yet at the same time there is nothing more solid. That limit, so elusive, is the rock of our existence.

To go the whole way through all there is, as Parmenides describes it, an utter innocence and simplicity is needed. For the extraordinary thing, the truth hidden from us so well, is that knowledge does have its ultimate limits—just as the path pointed out to him by the goddess has its ultimate goal.

To us this has become almost inconceivable. All we are used to, the only thing we know, is inquiries that go on and on for ever. Even if we manage to carry one particular search right through to its end, that's always only a half-way stage because we find ourselves straightaway at the beginning of another.

But the goddess is a goddess precisely because, unlike us humans, she delivers. When she presents us with her route of inquiry, she is not offering some infinite path that always keeps disappearing seductively into the distance. That's only the property of the paths she rejects.

This path of hers carries us all the way. By following it we arrive at the furthest boundary not just of ourselves but of everything there is. For it has its goal, its final limit and its very definite end, which is right here: in the stillness where we already are and always have been.

And so we come back to the one feature we were bound sooner or later to return to—the bonds.

Parmenides has laid out the basic elements of his teaching for us. All he asks us to do is to make the natural connections; to draw the inevitable conclusions. And once we see that what he is talking about is something real, something intimately related to us, once we put ourselves in the picture, add our own selves as the indispensable final ingredient, this is not at all hard to do.

On the contrary: it follows effortlessly.

You could say he is very unwise to expect us to do anything. And you might be right. But the fact is that this is how writers in his age used to communicate—giving listeners and readers the benefit of the doubt, leaving them to understand or not, letting them misinterpret if they are determined to, allowing them a little credit for their intelligence. It was only more recently that the laborious habit evolved of spelling out each detail one by one.

Parmenides is very generous with the hints and signs he offers. And he is almost obsessive with his language of fetters and bonds. They are everywhere: surrounding absolutely everything. He goes to the most extraordinary lengths to point out that existence is bound fast in a circular grip, is held tight in the bonds of great fetters and the fetters of a bond which keep everything exactly the way it is.

But, for reasons of their own, the generations of thinkers who came after him started interpreting this strange imagery as no more than symbolic in its quaintly ornate way of logic's inflexible rules; as simply symptomatic of Parmenides' fondness for flowery language.

What they have forgotten is that imagery has a significance, a life, an inner logic all of its own.

If this was only a question of the images he uses, then perhaps it would hardly be worth pursuing. And yet it's not. For his teaching about the nature of reality is a matter of practicalities, not theories; and so is his teaching about deception. The bound reality he is describing is not some intellectual construct. It's the reality we live and die in, that we can never escape for a single moment.

Because all existence is bound in fetters, so is our existence. Because reality is in bonds, so are we.

For Greeks, to be held in bonds implied something very definite. It meant being trapped, helpless, unable to escape. And the language they used for describing the situation was quite precise.

Just as their words for "bonds" and "fetters" were *peirata* and *desma*, their word for the helplessness of someone trapped and caught inside them was *amêchania*. Fetters and bonds, *desma* and *peirata*, were the literal or symbolic instruments that make us helpless. And helplessness, *amêchania*, was the result of being in bonds.

The connection between these words was so integral a part of the Greek language that poets constantly coupled them to describe the state of powerlessness; of futility. We even find the specific phrase *peirat' amêchaniês*, "the bonds of helplessness," being used to define the human condition in all its essential ineffectiveness.

The bonds of helplessness, so painful, hold us in their grip. Whatever we do or think—we humans who know nothing—is in vain, while the gods bring everything to completion exactly as they have in mind.

And perhaps you can see where this is leading. For those bonds featuring in the goddess' description of reality are only a half of Parmenides' story. The other half is her description of our helplessness, our *amêchania*: of our lostness as we wander around trapped and confused in our complicated existences.

In short, her account of reality is inseparable from her account of the human condition. And the fact that we could ever have doubted this, or considered the link between them insignificant, is just another sign of how we have complicated our lives. For even though we fail to see the connection because it's so very simple, everything she says is bound together.

8

There is only one reality: the one all around us.

Whenever we happen to feel helpless or trapped, that's because reality is held fast in bonds. And from these bonds there is absolutely no escape. Besides, even if there were, nothing else exists for us to escape to because all of existence is here—in bonds.

When things become too bleak or painful, in our very ordinary existence, there is no transcendental reality to get away to. We can go next door, or half-way around the world, or meet a goddess who will teach us the truth about reality and ourselves. But we will still be stuck in existence: prisoners of our thoughts and dreams.

Really to understand that we are trapped, held fast in bonds, that there is nowhere else to go, no possibility of transcendence, is devastating. It knocks the bottom out of everything we once thought we knew. All of a sudden we are faced, inescapably, with the horrifying reality of what before might have seemed such an attractive ideal—the terrors of completeness. For in the experience of completeness there is nothing to become. There is nothing else to look forward to.

The endless searching is over.

The greatest single trick of existence is to make us forget we are trapped, because then we are hopelessly trapped. When we keep believing we are free, that's bondage. And paradoxically the greatest freedom of all lies in knowing without the smallest room for doubt that one is trapped, because then the struggling and pretending stops.

But there would be no point whatsoever in becoming aware of how trapped we are if our awareness of the fact changed nothing. And this is where the infinite subtlety of the goddess' teaching comes into play. For in our helpless situation there is just one factor capable of helping us.

To Greeks, the ability to trap and bind successfully had a single name—*mêtis*. As a matter of fact *mêtis* and the mastery of bonds were so closely intertwined that, for an expert in *mêtis* who happens to be trapped, the most important issue is not whether it's possible to escape. The real question is whether it's possible to trap the trapper: to turn the tables, direct the strength of the more powerful force back against itself.

Our greatest problem as humans is that we are at the mercy of reality. We keep getting lost inside it; have forgotten how to finish what has been started, how to link the beginning to the end.

And yet all we need to do is to turn our awareness back, at every moment, to its source.

It only takes the slightest shift in consciousness, the subtlest movement of awareness, and instead of being bound and helpless we are binding the binder. We have completed the circle, inside and outside ourselves. Then the bonds and boundaries of existence are not in some far-off place any more, at the illusory edges of the cosmos.

They are wherever we happen to be. And we are absolutely free—not because we are free from something but because we contain everything, every perception and thought, inside ourselves.

This is the experience of utter stillness: more exquisite, more full, than anything under the sun.

And so Parmenides leaves us just where we found him, right in the middle of our very ordinary life. Or so it seems. For if you have understood anything at all in what he says, you will have realized that there is no leaving.

There are no comings, or goings; no goodbyes. And there most definitely is no death.

Finally, last of all, there is the key that opens and closes the whole of Parmenides' poem.

Of course I could stay quiet about it. It has been covered over for so long that no one would even miss it. But this is not the time for keeping silent any more.

With Parmenides the essential question has always been the same: how the two halves of his teaching, the one about reality and the other about deception, hold together. I already explained how they are linked in terms of *mêtis*, and also in terms of the great goddess who is mysteriously two as well as one.

But for such an essential question there is a more essential answer.

Reality, in all its truth and stillness, is held fast by fetters and bonds. This is the one half. The other half is that we live in a world of illusion: in a cosmos just as deceptive as the goddess' orderly words. And these two basic traits of existence—reality as held fast in bonds, the world that we live in as a deception—are far from unrelated. The only problem is our tendency to overlook the most basic things, just as we learn so easily to do without what matters most.

In Parmenides' time the idea of bonds and binding and fetters was still inseparably linked, as it had been for ages, with the notion of deception. In his time, and even for centuries afterwards, to talk of "binding" people was a standard way of saying that one was tricking them. If you wanted to describe the situation of being deceived you would quite naturally use the imagery of being caught in fetters, trapped in a bond, held fast. Expressions like "the fetters of deception," *apatês desma*, were perfectly routine. To bind was to deceive and to deceive was to bind.

But there was more to this, as well. For ancient Greeks, the language of deceiving and the imagery of binding shared one very specific factor in common. This is that they were both the most traditional of ways for referring to a magic spell.

The simple words "bind" and "bond" became key terms for describing magical procedures. From the earliest of times they were almost interchangeable with the terms "bewitch" and "bewitchment"—and referred in particular to spells that were accompanied by incantations. As for the specific word "deceptive," or *apatêlos* in Greek, used by the goddess to describe her teaching about this world of ours: that implied a great deal more than our modern ideas of intellectual duplicity. Deception, *apatê*, used to be the normal term for describing the effects of a magic charm.

And so we come to that other word she uses for summing up the human condition. For *amêchania* didn't only mean "helplessness." Neither did it just tend to suggest the helplessness of someone inescapably entangled in fetters and bonds.

The literal sense of the term is "without a *mêchanê*," which meant "without a trick" or "without a ruse." In other words it referred, as we have seen, to the predicament of someone caught out by a tricky situation and completely outwitted. So there should be nothing surprising about the fact that, both in and well after Parmenides' time, it was used as a common expression for portraying the state of someone who has been tricked or deceived: the victim of *apatê*.

And, more than that, it was also used to describe the condition of someone who has been charmed and bewitched.

Parmenides' language of helplessness and bonds and deception is perfectly consistent. And its implications are as all-encompassing as they are simple. The congruence, the harmony, the integrity of his poem as a whole is immaculate and complete—back all the way to his deliberate initial use of magical, incantatory repetition right at the start.

The solution to the riddle of how this teaching that he presents us with holds together could hardly be more accessible, any easier for us to reach. And it longs for us to touch it. But the price we have to pay for doing that is a heavy one.

It's every single idea we hold dear, including the reality of our own existence.

You may feel fully entitled to reject this magical dimension of his teaching; quite justified in dismissing it as hopelessly irrelevant to the work of a man so famous as the father of western logic. But that would be a shame. For without it we will always be outsiders to Parmenides' poem—wandering around, just as he describes, lost in a dream.

And, as for magic, this is not something we have outgrown. On the contrary: even our determined belief in its non-reality is simply a sign of how potent the magic is that we exist in the grip of.

The great problem with the approach of intellectuals to Parmenides has always been their belief that in describing reality as motionless and unchanging and whole and one, he was talking about some different world from the one we live in; about some other reality, some separate existence.

But for him there is no other reality, never could be. That reality is this.

There is only one single existence, which is the world we live in—surrounded by its fetters.

Reality is held in bonds. We are held in bonds. Reality is motionless. We seem to be surrounded by motion. The connecting thread between these statements is not at all obvious; but the reason for that is because existence is held fast in bonds. And of course the things Parmenides is talking about are bound to sound ridiculous to those who live their whole lives moving around entranced, enthralled, fettered, in a world of deception. For the key words in the two halves of his poem—bond and deception—are two sides of one and the same coin.

What can be described from outside as the binding of existence is experienced, from inside, as this: the wonderfully enchanting world you see and hear all around you.

And in that world Parmenides had a son.

As you may remember, his chief disciple and successor was someone called Zeno. This is the man who, we are told, died testing Parmenides' teaching in fire "like gold that's pure and true." And Zeno was Parmenides' son.

Or, to be more precise, he was his adopted son: a significant detail.

Parmenides belonged, just like those men with the ritual title Oulis who formed a continuous line of succession at Velia down through the centuries, to a priestly tradition that served Apollo Oulios. And Apollo Oulios—the god who destroys and makes whole—had his main centers of worship in Anatolia, above all in Caria.

Not too much is known about the priestly traditions of Caria or the surrounding regions in Anatolia. But there is one thing we do know. This is that the lines of succession tended to be based on the principle of teachers adopting their disciples and successors. To be initiated into such a line demanded total commitment; meant being introduced into a new family, starting one's life all over again. And your teacher became your father.

Zeno was a good son to his father.

Parmenides' central message had been that reality is whole and complete, utter fullness and simplicity. But, before even getting to it, he had been very careful in his poem to add one fundamental detail that people after his time became extremely efficient at forgetting—the fact that we don't stand the slightest chance of grasping anything about reality until we have become aware of how our beliefs and ideas are just a mass of self-contradictions.

One person didn't forget.

Parmenides had explained that in reality there is no movement, no separation between this and that, no time outside of now. As for Zeno: he didn't even bother to say anything about reality. He saw no need. He just argued that if we start from our own commonsense assumptions and take them seriously, then we end up having to accept there can be no movement; no separating one thing from another; no time apart from now.

He took a firm stand in what we think of as our ordinary reality, agreed to think the way we think—and then pointed out through a series of paradoxes that it's simply a mess of self-contradictions.

It's said he wrote forty paradoxes in all. And in spite of their absurdity, or rather because of it, they have kept worrying and fascinating philosophers and mathematicians and so-called logicians for thousands of years.

He argued that if you take the case of a moving object like an arrow on its way to a target, you will have to agree it happens to be quite motionless at every single moment of its journey. For, like any other object, it has to occupy a space exactly equivalent to itself; and this means it always has to be just where it is, which means it's perfectly still. Or he argued that if you are going to travel a certain distance you will first have to cross a half of it, then a half of the half, then a half of this half, and so on forever. And so you will never arrive.

His paradoxes evoke one single, instinctive reaction. This is the urge to dismiss them as wrong; the instant need to defend our familiar world by rejecting them as "fallacies," in other words as falsenesses. And that reaction takes one of two closely related forms.

First there is the temptation to reject what Zeno says on the basic grounds that, of course, everyone knows movement and time are real. But this is not too intelligent. All it shows is our willingness to act as happy victims of what could be a highly persuasive illusion—and that those who cry "fallacy" with the loudest of voices are quite liable to be the greatest fools.

Then there is the more sophisticated reaction: of searching for the worm in Zeno's bud, of looking for where he went wrong, trying to point out some subtlety he supposedly failed to notice. The only trouble is that whatever explanation somebody comes up with somehow never manages to satisfy everyone else. Soon it looks like just one more makeshift device for stopping up a leak in a boat until another set of holes starts appearing.

And besides, we have to understand that Zeno was only concerned to deny the reality of this world we get out of bed for every morning. He would never have wanted to deny the infinite ingenuity of human intelligence in inventing increasingly intricate ways of justifying its own existence.

Paradoxes are a very delicate affair. By definition they are something that upsets our perceptions; violates our accepted opinions about how things are. They can be ever so fragile, like a vase made of the finest porcelain. To stamp on them with the weight of our common sense because we assume that whatever stands apart from our idea of how things should be must be wrong: this is easy.

But then the flower in the vase will be crushed—and we will have denied ourselves one more chance to experience something of tremendous beauty.

Zeno's most famous paradox of all is known as the Achilles: it goes like this. No one could run faster than Achilles, the great hero. So in a race against a tortoise he was given a handicap, for the sake of fairness, and made to start from behind the tortoise. But when the race begins and he arrives at the place where the tortoise set off from, the tortoise has already moved on ahead. And by the time he catches up to where the tortoise got to when he had reached its starting-point, again the tortoise has moved a little further on; and so on. And so Achilles never catches up with the tortoise.

Whatever examples Zeno gave, there is one crucial fact we need to notice. This is that, just like Parmenides and just as with Indian logic too, he used logic in its truest sense; respected its original purpose. He used it not to fortify or justify our commonsense view of reality but to undermine it, destroy it.

And what's particularly interesting in the Achilles is that the faster runner never catches up with the slower. For it was well known to Greeks that there is only one factor capable of making the slower get the better of the faster. That factor is not strength or brute force. It's what they called *mêtis*: the subtlety that manages to achieve the seemingly impossible by reversing everything, turning all our expectations upside down and back to front.

But as for Zeno, he was not just performing some clever trick. He was revealing, with his *mêtis*, that this whole world we believe in is an illusion.

11

So many crazy stories have come down to us about how the earliest philosophers died that there is not too great a temptation to take them seriously.

It seems so much easier to dismiss them all as nothing but fictions, inventions. And this is what people have often been happy to do with the stories about Zeno's extraordinary bravery in facing death—and were free to do, until quite recently. For, a while ago, the situation suddenly and quietly changed.

The most detailed of all the accounts that survive about how Zeno died explains how he was brutally tortured when he was caught smuggling arms from his home of Velia down to Lipara. Lipara was the name of an island, due south from Velia and just off the north coast of Sicily, that had a unique religious significance for the ancient Greeks.

Along with the other little islands around it, it lay close to the center of the most dramatic volcanic activity in the Mediterranean—and was notorious for its connection with the forces of the unseen, with the vast fires burning in the underworld. It also happened to be responsible for inspiring some of the most vivid imagery about volcanoes and underground fire that eventually was to make its appearance in Plato's famous myth at the end of the *Phaedo*: the myth Socrates is supposed to have told just before being put to death.

The mention of Lipara in the story about Zeno dying hardly seemed worth attaching any importance to, until 1978. This is when some archaeologists working on the island found themselves faced with growing evidence that the Liparans had had the closest of ties with Velia. And it's no accident that one of the inscriptions found on the island included the word Oulis: a name only known from two other places in the whole of the western Mediterranean.

One is Velia, the other its sister-city of Massalia.

As the archaeologists were quick to realize, such a direct link between Lipara and Velia confirmed that the story about Zeno had not just been made up. And there were other details, too, in the traditions about Zeno's death that had not been made up either.

Nowadays the idea that Parmenides' son would have died testing his father's teaching in fire, like gold, is incomprehensible. And the reason is very simple. It makes no sense because we no longer understand that Parmenides' teaching used to be far more than something to be used for scratching the itch in our minds.

His poem, his teaching, was part of a sacred tradition.

And because this is no longer understood, we silently pass over another odd statement that also seems to make no sense. For no one has managed to explain what the writer of one ancient text could possibly have meant when he mentioned the supreme importance of being able, not only in our words but in our actions as well, to live "a Parmenidean way of life." And yet as soon as we start to rediscover what Parmenides' poem once was—not an exercise for intellectuals, but a guide to transformation—then all the details of what this writer says fall into place.

We can see just what he means when he goes straight on to talk about the divine power of deception that leads people astray; or about how our familiar human opinions are much more powerful and far less innocent than they seem to be because they are living beings in their own right, entities that promise us happiness and wisdom but lure us to our destruction; or when he talks about the way that, helpless in the face of these deceptive powers, we "wander around all over the place."

And it's easy to understand why, after delicately hinting at the immense value of living a Parmenidean life, he says something few people today would even dream of taking seriously.

For he warns that there is a tremendous element of danger involved in coming into contact with such a tradition, such a teaching. The result of approaching it with deep respect, with real attention, is wisdom. But the result of approaching it without them will be that you become more foolish than ever because you will have wasted an extraordinary opportunity.

And, as he goes on to explain, this kind of teaching is a riddle. If we miss the true solution, we lose everything. We end up, quite simply, destroyed—"not all at once, as in the case of people who died when they were devoured by the Sphinx, but little by little throughout the whole of one's life." The cost of solving the riddle is everything. And the price for not solving it is everything, too.

That's just what Parmenides' entire poem is: one great riddle reflecting the riddle of existence. It presents us with the most obscure enigma there is, the enigma of a teaching so practical that it reaches beyond all our ideas of practicality and seems completely impractical. But as the report about Zeno and Parmenides' teaching gently suggests, if something can be tested through death then the chances are it's well worth living for.

The only question is whether we are able to recognize its value while alive, or will keep on walking past it instead.

Of course there is one other riddle here, as well: the riddle of how this side to Parmenides' teaching ever came to be so totally forgotten. And for the answer we have to turn back to that story about Zeno dying while trying to smuggle arms down to Lipara. For we know who the enemy was that the Liparans were preparing themselves to fight; who the people were who soon would invade the island, devastate it. They were the Athenians.

And this is not the only evidence indicating Zeno's resistance to the Athenians; his wariness, to put the matter mildly, in face of their growing arrogance and thirst for power. But it has become almost impossible for us really to believe there could have been other Greek centers of culture, just as important in their own way, that fought to keep free from Athens—the city we have learned to idealize above all, to identify with everything significant and glorious, noble and good. And if those other cultures present us with the threat of something we no longer have the conscious equipment or the will to understand, then there is even more reason to forget.

As for Zeno, though: with his wariness he clearly had a strong sense of what was to come.

12

And as for Plato, in Athens: he clearly had a strong sense of what was important.

There was one man who, alongside his own teacher Socrates, impressed him more than anyone else—Parmenides. But it was not enough for Plato's purposes just to be seen as the bearer of Socrates' mantle. He also wanted the succession to Parmenides' teaching for himself.

This meant having to make a few minor adjustments.

Fortunately for Plato, he lived at a time when writing history and writing fiction were not yet the two separate things they seem to have become. The past was still fluid, available for shaping. Now we are forced either to repeat history or to rewrite it. Then history was still being written. And this is precisely what he did through the fictional dialogues, so life-like, that were to make him famous.

Disposing of Zeno, Parmenides' real successor, was easy for someone with Plato's inventive skills. Just a few deft words were needed, portraying him as immature and even touchingly apologetic for being immature: a man only too obviously unworthy of the succession. As for Parmenides himself, we are offered the picture of a very nice old white-haired man who not only loves splitting endless hairs but also enjoys contradicting himself—yielding so congenially, so conveniently, in the give-and-take of discussion to the soundness of Plato's ideas. And even though we know the details are Plato's fabrication, we can find it extremely hard to pull ourselves away from taking this portrait for reality.

But there was one other thing Plato realized he had to do if he was going to have his way. He had to kill Parmenides, the "father." The man who had said that reality in its perfection can never be violated would have to be murdered.

There was no subject more surrounded by taboo in Plato's time than patricide. But fiction is a wonderful tool, and through his writings he was able to carry out the murder without seeming to be responsible for anything. All he had to do was very delicately state what needed to be done through the mouth of an imaginary character: a non-existent visitor from Velia. And even now you will find scholars indignantly insisting that Plato himself is not to be held responsible for anything any of his characters ever say. They are, after all, just fictions.

It was the ideal crime; a crime only committed on a piece of paper with a watertight alibi. There were no bloody hands. But this murder was real enough. And it had to be real, because it was something that urgently needed to be done.

Plato's fictional visitor from Velia explains quite clearly why Parmenides had to be got out of the way. The teaching presented by him in his poem had placed a roadblock in front of the mind. In saying that everything simply is, by denying the existence of non-existence, Parmenides had ended up denying our thoughts the slightest room for manoeuvre. There was nowhere to go, backwards or forwards or sideways. The mind was trapped—in reality.

And that was an essential aspect of his teaching. For the way Parmenides worked, much the same as Zeno did, or Socrates, was to challenge the mind only to undermine it; was to paralyze it, silence it, bring it face to face with stillness.

Plato's genius was to realize this was no longer enough. The intellect of the people all around him had become much too powerful, too irresistible. The only way to master it would be to go with it instead of trying to stop it, would be to trick it into believing it really could do something useful. And as Plato made his fictional Velian visitor explain, Parmenides had to be murdered so we could bring non-existence in again through the back door: so we can safely say that even if something exists "in one sense," it doesn't have to exist in another.

With this little "in a sense"—so appealing to reason and to what soon would be known as common sense—the philosophy we are now familiar with could come into being. All the seriously complicated edifices of the western intellect could be built. Plato was able to start structuring a whole world of separation, to begin theoretically articulating the principle of transcendence: of the need to get from here to there even though there is no there apart from here. Our minds had been given permission to play hide-and-seek with themselves.

He did this according to the same principle we use when we give a dog a ball to keep it happy. The growing western mind was restless for experience, for complication, so it was best to give it what it wanted. Parmenides' teaching had been that logic is something divine, a gift from the gods. Plato took logic and put it in everyone's hands: encouraged people to think and argue for themselves.

It was a tremendous achievement. It required all sorts of distortions, falsifications, obscurations—which his successor, Aristotle, was soon pursuing to perfection. And yet, at the time, these were a small price to pay. For through his writings Plato was able to transmit revealed teachings, traditions, ideas, in a way that would make them not just accessible but also intriguing to the mind.

He had given people something wonderful to play with. And soon it was obvious to almost anyone that the way to get to the truth in those ideas was not through entering some other state of consciousness but through thinking. As one historian has described his achievement, in terms that are accurate enough, Plato was the man who "by a truly creative act transposed these ideas definitively from the plane of revelation to the plane of rational argument."

But now, after over two thousand three hundred years of thinking and debating and rational argument, the time has come for a little honesty.

In all those years our minds have allowed us to do great things. We can build bridges and fly, heal and kill ourselves in thousands of new ways. As for reality, though, and the soul, and all those questions that Plato insisted mattered most: we have got absolutely nowhere. We have plenty of theories, endless discussions of problems about problems about problems. But the simple fact is that through our minds we have not managed to understand one single thing.

And the time for thinking and for reasoning is over now. They have served their purpose. They have kept us busy, allowed our minds to grow, carried us a little way further on the route towards greater individuality and self-consciousness. The problem is that we still know nothing.

It's no longer enough to read what Plato or others say and be inspired, intellectually stimulated, emotionally touched, stirred by a longing for reality. The time for all that searching and struggling is past, finished. The reality is here, in the middle of the illusion; has been all along, longing to be recognized. Now we need to become that reality, take responsibility for it, make it real again.

II

SOWERS
OF
ETERNITY

SIX

I know that truth is with the words
I will be saying. But, for humans,
the rush of assurance towards the seat
of their awareness has become so
very troublesome: so undesired.

EMPEDOCLES

1

This book is simply an expression of that line Parmenides belonged to—which survives individual people in the same way trees survive the winter.

And it has nothing to do with the words you can read on the page.

If you look, you will see that everything you hear or read is meant to entertain; amuse; inform; inspire. We always expect it to give us something. But nothing is enough. We pick up a book one day, then put it down and move on.

This book offers nothing of the kind. The information it contains is far more accurate, to be sure, than anything you will find written anywhere else about the subjects that it touches on—and is utterly unimportant. All the details in it are just a trick. But what it does offer is the space for you to create a nest in it, make yourself at home.

Then there will be no need to pick it up or put it down.

The reality behind these words is quite different, I can only remind you, from whatever you are able to understand through thinking: has nothing to do with the impressions that tumble into your mind and then, sooner or later, filter off again through your awareness.

Every word in this book carries the consciousness of its unimportance. Each one of them prostrates to reality; bows until its head touches the floor of oneness. And their message has nothing to do with sounds, or even with apparent meanings. Neither does it have anything whatsoever to do with thoughtful responses, careful reactions, considered judgements.

On the contrary, it lies in the utter stillness that can only be approached when you allow yourself to be shaken by what has been spoken quite silently for thousands of years.

As for the essence of that tradition Parmenides belonged to: it neither died out nor stayed confined to Velia. In fact with the passing of time it traced a strange, neglected path.

You can search as hard as you like for a description of the course it followed. You won't find one. You can look high and low in the textbooks for some account of it, some explanation. But all you will be presented with is something else—the crudest of substitutes, clumsy attempts to lump Parmenides together with people whom in reality he could hardly have had less to do with.

You will find him, a man who brought the unshakable knowledge of reality back intact from another world, thrown into the company of wandering entertainers who made a deliberate point of cautiously insisting that no one could ever reach any certain knowledge about anything of the kind; or of people who soon would be treating his teaching as if it was some sort of crossword puzzle to be played around with in their spare time. And the most interesting thing is that none of these inconsistencies or incongruities was of the slightest genuine concern to those who patched together our histories, organized our past.

Their overriding interests lay in quite another direction.

As for us, now: we have become so used to fictions and substitutes that we just do the best we can to make do. After all, not much matters any more where the earliest of philosophers are concerned except the one compelling need to turn them into so many human milestones on an evolutionary highway heading nowhere.

You don't want to follow that route, though. For the real path traced by the line Parmenides belonged to followed a very different course.

Once, the direction it happened to take was still known about. But that was a long time ago. And now there is no way you could even start to discover it again through reasoning, because reasoning is precisely what covered it over in the first place; is what did everything possible to obliterate its traces.

The only way to find it is through your neglected sense of smell. I am not talking about the kind of smell used to tell where your territory begins and someone else's ends, but about something even more instinctive: the scent of recognition, of rediscovering ancient links and affinities long forgotten.

And with this recognition comes sweetness—along with the knowledge that things will be simpler now. The hardest part is already over.

The greatest struggle is behind us, and what lies ahead is like the joy of opening your mouth to rain or of running effortlessly down a gentle grassy slope.

2

Usually, when something embarrasses us we react by coughing or smiling; becoming self-conscious; getting angry.

But when something embarrasses us deeply, for a fraction of a moment we go quite silent and still. Then we go on doing the same as we had been before, furiously trying to pretend that nothing has happened.

It's as though a strange man were to open the door into a room where everyone is enjoying a party. The people all sense that he doesn't belong there—without even knowing what they are sensing. And the thought of his strangeness disturbs them so much that they go on behaving exactly as they had been before. But now they are partying a little more intensely. They talk louder; they start drinking more quickly.

There is a man who, twenty-four hundred years ago, stepped into what we consider the sophisticated party of western culture just like this. And the resulting embarrassment, the unease, could hardly have run deeper. Here is a man who would make a unique, unparalleled contribution to the intellectual development of the western world. He was to play a major role in forming what were soon to become known as the distinct learned disciplines of philosophy, rhetoric, medicine, chemistry, biology, astronomy, cosmology, psychology, religion. But there is one slight problem.

He was a magician.

Or to be more precise, considering how we have come to think of magic as nothing but funny performances and cheap tricks, he was a sorcerer: a man with certain powers we would be hard put even to start making sense of. And just to make things worse, he said he was immortal. He explained that he had realized his divinity. He announced he was a god.

Since then, historians and philosophers have managed to keep very busy performing their familiar role; playing their usual part. They furiously occupy themselves with arguing about the tiniest details of what they imagine were his ideas on this or that, his theories, his intellectual concepts and contributions. As for all the rest: they try even more furiously to act as if it doesn't exist. Their embarrassment is so profound that it forces them to devise more and more sophisticated tricks for trying to make his magic vanish, for getting the sorcerer to disappear.

But, like a haunting nightmare, this man's magic will not go away.

His sorcery is here to stay. It will outlive all our rationalizations and intellectual complications by a long, long distance for the simple reason that in comparison with it all our powers of reasoning are unspeakably feeble. And, as we will see, it shows in the most down-to-earth way imaginable that there can be no real search for wisdom without the help of extraordinary powers—just as there can be no serious enquiry that doesn't end in the discovery of one's own divinity.

The man I am talking about came from a city called Acragas on the southern side of Sicily: an island that had close ties with the Phocaeans and with Velia in particular.

He was a little younger than Parmenides. Just like Parmenides, he was a poet; and, as with Parmenides' poetry, only parts of what he wrote still survive.

It has become a common complaint from those who try to study him that the surviving parts of his poetry are not enough to provide a clear idea about his teaching. But for them nothing will ever be enough. They are always speculating restlessly about what's absent—and miss the fact that their failure to come to any real understanding of the things he said is not because they lack the necessary material.

It's because they have no notion of how to approach the material they already have. For, in this perfect world of imperfection, nothing important is lacking. We are provided at any given moment with exactly what we need to know. And that man's teaching is just as alive now, as powerful, as accessible as it ever has been.

As well as being a sorcerer, and a poet, he was also a prophet and healer: one of those healer–prophets I have already talked about.

He was someone who had the ability to bring back the power of healing from another world. But his main concern was not just to free people from illnesses. It was to free them from themselves. He wanted to heal them from their illusions about time and life and death. And yet there was one precondition for receiving his help.

You had to be prepared to leave all your ideas about yourself behind.

If you are not prepared to do that now you should run as far away from anything to do with him as you can. There is one problem, though. If you want to run away from him you will also have to run away from the air and the trees and from your own nature. For all these things expect of you exactly what he expected. They ache for you to become conscious.

As I said: he is a sorcerer. And, from a sorcerer like him, there is nowhere to run. But if you want to learn from him then nothing could be easier, because every single thing you can perceive is waiting to help; is longing to wake you up.

Often this man is described nowadays, with a nervous smile and an anxious laugh, as a colorful personality. And yet he was most at home in a world where there is no color as we know it. He is considered quite an eccentric character. But the strange thing is that there is no one you could name in the whole history of the western world who happens to be saner: who is endowed with such genuine common sense.

Welcome to Empedocles.

3

Until a short while ago people thought they at least had the most basic outlines of Empedocles' teaching neatly marked out.

The general assumption was that he had written down the central part of his philosophy in an essentially scientific poem; rational, level-headed. His eccentricities and extravagances, the religious mystery and magic and hocus-pocus, might perhaps show their face in the poem here or there. But they had no real place in it: they belonged elsewhere.

There was any number of signs that such a distinction couldn't possibly be true—a whole stream of details indicating that the attempt to split Empedocles in two was wrong. And yet to follow those indications, and follow them not just casually but right through to their logical conclusion: that was something no one had the stomach to do.

Then, not so long ago, a few words from this poem of his were found on tiny fragments of papyrus that had been stored away unrecognized for years in a European library. Initially they were hailed by historians of philosophy as the find of the century. But soon, like in the case of a child with a brand new toy, the excitement started giving way to disappointment. The papyrus was so fragmented that it raised as many questions as it answered. The old ambiguities surrounding Empedocles were as overwhelmingly bewildering as ever.

Even so, those pieces of papyrus presented one major discovery. For they showed what ancient writers such as Aristotle had tended to leave out when quoting individual lines or passages from Empedocles to illustrate his views on specific topics like cosmology, biology, physics.

They revealed how his apparently factual comments on one subject or another had, to begin with, been interspersed among other lines of poetry; other comments. They showed how Empedocles himself had alternated the most careful descriptions and thorough explanations of this world we seem to live in with the cry of the soul aching, longing, for its home.

And the papyrus shreds showed more, even though they were only revealing what should have been quite obvious for thousands of years.

They demonstrated that Empedocles' entire account of the universe was bound up with the fate of the soul. All those themes and ideas in his supposedly rational poem that soon were to prove so important, that were to provide a platform for early physics and chemistry and science, were not there to offer factual information.

They were there to save the soul. The cosmology was being offered not for its own sake but to help us see exactly what, in this strange world of ours, is what: to indicate where we belong, where we don't, what things bind us and how, the ways we manage to trap ourselves and end up deceived. Everything—the composition of flesh and bone, the harmonies and imbalance of the body, the nature of the sun and moon and stars—was being explained to help us learn what we really are and be free.

Even now, the experts still don't see what these pieces of papyrus have to tell. Instead, they get caught in the fuss and the buzz of speculation: of trying to rearrange the new pieces in their jigsaw puzzle so as to arrive at some modified, updated version of Empedocles the philosopher writing his philosophy.

But what they have managed to avoid, and wisely so, is noticing the larger picture. For if they were to catch a glimpse of it they would realize Empedocles has nothing to do with any of our modern notions about philosophy.

And they also haven't noticed whom, or what, the evidence allies Empedocles with. It links him with the ancient Gnostics, who tend to be seen nowadays as little more than offshoots of Christianity even though—as many of them knew and admitted—their roots reached back much further into the past.

There were certain Gnostics who taught cosmology in the same basic way as Empedocles: for the sake of the soul. They saw themselves as messengers, lawgivers from another world, as divine healers with magical powers. And it's no coincidence that they described themselves, like Empedocles, as prophets.

And yet even this is not important. Everything to do with those fragments of papyrus, their immediate significance as well as their vaster implications, is ultimately just child's play. Even the fascination of seeing where Empedocles' real connections lay soon turns into yet another distraction, a further betrayal of what he stood for, one more way to avoid the simplicity and timelessness of his message.

There can be no doubting what that message is. But if we want to hear it, we have to approach it in the right way. And that, fortunately or unfortunately, means having to approach it on Empedocles' own terms—not ours.

We have to trust him, put ourselves completely in his hands. If we approach what he said thinking we are cleverer than he was, we will end up total fools. And this is much more than empty words: I will show you.

It also means we can no longer decide where to tread, what to take seriously or simply dismiss. We can no longer stick to the aspects of his teaching we feel comfortable with and rationalize the rest; keep to some safe ground.

There is no safe ground.

And it means, as with Parmenides, that we have to begin at the beginning. For we know, whether we want to or not, what Empedocles said towards the start of his supposedly philosophical and scientific poem. He opened it with a direct address to a disciple called Pausanias; and in this opening address he explained why the detailed account of his teaching that he was about to offer is not for everyone.

He underlined the fact that, on the contrary, this particular poem is esoteric. Most people will inevitably, automatically, get confused by it because they lack any of the necessary qualifications for understanding it. Its teaching is only for the rare individual who has the capacity to approach it rightly: who is ready to make the necessary effort, is desperate enough to be willing to be changed by it.

Others can waste their time as they choose—not yet aware that they are nothing but those rare individuals in disguise.

4

Palms—so narrow and closed in—have been
poured over people's limbs. But countless
worthless things keep crashing in, blunting their
cares. During their lifetimes they see such a
little part of life and then they are off:
short-lived, flying up and away like smoke,
totally persuaded by whatever each of them
happened to bump into while being driven
one way, another way, all over the place. And they
claim in vain that they have found the whole.
Like this, there is no way that people can see or
hear or consciously grasp the things I have to teach.
But as for you:
because you have come aside here, you will learn.
Mortal resourcefulness can manage no more.

And here you have them.

You can go from side to side and around and around for as long as you want. But sooner or later, against your will or not, you will have to come back to them: the preconditions for receiving any real knowledge that, even though they are only preconditions, already contain more wisdom than all the learning in the world.

Empedocles sums them up in a nutshell. To state them as directly as possible is simply his duty. But this is not to say that what was simple for him is going to be simple for us; and I have made no effort to soften the bizarre effect of these opening words that stood so close to the start of his great poem.

There is a surreal quality about the initial image in particular—and very deliberately so. For those palms, poured over our limbs, are not something we can see or recognize like the little hollows of our hands or the other parts of our body. They are what we use to see and recognize everything else.

If perhaps they seem somehow disturbingly familiar, that's because they are the basis of all our experience; of all our knowing, of everything we so confidently consider reality. But at the same time they are unfamiliar because they are too much a part of us. They are just far too close.

They are the unperceived perceivers: the mysterious powers embedded in our being that we spend our whole lives observing and experiencing everything else through while staying perfectly blind to.

In this enigmatic situation of ourselves being presented to ourselves, nothing could be more urgent than to realize that some words are much more than ordinary words. And nothing could be more vital than to understand that some encounters are infinitely more significant than random meetings. For there are some words that, instead of only expressing tiny aspects of our existence, manage to encapsulate the entire known universe; and there are some encounters that date back to well before we were even born.

If you think you can just bump into these words of Empedocles and understand them before bouncing on to your next experience, then the next, you are mistaken. You know nothing. You don't even know how to search for real knowledge—and as for finding it, you wouldn't even recognize it if you did.

Everything you do is a charade. Even your modesty is false and, when with apparent humility you declare how little you know, you are only trying to conceal the fact that really you are claiming the opposite. For your lives as you live them are like a torn bedsheet; a little mound of earth left behind by a mole; the corner of a children's playground where the bullies beat you up; the furthest end of a dead-end street.

And our lives are so very short.

Empedocles states the position quite clearly. "Like this," we will never see or hear or be able to understand what he has to teach. But of course every scholar and philosopher is deaf to his warnings, ignores these opening words with their simplicity, rushes blindly on ahead to get lost in what they each imagine is the main part of Empedocles' teaching. As soon as he starts describing the cosmos, the creation of humans and animals and plants, they set about discussing what he says to their heart's content. But as for this introductory passage: instinctively they avoid it, sensing how intensely undesirable its message is.

In all the thousands of pages pumped out by experts on the subject of Empedocles, there is hardly a passing word about it. Mostly they keep away from it like a poison; a plague; an abandoned desert. And when the occasional commentator does happen to bump into it, the result is utter chaos.

Somehow, by some strange magic, people have managed to persuade themselves that these absolutely necessary pre-conditions for any genuine understanding have nothing to do with them. They misunderstand what he says, mistranslate it, distort its meaning and discolor its sense—even try, just as there are those who expect us to believe that when Parmenides criticizes the human condition he is only criticizing Heraclitus, to imagine Empedocles in these lines is only criticizing Parmenides. And, as if that hasn't been enough, the extra step was taken early in the nineteenth century of simply altering the Greek text.

So, in most editions of Empedocles published during the last two hundred years, you will find his crucial final statement here has been thoughtfully altered. He is made to tell his disciple that "because you have come aside here, you will learn no more than mortal resourcefulness can accomplish."

But Empedocles has already described what mortal resourcefulness is, and can accomplish. It's chaos; achieves nothing. It's what happens when men of learning bump into his teaching and choose, without so much as seeing what they are doing, to alter it to suit their own small ideas and preconceptions.

Even his ability to portray the oppressive limits, the terrible narrowness, of human resourcefulness should be a clear sign that he has access to something more—something far vaster. And in fact he is that perfect paradox: a human pointing to what lies beyond the human which, even though it exists outside the little sphere of our human capabilities, is completely available to us if we want it.

5

I have not yet told you the whole story, though.

Empedocles' portrayal of the human condition is coherent enough as a general picture of our usual, lost existence. But it also has another side to it—a concealed underbelly studded with diamonds and precious stones, encrusted with the most skillfully crafted jewelwork you could imagine.

All the key words he uses are intimately linked with each other in a glittering network of hidden meanings. The trouble, now, is that with the passing of thousands of years the sense of words has slipped; changed. Structures of significance have melted away only to recrystallize in different shapes and forms. What used to yield its secret naturally to a perceptive intelligence has drifted off into unfathomable mystery, and absolutely needs some explaining.

The best thing will be to begin at the beginning—with that peculiar mention of "palms."

This word used to mean a great deal to ancient Greeks. For them, a palm was not just the hollow of a hand. It also meant the unshakable power that gets and keeps the upper hand even in the most difficult situations, the steadiness that calmly manages to master instead of being mastered. And at the same time it was the part of the body used by artists or craftsmen to manipulate, shape, perfect; was what allowed them to transform their raw material into a work of art by making the subtlest of adjustments from moment to moment. It was the instrument they needed for manifesting their *mêtis*.

But, even more importantly, the palm is what allowed tricksters to deceive and cheat—to hide things away by sleight-of-hand only to produce them when no one was looking or expecting. This is why, in the Greek language of Empedocles' time, "palm" happened to be the standard word for an ingenious device; a trick; a cunning scheme.

And it was a word inseparably associated with *mêtis* for the simple reason that whatever *mêtis* implied in terms of agility and skillfulness, trickery and cunning, it implied as well.

Then there is that dazzling image of palms being poured all over our limbs. It might seem little more than a bizarre joke; a brilliant game of imagery. But as we have seen with Parmenides, jokes sometimes tend to turn into rather serious matters. And in fact, by producing this comical picture of palms being poured over people's bodies, Empedocles is doing something very deliberate.

Ever so carefully he is evoking what once were notorious scenes in Homer's poetry: scenes describing how, in exceptional circumstances, divine qualities can be bestowed on human beings as gifts by being poured over their bodies. And these acts of bestowing, so gracious, are always performed at the hands of gods who happen to be supreme experts in *mêtis*.

If you choose to follow what Empedocles is hinting at through this skillful crafting and shaping of well-known imagery, you will see he is portraying us humans as graced by the gods with a potential at the core of our being; with a gift of *mêtis* that penetrates our bodies, makes us virtually divine. And in what he is saying there is a tremendous sense of promise, of hope.

But a promise is only a promise.

Those palms we have been graced with are constricted, closed in. The essential instruments we need for openness and perceptiveness, for mastery, that can even make us divine, are shut. Instead of being able to see or hear anything intelligently, we are bombarded and overwhelmed by our own perceptions: instead of mastering them, they master us. All our cares and best intentions are dulled, dimmed, deadened. And before we even know it, we are dead as well.

Everything that could go wrong has gone wrong. Our whole lives are a contradiction; an undoing of their own potential; an absurd, back-to-front joke. The very fact that the promise inside us is unfulfilled makes it act, paradoxically, like a curse. Instead of helping us, it works against us and destroys us.

And yet, with Empedocles, there is significance even in all this confusion.

For one single strand of meaning runs right through the middle of it, reaching back the whole way to his opening image of those palms as "narrow" or "closed in."

The word he uses here to describe their narrowness is a rare one. In the earliest Greek poetry it always conveys a quite particular, oppressive sense of danger: of a grave threat just out of sight, of trickery and deception. And there is nothing accidental about the way that very soon Empedocles will be describing how humans keep "bumping into" things as they are "driven" all over the place—because by far the most vivid as well as memorable example of this unusual Greek word for "narrow" comes in a famous passage, towards the end of the *Iliad*, where Homer emphatically repeats it right alongside the identical expressions used here by Empedocles for "bumping into" and being "driven."

The passage is a dramatic one. You may already be on the verge of remembering it. It begins with a hymn of praise to *mêtis*, then goes on to describe the notorious chariot race where the contest is decided not by speed but by *mêtis*: where the winning charioteer cunningly manages to ride on past his competitor along a narrow stretch of road by threatening to bump into him and force a fatal collision while driving his own horses and chariot at full speed ahead.

As you can see, Empedocles has brought us back onto familiar ground. For running through his account of the human condition is a constant stream of references not only to the particular theme and qualities of *mêtis* but also to the very same passage in Homer already referred to so subtly and mysteriously, so pointedly and humorously, by Parmenides.

According to Parmenides, the entire human condition can be defined as a lack of *mêtis*: as the total absence of *mêtis* absurdly pretending to be its opposite. For him, helped by a goddess, nothing could be easier than to ride on ahead of us mortals and outstrip us. But Empedocles, for his part, goes into rather more detail; is a little more explicit in his delicately, devastatingly implicit way.

According to him, in this contest of life we are not even the losing charioteers. In fact we are not even driving a chariot and horses. On the contrary, we are the horses and chariot that are being driven—all over the place. For we are not even the team of horses that loses. We are the horses that are totally lost.

And this lostness is the most our human *mêtis* can manage.

6

And, still, I have not quite told the whole story.

To translate the final, crucial statement in this opening passage as "Mortal resourcefulness can manage no more" is accurate enough—as translations go. Technically speaking it could be considered more than fair.

But it hides far more than it reveals.

Behind that translation "resourcefulness" lies one very specific word in the original Greek. It should be a rather old friend by now: the word is *mêtis*.

You might perhaps have wanted to think I was making up all those connections between palms and *mêtis*, pouring and *mêtis*, narrowness and bumping and being driven and *mêtis*. I was not. Each of those words and phrases was just a delicate hint awaiting its explicit confirmation, one small part of a puzzle waiting for its completion in this culminating line. For if Empedocles was a supreme expert at subtlety, at secretive understatement, he was also a master of being absolutely explicit at the right time.

As we will see, he leaves very little up in the air. He can be almost brutally frank and down-to-earth in stating what matters; in hitting the nail on the head. And yet he knows there is nothing to worry about. People will still find a thousand ways of avoiding the things he says.

But of course it's not only a matter of one word, *mêtis*, suddenly clarifying all the elusive references in the few lines that came before. This is the least of it. For here is the exact term that—with its impossibly subtle connotations not just of exceptional resourcefulness but also of intense awareness and alertness, of cunning and trickery and deception—runs through the whole of Parmenides' teaching like a golden thread. And you should be in a good position now to appreciate how significant it is that the very same word which proved so crucial for understanding Parmenides and his poem, which expresses the essence of everything he had to say far better than any other term, which Parmenides himself hints at and plays with in the most exquisitely roundabout of ways, occurs here right at the start of Empedocles' teaching: spelled out without any ambiguity, in black and white.

Empedocles is sounding the magic note of recognition. He is taking up the almost invisible thread that everyone else has forgotten even exists and, deep down, would dearly love to go on forgetting. Before moving on, he is picking up at the beginning of his own great poem the key to the poem of Parmenides.

He is continuing the line.

And so we can start to see exactly what he means when he sums up his grim account of the human condition with the statement that "mortal *mêtis* can manage no more." For he has already told us, through his brilliant manipulation of images and words, what mortal *mêtis* is.

It's a potential never realized; a pitiful joke; an inattentive alertness; a faculty of perception which is blocked up; a mastery that consists of helplessness, a refinement which is all clumsiness, a cunning that deceives itself.

Just like Parmenides, with his mocking references to our "much-experienced habit" and to us helplessly "steering" our "wandering minds," he is trying to explain to us mortals that mortal *mêtis* is the most perfect contradiction in terms. Exactly like Parmenides, he uses the vocabulary of *mêtis* with extraordinary *mêtis* to make the identical point already made by Parmenides in his own way—that the *mêtis* of humans is no real *mêtis* at all.

The most it can manage to accomplish is nothing.

And yet even this, as you may have sensed, is not the whole story.

Mêtis is never simple or direct, least of all when it seems simple and direct. Its language is cunning and ambiguity, hiddenness and complexity. So when Empedocles uses the word *mêtis* itself, so directly, so openly, you can be sure he is hinting at more than meets the eye. And in fact his statement that "mortal *mêtis* can manage no more" has another significance, a second meaning, a double sense.

It contains inside it a fundamental ambiguity: not the type of ambiguity you can resolve with a focused effort of your mind, but the lingering kind. The more you ponder it, the more it gets under your skin. The more you try to avoid its implications, the closer it dogs your steps and snaps at your heels.

In that phrase "can manage no more," the Greek for "manage" has the basic sense of being able to move; of stirring oneself to act. And Empedocles' string of references to the passage in Homer about the chariot race and *mêtis* leaves no doubt as to the underlying implication of his statement, here, that "mortal *mêtis* can manage no more." It means that everything human *mêtis* attempts to do results in chaos. Our power of movement, all our scope for action, is strictly confined to letting ourselves be pulled and pushed around in every direction—while fooling ourselves that we are responsible for what we do.

There is nothing that we ourselves can do.

And yet this is not completely true.

For there is one single action we can take. We are quite helpless, but the one possibility within our power is that we will realize how helpless we are and take the initiative of stepping aside to where we can be helped. The one and only movement we can truly, consciously, make is to take that step aside; is to realize we will never get anywhere by drifting along in the unconscious hubbub that everyone calls life; is to gather the little energy we have and draw aside to where we can start to learn.

The statement that "mortal *mêtis* can manage no more" contains not the slightest reference to any limitations on the part of Empedocles' teaching. It has no relevance to him. What he has to teach is way beyond anything mortal *mêtis* can even imagine, because its source is divine.

What this statement does refer to is, first, the utter incapacity of human *mêtis* to manage or achieve anything genuine by itself. And, secondly, it refers to the summit of all human achievement: the remote chance that we will grasp the appalling helplessness of our situation and take the crucial step of "coming aside," of finding the place where we can ask for help.

When we realize we simply can't go on alone, can get no further under our own steam, that is as far as human intelligence and power can reach.

Mortal resourcefulness can manage no more.

When every scholar who comes into contact with Empedocles' comment that "Mortal *mêtis* can manage no more" automatically makes it apply to Empedocles himself and the mortal limits of his own teaching, when they even alter the original Greek text to make him tell his reader that "You will learn no more than mortal *mêtis* can manage," there is no mystery as to why.

It's the crazed, unconscious attempt to keep us trapped in our mortality: to go on playing the desperate game of pretending that nothing exists or can exist outside the prison of our self-deception.

And yet the whole point of Empedocles' teaching is that outside our little world something else is waiting for the one, decisive moment when we not only realize the futility of whatever we attached value to in the past but also become so tired of its futility we can no longer go on living the way we had before.

That something else is the teacher.

Parmenides had already described how, if we want real knowledge, we have to leave that little world behind; have to find the path leading "far away from the beaten track of humans" and then follow it all the way. He had also made it as plain as he could that only one type of knowledge has any genuine substance or value—the kind originating directly from a divine source. And he even hinted, through the goddess' careful words about his special bond with the Daughters of the Sun, that during the course of his journey he himself had somehow crossed the boundary between the human and the divine.

But Empedocles leaves no room for hints any more. When we come to him, the teacher is no longer a goddess in some distant or mysterious realm. He is the teacher. And you don't have to travel to the furthest edges of the universe to find his teaching. On the contrary, you can only find it right here.

To encounter the teacher, all you have to do is come aside "here." From the point of view of the disciple, that place can seem to be anywhere. But for the teacher it's always here, in the space of utter silence and stillness where one already is. And through this you can see what a major change in emphasis takes place as the tradition passes from Parmenides to Empedocles.

Parmenides' poem begins with a journey that appears to take us as far away from here as possible: to the limits of existence, to the mythical roots of all there is. Only with time does it start to become clear that his "there" is really "here." But with Empedocles the teaching starts here. He takes full responsibility for it from the very beginning. There is no more talk of paths that turn out not to be paths—none of those engaging riddles about journeys all leading nowhere. He has incarnated the teaching in himself.

And he assumes complete authority for it as the more-than-human teacher.

This is how the line progresses. Parmenides warms. Empedocles burns. With him, there is no more room for any manoeuvre.

He dares to take the step of saying that to find the truth is not a matter of entering another level of reality, of travelling beyond time and space, of tuning into another dimension. What matters most is to come face to face with a human being who has realized that truth and embodies its power; who has discovered the immortal at the heart of the mortal, the divine in the middle of the human.

Instead of being told by a goddess that human existence as we live it is totally futile, now we are being told this by someone who seems quite human like us. And yet Empedocles can say that because he knows human existence is not an end in itself.

If we were only human beings there would be no problem, no confusion or despair. We wouldn't be at war with ourselves, living a gentle nightmare at the mercy of our own power. But we are not. When we grow up and build a home for ourselves, a family, a career, follow all our dreams, this is not life. This is nothing to do with what life is really about. It's not even the beginning of life. And to say that everything we call experience is no more than a chaotic dream is not to be negative. On the contrary: it's just the attempt to save a little time, to save a lot of suffering, to help hurry things along.

For we are the seeds of so much. Human existence is nothing but the divine life unlived.

And to start to live it, you have to come aside while you still can. You have to find the sacred spot where teacher meets disciple and the real learning begins—a learning that has nothing otherworldly about it. In actual fact it's not so much a process of learning as a stripping away of all the teaching you have ever had until you are left quite naked, facing something far greater than yourself.

From then on, life without the teacher is impossible any more; unbearable; inconceivable. And there are no approximations to this unending relationship, no near hits or near misses. Either you come aside or you don't. There is no half-in, half-out, no voyeurism, and absolutely no bargaining. You either accept the terms you are offered or had better leave. For, as we will soon see, tricks and devices exist to make sure that those who insist on laying down their own conditions will end up staying far away.

So there is a warning, and there is a promise.

The warning is that, until you experience your total powerlessness, you will never discover your real power. Instead, you will just mess everything up; turn any help you are offered into yet another form of helplessness; misinterpret, even with the finest intelligence, whatever you hear; will change it, get everything back to front. For this is how the tradition works.

The promise is of discovering something new, not simply about the world around us but about what we are. And as Empedocles' opening passage makes clear, what we learn will no longer be partial or fragmented or clumsy.

It will introduce us to a vastness we have never fully experienced before, will give us a sense through our little lives of what lies behind them, will bring us face to face with a mysterious quality inside us of intense presence and awareness we never knew was possible—let alone that we have always possessed.

Above all, though, it will show us how we have been tricked and how we keep on ceaselessly deceiving ourselves.

SEVEN

The helplessness is tremendous.
And this affair will only be brought to
completion through immense struggle.
There will be fighting and violence and war.

OLYMPIODORUS THE ALCHEMIST

Empedocles' explanation of the cosmos is so terrifying in its symmetry and simplicity that it could hardly be allowed to survive intact in our complicated modern world. But I will do my best to keep it simple.

The universe works like this.

There is an endless cosmic cycle of uniting and separating, coming together and moving apart. The uniting is the work of Love. The separation is done through Strife: the power of hate and fighting and hostility. And there are four fundamental "roots" of all existence—earth, water, fire and air. They blend and merge with each other through the power of Love. Then they divide again under the influence of Strife until earth is left alone and heavy at the center, embraced by water and then by an envelope of fire, with purest air surrounding everything on the outside.

Nothing else exists.

And this process of uniting and moving apart is all that ever has happened or will happen. Absolutely anything and everything is a part of this endless cycle. Each little fizz or bang or cataclysm is just another blip along the way.

But there is room here for a little warning.

Because the same identical process keeps repeating itself at every conceivable level, down through the life-cycle of the stars to the tiniest insect as it breathes in and out, you can never be too sure that the grand events all around you are actually what you think they are. For it might well be that what looks to all intents and purposes like a drama of cosmic proportions—is studied most accurately, measured scientifically—is in fact no more than the collective sighing of humanity.

As for earth being in the middle, you might think this is a plain sign of Empedocles being ever so primitive and naive. But there is far more to the matter than that.

In reality there is nowhere else it could be, because this is where we are: at the center of everything we see. Even if we leave it to travel somewhere else, our eyes will still be made out of earth. Whatever we discover, or believe we discover, however wonderful the life forms we might happen to bump into, they will all only be the creation of our terrestrial perception. We are the most naive of devils if we imagine we will ever find reality by drifting around in outer space.

And then we come to the most important point.

In the whole of existence there is nothing, absolutely nothing, that is not divine.

Love is divine. Strife is divine. Each one of the four elements, or roots, is divine. So whatever you see or hear is divine. And whatever you see or hear with is divine.

This means that when you manage to separate your awareness into one pure element—not by thinking about it, simply by doing it—you are pure divinity. When you identify with several elements in combination, or perceive more than one at the same time, you are a complicated divinity. You are likely to be a confused divinity, apparently quite mortal.

But still you are divine.

You might seem to change. But one day, if you are still enough, you will discover that in essence nothing whatsoever changes.

And yet, for the moment, let's pretend I never said that.

Empedocles knows his way around eternity like a wild cat around its lair. He defines his ground with the clarity of someone whose eyes see straight into another world—and with the faultless consistency that only a true sorcerer has the power to value or understand.

The process of coming together and drifting apart, of breathing in and out, of being born and dying and being born and dying again, goes on and on. Like anything else that never really happens, it has no end. But even so, every single time that Empedocles refers to this cycle he describes it in just the same way: presents it in precisely the same sequence.

First there is the joining through Love. Next, secondly, subsequently, comes the destruction and dissolution by Strife.

Time after time, when referring to the whole of existence or to the elements that make it up, he talks about the movement towards union as coming first and only then being followed by the opposite process of scattering.

I will tell a double tale.
First it grew to become one alone out of many
and then it grew apart to become many out of one.

Or

They keep changing and changing without break
or end, never stopping: now all coming together

through Love to be one, then each of them being carried
away again and left separate by Strife's hate.

And ever so occasionally he starts not with the process of Love bringing everything together but, instead, with the state where everything already happens to be separated out—which amounts to just the same thing.

In the time of Ill Will they are all distinct,
apart. But then they come together in Love and
yearn for each other.

Perhaps, though, you will wonder why I make such a fuss about a straightforward matter of ordering and sequence. For, to be sure, this is Empedocles himself speaking and saying things just as he wants.

But if you look instead at the massive modern literature dedicated to his philosophy you will find a very different story.

You will be told how his account of cosmic history begins with the state of pure Love and ends, after Strife's unfortunate interlude, with a joyful return to the state of Love. This is so much more understandable and understanding. It expresses our values so much more faithfully; reflects so much better all the things we love and hate.

Here or there, it's true, a rare scholar has noticed Empedocles' own clearly stated sequence—and even realized that it reflects with perfect precision the detailed ordering of cosmic events as presented in his poem. But to notice the point in passing and to stay true to it, not forget it: these are two separate things. And soon even those rare scholars lose their grip on what they have noticed, let it go, sagging under the sheer weight of all our collective assumptions and preconceptions about what Empedocles should have said.

Then there are the learned experts who state, quite baldly, that to view Empedocles' cycle as beginning with the state of Love and also ending with the state of Love is only "logical." But whatever logical reasons they try to give, their real logic is this: we love love and hate hate. An original state of pure love sounds so much more reassuring than a primal condition of hatred and separation.

And, above all, nothing could be more disturbing than to allow Strife the final word. That would be too bleak a prospect to bear.

In other words to be logical, as people like to use the word, means asserting what we want to be the case. It means explaining Empedocles' philosophy while disregarding what he said; substituting the familiar for the unfamiliar, safety for the lurking shadow of infinite danger.

And so you can start to see how much of our written history is a memorial to wishful thinking.

In a sense this hardly matters. It's only human to believe what we want. But in another sense nothing could matter more. For there is nothing that can silence or calm the howl of infinite pain, deep inside each one of us, which is our own very human response to all the atrocities committed by century after century of reasonableness and so-called logic: of forced and artificial neatness, of violating the wild spaces in our hearts.

So, as I said to begin with, the situation is quite simple. There is the Empedocles you can read about. And then there is Empedocles.

And for Empedocles himself the cosmic drama, in all its endless repetitions, ends every cycle not with Love but exactly where it began—with the stage of total Strife.

3

It all begins with the four different elements utterly pure, divine, immortal, quite separate and apart. This is also just how they will be again, when everything has been said and done, at the very end of the cycle.

Pure air, or *aithêr* as Empedocles called it, was up in the heavens where it belongs—with the other three elements ranged well below it.

And then the purity was over.

There is a timeless oath, sworn and agreed by the gods, that has to be obeyed: whenever one power reaches its fullest expression it has to give way and withdraw. So Strife started retreating meekly to the furthest edges of all there is while Love expanded, slowly spinning outwards from her position at the center. The age of hating was finished.

A new cosmos is about to begin as Love seductively, charmingly, so gently and persuasively overcomes every trace of resistance.

> *On came the soothing, deathless assault of faultless*
> *Love. And what before had learned to be immortal*
> *all of a sudden became mortal. What before had been*
> *unmixed changed its paths: was shaken and stirred.*
> *And as things blended with each other ten thousand*
> *swarms and tribes of mortals streamed into being,*
> *fitted together in all sorts of shapes and forms—*
> *an astonishing sight to see.*

The creation, if you can call it a creation, is like a half-forgotten fantasy. Or rather, it's like some dimly remembered nightmare: the shadow of this world we know. Earth flies up and mixes crazily with water and fire. The air is pulled down in spirals out of the heavens, dragged into the depths. The four elements become lost to themselves as they find themselves in the completely unfamiliar situation of having to abandon their own familiar realm, of being

made to wander away from their own kind
and be born as mortals.

They mix and interact at random, creating strange forms of life that come into being only to disappear: phantoms belonging to a world of dreams.

There were so many of them—double-faced,
double-chested. There were ox-creatures with faces
of humans; and others that sprang up were just
the reverse, human creatures with ox-heads.

And in this swirl of immortal things becoming mortal, of what once was pure being mixed, any original sense of identity or trace of freedom is gradually left behind. Everything enters a great womb, everything becomes the womb, is forgotten in the womb of itself. And Love has her final victory, her total domination over all there is.

Whatever exists has been subdued, denied the expression of its own nature, stripped of all its dignity and power for the sake of an oppressive union; "has been brought under," to use one of Empedocles' expressions, as if into some gigantic underworld or cave; "is firmly fixed, hidden in dense obscurity."

And this, to use another of his words, is perfect "harmony."

But it would be good not to have too many illusions about what harmony is. For us, now, the word means pure sweetness and balance: refinement and delight. But in Empedocles' time it also referred to the very concrete state of being bound together and joined fast. Love is the joiner who will fit you together, when you have quite forgotten yourself, with all her other pieces in her dark cave of dimly remembered terrors.

And as for the consistency of this universal mixture that Love produces at the peak of her power, it will be good to keep the record straight because there is such an irresistible desire to idealize her; to romanticize her work and think how idyllic her reign must be; to imagine that her joy in subduing the elements must have been the elements' joy in being subdued.

The consistency of the four elements in this perfect mixture is more or less identical to the consistency of flesh. But there is one substance that it resembles even more closely—blood.

The goddess of love has produced a cosmic blood bath.

4

Then comes the time of return. The immortals are about to start their journey home.

Suddenly there is a changing of the ways. The cosmos shakes; every direction is reversed. The centrifuge begins.

Faultless Love yields to faultless Strife with the same un-yielding certainty that makes us keep on breathing in and out even while asleep. And, at last, there is the promise that a little light will gradually emerge for the first time in ages.

Just as the four roots had all been forced to come together and tangle, they start separating away from each other instead. But there is a mysterious, paradoxical difference now. For this movement is not a result any more of things being persuaded; pressured; coerced.

It's because they want to move like that.

Fire starts separating away from the chaotic, murky mess. It shoots out and up where it can, expansively, instinctively— free at last, "wanting to reach its like." And in its upward volcanic rush it brings to what could be called the original surface of our earth some "whole-natured" creatures, as Empedocles describes them: complete, undifferentiated, no distinction in them yet between female and male.

Like souvenirs of Love's perfect harmony, they are the integrated nature that lies at the source of what we refer to as humanity. And for many Greeks they automatically will have evoked through their wholeness, their undivided simplicity, a kind of golden age; a primordial state of innocence.

But Empedocles makes it quite clear that this is no idyllic golden age. These whole-natured beings are the "young night-time shoots of men and women who will shed and be the cause of many tears." They belong to night because there is no sky yet as we know it, no heavens: no sun. And they are the origin of many tears because they contain the germs of seemingly endless suffering.

There is another touching detail, too, that he adds to his picture of these primordial creatures; such a fine detail but so telling.

Not yet
did they display the beloved shape of lovely limbs.

This simple statement about the absence of beauty, along with any of the love it arouses, could hardly be more significant or pregnant in meaning. For we happen to know that Empedocles gave a second name to the goddess he refers to as Love.

That other name is Aphrodite: the queen of love and charm and sex, of desire and infinitely tempting beauty.

And so you may be able to see what an extraordinary story he is unravelling—story inside of story, paradox inside of mystery.

Those undifferentiated, integrated, whole-natured beings are among the most perfect of mortal creations produced by Aphrodite while her power is still fairly strong. But for them there is no dance of sex: there is no need. It's only when her influence has already weakened, after the dividing of her unitedness by Strife has got well under way, that the dance begins.

For Greeks, sexuality was the uncontested domain and undisputed realm of Aphrodite. For Empedocles it simply is her last stand. The sheer gripping intensity of sex—the passionate attraction, the desperate lunging for physical union before being torn apart from one's partner and left separate again—is nothing but Love's quick taste, her briefest re-enactment, of what she once was able to accomplish when she seduced immortals into becoming mortal.

It's the best that she has left.

And now we are those separated women and men of many tears, making do as well as mortals can hope to do in a world steadily being torn apart by Strife. For this is where we are in the cosmic cycle: no longer simply divine and no longer whole, heading towards total separation.

To us, as mortals, the situation could hardly be more dreadful. The world goes on speeding up as we keep on changing bodies, being reborn, going from life to death and then from life to death and life again, carrying the traces of all our suffering and wanting inside us. To mortals, Strife's rule is just as terrible as Love's rule was to immortals.

The prospect for us humans is appalling and will only go on getting bleaker, with more and more disintegration ahead until no memory of life as we know it is left.

And, eventually, there will be nothing but the return to pure immortality. The *aithêr* will be back in heaven, free again. The other roots will be just where they belong. And if we can only learn how to stay conscious, we will be confronted with the strangest prospect of all—the death of our mortality.

5

There is the story of the cosmos. And there is the other story woven into and around it by Empedocles, the story of the soul.

The two tales are so obviously linked for him, so unmistakably interrelated, that it's clear they are only aspects of one single tale. But as to how exactly they are linked—that is the question.

There is one particular word he happens to use in referring to the soul: a term he was also free to apply with equal logic to any one of the four primordial roots behind the whole of existence.

This is *daimôn*. For, in the ancient Greek language of his time, the word still meant "divine being." That was well before it started being turned with the help of early Christians into our familiar term for a demon.

Empedocles presents himself quite openly as a *daimôn*, as someone who knows he is divine. And he does so with such authority and dignity that it can seem very tempting to suppose he may be thought of himself as belonging to an exclusive group; to some closed circle of immortals. This would seem to leave plenty of room for doubt that according to him we apparently ordinary humans might perhaps, by contrast, just be what we seem to be and no more.

But there is no room for doubt. There is no perhaps or maybe. For Empedocles makes it quite clear, to anyone willing to see, that we are all *daimôn*s who keep passing from life to death and then from life to death and life again; who have ancient ties with each other from times we no longer even remember. This is the only reason why he cries out, with a voice so raw in its immediacy, for people to stop killing and eating animals.

> *Won't you stop the*
> *terrible sound of your slaughter? Don't you*
> *see how you are devouring each other*
> *in your careless mindlessness?*

And this is why he describes, with such fine ambiguity, how a man can "raise" an animal over the altar without even realizing that in raising the creature from its birth he was raising a being who once had been his own son:

> *Father raises dear son—shape changed—*
> *and slays him with a pious prayer,*
> *the big fool.*

Every single human is an unconscious immortal. But this is the least of it. So are animals and even plants. Everything has its role to play, lifetime after lifetime, in the great reincarnation process. We are all involved in this, whether we want to be or not. There are no special clubs.

And yet the one, crucial point for Empedocles is that we have gone blind: have forgotten what we are. We don't see the divine inside ourselves, except in occasional glimpses that terrify us through their haunting intensity, any more than we see it all around us.

Immortal life is everywhere, sacred, inextricably entangled—and aching in the depths of its being to return home, to be back again where it comes from. For there should be nothing too surprising about the fact that Empedocles' story of the soul takes the form of a perfect cycle.

There used to be a time when the soul was free. And there is a time when it will be free again.

6

It all begins with the soul utterly pure, divine, immortal, sharing the company of other pure souls but otherwise quite separate and apart. This is also just how it will be again, when everything has been said and done, at the very end of the cycle.

The pure soul was up in the heavens, where it belongs. For the original home of the *daimôn* is not here on earth: quite to the contrary. The heavens are where it comes from and, Empedocles explains in no uncertain terms, are where it will eventually return when individual human beings become so purified during their final incarnations on the earth that they "spring up from there as gods"—as immortals again with their own full power and dignity restored to them at last.

And then the purity was over.

There is a timeless oath, sworn and agreed by the gods, that has to be obeyed.

> *Whenever it happens that any*
> daimôn—*one of those beings who has life*
> *for a long, long time—through some failing*
> *pollutes its own dear limbs with blood,*

this is when it has to leave its home behind. Empedocles describes the offence, the fault, the failing with such enigmatic simplicity that even in antiquity people were clumsily trying to fill out and elaborate on what he said. All we are really told, though, is that the *daimôn* has to suffer after it pollutes its limbs with blood.

But you shouldn't let this mention of the *daimôn* with its limbs mislead you into thinking it has some human form. To be sure, it has a physical existence: everything does, whether we can see it or not. And yet Empedocles can talk quite freely about the "limbs" of the sun or even describe disembodied divine awareness at its purest as having "limbs." As we will see, the *daimôn* has no human form—not yet.

Once the pollution with blood has happened, this is when the nightmare begins. The soul is

> *made to wander away from the blessed ones*
> *and take on all sorts of shapes and forms of*
> *mortal existence through the course of time,*
> *exchanging one hard path of life for another.*

What had been pure and immortal becomes mortal; is pulled down out of the heavens and dragged into the depths, utterly lost to its own kind. It cries out with longing for its own familiar realm and cries out even more when it sees the "unfamiliar place," to use the expression used by Empedocles, that it has been drawn into. It finds itself surrounded by phantoms: plunged into a world of dreams. Any original sense of identity is gradually left behind as the soul is deprived of all its dignity, stripped of its joy.

And it becomes aware that it has been brought inside a vast "covered-over cave." It has entered a grim, oppressive underworld where strange shapes and the terrifying events that take place can only be seen very dimly "through the darkness." And in the obscurity of this covered-over cave the soul is about as far away from its home, its own freedom, its original simplicity, as it possibly could be.

But that's not the end of its suffering; not by a long way. For one particular event is about to take place here in this dark cave of terrors.

The *daimôn* is about to be wrapped up and inserted into a whole sequence of bodies made from flesh and blood, to be coated with earth and dressed up in robe after robe of flesh that will fit it to perfection but—and this is the paradox—always remain alien to what it really is.

7

Then comes the time of return. The immortal soul is about to start its journey home.

The first we plainly see of it in its new, incarnated form is on what at that time was the surface of the earth. But, just as plainly, things were very different from how they are now.

It was an age of what could be called almost perfect harmony. There is no conflict—yet. There is only one dominant power that humans either want to, or are able to, acknowledge: one queen. She has their exclusive, undivided devotion.

> For them no Ares was god, no
> Battle-Panic, no King Zeus, no Kronos, no
> Poseidon; but Aphrodite was their queen ...

So they honor her with scents, with incense, by pouring honey on the earth. And through their peaceful simplicity they naturally seem to evoke a kind of golden age; a primordial state of innocence.

But, even so, Empedocles manages to make it clear that this is not some purely idyllic golden age. Apparent innocence is tempered with a sharp awareness of what is wrong; what has to be avoided. To kill animals and eat their flesh is not just an abomination but "the greatest abomination of all." The gentlest signs of tension are already present, of a potential conflict lurking in the wings that eventually will give rise to so much suffering.

One little point deserves mentioning here, as well. There are scholars who have become so infatuated with Empedocles' description of life under Aphrodite's pleasant rule that they simply equate the state of these freshly incarnated human beings with the state of the *daimôn*s at home in heaven. Visions of happiness can sometimes have this effect on people. And then, when they notice the differences between his accounts of those two states, they turn around and accuse him of inconsistency: of being confused.

But the confusion is only theirs.

For Empedocles the entire fate of the soul revolves around one single theme—the theme of incarnation, of immortals becoming mortal, of the divine being incarnated and made human. Incarnation as human beings is, very specifically, a punishment for the *daimôn*'s failing. And the peaceful inhabitants of Aphrodite's age are, just as specifically, incarnated human beings.

In other words we are not being faced with two alternative ways of describing one and the same primordial state. On the contrary, we are being presented with two separate stages in the cycle of the soul.

That means something rather striking, and quite precise.

It means that when the soul violates the strict ban on destroying life and eating flesh in Aphrodite's charming realm—which it certainly will—this will not be its first fall from grace.

It will be the second. And in fact the whole destiny of the soul, as Empedocles so skillfully portrayed it, is a history of two falls: the fall of *daimôn*s from heaven followed at the opposite point in the cycle, with delicate symmetry, by the fall of incarnate human beings.

This scheme of a double fall might, to us, seem strange. But really it should not. For it has its almost exact parallel in the theme of two falls, structurally symmetrical and closely interrelated, that was to become so significant in Christian tradition—the fall of angels not only followed, but also mirrored, by the fall of humans. And yet between Empedocles and the Christians there is one crucial difference.

In his case the humans are also the angels.

And with the second fall there is no going back. Of course there will be the moments of anguish and regret. Nothing could be more human. But once Aphrodite's realm of innocence has been disrupted, that is that. Violence only leads to more violence; bloodshed to bloodshed; hate and anger to more and more strife.

Now we are those women and men who have fallen a second time, making do as well as mortals can hope to do in a world steadily being torn apart by strife. For this is where we all are in the great cycle of the soul that Empedocles is describing: no longer divine and no longer innocent, heading towards greater and greater destruction.

And the worst part of it all is that we are not just punishing ourselves, or each other. Because there is nothing that is not related to everything else, even the world punishes us. The great bodies of the elements, to the extent that they have already become separated from each other, themselves reject the soul because of its impurity:

> *The might of* aithêr *chases it into the sea,*
> *sea spits it out onto solid ground, earth spits it*
> *up into rays of the radiant sun and the sun hurls it*

into the whirlpools of aithêr. *One receives it from another, then another from another, and they all hate it.*

They throw it here, there, forwards and backwards, as if in some gigantic winnowing machine. And so we are left incapable of staying put, restless, searching for a home we are somehow never allowed to find.

The prospect for us humans is appalling and only seems set to go on getting bleaker. But this is precisely where Empedocles steps in, to point out the hope in the middle of the hopelessness; to indicate the next stage.

For he comes as a messenger to remind us of our real origin and call us to become free again, to show how to make the journey not to some happy human state but to something far vaster. He is confronting us, if we can only learn to understand it, with the strangest prospect of all—the death of our mortality.

8

This is where the stories and the storytelling end. For I have gone into enough detail already about these two tales that have done so much between them to shape and inspire, entertain and offend, the western mind.

We have to remember with Empedocles, and keep remembering, what can be so extremely easy to forget. He was not just a storyteller. He was a magician. And a magician's tales have the power to wake us up or send us straight to sleep, to take us to a place inside ourselves that we never knew existed or—if we are not careful—lead us right up the garden path.

When a culture dares to take its stand on a magician's tales, allows itself to be influenced even slightly by a magician's words, you can be sure that its foundations will never be as stable as they might seem. For at the basis of all its seriousness, of its immense investment in solemn continuity and learning, there may be nothing more substantial than a sorcerer's joke.

As for Empedocles, you will have gathered by now that he loves presenting riddles. In fact his whole teaching has always been just as much of a riddle as the rather fragmented riddle it was soon to become. From the very beginning it has been no less of an enigma than Parmenides': a teaching that might appear straightforward but is littered with traps, that could seem infinitely complicated but is only reflecting back to us the complications in our own minds.

And with Empedocles' two stories we come to the biggest riddle of all—to what historians quite freely acknowledge is the central question posed by his teaching as a whole, the crucial question, the one that promises to clear the way for finding answers to every other major question about what he once taught.

This is the question of how, if at all, his story about the soul and his story about the cosmos fit together.

The answer itself, if you look for it with absolute sincerity, can be found in half a minute; half a second.

Or to be more accurate, if you look for it with sincerity it will come and find you. And, once it has, it will do exactly what Parmenides aimed to do: from then on, everything in your life will be turned upside down.

But century after century, generation after generation, experts have kept going around in circles looking for some answer to this one essential question as to how or whether the two stories fit together—bumping into the evidence and trying to make sense of it, confusing every issue they conceivably can. This is nothing to be surprised at. The truth is that they don't really want the answer at all. For you don't need any razor-sharp vision to see how the two stories fit together.

What you do need is the ability to surprise yourself. Or rather, you need to be able to trust the evidence more than your own assumptions.

And the same fundamental assumption is always made. It seems such a natural one to make, so unobjectionable, so reasonable: that Strife must be the cause of the soul's incarnation and dear Love its only hope and salvation. Love is quite obviously the source of all good and bloody, violent Strife the cause of evil.

Never, in the whole scholarly literature, will you find a word said against Love. Never would anyone dare to express a single doubt about her. And there is something quite amazing about the way that even the most hard-nosed of philosophers, the most professional of logicians, will go weak at the knees at Empedocles' merest mention of Aphrodite.

If you can stop for a moment, though, and put aside all your innocent assumptions, you will begin to catch a glimpse of a totally different picture. If you allow the outlines of Empedocles' cycles—beginning where they begin, ending where they really end—to tell their own story, you will see that the power responsible for drawing the soul out of heaven is not Strife but Love.

And the one power, the power of absolute terror and fear, that can finally get us home is not Love but Strife.

Nothing could sound more horrifying. And the most difficult thing of all is to know what to be more horrified by: whether by the picture of the soul's destiny that Empedocles is presenting or by the total failure of ancient and modern readers to see through to what he is saying. For it's not just that the basics of his philosophy have been got wrong. It's that everything about them has been got completely back to front.

That question as to whether or how the two stories fit together is not the real question, and never has been. They do fit together with an appalling simplicity because Aphrodite is the power that traps the soul and Strife is the one that sets it free.

The real question, the question behind the question, has always been how many thousands of years it would take for that simple answer to be found and explained—before it's covered over and forgotten all over again.

EIGHT

It's Aphrodite who deceived me

Gnostic Text from Nag Hammadi

Already my heart had turned:
I wanted to return, back home again.
And I grieved over the deception handed me by
Aphrodite when she led me away
from my own dear home.

Homer's Odyssey

1

Aphrodite was well known to the Greeks for her unique ways of getting things done; her ways of Love.

She forces whatever she likes, whatever she wants, to act against its own will and better judgement—but without appearing to exert the slightest force. She displaces, tears away, drags together with perfect grace and subtlety. This is the nature of her charm.

Empedocles describes with fine precision how when her time comes round for taking control of the cosmos once more, for making what had learned to be immortal become mortal all over again, on she comes as a "soothing" assault of love: like a soothing drug, gentle in the way that only Aphrodite knows how to be. But we know a great deal from the ancient Greek poets about this gentleness of hers. It's all sweetness and seduction, cunning and persuasiveness, the purest deception.

And this is where everything that anyone understands or has understood about Empedocles becomes the purest misunderstanding.

If you managed to follow Parmenides through his goddess' tricks and deceptions you will have no problem, now, in approaching Empedocles' Aphrodite. Otherwise you don't stand a chance. For what he is presenting with his magic poetry, and above all through the esoteric teaching he dedicates to his disciple Pausanias, is not some interesting story or philosophical treatise but something perilously real.

Aphrodite is one of the key players in his teaching, in the sense that in her hand she holds the first key to unlocking its mystery. And yet Aphrodite is Aphrodite: you need to keep your wits about you if you are not going to end up one more of her helpless victims, her sweetened fools.

Already in Homer you will find the plainest of references to the basic theme that other poets before, during, after Empedocles' lifetime would keep coming back to again and again. This is the trickery Aphrodite resorts to so as to get her way.

Even the greatest of the gods, members of her own family, have to approach her with special respect because of the unique gift she has to offer:

> the love and the desire you use to
> overpower immortals and human mortals alike.

And the Greek word used here by Homer for her supreme weapon—which is "love," *philotês*—just so happens to be the very same word given as a name by Empedocles to that other great cosmic power he places alongside of Strife.

Or, at least, Love is the name he gives that power provided he is not simply calling it Aphrodite. And it can be helpful to remember that whenever ancient Greek poets mentioned *philotês*, or love, in the context of Aphrodite they tended to be well aware they were evoking the most exquisite form of deception.

Aphrodite is the goddess of attraction who stands innocently by and tricks you completely. She is the one you can never be too sure of. Her gentleness is her unstoppability. And her power of love and deception, as the Greeks were quick to realize, is nothing short of magic.

There is one delightful scene in Homer that shows her enumerating with careful precision exactly what her magic charms consist of:

> love, desire, sweet talk,
> deceitful words that steal away the intelligence
> even of those who are most cautious and wise.

But there is an important difference between Homer and Empedocles.

Through his poetry Homer talks about, describes, humorously portrays this ability of Aphrodite to fool those who think themselves cautious or intelligent and snatch away their wits. But Empedocles, like Parmenides, doesn't just talk about things.

Through his poetry he demonstrates them.

And the people fooled by her are not some mythical figures in a story. They are us.

2

How on earth Aphrodite managed to pull the wool so complete-ly over people's eyes and persuade everyone reading Empedocles that she must be the liberator, sweet savior, of the soul—this is a downright miracle.

No one could possibly accuse Empedocles himself of being vague or indirect. On the contrary: he is the perfect incarnation of clarity when he describes how, through Love, what had been immortal "all of a sudden became mortal."

As he constantly makes plain, Aphrodite is the force that incarnates. She is the one who designs and creates our short-lived bodies. With an astonishing degree of attention to detail she "binds" them, and us. She "fixes"; "solidifies"; "glues"; makes everything "stick fast"; "fastens together" mortal exist-ence with her bolts and nails, her "bolts of love."

She is earthy and earthly, the power of physical fulfilment and fertility, of pleasures and delights. And never in the slight-est way does he contradict her absolutely conventional role, so well established by the literary and religious traditions of his time, as the goddess of sex and sexuality. He only emphasizes it and, just like Parmenides, extends and elaborates it even further.

She is the being who, as Empedocles makes clear through-out the poem he addresses to Pausanias, brings everything in the universe together whether it wants to or not. She is the goddess who uses whatever force is needed to play her role as creator of our world; as absolute dominator of mortal existence.

She is the cosmic matchmaker.

And he refers to her with the most delightfully earthy humor. But we have such lofty ideas in our heads about the nobility of philosophers, about the severe solemnity of their teachings, that somehow nobody manages to notice.

There is an important point towards the beginning of this poem for Pausanias where he briefly lists the four elements, passes quickly over Strife, and then devotes a lengthy passage to Love. Even the most seasoned scholars become so excited and misty-eyed at this obvious expression of enthusiasm, on Empedocles' part, for his favorite divinity that they fail entirely to read what he says.

They also forget that someone like Empedocles will never say anything at all except for a very particular purpose. So, when he urges his disciple to listen attentively to what he has to say about Love, this is just what we should do.

> *Watch her with your consciousness! Don't just*
> *sit there in a daze staring blankly with your eyes!*
> *Even mortals acknowledge her as implanted in their*
> *members, as she through whom they think thoughts of*
> *love and perform their acts of joining. They call her*
> *Delight and Aphrodite. But actually to perceive her*
> *spinning around in the mid-parts: this is something no*
> *mortal has ever done. As for you, though, listen to the*
> *undeceptive arrangement of my words.*

You can read this passage without really reading it and go away—as everyone does—quite satisfied that Empedocles is praising the spiritual goodness and beneficence of his preferred divinity, her mysterious power and omnipresence, to the highest heavens. But if you stop to pay it a moment's attention, you will see it offers a little more than first meets the eye. In fact there is no need for a nudge, or a wink, to convey a sense of precisely what human thoughts and actions Empedocles has in mind. This divinity known to mortals as Delight, as Aphrodite, is the goddess of sex.

Take a quick look under the bland surface of his reference to nice thoughts, to acts of love, and you will start to catch a glimpse of his exquisite humor. The word he uses for "members" is just as loaded with connotations, in ancient Greek, as it is in English. Under different circumstances it could quite easily mean human limbs and nothing more. Here, though, in such a delicately obvious context of love and sex it has the far more specific sense it often has elsewhere: the sense of genitals. And this is not even to mention the other word he evidently goes on to use, a moment later, when he describes Aphrodite spinning around with a spiral-like movement "in the mid-parts."

In one sense there is a direct reference here to her basic location at the midpoint of the cosmos. But we also happen to know that this particular expression, "mid-parts," was a very specific Sicilian slang word for the genitals.

It's healthy to remember that Empedocles was a Sicilian; and to remember, as well, how the most ancient images of the great goddess which sometimes are referred to as "Venuses" used to depict her. This sacred imagery, not only on Sicily but throughout the Mediterranean and Near East, showed her with a simple spiral marking her genitals—the spiral that through its irresistible spinning draws life deep into the great womb before at last releasing it again.

In other words Empedocles is doing what he can to make his disciple perceive directly, with his own conscious awareness, something already treasured as a revealed truth for thousands of years.

Perhaps his casually expert ease in pointing to the power-house of sex at the heart of creation, his light-hearted subtlety in touching on such a pleasurable subject in such an enjoyable way, will make you feel relaxed and quite at home with what he is saying. Perhaps you will even feel so at ease that you go on forgetting for a while longer about the fate of the soul.

But maybe you will also begin to understand why for Gnostics it happened to be love, pleasure, sex, the power of Aphrodite, that draws the soul down into incarnation—only to make it forget itself, its real nature, its identity, its past.

And maybe you will be able to appreciate why Platonists too, however politely they managed to treat the subject in their particularly polite Platonic way, found themselves describing Aphrodite as the goddess who "arouses in souls the desire for earthly life": who "through enjoyment bewitches our souls."

3

Empedocles warns us.

Early on in his famous, and yet esoteric, poem he not only brings up the subject of Aphrodite's involvement with the mysterious power of sex. He also prepares us quite specifically for her grand deception: explains just what happens as she mixes the four elements of existence together, with her artful "harmony," to create this beautiful world we suppose we know so well.

But of course, for any warning to work, there has to be someone present to notice it. And there is no one. The most intelligent of readers listen to his words without even remotely registering what he is saying, as if in some kind of daze. His plain indications that Aphrodite is a deceiver go in through one ear and then right out through the other.

So I will simply repeat his warning; give it another chance.

Just like when painters
work on intricately ornamented pictures—
professionals, well skilled in their craft through
mêtis, who take special paints of various colors
in their hands and mix them with either greater
harmony or less to produce shapes and forms
resembling anything or everything, creating
trees and men and women and animals and birds
and water-nourished fish and long-lived gods
who have the highest of dignity and honors—
just so, don't let deception overthrow the seat

384

of your awareness and make you believe that
whatever you see, all those countless numbers of
mortal beings around you, has any other source.
But know this, and know it clearly, once you have
heard these words spoken by a god.

Empedocles describes the situation very nicely, beautifully. That happens to be his privilege as a poet. But the barb concealed inside his words adds a sharpness to their poetic form. For this story he is telling is the same one we have already heard from Parmenides.

We live in a world created by the *mêtis*, the supreme cunning, of a great being: a goddess called Aphrodite. And in general we are totally at the mercy of her deception, her *apatê*.

Now you will be able to appreciate the significance of one crucial detail I skimmed over a little while ago. It has to do with that same passage where Empedocles broaches the mysterious topic of Love spinning around at the center of the cosmos.

After suddenly snapping his disciple to attention and preparing him for the vision of what no mortal has ever seen, of what no mortal perception ever can see, he brings his comments on the subject to an equally abrupt close by insisting that Pausanias listen with absolute attentiveness to "the undeceptive arrangement of my words." Scholars have looked, as usual, in all the wrong places for some clue as to why he should go to the trouble at this particular point of putting such a dramatic emphasis on the fact that his instructions are not deceptive: not *apatêlos*.

But the answer is right in front of us.

Aphrodite, the invisible spinner, the goddess whose mystery he has just been describing, is the mistress of *apatê* or deception. Everything about her is sheer deception. Her *philotês*, her notorious love, is the epitome of cunning and trickery. And there is only one way to come to a real perception of her: with the help of a teaching that manages to look straight through her ruses, that refuses to get entangled in the web of illusions she spins.

To understand the deceiver, come near to seeing her as she is, you have to find a powerful protection against being deceived. For this *apatê*, this deception, comes from a goddess.

And that—according to Empedocles', as well as Parmenides', own terms of reference—means something quite precise.

What it means is that no one but a divine being has the slightest chance either of perceiving her as she is or of revealing her nature to others. It takes a goddess, or a god, to see through her.

Empedocles' reason for placing so much weight on the fact that no mortal has ever grasped her true nature could hardly be simpler. A mortal is, by definition, someone who is trapped by her: is one of her special mixtures and creations, yet another of her pretty men and women all lined up in a row. For it's not just that, as mortals, we live in a world of illusions.

This would be nice if it were true; an extremely engaging illusion to live in and be entertained by. But the fundamental point is that, as mortals, we are illusions too. Whether we are intelligent illusions or not, we are still illusions.

What Empedocles is indicating, insisting on, demanding, is that if we want to understand anything about the cosmos we can no longer go on seeing things in the same way. And it's not a question of learning to see better, of expanding or improving our mortal perception. If we try to improve our usual way of perceiving we will only end up with an even bigger and better version of the total chaos he described at the start of his poem:

the chaos that sums up and so elegantly defines the human condition.

His aim is not to help us extend what we imagine are our existing faculties, refine them, push them to their limits. There is no gradual, comfortable progression towards the type of understanding he has in mind. For the essential purpose of his teaching is to awaken an entirely different form of cognition, one we have forgotten, that sees everything in a totally different light and from another perspective altogether: the perspective of immortality.

There is simply no other way of learning to watch the bewitching painter of this world—or even of getting to glimpse the painting.

4

Telling love's story is a strange affair.

It has no plot because every single plot is contained inside it. And the only way to tell it is by spinning around in circles—returning, again and again, over ground already covered.

We have already seen how, right at the end of that passage where Empedocles introduces his disciple to the queen of love and sex and delight, he warns him to hold fast to the undeceptive reality of his words. But he also says something extremely significant at the very beginning of it. "Don't just sit there in a daze."

The expression he uses for "in a daze" takes us back a long way. It happens to be the same as the one already used by Parmenides, towards the start of his own poem, to describe how humans spend the whole of their lives carried around "in a daze"; utterly helpless, bewildered and confused, deaf and blind to the divine reality governing every aspect of their existence. And considering the closeness of Empedocles' relationship to Parmenides, bearing in mind their almost identical ways of portraying the human condition, this is no coincidence.

But we already saw that people's helplessness or *amêchania*, as described in Parmenides' poem, has more than a little to do with the overpowering influence exerted on them by the binding charms of Aphrodite. Here, with Empedocles, you might perhaps want to think we are being told a different story.

We are not.

Empedocles doesn't warn Pausanias against sitting in a blank, unconscious daze when he is telling him about Strife; or when he is talking about the elements. But as soon as he brings up the subject of Love, of *philotês* with all its notoriously deceptive power, of Aphrodite, of delight and sex, the urgent instructions come straight into play.

And it's not hard to see why.

We have done quite a job over the past thousand years or two of rationalizing love—not to mention turning ancient Greece itself into a glittering manifestation of rationality. But this does nothing to change the fact that Greeks often had an intense concern with the influence which magic in general, and love spells in particular, could exert at any moment on their awareness. They were sensitive to mysterious effects and threats that for us seem not to exist.

Professional magicians had to make special efforts, for their own part, to protect themselves against the devastating impact of perceiving divine beings and realities directly. They were quite likely to be left with their consciousness over-whelmed, above all with their eyesight dazzled and dazed, unless they were very careful. But for most Greeks, especially men, one of the greatest dangers was something they had no need to invite or go out of their way to search for.

This was that they would be overpowered by Aphrodite: left sitting around "stunned and senseless" by her love magic in a blank stupor or daze.

The fact that when Empedocles starts revealing to Pausanias the cosmic reality of Love, or Aphrodite, he instructs him to use his awareness very consciously so as to avoid being left in a daze is no more accidental than the fact that, when he finishes, he sharply warns him not to be deceived. Empedocles knows what he has to do to guide him; guard him. And this ability to protect his disciple, to snap him out from an overpowering state of deception and bewilderment, is what one would expect of an experienced sorcerer—with one significant qualification.

The qualification is that Empedocles is not simply trying to help him shake off the effects of a single but dangerous encounter with Aphrodite. He is trying to wake him up to the fact that, like absolutely everyone else, he has been under her spell for the whole of his life.

And so you should be able to see how everything he says fits together with the most perfect logic. When he insists "Don't sit there in a daze," just as when he goes on to demand that his disciple keep listening to his "undeceptive" words, he is only formulating in a very slightly different vocabulary the same warning he is so quick to express about Love's cosmic trickery: "Don't let deception overthrow the seat of your awareness."

All he can do is offer warnings, and hope they might be heeded.

We may not choose to pay them much attention. And yet the instruction he offers is utterly consistent and systematic. Empedocles is facing a magical power of cosmic dimensions— and is being confronted by the task of initiating someone into a familiarity with that power while, at the same time, needing to safeguard him from its predictable effects.

Of course that makes him a magician in his own right. As we happen to know, though, this is precisely what he was. But we have been so hypnotized by the absurd idea of Empedocles as a rational philosopher, which is only the historical result of some intellectuals in the ancient world imagining they could analyze his writings from a perspective quite different to his own, that we are no longer able to see him or his teaching for what they really are.

And, in general, this is probably all for the best.

Those who like to believe he was just an interesting thinker, his poetry nothing but the product of a vivid imagination and a passionate engagement with theoretical ideas, are well protected by their beliefs. For to be a sorcerer, in the sense that Empedocles understood it, meant confronting a world of realities and dangers beyond our remotest comprehension.

To him, sorcery was not some imaginary option for unbalanced people who have lost a grip on the facts of life.

On the contrary: it was the only option left, the only available way to function, for those rare individuals who have made the irreversible discovery that what we consider reality is a total illusion.

5

Empedocles is quite right in the way he describes Love's influence: as like a soothing assault, a gently irresistible stream of illusion.

Of course we think we are impervious to any such nonsense. But this is a crucial component of her deception. First she makes us humans and then, as if that was not enough, makes us imagine the things we think really matter.

She encourages us to suppose we know a great deal. And so, for example, we believe we understand what it means to be objective. But what goes by the name of objectivity is only the result of our awareness being drawn along certain channels, in quite specific directions, by forces we are not even aware of.

One simple way to become alert to this process, bit by bit, is through noticing little things: by observing the small details that usually no one cares to notice, let alone put together and connect. For there are far fewer random events or coincidences in existence than we tend to think. And through these little details runs an almost invisible stream—linking them with the same quiet certainty that ensures Aphrodite's fondness for deception will somehow, miraculously, keep slipping the mind of anyone reading Empedocles.

I will just mention a couple of them for the moment. With time you may be able to catch sight of the connecting stream and, out of the corner of your eye or face to face, glimpse the power that operates behind them: definer of our rationality, shaper of our thoughts and dreams.

The first of these details comes in a passage where Empedocles is explaining how the various pieces and portions of the
four primordial elements, that once were completely separate,
have been made to come together and blend.

Those that are ready for mixture
have become affectionate towards each other, made
alike by Aphrodite.

Or, at any rate, this is what he is said to have said—even
though he said nothing of the kind. For his words could not
possibly have any such sense. There is no ambiguity in his Greek:
only one single meaning the words can have.

Those that are resistant to mixture
have become affectionate towards each other, made
alike by Aphrodite.

And yet what he said has been gently modified by each translator and commentator. Resistance, as you will notice, has been
converted into readiness.

One scholar happened to note the real meaning of these
words over thirty years ago. But his comments were quickly
swallowed up and forgotten. Our confident assumption and
fervently held conviction that scholarship keeps making steady
progress is just a myth, another self-deception: what real progress there is tends to come in spite of scholars, not because of
them.

And in this specific instance, so quintessentially symbolic,
apparently so insignificant, any opposition to Aphrodite's
influence has been wiped away.

I said I would mention one other detail. It comes from the passage where Empedocles describes how Love first asserts its power by spreading out through what had been Strife's universe, forcing what had been immortal to become mortal— and makes things start moving together "not at once but at will," in other words just when it suits them.

This is what everyone, without exception, makes Empedocles say. But it, too, is not what he said.

The Greek word translated as "at once" also has, built into it, the sense of "spontaneously"; "willingly"; "without hesitation." As for the word translated as "at will," really it doesn't mean that at all. What it does mean is "willingly," "spontaneously," "without hesitation." So what Empedocles would be saying here is that under Love's influence all the elements come together "not without hesitation but without hesitation," "not willingly but willingly." And this is nonsense. The two different Greek words are as close as possible to meaning the same thing: there is no room for any genuine contrast or opposition.

It should have been only too plain, all along, what he really is saying.

Ancient Greek used to be written without spaces between the words, as a single unbroken stream of continuous text. And when we break up his words here as we must, not into *alla thelêma* but into *all' athelêma*, we are left with the most perfect sense expressed in the most perfectly elegant Greek. Through Love

everything comes together to be one alone—
assembling from all different directions
not at once, but reluctantly.

It's also no coincidence at all that this particular way of portraying Aphrodite, as obliging the victims of her power to yield to her and unite not willingly "but reluctantly," happened to be a standard feature in ancient Greek magical texts.

Everything that exists, according to Empedocles, was once profoundly unwilling to be overpowered by Aphrodite. It had no choice, though. And what happened then goes on repeating itself now. The smallest traces of reluctance and resistance are washed away. Scholarly minds are quite happy to help with this because, at an unconscious level, we will still do anything for Love—break the rules of sense, cling to meaningless meanings, mistranslate someone's words and even change them without being aware of what we are doing or why. The mistakes, the apparently isolated lapses in judgement, always seem so easy to explain away. But through them we become Love's unwitting accomplices, magically concealing her magic, making everything appear fine and okay.

For the truth is that we have come to love being deceived.

In the deepest nature of everything there is the instinct to resist what Aphrodite has to offer and to want something else, which is the secret behind her creation. Now, of course, we are quite used to the way things are: to this charming deception. Or we almost are.

And yet once, long ago, before the spell, it was all very different.

6

Empedocles' teaching, as you may have begun to realize, is like a road without an exit.

There is no passing through it and coming out at the other end untouched, unchanged. You are the raw material for it: not it for you. And if the idea that you are being affected and always have been influenced—quite unawares—by the forces it describes strikes you as profoundly disturbing, this is all for the best.

Disturbance is one essential component in the process of being changed.

The world around us can seem so familiar, solid, real. But such a sense of familiarity is purely illusory; is like the effects of a drug. For the frightening fact is that things are only the way they are because of how we perceive them.

We see mixture all around us, shapes and forms and colors coming into existence and dying. But this is not because anything is really like that. It's simply because our perception, itself, happens to be mixed.

And Empedocles explains just why we humans happen to perceive things the way we do. When the four elements are blended in a perfect harmony they produce blood; and,

in the oceans of throbbing blood, this is where
you will find what usually is called awareness by
humans. For consciousness, the consciousness
of humans, is the blood around the heart.

You will note how insistent he is, how careful to emphasize and then repeat, that he is describing the awareness of humans. He is not talking about the awareness of dragonflies or fish. And he is not talking about consciousness in general, either. For, as we will see later, he taught that absolutely everything is conscious. Everything, regardless of whether to our perception it seems alive or just a lifeless object, thinks. Everything has its share of intelligence.

Of course you might be tempted into thinking, as commentators often do, that by human consciousness Empedocles means the highest possible form of consciousness in existence. This would not be a good idea, though. For as Empedocles never tires of pointing out in his consistent attempt to penetrate and puncture our boundless vanity, human consciousness is only mortal consciousness.

And that hardly amounts to very much.

Human consciousness is what sends us careering around in our knowledgeable, well-intentioned confusion. It's Love's supremely crafted product: the awareness we use through every moment of every day for relating to all the painted shapes around us without even realizing they are an illusion. Here, in the throbbing blood of humans while they live, is the perfect manifestation of Aphrodite's thinking—perfectly blended and balanced, perfectly impure and mortal, the perfect instrument of deception.

Or it might be better to state the situation another way.

This ordinary everyday awareness that we use for identifying and understanding everything, including ourselves, is not ours at all. Whenever we happen not to be overwhelmed by the effects of Strife, our consciousness and intelligence are Love's intelligence and consciousness. Until we learn how to take responsibility for our thoughts, how to start perceiving the world around us with the awareness of which we really are capable, Love is thinking and perceiving for us and through us and as us.

In short, we go through our lives without any thoughts or awareness of our own.

What we like to call objectivity has no real claim to the name at all, except in the specific sense that it helps to serve Love's objectives. And this is why, although our usual consciousness is just fine for helping us understand texts about politics or mechanics or farming, to understand Empedocles a different kind of awareness altogether has to be cultivated and created.

To explain the need for that new form of awareness, describe how to develop it, is the whole point of his teaching. Unless we appreciate this, everything is bound to go wrong.

So there should be nothing too surprising about what happens when philosophers use the old awareness they have been given for trying to discover the exact nature, according to Empedocles, of our immortal soul. Without fail they tend to look in precisely the wrong direction—and assume the answer has to lie with Love.

In fact there is no more improbable place to look if we want to find out what, for Empedocles, immortal consciousness consists of. But when enough people are willing to believe the improbable then even the impossible ends up becoming likely.

The answer put forward, as and when any answer is proposed at all, is that for Empedocles the immortal soul or *daimôn* has to be a portion of Love; must somehow represent the most perfectly blended and harmonious form of consciousness. There is just one little problem, though.

We already have Empedocles' own, plain description of consciousness at its most perfectly blended and harmonious.

Blood around the heart, the blood we use for thinking right now, is the finest mixture of the elements. It represents the pinnacle of Aphrodite's achievement. And it happens to be as body-bound and incarnate, as fleshy and mortal, as anything could be.

Or to state the matter a little more crudely: if this bloody awareness we know so well were able to free itself from the human body and return to some separate or disincarnate state, then pigs would be able to fly.

7

Watching the tides and coursings of history from the point of view of eternity can be a lonely business.

But it has its consolations. Sometimes the oceans of learning throw up a single jewel before sucking it back, lost again and forgotten, into the depths. And this is just what happened when, in the year 1805, Friedrich Wilhelm Sturz published what was to be the first modern scholarly edition and commentary dedicated to presenting Empedocles' poetry.

With the open eyes and daring of someone standing close to the dawn of a new enterprise, he looked questioningly at what Empedocles had said about Love. In particular he looked at what he had said about the state of seeming perfection that occurs once in every cosmic cycle when Love has brought everything together into a completely harmonious, integrated, spherical whole.

Then he looked at what generation after generation of well-meaning Platonists had already written about this state of Empedoclean love—idealizing it for its marvellous harmony, for the utter purity of its spiritual oneness. And he realized that those writers, for all the complexity and apparent sophistication of their thinking, were talking sheer nonsense.

His own definite conclusion about Empedocles' perfect sphere of love, a conclusion he kept coming back to and re-stating, was very direct. "I reckon it has to be explained as being a state of crude and chaotic matter."

And so, even if only for a few passing moments, open challenges were being issued to the dogma that—regardless of

Love's sheer delight in her oppressiveness, in the ability of her harmony to make all the elements helpless by not only compromising their immortality but also snatching away their freedom, and in spite of the fact that her rounded womb contains all the darkly hidden ambiguities of Parmenides' bound reality— Aphrodite must be the kindly liberator of the soul.

Then Friedrich Sturz took another step. And the comment he made deserves to go down in history for the way it was to fall on so many future generations of deaf ears.

What he said is that Empedocles himself must have looked for liberation not to Aphrodite but to Strife, because "his hope was not that his own soul would be drawn back into chaos through Love. His hope was for his soul's immortality."

And, as we have seen, he was quite right. The soul is freed, returned to its original state of purity and immortality, not by Love but by Strife. So if we really want to know what the soul is made of, then we are going to have to look to the point in the cosmic cycle right opposite Love's harmonious womb— to the stage when the four elements exist in a state of complete purity and immortality and separation.

As for discovering what particular substance the soul consists of, nothing could be simpler. The soul comes from the heavens; and it returns there again at the end of each cycle. The heavens, for Empedocles, are made up of the element he called *aithêr*. And whenever ancient Greeks from virtually any or every period in their history speculated about the physical substance of the immortal soul, they would always keep coming back to the same basic answer: the soul consists of *aithêr*.

You might wonder why, if for Empedocles himself the nature of the soul was such a straightforward matter, he refused to state his position clearly. And if his purpose had been to offer a plain, rational exposition of his ideas then of course such lack of clarity would be inexcusable.

That was never his purpose, though.

We consider it our right, our privilege, to be handed the truth on a plate. To Empedocles such an attitude could hardly have seemed more naive because he knew any real teaching can only be received once the ground has been prepared for it first.

His teaching is esoteric. His words have the power, by themselves, to draw someone into the realities they point to. They are a riddle to be pondered, meditated on, cared for, lived with, patiently nurtured until they unfold into their own solution. And that solution is not a matter of theoretical data, conveniently supplied as if in some textbook, but a question of direct experience.

This is why it's so important that we approach Empedocles' teaching on his terms, not ours.

You might also wonder about something else.

If for Empedocles the soul is a fragment of *aithêr*, it might seem strange that he describes the four great bodies of the elements—*aithêr* and water, earth and fire—as all rejecting it in turn and throwing it from one to the other. But here, too, the answer could hardly be simpler.

Those four great elemental bodies in the world around us are already, relatively speaking, very pure. And only what is pure, as Greeks would say, will be allowed into the company of what is pure. We for our part, still swimming with our awareness in the blood around the heart, identifying ourselves as mortals, are anything but pure. We still have a long way to go before the *aithêr* inside us can join the *aithêr* already up above in the heavens: uncontaminated, pure, soul with soul, all together again.

Strife has a great deal of work left to do.

8

And so we come to that other cosmic principle quietly lurking behind all the glitter and glamour of Love.

Strife, as a force at play throughout the universe and in the lives of humans, already had quite a reputation for ambiguity by Empedocles' time. There were writers who had discussed its good sides along with its bad ones; had emphasized its virtues and importance as well as the sheer, brutal fact of its inevitability.

At first sight, though, there seems nothing in what Empedocles himself has to say that could be considered too ambiguous. Strife belongs in the shadows while Love takes the limelight. As commentators delight in pointing out, Aphrodite is only too obviously the divinity he favors.

But we have already seen that few things could be less obvious—or more ambiguous.

It's not just a matter of having to appreciate how Strife's role in separating out the elements is ultimately as essential for the existence of any orderly universe as Love's role is in combining them. This kind of purely mechanical consideration is valid enough in itself, but little more than child's play. Far more important than any such considerations is the fact that with Love nothing is what it seems.

When Empedocles appears to be praising her, he is also warning about her at the same time. And if Aphrodite with all her beauty and charms is the first mystery in his teaching, Strife happens to be the second. So if you were thinking that the need to see through Love's illusions is the only challenge posed by

Empedocles' teaching, you have been very pleasantly deceived. The real work of understanding him, of waking up to what this sorcerer is doing, has only just begun.

Fairly early on in his poem for Pausanias, with all the clarity he feels would be appropriate, Empedocles delivers a statement on the crucial issue of existence and non-existence; of life and death.

> *No one*
> *who was wise about such matters would*
> *prophesy in his chest that for as long as people*
> *live what they call life they are, and experience*
> *bad things and good, but that before being*
> *fastened together as mortals and after being*
> *released they are nothing.*

You will notice how delicately, and deliberately, he structures what he says. And his reference to prophecy—in the chest which was known to Greeks as the seat of prophecy, where breath and inspiration reach the heart—should have us on our toes. To skim over these words of his rather than stopping, for as long as it takes, to uncover their meaning would not be too intelligent an attitude.

After all, we happen to be reading the writings of a prophet.

He starts with a negative and also finishes with a negative. So instead of being told directly what would be prophesied, we are only told what would not. And this method of communicating by phrasing things in an obscure and roundabout way is typical of prophetic statements. The prophet uses the language of oracles and riddles to do no more than softly hint.

Here, at least, the central riddle is quite clear. We are being presented with the blatant enigma that we live beyond the lives we seem to live.

We are beyond what we are.

And just as clearly, for anyone with a little intelligence and patience, there is only one solution to this riddle. We not only go on existing but also go on experiencing good things and suffering bad beyond what we call life because we survive as suffering, experiencing beings.

Of course anyone is perfectly free to deny that he is asserting a belief here in our own survival after death. One of the greatest beauties about a prophetic riddle is that we can always choose not to follow the gradual process of its unfolding and to walk away from it instead. But this does nothing to alter the process itself, which has all the naturalness and inevitability of a seed developing into a plant.

And so far, with this particular riddle about life and existence, we have only watched the initial stage of the seed turning into a shoot. The blossoming is still to come.

The real secret, the central mystery at the core of this prophecy, lies in the exact words Empedocles chooses to use when hinting at how people continue to exist "before being fastened together as mortals and after being released." For "fastening together," in his poetry, is a technical expression he only ever uses while referring to the work of Love. And "releasing" is of course the work of Strife, undoer and unbinder of her creations—just as it also happens to be the standard term in ancient Greek for undoing a magic spell, for dissolving obstacles, for freeing the soul from the body and for liberating those who have been polluted from their state of impurity.

In other words what Empedocles is gently indicating here with his enigmatic style is that we not only exist while we are incarnated as mortals by Love. We also go on existing and living when we have been released from our bodies by Strife.

This little prophecy takes up just a handful of lines. But it confirms with small-scale precision what already became so clear from comparing the entire cycle of the cosmos with the cycle of the soul.

Love fastens the soul in the body. Strife is what sets it free so that, unsuspected by us, it can live out its real destiny beyond the restrictions of incarnated existence.

And yet, magician that he is, Empedocles says this without ever saying so. He is a man whose teaching has been analyzed and discussed for over two thousand years but during that time has gone quite unnoticed, because his real words are made of a substance far too pure for anyone to see.

9

Strife stalks Empedocles' universe like a ghoul.

It embodies everything we fear most—death, destruction, the undoing of Love's infinitely careful work, the gruesome process of organic life being torn apart and dismembered.

But then we have to remember.

Behind Aphrodite, for Empedocles, stands death in the form of Strife. Behind Aphrodite for Parmenides stands his mysterious, unnamed guide: Persephone, the queen of death. And according to Parmenides there is only one way of getting free from Aphrodite's magic grip. That way is with the help of her polar opposite; is through the knowledge only found at the other side of life as we know it.

This is why he makes such a ceremony, right at the opening to his poem, of describing an initiatory journey into the world of the dead. The journey he portrays is not some literary ornamentation for his logical philosophy, some fancy decoration, as historians love deceiving themselves into believing. It represents the essential first stage, the unavoidable prerequisite, for whoever wants to understand the reality behind illusion.

You have to die before you die.

And one thing we should never do with regard to this journey is underestimate it. Nobody in his or her right mind would want to contemplate it, let alone make it. For even though the only real freedom from loneliness comes through travelling this route, as it leads away from Aphrodite and past all her illusions, at least to begin with there is nothing in the world that could be so lonely. Whatever gave a sense of fulfilment becomes emptiness. And everything, without exception, is reversed. To travel this way means heading in exactly the opposite direction from whatever we call life; swimming against the stream of all existence.

And it marks the death of running from what we fear.

Collectively, without even knowing what has happened, we have trained ourselves to turn our backs on the things that seem to threaten us most: to keep finding ways of postponing, avoiding, wishing them away. But the way of the initiate is to head straight towards them—is to penetrate and pass right through them until one comes out at the other side.

This is why Parmenides lets himself be taken directly to the underworld. There is nothing safe in what he is doing; nothing even remotely reasonable. And yet he does it not only because he has no choice but because he also knows that, with the protection and guidance always given to someone who has the right motives, the journey can be made and has to be made.

We spend most of our lives, without even realizing it, longing to go back to some Garden of Eden. But as early Christians understood very well, there can be no returning to Eden; and even if there could, nothing would be worse for us. This is why it often used to be said that Eve's and Adam's fall was, when all is said and done, the greatest possible blessing. Otherwise they would have stayed innocent little children and never had the chance of growing up.

We can complain for the rest of our days about how hard things are, with plenty of justification. But it was only because of what happened, through all this suffering, that we will be able to make our way back at last to where we really belong.

And that means being prepared to take terrible risks.

We love taking things easy—will even spend the greater part of our available time working ourselves into the ground just so that we can sit around in a little comfort and security right at the end. But this is a fool's game. We will have the shock of our lives when, sooner or later, we realize that what had seemed so perfectly safe is in fact the perfect illusion.

Everything we look to for safety or comfort: this is Love's trick. And by refusing to take any true risks we end up ironically taking the most dangerous course there is, of placing all our trust in our deceiver.

We live in a ruthless universe. There is great beauty and there are absolutely no guarantees. Everything is masquerading as its opposite. And nothing could sound more unlikely but also be more unavoidable than Empedocles' mysterious message— spoken by him without even being said—that Love traps the soul while Strife sets it free. No message could be so plain and so concealed, so transparent and so ignored at the same time.

For this message of his is just like the call of the soul itself: impossibly faint and distant, but closer to us than anything else.

NINE

A disciple of Empedocles asked him:
What is the noblest thing to know?
He answered:
What people neglect the most.

SHAHRAZURI

Talking openly about mysteries after they have been kept hidden for so long is not an easy or comfortable thing to do. It would seem much more sensible, a great deal simpler, just to sit down and stay silent.

This may have been possible, once—but not any more. The secrecy has served its purpose. And now is the time for bringing what has been hidden back out into the open.

Looking over my shoulder at the ground covered so far I would be a fool if I failed to wonder what good reason you could have for believing the things I have said about Empedocles' Love, or Strife. And of course the answer is that there is none.

Countless very intelligent people have written about his teaching. I am stating the opposite of them all. Statistically, the chances of my being right and their being wrong are not only negligible. They are not worth calculating. Even to dream of taking a stand against the massed apparatus of so much learning would be quite absurd.

One of the greatest, and certainly most famous, of such people was Aristotle. There could be few better examples of human intelligence at work: of rationality at its sharpest and most efficient.

His attitude to Empedocles was, not surprisingly, rather complicated. He admitted to a kind of grudging admiration but loved barking at him about all the various aspects of his poetry that he hated. And there were plenty.

He intensely disliked him for writing as a poet; for using ambiguous expressions; for his oracular and prophetic language. Luckily, though, Aristotle had the special gift of being able to understand him better than Empedocles understood himself. As he so masterfully sums up his perception: "Anyone who follows Empedocles and understands him not on the basis of his inarticulate babbling but on the basis of what he really means will discover that Love is the cause of good while Strife is the cause of evil."

And there has never seemed the slightest reason to doubt him.

Then there is Plutarch—an enormously learned man who was also a high-ranking authority and religious official in his time. He prided himself on his ability to penetrate the hidden meaning of riddles; of mysteries. He wrote a massive work on Empedocles in Greek. And, as has often been pointed out, if one is to trust anybody's interpretation of Empedocles then this is the man to place one's faith in.

So there is a profound significance in the simplicity of his conviction, expressed without the slightest wavering or uncertainty, that "Love is the name Empedocles gives to the power responsible for doing good" while "Strife is his principle of evil."

But Plutarch, the good man he was, suffered from one particular problem. This is that the only mysteries he ever solved were the ones he created for himself. He would not have been able to recognize a true mystery even if he tripped over it in the street.

And there is one specific mystery whose existence he would never in his wildest thoughts have imagined finding in the writings of Empedocles: an esoteric principle that, during the centuries after Empedocles had died, slowly started spreading out over the seas of rationality like an oil slick.

This principle, well known to ancient Gnostics in particular, is the mystery of inversion. The idea behind it is that truth must never be stated directly but always through its opposite. So when somebody wise says something is good, then that means it really is not good. And if something is described as bad then that means it is good. Or as one famous Christian pope and saint, Gregory the Great, tried to explain it in his own writings: "Outwardly to approve of something means, in the language of mystery, to oppose it. And to refer to certain actions in negative terms is, mystically speaking, to encourage them."

Needless to say, for anybody nowadays to take such a ridiculous principle seriously would be utter foolishness. And to think of finding it at work in the teaching of such an influential philosopher as Empedocles would be sheer insanity.

But in a world where rationality and common sense are illusions and objectivity is a dream, perhaps this is not such a bad thing. And as a matter of fact there is no need whatsoever for us to try imposing any such principle of inversion, or contradiction, on Empedocles' teaching.

It's already there, all ready and waiting for us—right at the heart of everything he says.

2

The way we respond to Empedocles' poetry is a perfect reflection of our attitude to life. And the degree to which we are tricked by one mirrors the extent to which we are deceived by the other.

The sheer breadth and scale of his teaching can be stunning. But running all the way through it is the thread of humanity that makes whatever he says so approachable; gives it its sense of rightness. This is the thread that ensures the most crucial details in his teaching will always be the ones we are able to recognize, relate to, instantly identify with.

Love, as he describes it and as we know so well, is gentle and kind. As for Strife, he seems less keen to talk about it than about Love—which is very understandable. When he does, though, his judgements are perfectly appropriate. Strife, the dismemberer, is evil. It happens to be the direct cause of death which is wretched, miserable, ill-fated. And, as he so rightly portrays it, Strife is ruinous and accursed just like death itself: hateful and abominable.

Of course there is no need for him to tell us such things. We know them already. But he does. He understands our feelings as well as we understand him.

Catching the general drift of what he describes is just like breezing through another routine, if interesting, day. From the first moment we wake up in the morning there is experience after experience waiting for us; different situations to take in our stride whether we like them or not; all kinds of events to trigger our usual emotions.

And then—out of the blue on such an average day, under a bright and sunny sky—the realization might come that something is terribly wrong.

It should have started when the alarm rang, or when you were brushing your teeth. Even though things might seem quite normal, somewhere inside yourself you know that none of this is really happening. Perhaps you are playing the role of someone else. Maybe someone else is playing yours. But, either way, you are not yourself at all.

Everything is just a dream: the strangest of mistakes.

Empedocles was trying to warn us this would happen. He had already been sounding the alarm bells loud and clear, right from the start of his poem for Pausanias, when he presented his horrific portrait of the human condition.

The appalling image he offers of people going through their whole lives without a shred of *mêtis*, of genuine alertness or intelligence, is unflattering—to say the least. And yet the one statement he makes that cuts straight to the heart of the matter, a comment so disturbing some scholars even try to remove it from his text, comes when he describes how people in general "during their lifetimes see such a little part of life."

Certainly there is a hint here, in this mention of "lifetimes," that none of us only lives a single life. But even more significant is the very noticeable distance Empedocles has started to put between his own understanding and others', between the lives people think they live and life as he knows it. Life for him is not the same as life for them.

And then comes his prophetic riddle about existence and non-existence, where he subtly points out that those who are content just to "live what they call life" have no genuine wisdom or insight at all. Suddenly Empedocles is whispering in our ear, with greater clarity this time: Don't be fooled.

Whatever you think of as life is not really life. What you mean by life and what I mean by it could hardly be more different.

The distance is growing larger.

But this is not even to mention what he says about death. There is one little passage where he tells Pausanias what we should have been able to guess.

> For all mortal beings, there is no such thing as
> birth. Neither is there any end for them in hateful,
> destructive death. There is nothing at all but
> mixture, followed by rearrangement of the things
> that have been mixed: "birth" is just the name
> applied to those events by humans.

Now the whispering has turned into a sharp tap on the shoulder. Empedocles is saying out loud: When I describe death as being ruinous and hateful, accursed, abominable, don't believe me. In reality it's none of these things. And when you hear me talking about death, you mustn't believe me either. For there is no death.

And so you should be starting to get a sense of the sheer scale of his apparent nonsense.

He will talk to us at great length about the beauty and goodness of life: the life manufactured for us by Aphrodite. But for him this is not life.

He will keep on referring to death as terrible and atrocious, horrific and appalling. But there is no such thing.

He scares us with his language but says there is nothing to fear, makes repeated assertions only to whisper the exact opposite in our ear, describes something with total confidence while prodding us and announcing it's a lie.

And if we had any wits about us we would realize he is creating a tremendous sense of confusion through this double talk of his. With his conflicting signs and messages he is saying yes, but no; absolutely so and absolutely not. He is placing everyone in an intolerable position, systematically splitting his listener in two. And he is planting the seeds of strife not in the outer world but in our inner being: the seeds of a conflict that can wake us up, separate our consciousness from our unconsciousness, free us from ourselves.

The crude manifestations of Strife—death and destruction—are always enough to shock us out of our sleep for a little while until we crawl back again into our womb of comfort and routine. But what Empedocles is doing through his words is far more subtle; is inwardly instead of outwardly destructive. The only problem is that it requires from us a certain degree of alertness and conscious cooperation to begin with. And these qualities are strikingly rare.

So we may think we are reading Empedocles while we wander through another usual day. But it turns out that nobody woke up this morning, after all.

As I mentioned, everything is a dream.

3

Empedocles himself offers the clearest possible explanation for his bizarre, contradictory behavior. But of course, as always, we have to open our eyes if we want to see it.

In another passage from his poetry that has been preserved for us through all these thousands of years, he states quite frankly what he is doing. Without the slightest concealment he explains just where he stands in relation to ordinary humans and their very familiar concepts.

> *When light has been mixed in the form of a*
> *human, or any kind of wild beast or shrub or*
> *bird, and then comes into contact with* aithêr,
> *this is what they call "coming into existence."*
> *But when those elements are separated again,*
> *they call that "ill-fated destiny." What they say is,*
> *for them, quite right; and I myself conform to*
> *their convention.*

Through these lines he might seem to be talking about elemental processes: about how when light, which is a name he gave to the element of fire, comes together with *aithêr* then organic life as we know it is born. Really, though, he is talking about something quite different—not about the process of life being brought into being but about the process of humans creating and giving names.

And, just like Parmenides, he is making the point that with all our usual acts of naming we impose impossible limitations on reality. We contribute, quite willingly, to tricking ourselves.

Those names we invent have become such second nature to us that we never doubt or question them. But they are wrong. There is no coming into existence because existence always is. And there is no "ill-fated destiny" called death because death is not our destiny and the only ill fate we have to suffer is our ignorance of what that destiny is.

All our familiar terms like "bad" and "good," "death" and "life," are utterly deceptive in the ways we always use them: they turn everything upside down and back to front. But Empedocles makes an extraordinary choice.

First he explains, with clinical care and objectivity, precisely why they are wrong. Then, instead of avoiding or denying them, he does the exact opposite.

He accepts them. He embraces them with a completely clear consciousness of what he is doing. These terms are wrong, deceiving; as misleading as could be. But for humans they are quite right because they are the norm.

And he makes the formal decision to join in.

People have read this simple statement, "And I myself conform to their convention," for centuries. But its significance escapes them like water pouring through a sieve. For us the frame of reference created by our usual, commonsense expressions is so solid and real that we unconsciously assume Empedocles must always have been a part of it. And yet he is not.

For us, all the concepts of our familiar language point to some reality. To him they are a web of illusions. But because

he chooses to join our consensus we manage to convince ourselves quite automatically, in spite of everything he has said,
that he belongs to it. And yet he doesn't.

He is simply infiltrating our illusory existence, sabotaging
it from the inside.

He has to communicate with us somehow. He needs to
build some kind of bridge between his own awareness and
the normal human awareness we like to imagine is the only one
that exists. So he deliberately lowers himself, or raises himself,
to our level; agrees to speak in and on our own terms.

Consciously he bows to our unconsciousness. And because
we are unconscious we forget that he is conscious before we
even remember it.

He is adopting our habits, adapting to our norms. And
because these norms and habits are so natural to us, we fail to
realize how unnatural they are for Empedocles. But, as his job
is to reach into the depths of our illusory world, he puts aside
his own understanding; cloaks his own knowledge; conceals
his inner awareness.

And he speaks to us in our infinitely deceptive language.

We are so used to being the helpless, blind victims of this
deception that we are unlikely to see just what his action means.
In reality it implies that when Empedocles speaks to us, this is
not him speaking.

It's us.

His process of conscious adaptation is something we can
spend forever minimizing, playing down and justifying, explaining away. These are nothing, though, but token gestures
on our part to make ourselves feel a little better; to try and
make our illusion seem a bit more solid. For the chilling fact is
that we are not really reading Empedocles, whatever we like to
think or imagine. He mentions a few riddles at the beginning

of his esoteric poem for Pausanias, then leaves the occasional scattered hint about what he is doing which of course most people choose to ignore.

And he is off. In essence he is talking the way we talk and saying what we expect to hear—not what he really means.

He has disappeared.

We may insist that of course we have Empedocles' own teaching. But if we believe this then we have been deceived, because we have nothing of the kind. All we have is the cloak he used for disguising himself and left behind after he came to visit.

Empedocles, as you should remember, was a sorcerer. He was a perpetual shape-changer, a trickster, a master of illusion who was always showing himself in different forms and guises. To him nothing could be easier than to present himself as a god and, by putting on his cloak of invisibility, appear to us in the very next moment as just a gifted human being.

4

To see that Empedocles says the most important things without even saying them: this was bad enough. But with the realization that he is not even saying what he appears to be saying comes the inevitable feeling of being drawn into deep and muddied waters.

There is no need to worry, though.

The sense that everything has become hopelessly complicated and confused is only an illusion, because a very simple logic is at work here. And this logic can be expressed in the form of one single principle.

That principle is the mystery of reflection.

Empedocles might seem to be using a whole arsenal of sophisticated tricks for hiding what he really means behind its opposite—esoteric techniques, deceptions, methods of communicating on different levels at one and the same time. In fact he is doing nothing of the kind.

All he is doing is using a simple little mirror, the type you have around your home or can pick up for next to nothing in a shop. He just holds it up to whoever reads his poetry.

And the reflection does the rest.

It makes no difference who we are: ordinary readers or great philosophers, living now or thousands of years ago. Human nature comes in all sorts of different shapes and forms and sizes but, as for its essence, it always stays the same. We see what we are familiar with reflected back to us and instantly fall in love with our reflection. We glimpse ourselves, our normal but extraordinary existences, and immediately we fall asleep.

It's just like in a fairytale. The pull of the reflection is irresistible. Empedocles warns us, then warns again. He waves his arms up and down, announces precisely what is about to happen. He says: I am going to use your deceptive, illusory language so don't believe what you hear. I am going to conjure up fantastic specters of death and life that have no genuine existence, so don't for a moment believe what you think you see.

But we are so used to specters and deceptive words, so drugged by the hypnotic illusion of familiarity, that we forget all the warnings as soon as they have been spoken. Empedocles might just as well never have bothered with them.

Viewed from a distance, with a certain sense of detachment, the situation can seem almost incredible. At one moment he is saying there is no death and that what we call life is not life at all. In the next moment he is talking about how awful death is and painting the most vivid images of what we call life—but no one so much as pauses to consider the real significance of such an incongruous contradiction. We have to understand, though, that this is not simply a matter of our failing to notice the obvious.

Things would certainly be that straightforward if we had the objectivity we believe we possess. But they are not. And this is because in reality we have no minds of our own.

Even the idea that we do have our own minds, can think for ourselves, is a result of the cosmic illusion we believe we live in. We are all Aphrodite's playthings. And the reason why her spell stays so powerful is because, great minds and small alike, we are completely unaware of it.

You will note that Empedocles is not at all underhand in what he does. On the contrary, he is careful to warn us—just like Parmenides' goddess when she tells us she is about to start talking deceptively before she even begins.

He is a model of undeceptiveness.

And yet he deceives everyone. He is the most accomplished of tricksters who does all the correct and decent things but still manages to fool everybody without exception into believing he is saying, quite seriously, that life as we know it is good and Love is perfect; death is bad and Strife is evil. For of course there is no reason whatsoever why he should need to trick us.

All he has to do is be perfectly honest and leave it to us to deceive ourselves.

Empedocles' reputation as a magician, his role as an initiator into esoteric mysteries: these are not aspects of the man that we can put aside and hope will go away. His teaching is pure treachery because the whole world we live in is treachery. And the clue to understanding this teaching of his is that if we can see how it works then we will be able to see how the world around us works. For what he has managed to do is to compose his poetry as a functioning model of the cosmos. While the universe traps us on a large scale, his poetry catches us in miniature.

Once we start to appreciate this fundamental point, then we are coming close to the heart of his teaching—and also to appreciating what it is not.

The inevitable impression is that he is offering us something through his poetry. But really he is offering nothing we can name. We may think we are approaching him for his own views and opinions. But he is hiding them. It seems obvious to us that he is stating exactly what he is saying. But the main purpose of his teaching is not to give us information. We can gather from it all the facts and ideas and details that we want.

And yet his physical explanation of the universe is only the most exoteric part of a very esoteric teaching: something to keep our minds busy and occupied, a few crumbs tossed under the table for stray dogs.

They are not the meal, though.

Empedocles belonged to a tradition that aimed to give something to everyone, on the level at which each individual is able to receive it. Those who want to be deceived will go away deceived. But the central purpose of his teaching is to test us; is to find out what substance we are made of.

If we manage to see what he is doing, if we are able to realize how completely we have been fooled not just by him but by everything, then he will have given us the most precious gift of all—ourselves.

The only trouble is that most people, if offered themselves, will snap out in anger. But if they are presented with scraps of information and theories that they can argue about, that will give them some sense of superiority and self-importance, they will go away quite happy.

This is the mystery of reflection.

5

Nothing could be less noticeable than this process of reflection while one is not aware of it. Nothing could be more fascinating, when one is.

There is no need to provide any specific example of the process at work: Empedocles' entire teaching is, itself, the most perfect demonstration. But I will give an example anyway.

It will take us back right to the very earliest phase of his teaching as a whole—to the critical point where he initiates his listeners, or would-be listeners, into its most basic features and themes for the first time. Here is where he starts his narrative about the cycle of the soul and gives the initial touches to his portrait of the *daimôn*, the divinity inside us all that was thrown out of heaven once it became polluted.

And here is where, in a climactic gesture full of drama, he introduces us to the figure of Strife.

He describes, as we have already seen, how the fallen soul is made to suffer by wandering from body to body; is never able, in this world now so familiar to us of diminishing love and increasing hate, to find a home for long; how neither *aithêr* nor any other element is willing to accept it but kicks it around like a ball.

And then comes a famous autobiographical statement by Empedocles that would be a great deal more famous if we only realized what he is saying.

> *The might of* aithêr *chases it into the sea,*
> *sea spits it out onto solid ground, earth spits it*

430

up into rays of the radiant sun and sun hurls it
into the whirlpools of aithêr. *One receives it from*
another, then another from another, and they all
hate it. This is the way that I too am now going,
an exile from the gods and a wanderer, placing my
trust in mad Strife.

There can be no real uncertainty about Empedocles' meaning here: not the slightest grounds for doubt. He is being, as always, very precise. The sense of the passage is not open to negotiation. He is describing the terrible experience of being banished from his home in the heavens only to find himself being mercilessly thrown from element to element. And, faced with this appalling situation, he is placing all his trust in mad Strife.

That, at any rate, is what he said. But as for what people say he said: this is quite another matter.

If you look in the standard textbooks on the history of philosophy, you will be told that "Empedocles is forced to wander far from the gods because he allowed himself to be persuaded by furious Strife." You will learn how he is "a wanderer, because he once trusted to insensate Hate"; how he presents himself, full of shame, as his own best example of a *daimôn* that "fell because it 'trusted in raving Strife.'" Every one of these interpretations is based on this same, single passage—where Empedocles' own words are routinely translated so as to make him say he is "a fugitive from heaven and a wanderer, because I trusted in raging Hate," "an exile from the gods and a wanderer, having put my trust in raving Strife."

And if I were to quote every mistranslation I would fill a book, because he is saying nothing of the kind.

The exact word he uses here for "placing my trust in," *pisunos*, had an extremely specific meaning in ancient Greek. To become *pisunos* in something, to decide to trust it, is what you do when a dangerous or difficult situation calls for a special kind of help. The object you pin your hopes on is not what got you into trouble in the first place.

On the contrary, it's what you expect will get you out. And the particular scenario, which also happens to be described by other Greek writers living in or around Empedocles' time, of an "exile placing trust in" something is the direct result of that something being the exile's one and only hope of finding safety.

As for Empedocles himself: he even emphasizes that he is doing the trusting "now," not at some remote time in the distant past. In short, he is not saying he is an exile because he trusted in Strife. He is saying the exact reverse, that he trusts in Strife because he is in exile.

And he is placing his trust in strife, mad Strife, to get him out of this appalling situation he has been thrown into.

Naturally, though, the prospect of him or anyone trusting in something as untrustworthy and utterly dangerous as Strife is horrifying. It runs counter to all our normal expectations. So what he says has, for around the last two thousand years, been changed; completely inverted.

You will note how open he is about the fact that he is trusting in Strife.

But because this is not what we want to hear, we don't hear it. This is not what we are accustomed to because it flies in the face of too much. He gently caresses us with his meaning. And yet his caress is like being touched by a wild animal—something we are not able to tolerate. So we turn what he says back to front.

432

Here you have esotericism at its most perfect.

Empedocles lays everything out on the table; hides nothing; is totally honest. And no one notices. In the biblical language that Jesus is said to have used when explaining the parable of the sower and the seed, "they see without seeing and hear without either hearing or understanding."

Or to quote Empedocles' own words at the beginning of his poem for Pausanias about men and women who are so full of their smallness that they are unable to glimpse the vastness lying behind their little lifetimes, so unconscious of their lack of awareness that they insist on endlessly repeating the same chaotic routines:

> *Like this there is no way that people can see or*
> *hear or consciously grasp the things I have to teach.*

6

The time for finding something, or somebody, to place one's trust in is when reliable help is needed. But to be faced with a dangerous situation and decide to place all one's trust in something dangerous calls either for stupidity—or for one very specific quality.

That was the quality referred to by Greeks as *mêtis*.

The route Empedocles is following, of trusting in mad Strife, could hardly be more dangerous. To travel this way is to play with fire. It means deliberately invoking danger so as to escape from danger. And that needs every ounce of cunning and awareness, flexibility and alertness, one can find.

But to trust in Strife is not a decision Empedocles makes because he enjoys flirting with danger. He does it because he knows he has to.

We live, as he explains so thoroughly, in an age of growing Strife. There is no standing still, and no going back either—certainly no going back to some idyllic state of innocent harmony and love. A new energy is spreading through the cosmos and we can't stay asleep for ever, lulled by Aphrodite's magic.

Things are changing, slowly but surely: whether we want them to or not. We are faced with the destruction of our illusions in one way or another.

And there is only a single choice we have now. Either we can follow Strife unconsciously or we can follow it with a real awareness of what we are doing.

In fact Strife, for Empedocles, is just as ambiguous as it ever was for any of the writers who had discussed the topic before him. It can be good; it can be bad. There is nothing worse and nothing better. It can destroy us or save us. For Strife is what has the power to take us home, set us free.

So the one choice we are left with is to let Strife do its work either with our cooperation or without: either with our deliberate trust and awareness or in spite of us, dragging us along by the heels. But the more we try to run away from it and hide, the more trouble we will be creating for ourselves in future.

The situation is starkly simple. If we let it have its way without cooperating, then Strife will manifest as violence and destruction all around us. But if we are willing to cooperate, we can consciously channel its energy instead into destroying ourselves—our beliefs and illusions, our attachments, our clinging to the ways things are. For what can be so difficult to realize is that the very act of becoming conscious is, itself, a process of destruction; of separation; of learning to die before we die.

In this unavoidable situation of increasing Strife, absolutely nothing is fixed or certain. Good is no longer just good, bad bad. The reality is far more subtle than that. What appears bad may be the greatest good and what is bad at one moment could become good in the next. In short, nothing can be more dangerous or ambiguous than to follow the route of Strife. And no teaching that talks in these terms could be more vulnerable to misunderstanding.

This is why Empedocles has to be so careful about how he formulates his message. For him to come out into the open with a statement, however poetic, that the route we need to follow is the path of Strife would be totally irresponsible. Most people would misinterpret him rather than realize what he is hinting at: would take his message the wrong way.

And here is where we can start to appreciate not just how subtle the reality is that he is pointing towards but also how subtle he is in pointing to it. For he does come right out into the open and announce this. In fact he states, as clearly and dramatically as possible, that he is placing his trust in Strife.

But the mystery is how he manages to do so in such a way that no one notices—that what he says is systematically turned upside down and back to front.

This is his magic; his trick of invisibility. He conceals himself by concealing nothing. You might want to believe that all the repeated misunderstandings and mistranslations of his statement about trusting in Strife are just an accident. And yet they are a great deal more than that. Or, instead, you might think he is playing a trick that would be easy for anyone to pull off. And yet nothing could be more difficult.

This type of unambiguous ambiguity is only possible for someone who, like Strife itself, haunts the edges of existence and is familiar with the shorelines of our consciousness where the illusory world we are so used to borders on reality; where life as we know it disappears into the unknown.

By talking from that place you can say black and people will understand white, green and everyone will see red. Empedocles was only too familiar with those grey regions where the age-old game of reflection is played out: of letting people see and hear what they want to see and hear while at the same time managing to deceive them even in their deception by somehow, impossibly, miraculously, allowing something else to creep in ever so slowly through the gaps.

And so, as you may be able to see, everything comes back to *mêtis*.

Mêtis is the one thing needed if we are going to travel such a dangerous path without being destroyed by the forces we encounter.

Mêtis is also the one thing needed for indicating the existence of such a path in a way that will only lead to harmless, rather than harmful, misunderstandings; in a way that ensures the real message will be heard by those who are ready to hear it but go straight out through the ears of those who are not. This is the *mêtis*, magically built into the fabric of Empedocles' teaching, that guarantees it will be able to protect itself.

And, last but also first, *mêtis* is the alertness we have to cultivate if we are going to recognize his tricks. For it needs just as much *mêtis* to understand what Empedocles is saying as to take one single pace on the path he is pointing out.

So the magic circle is complete. The very existence of a path that can only be trodden with the help of *mêtis* stays neatly hidden from everybody lacking the *mêtis* to recognize it. And of course even Empedocles' clear warning—when describing the human condition so vividly right at the start of his esoteric poem for Pausanias—that lack of *mêtis* is the one crucial factor responsible for keeping us mortals trapped in our aimless and upside-down existences is ignored, turned upside down and back to front.

This is exactly the way things should be.

7

And all we are left with, now, is the madness. For there is no avoiding it any longer—this monster that might turn out not to be such a beast after all.

If the notion of Empedocles following Strife is hard to swallow, the idea of any respectable philosopher placing his trust in "mad" Strife is more or less unthinkable. And unthinkable is what it already was for Plotinus, the man often considered one of the greatest mystics the West has ever known. The better part of two thousand years ago he, too, innocently turned Empedocles' message upside down—misinterpreted him as saying that the soul's original fault was to have fallen from heaven "trusting in mad Strife."

Plotinus may have been a mystic; but he thought he could be a very reasonable mystic. So he fell, along with everyone else, straight into the trap. The mistake is so subtle, so seemingly natural, it just slips off the tongue unnoticed. And it was that much easier to make because Empedocles had been so careful to grease this route of misunderstanding you might, even now, want to swear there are no misunderstandings in sight.

For the truth is that one has to be rather crazy, in the first place, to see what he is doing.

But madness is what we are faced with. And where Plotinus' thinking comes to an end is where we have to begin. In fact he would have done much better here to remember the famous theme already made popular by his teacher, Plato: that there are two basic kinds of madness. One is the pathological madness we are fairly familiar with. And yet there is also a divine kind that has the ability to pull us out from our routine world of habit and bring us close to the gods.

Plato himself, with his love for order, went on to try tidily subdividing this divine madness into various types. But the underlying point we need to bear in mind is that madness for Plato is as ambiguous as Strife was for Empedocles.

They both have two apparently different faces. They are both able to make us less than human, or much more. And if madness can drag people into the humiliating depths of insanity it also, as Plato makes very clear, has the unique ability to purify—to ferret out with the unfailing insight of a prophet whatever has been hidden away behind the scenes, to bring freedom and final release from the most ancient of impurities.

This emphasis on purity and prophecy has such an uncanny similarity to Empedocles' own ideas that we should hardly be surprised when it turns out he too, in a lost part of his poetry, said there is more than one kind of madness. A medical author, writing in Latin, has helpfully summed up for us what they are.

"One kind is caused by the purification of the soul. The other is the result of mental alienation and has a physical cause, namely imbalance."

But if this brief report has often been looked at and commented on by scholars, what has not been noticed is the logic that lies behind it.

The second case, physical imbalance, is of course the work of Strife. This is what happens when the perfectly harmonious mixture of the blood, so lovingly created for humans by Aphrodite, is upset and the mental equilibrium disturbed. But the first case, which the medical writer is careful to explain lies outside his domain, is when the soul becomes purified: freed from its contamination.

And release of the soul from what has been polluting it for ages is also, as we have seen, the work of Strife.

The one factor that makes this report about Empedocles' two kinds of madness so intelligent, so entirely logical and consistent, is the way they both are the result of the same influence. Strife causes the first; Strife causes the second. And now we can start to understand why Empedocles attaches such crucial importance to the act of "trusting in mad Strife."

Madness, just like Strife itself, can make things much worse through its imbalance. Or it can make them far better. It has the power to throw us to heaven or to hell. It can add to all the existing contamination by drawing us into mindless anger, bloodshed, vicious circles of violence.

But it can purify us, too. It can loosen Love's forced balance; restore us, with a little apparent effort, to our natural state free from the slightest effort.

Strife is absolutely destructive. We can either use it, or be used by it. It has the power to dismember us: tear us apart. And yet this is where we have to bear in mind that, not only for shamans but also for the types of mystics and magicians whom we know Empedocles had close contacts with, dismemberment happened to be a recognized form of initiation—of dying while still alive.

And at the heart of shamanic traditions is the idea that, if controlled, madness can not only heal but also give access to another world. The greatest evil, the most disruptive of forces, serves the greatest good when used right.

But madness is still madness.

Few things could be more dangerously deceptive than to talk about madness in terms of a "good" or "right" kind as opposed to a bad or wrong one. For what we end up doing is rationalizing something that lies beyond reason and our normal understanding; pasteurizing it; presenting it in some safe, attractive package.

Madness is a tremendous power, and to keep one's focus in the eye of the storm also requires tremendous power.

To try controlling it with our thinking minds is hopeless because something far deeper is needed: a trust and sense of direction that only come from the soul. One light brush with insanity is enough to smash every neatness to pieces. It crashes through our objectivities and common sense as if they were made of paper.

Madness is to know what it means not to have been born and never to have been born, to watch the stars turn to dust and attach no significance to this whatsoever. Clinical insanity is simply the inability to hold the purity of such a state: is to walk through the gallery of thousands of years and, without realizing you are all the things you see, make the mistake of identifying with some dark corner of existence.

For madness is not only insanity. It's also what brings release from all our little sanities—and gives sorcerers the freedom they need to do the impossible.

It's what calls to us, crying out for us to come home. And it's what takes us home, at last.

Madness is a strangely restless creature. It finds no satisfaction in the activities that keep sane people contented, searches for jewels through the garbage they throw out, chases after flowers where the ground is all withered with drought.

And the difference between the two types of madness mentioned by Empedocles is that one of them never finds what it looks for.

The other does.

Plotinus' very reasonable misinterpretation is, quite clearly, the end of the road for any real understanding of those famous words by Empedocles about trusting in mad Strife. The prospects that some genuine idea of what Empedocles himself had once meant would ever emerge out of it stand at zero.

But this is to make no allowance for the seemingly impossible.

Most scholars recoil with horror at the sight of what happened when early Greek philosophical traditions started drifting into the Islamic world. To be sure, occasional details were preserved. You can also find some faithful translations. But this is where old misunderstandings began giving way to new ones thanks to all the problems in transmitting ideas from one language and culture to another.

And yet sometimes wonderful seeds spring up from nowhere, suddenly shooting out of what had seemed nothing but desert.

Plotinus' own writings resurfaced in an Arabic version. Partly this was a result of literally translating the Greek. Partly it was a free rewriting that often owed as much to Gnostic and Hermetic ideas as it did to anything in Plotinus. At one moment the translator manages to pay close attention to the text in front of him. But then he wanders far away before pulling himself back again.

And when he arrives at that point where Plotinus inverted Empedocles' comment about "mad" Strife—making it contribute to the soul's fall instead of its salvation—you can see how sometimes two wrongs do make a right.

For, in just the same way that Plotinus had turned what Empedocles said about madness upside down, his own translator now does the same to him. All of a sudden he is presenting us with a graphic portrait of Empedocles, himself, that has no correspondence in Plotinus:

"When he came down to this world he came as a help to those souls whose minds have become contaminated and mixed. And he became like a madman—calling out to people at the top of his voice and urging them to reject this world and what is in it and go back to their own original, sublime and noble realm."

In an instant the whole landscape has been transformed. Instead of madness as something to correct or overcome we are confronted with Empedocles, the inspired madman, calling to people from the streets and rooftops to remind them that this is not their true home.

And he comes as a "help": a fascinating little word because it already had such a specific, very technical sense. In Gnostic and Hermetic circles it had been a term used for centuries when describing the great prophets of each age who come as messengers to remind people about the reality they have left behind and point them back to it again. And soon, in Sufi circles, "help" would become a standard way of referring to the Pole—

the supreme guide and spiritual teacher in any time, the shaikh of shaikhs around whom the whole of existence revolves.

Then there is that telling little detail about Empedocles coming like a madman to help those whose minds have become "contaminated," "mixed." For we know from his own poetry who was responsible for this state of forgetting and confusion: Aphrodite, the queen of mixture.

And as to how such a simple understanding of Empedocles managed to survive after so much had been done to obliterate it, the answer is just as simple. While philosophers in the West crucified his prophetic teaching on the cross of an imagined rationality, something else was silently transmitted down to Egypt and from there into the Islamic world.

This was the knowledge that his teaching was alive, needed to be lived.

Among Arab alchemical circles in the ninth or tenth centuries we hear of "Empedocles groups." Then, during the late tenth century, a Persian writer mentions the members of an esoteric religious circle who took Empedocles for their supreme guide: "They regard themselves as followers of his wisdom and hold him superior to all others, claiming he has enigmatic allusions which can very rarely be understood." We have already seen enough examples of these "enigmatic allusions," of his hints and riddles, secret messages, coded language.

And in the Persian world an unbroken tradition, extending down through the centuries to modern times, viewed Empedocles as one of the greatest spiritual teachers or true shaikhs who had ever lived.

Often these people had very strange ideas about the exact details of Empedocles' historical teaching. With the type of factual information at their disposal that was bound to be the case. But what is far more extraordinary is how, after fifteen

444

hundred years or more, there were individuals who would still look back to him as someone with the power to guide and help them. This type of thing never happens just by accident; and the reasons why such a strong sense of Empedocles as a spiritual teacher survived for so long are a mystery that will always remain as much a mystery as the teaching itself.

So we are brought back to the same basic point we were brought to by Parmenides' teaching, by the tradition about Zeno being prepared to die for the sake of it, by the ancient reference to "a Parmenidean way of life."

Empedocles' teaching, like Parmenides', was something that had to be lived because it was something with the power to change one's life.

Nowadays this crucial fact has been crushed. Even to mention it is enough to bring the anger and contempt of western experts tumbling down, because they know inside themselves that they have lost the essence. Jealously they hold on to Empedocles, try to convince everyone their ugly duckling is only a duckling. They cling to their patient analysis of details, which on every important issue is invariably wrong, and fail to see that these ancient teachings were real; were intended to be real; and, most significant, that there is no possible way of understanding them unless one is prepared to live them out.

For the truth is that unless they are lived they are like seeds without any soil. They will never grow into anything.

9

Human nature always wants to know just where it stands: what is right, what is wrong, what is good or bad. But the moment we come face to face with madness even the hope of finding any final assurance is blown away.

First, in Empedocles' teaching, comes the apparent certainty that Love is good. And yet when we peel away the outer layer of its skin we discover this is wrong. Then comes the seemingly more certain knowledge that Love is not good.

But that, too, has to go.

To embrace Love as good is bad enough: is to be taken in by a magical power of illusion. To reject it as bad is even worse, though. For while to run away from Strife is to run from ourselves, to try running from Love is simply to add to its power and end up making its illusions all the more real.

The normal reaction on realizing one has been trapped is just to search for some way, any way, to escape. But Empedocles is no normal person. He is a magician; and magicians lose their power if they run away. He knows very well there is only one real method for getting free. This is to observe your capturer's habits and techniques, to study them in the greatest detail and then turn what you have learned to your own advantage at the appropriate moment.

So, just as he has to use Strife if he is going to avoid being used by it, Empedocles also has to know how to use Love.

And this is where he leaves every philosopher standing, unable not only to follow him but even to see where he went.

Historians in the West have always tended either to turn a blind eye to the problem of why he made Love and Strife the basis for his teaching—or to offer the lamest of excuses for him instead. If they were only to accept he is a sorcerer, not some abstract thinker, they would understand the reason straight away.

The dual forces of love and hostility, attraction and rejection, union and separation, binding and releasing were the fundamental principles underlying Greek magic through the whole course of its history. Knowledge of them was considered indispensable for any successful magical operations. And the whole point of this knowledge is that every coin has two sides.

To know how to free, you have to know how to bind. If you want to break a spell you have to be able to make one.

A few stories of Empedocles' magical exploits used to make the rounds in the ancient world: tales about saving people from sickness or plague that it can seem hard nowadays to take seriously. But sometimes they tell us more about him than all the learned Greek philosophers put together.

Among these stories are accounts of him using binding magic, in particular. And that makes complete sense. For he was well aware that, to get by in a universe where Love still has a grip, we have to use Love's tricks.

To break all bonds, leave every illusion behind, fly off into the freedom of total madness: you might have thought this is the end of the story for Empedocles. And of course you would be wrong.

Trusting in Strife, mad Strife, should hopefully lead to the knowledge of what lies beyond death. But then the knowledge of that reality has to be brought back into this fragile world of illusions.

For Empedocles' teaching is, after all, something that has to be lived. After experiencing death while still alive you have to bring that understanding back into life, or what people call life.

For any shaman, initiation through dismemberment is not an end in itself. On the contrary, it's no more than a prelude to the ritual act of putting back together the body's scattered parts so as to be able to function again in this world of the living. And in just the same way Empedocles, who knew as well as anyone what it is to be free of the body, became a healer of the body—a master of balance as well as imbalance, of the extraordinary but also of the mundane.

First, madness has to be experienced; then controlled. And to do this is to discover all kinds of sanities, of ways for operating skillfully in the world.

Empedocles explained how when the elements are perfectly blended in different parts of the human body they create effective speakers, or manual workers. And to understand such a principle is to know how to become effective in many kinds of ways. For the ability to control madness is also the power to control sanity: to adapt to different forms of normality as required.

To be controlled by insanity is to be feeble. To be controlled by sanity is to be even feebler. But when you have become so mad you are prepared to leave the purity of your madness behind then the memory of it, preserved in every cell of your body, will stop you ever becoming contaminated by sanity.

This is what it means to live in two worlds and not be limited by either; to use Love and Strife instead of being used by them.

And this is the freedom that lies beyond freedom—such a mystery it can never be understood by people who are trapped in sanity or insanity. For they will only see what they are able to see: shapes flitting by in front of their vision. As to where any such shape comes from, or happens to be going, they have no clue because they assume their little field of perception is all that exists.

To go in and out of madness like this is to have the power to play endless magic tricks. And the funniest thing is that those who know the ins and outs of reason, its back doors as well as the front ones, have a far better grasp of it than those who stay trapped inside it for the whole of their lives.

So at a certain point in Empedocles' teaching, just the same as in that teaching given to Parmenides, you have to come back again into the deception—Aphrodite's deception. But the secret is to be able to see this whole world as an illusion and still function in it as if it's real; to seem bound while inwardly staying quite free; to act bewitched like everyone else but, in doing so, to be deceiving rather than deceived; to play the game of performing as a human while scrupulously abiding by Aphrodite's rules.

And she has very precise rules. One of Empedocles' favorite images for describing her *mêtis* was the image of a skillful shipbuilder. The bodies she builds for us are ships: ships we need for crossing this illusory ocean of existence.

On it we have to navigate well, steer straight and true. To smash our ship on the rocks before the journey is over would be to break the most important rule.

10

To get angry with Aphrodite for deceiving us would be child-ish. To be upset with her because she has trapped us is pointless.

Empedocles would be just as likely to reproach her, to level accusations at her, as Parmenides' goddess would. The illusory world manufactured and governed by Aphrodite is an insepa-rable part of reality: there is no rejecting one aspect of reality without rejecting the whole.

So he acknowledges her cunning creation with the respect reserved by one magician for another. To him the main ques-tion was never how to evade her tricks but how best to adapt to them, how to use them to the full.

And we have one supreme example of him adapting to the world she has conjured up. That, of course, is the teaching he left behind in his poetry; the words he so cunningly wove together into verse.

Through them he paints an amazingly intricate picture of her wonderfully intricate creation. He explains in immense detail how the deception works, ignores nothing.

But because this is Love's illusory world, the only way for him to describe it in such detail is by conforming to the illusion.

As for us deceived human beings: he makes the greatest effort to speak in terms we will understand. He communicates on a level we can relate to, uses the kind of normal language acceptable and appropriate for mortals to hear.

If he were able to say directly what he knew he would scare the living daylights out of us. So he gently bends, instead, and adopts the mortal point of view.

But because all we know is how to be deceived, he too has to go on deceiving us. Because this is Love's deceptive world, the only way he can function in it effectively is by using deception.

In other words he has to adapt to the human point of view so as to undeceive us. And yet, through the very fact that he does so, he is bound to deceive us.

He wraps himself in the most natural of ordinary values, accepts our most fundamental concepts and names. At the beginning of his poem for Pausanias he is very careful to warn explicitly about what he is doing: to emphasize that basic human concepts like "life" or "death" are fantasies, illusions, the products of deceived and deluded minds.

But then he goes on to do just what the goddess had already done in the second half of Parmenides' poem.

Suddenly he starts hauling back in all the names and expressions he had gone to such trouble to throw out. And, once the dust has settled, Empedocles is transformed into what we can see and understand—an almost fully functioning human being.

He could never function as a human completely, though. For him to do what authors of stories or dramas find themselves doing, when they are forced to be consistent in acting out the roles of their chosen characters, would be far too restrictive and limiting. Instead, with astonishing agility, he slides silently into and out of identifying with the human condition. Now he is speaking with passionate intensity as a mortal. Then he is explaining in detail what mortals think and believe with the matter-of-factness, the dry objectivity and distance, of someone inwardly quite detached from the views he happens to be mentioning.

Then he is noting things mortals don't know or leaving behind yet another reminder not to be taken in by all this deception.

But throughout the whole of his strange dance, which can never be rationally understood, he is adopting the upside-down standpoint of humanity. He has committed himself to the mortal perspective. Even when he is doing as much as he can to correct it, extend it, he is not able to say openly what he means. He has to keep disguising himself, adjusting, just hinting.

And hint is what he does.

He points to the existence of another life beyond what we call life, another intelligence behind our normal human intelligence, an entire reality waiting for us outside what we consider reality.

He even indicates through the words he uses that there is another harmony, another peacefulness, apart from what we know as peacefulness and harmony; another togetherness and oneness quite different from whatever we think of as oneness, or togetherness; a longing and yearning totally distinct from anything we experience in our normal lives as longing, as yearning.

And, if we care to look, we will be able to see why.

Thanks to Aphrodite's deception, everything in this world is essentially back to front. What to us seems most natural is, to the divine awareness inside us, quite unnatural. If we think we are free, we are being forced. For behind her softness Aphrodite is sheer ruthlessness: the purest violation of our inner nature.

As for Strife, what we perceive as ruthlessness or violence is also the movement of our deepest nature longing to be freed from force and to go home.

But our words, too, are just as opposed to reality as the values they reflect. Empedocles states in no uncertain terms that the names and words we use are utterly deceptive, so there is a certain gentle irony in his choice of the word "Love" to describe the action of Aphrodite. And yet there is an even greater irony in the way everyone takes this name at face value.

For love, to us, is no more likely to be what love is to Empedocles than our yearnings will be his yearnings; our longing his. But, committed as he is to the mortal position, he can say nothing about this.

And even if he could, he would only be polluting something infinitely precious with the contamination of human names and words.

We can never afford to forget that Empedocles' teaching as a whole is nothing but an elaborate trick, an illusion hiding a reality, a superimposition of apparent rationality on a background of sheer madness. Even its seeming sanity is simply madness in disguise. And what he talks about most: this is for our own benefit. What he neglects to mention—that is what matters to him most.

What we refer to with such ease as love is not real love at all, any more than what we call life is really life. But this is the secret that most people, from the time they are born until the moment they die, are so dazed they never know.

11

Empedocles' teaching has always struck people with the crudity of its dualism: Love versus Strife, good against bad. But the crudity of this duality is not really his.

It's ours reflected back to us.

The magic of his teaching makes sure that to begin with, from whichever angle or position we view it, we will feel very confident we know exactly what he is saying. Only after walking quite a way down its hall of mirrors will the cracks start appearing in our self-assurance—as an understanding slowly dawns that this teaching of his is nothing but a trick inside a trick inside a trick.

After the certainty that Love is good and Strife is bad comes the conviction that Love is bad, Strife good. But after this certainty, too, has come and gone we are left with the growing sense that Empedocles is concerned with something far subtler than any fixed identification of either as simply good or bad.

It all comes down to the need to discover, in each single instant, what happens to be good or bad for that particular moment. And only one factor can help us now. This is the razor-sharp awareness, the totally focused sensitivity to the present moment, known to the Greeks as *mêtis*.

And that allows no room even for a moment's complacency.

Strife is blatantly untrustworthy but has to be trusted. Aphrodite's smile is an utter illusion but she has to be smiled at. She is a force of *mêtis*, and so we need *mêtis* to see through her tricks. *Mêtis* is needed if we are going to trust in Strife, and even for us to see that this is what we have to do.

Otherwise they will either trap or destroy us.

The real axis around which Empedocles' teaching revolves is not the polarity of Love and Strife. They are just two flags flapping in the wind.

It's *mêtis*—the single principle running through the universe that we either learn to use or reconcile ourselves to becoming victims of. This is why Empedocles presents it with such emphasis at the start of his esoteric poem; why he makes it feature so prominently not only as the one, crucial factor distinguishing his knowledge from the knowledge of any ordinary human but also as the one fundamental requirement for understanding what he has to teach.

And, needless to say, *mêtis* is as silently meaningful to Parmenides as it is to him. To both of them it embodies all the qualities of subtlety and cunning and alertness that are essential if we want to avoid being caught in a world of endless deceptions. As a matter of fact it lies so close to the core of both their teachings that we could almost say the apparent differences between them are more illusory than real.

But fortunately, or unfortunately, any appreciation for this kind of subtleness has always been kept out of the public eye.

The first people in the West to label Parmenides and Empedocles as thinkers, to start categorizing them according to their dogmatic positions, their supposed opinions on this or that, got to work quite soon after they had died.

They were professional show-offs and entertainers, flagrant exhibitionists and know-alls. But Plato was quick to realize that such slick definitions could be endless sources of amusement and he enjoyed making humorous use of them in the dialogues he wrote.

It was Aristotle, though, who—disarmingly superficial, disastrously influential—converted the playful trivialities into serious statements of doctrine.

And so the foundations had been laid for what would come to be known, with great respect, as the history of western philosophy. Parmenides was defined as a "Monist," meaning he only believed in one single principle that never moves or changes. Empedocles was named a "Pluralist" because, with his Love and Strife and four roots of existence, he believed in a number of separate principles. But to call Parmenides a Monist means either having to ignore what he says about deception in the second half of his poem or having to dismiss it as quite insignificant. And to call Empedocles a Pluralist is to show no awareness of the fact that his teaching, too, is something organic; has a life of its own; keeps constantly changing and growing as we change and grow in understanding.

Above all, though, to imagine we can define him and what he has to offer with some convenient label is to forget that he happens to be a trickster.

To judge from the outside of Empedocles' shop, it looks as if he has all kinds of fruit and vegetables for sale. And when you go in he will show you a fine selection of produce. But let yourself be drawn further inside the store and you will discover he is giving away things infinitely more precious than vegetables.

If you are not able to believe what you see and leave, then come back the next day to check if what you thought you had seen is real, you will find nothing. The shop front will still be there; the advertising sign will be creaking in the breeze. But the inside of the shop will be empty. Everything will have gone.

For Empedocles is a sorcerer. He is not going to wait until a time that suits you. Unless you take advantage of the opportunity while you still have the chance, the moment will have slipped you by.

The reality of his teaching is pure hiddenness. But he manages to keep the hiddenness well hidden. He knows people are easily satisfied and, when you first come to his teaching, he will be glad to serve you with whatever you want.

If you would just like something to analyze and criticize, he will give you that with the simplicity of someone giving a child a piece of fruit or a dog a bone. This is the wonder of a teaching based on pure illusion: that it provides you with whatever you feel you need while making you believe your own understanding is perfectly complete.

And if you are sincere enough that you want something to live by but have little appreciation for subtlety or tricks, he would never dream of offering you more than you are comfortable accepting.

To anyone not able to follow his teaching all the way he will give the most careful instructions on how to honor Love's illusory creation; on how to appreciate its incredible beauties and treasures; on the absolute importance of avoiding bloodshed and doing no harm.

For if you are not yet ready to discover what lies behind your humanity the next best thing, the most important thing, is to become a good human being.

If you are willing to follow this teaching all the way through its spiralling of trickery and deceptions, you will find yourself being brought back at last to one little statement. Seemingly straightforward, its apparent innocence is like the thinnest of coverings over a bottomless abyss.

When Empedocles turns to describe Aphrodite for the benefit of his disciple, he starts by warning him not to sit in some blank stupor or daze. And then he ends his comments about her by urgently insisting: "listen to the undeceptive arrangement of my words."

For a long time scholars have noticed how he is referring back to that one, crucial point in Parmenides' poem where the goddess turns to describe Aphrodite's world and calls on whoever has managed to follow her to listen now "to the deceptive ordering of my words."

The formal contrast between her open admission of deceptiveness there and Empedocles' reassurance, here, of his undeceptiveness is so clear historians of philosophy have not hesitated for a moment to see in his words a direct attack on Parmenides: Parmenides may have dismissed the universe as a sheer deception but Empedocles, a far greater optimist, a wholehearted lover of our world, was convinced it could be explained without a trace of deceptiveness.

And there could be few better examples of how easy it is to be fooled by appearances.

As for Parmenides' goddess, we have already seen how much naivety is needed to avoid noticing the complexity of her statement that she is about to deceive. Through admitting, in all honesty, that she is about to talk deceptively she has produced a brilliant inversion of every ordinary trickster's attempt to deceive by pretending to be honest. The undeceptive deceiver, she is posing a riddle that means we have to believe her but not believe her at the same time.

As for Empedocles, take his comments about being undeceptive out of context and you are certain to feel instantly safe. Such an unqualified assurance can instil boundless feelings of illusory confidence and the deepest sense of trust.

But it also is helpful to consider the realities of the situation.

Empedocles' immediate motive in insisting on such complete attentiveness to his undeceptive words is the fact that he has just invoked the most potent and perilous of magical powers: Aphrodite, queen of deception. This is no time for basking in the sense that we are safe, because we most definitely are not. Empedocles has done nothing but draw the thinnest line of undeceptiveness through the heart of deception—has extended his hand for a moment to help snatch us out from a world of utter illusion.

If we let go of the hand we will be back just where we started. But the joke is that if we take it, allow ourselves to be guided by him, then our real troubles begin. For Empedocles has only one way of leading us out from Aphrodite's labyrinth of deceptions.

This is by tricking us; tricking us beyond belief.

And yet, you may say, we have his assurance that he is not tricking us. For someone who claims not to be deceiving us to be deceiving us is inconceivable.

But that only shows how gullible we have become.

In Empedocles' time, just like Parmenides', people tended to be a little shrewder. Declarations of honesty were not quite so naively embraced. And this is not even to mention what an exceptional case Empedocles is.

As soon as he starts his poem for Pausanias he is already insisting that we need *mêtis* to understand him: more *mêtis* than humans are capable of. And *mêtis* means, above all, experience in the arts of deception. There is no need to look any further than that divine embodiment of *mêtis* who was Apollo's little brother, Hermes—always deceiving, inverting everything by turning it back to front, upside down, inside out, and who brings all his lying tricks to their climax by assuring the gods with a perfectly straight face that

> I will say the truth, to be sure. For I am
> unfailingly truthful and have no notion of how to lie.

Here we have in a nutshell what would become, and remain for thousands of years, the quintessential form of rhetorical trickery: the sheer deceptiveness of pretending to be undeceptive.

And yet this is not the end of the story. For if I were to suggest Empedocles lied in saying he was being undeceptive I would be quite wrong.

Just like Parmenides' goddess, he well knows how to deceive. But, just like her, he only starts the deceiving after warning us very plainly that this is what he is going to do. If we choose to ignore his warnings and wander off again down the labyrinth of illusions, that's not his fault but our own undoing.

It may seem he is deceiving us. And yet this is just as much an illusion as the belief that he is being perfectly straight-forward and true, because he is not tricking us. He never has. We are deceiving ourselves.

But the story has still not come to an end. For to say we are deceiving ourselves is ultimately no more correct than to say we are being deceived by Empedocles, because that "we" is itself just another magnificent illusion created by Aphrodite. These humans we think we happen to be, so carefully pondering the nature of deception, are her most cunning deceptions.

And so it all comes back, for Empedocles as well as for Parmenides, to Aphrodite.

In claiming to be deceptive about her, or undeceptive, they both mean exactly what they say but are also saying the exact opposite of what they mean. What at first looks like a simple case of Empedocles contradicting Parmenides is in fact an example of flawlessly coordinated humor—of total solidarity in the shared understanding that, where Aphrodite and her cosmos are concerned, deceptiveness blurs and merges into honesty.

For this is the way the tradition works. The more Empedocles appears to disagree with Parmenides, the more he really agrees. What seems like polemics is an endless dance of pirouette on pirouette by two people who know that the greatest deception of all is to tell the truth and who laugh with each other in the awareness that the greatest truth is to deceive.

TEN

*And the bones
of the Sophists long ago turned to dust
and what they said turned to dust with them
and the dust was buried under the rubble of
declining Athens through its fall ... buried
so deep and with such ceremoniousness and
such unction and such evil that only a madman
centuries later could discover the clues needed
to uncover them, and see with horror what
had been done*

ROBERT PIRSIG

Possibly one little problem has been bothering you.

If, for Empedocles, each cosmic cycle comes to an end then there is no point in making the effort to do anything. Every contaminated soul will eventually be purified and returned to heaven. Trying to purify oneself, become better or wiser, seems futile: we might as well just sit back and wait. And for Empedocles himself to go to the trouble of being a teacher, acting as a prophet, tricking us so as to try and wake us up, is useless.

In other words, if everything is basically predestined this leaves us with no real free will.

The problem of choice and necessity is an ancient one. Theologians and philosophers have scratched their heads and pulled their hair out over it for ages.

And yet the solution to the problem is utterly simple. We have no free will at all; but we are predetermined to think we do.

The whole question of free will and predestination, of individual choice and necessity, that has eaten into the West for the past two thousand years is sheer vanity. Free will is an illusion. And the illusion of free will is a part of the cosmic necessity.

The only reason why we make any effort is because the effort is preordained. And our only genuine freedom is to cooperate with necessity. Of course that sounds terribly restrictive to us as humans who want to be separate, individual, different from nature: different from everything. But this is because we have already restricted ourselves by wanting to be so many things. For it's only when we realize we are not separate at all that we start to become free.

There is no individual freedom whatsoever at the beginning of each cosmic cycle. We are forced to participate quite unconsciously, altogether against our will. But towards the end of each cycle we are under a cosmic obligation to become conscious. So Empedocles has no choice except to make every effort he can to lure us out of our confusion into some greater awareness.

And we are bound to do whatever we can to become more conscious.

As for that original fault or primordial failing of the soul before the beginning of creation in letting itself be polluted: this was nothing it could avoid. In fact ancient Greeks were very familiar with the notion, so paradoxical nowadays to us, that our faults and failings are actually caused by the gods.

But the important thing to understand is that even if the blame for what once happened or happens now is not really ours, we still have to take full responsibility for our illusory failings and suffer all their illusory consequences in this world of total deception.

All our apparent choices have been made for us. And yet we are still obliged to go through the routine, the charade, of seeming to make them. Everything is decided for us—even whether to go on reading this book or not, whether to move our arms, object or agree, get up or stay sitting, think about next week.

Even the longing to become free, to grow in awareness, be more conscious, is predetermined by our inner nature; is our own divine self drawing us to itself. And to become one at last with that inner nature is to realize everything is bound by absolute laws.

Then we are free: free from the illusion of having to choose, free simply to be ourselves.

But when every soul is dragged out of heaven once more at the beginning of a new cycle, as it most definitely will be, the illusion will start all over again.

2

And with no choice there seems no point.

The belief that our decisions can make some difference is the greater part of what makes life feel worth living. Not much could be worse than for every attempt to learn, discover freedom, grow more conscious, to come to nothing as another cosmic cycle drags us back down into unconsciousness.

One fall from the divine world might sound like a tragedy. A single return could look like a challenge. But to keep having to go down and up, down and up, cycle after cycle, becomes rather tiresome after a while. It means that every illusory effort of ours to become free is only the prelude to being trapped all over again.

Nothing could be more pointless.

There is a cosmic law, though, which states that whenever you come to the point of total pointlessness some other point is always lying behind it. When purposefulness gives way to futility, a greater reality is just outside of view.

And Empedocles indicates, quite clearly, what lies beyond this pointlessness. In fact he goes to the trouble of mentioning it more than once: even the few scattered fragments from his poetry that still happen to survive show him repeating exactly the same words for special emphasis.

But what he says is so paradoxical, so contradictory of everything else he appears to say, that no one knows what to make of it. And as is bound to be the case with something so precious, so essential, it stays almost completely neglected.

He already points it out when presenting for the very first time his central idea of a cosmic cycle that keeps shuttling all things in existence, without exception, unceasingly backwards and forwards.

They keep changing and changing without break
or end, never stopping: now all coming together
through Love to be one, then each of them being carried
away again and left separate by Strife's hate. So to the
extent that they are familiar with becoming one out of
many, then become many all over again when the
oneness grows apart, to this extent they come into being
and have no lasting existence. And yet, to the extent that
they keep on interchanging and exchanging places
without break or end, to this extent they always are
motionless throughout the cycle.

Right in the middle of introducing his principle of endless motion, Empedocles suddenly mentions total motionlessness. As soon as he starts describing the phenomenon of constant change, he almost defiantly points to a state quite free of any change.

Something could seem, to say the least, rather wrong here. And yet nothing is wrong, except for the failure to understand that Empedocles' reference to motionlessness is not a matter of theory or rigid doctrine.

It's a matter of perception.

When we are absorbed by everything happening all around us and excited with so many changes taking place in front of our eyes—the unions and separations, gains and losses, lives and deaths, the tragedies and redemptions, illusions and breaking free, the yearning for adventure followed by the longing to go home—there is always movement.

But when we start to glimpse the endless repetition behind our restless thirsting and questing for change, this is to catch sight of the motionlessness at the heart of all motion. For what can be so hard to appreciate is that motionlessness is not some different reality, some other level of existence, separate from the world of motion.

On the contrary: the more we try to discover stillness by leaving movement behind, the more movement we end up creating through the very act of running away from motion.

And, just as Parmenides knew that the easiest way to experience the stillness seemingly denied by this world of the senses is by using our senses to the full, so Empedocles knew how to look for it in the place we would least expect to find it.

To observe life with complete awareness is to see that, once movement has repeated itself long enough, the motion turns to motionlessness. Through accepting movement totally, not just partially, we discover nothing but total stillness.

Then there is nothing to go after any more, and nothing to avoid. You will never believe anyone who tells you incarnation in this world of illusory beauties is good—because you have experienced the terrible, agonizing call of the soul longing to be free.

But you also know that the return of the soul to freedom is just as transitory; just as illusory.

And, ultimately, it makes no difference at all if you are up or down. For in reality nothing matters. We simply are where we are. And as a part of the illusion we keep on doing what we have to do.

We go through the apparent motions of making unreal choices and decisions, being glad or disappointed, seeming to prefer this to that or that to this.

But inwardly it's all over. The drama has no substance.

To find that stillness means neither being drawn into the illusions nor trying to escape them. It means that, even when trapped, we are free.

And even while apparently incarnated we know what it is, at any moment, not to be incarnated. For we are not only where we are.

We are exactly where we always will be.

3

This tradition is an endless source of surprises.

Parmenides begins with total stillness and then slips into movement. Zeno starts with movement and, without ever leaving it, dissolves it. Empedocles, too, makes movement the starting point and cornerstone of his whole teaching—only to touch repeatedly, in passing, on the utter motionlessness behind it.

Everything about this tradition is subtlety. It slides as smoothly from one position into another as a snake, shedding its skin so many times you can find yourself wondering which is the skin and which is the snake.

But behind the sliding is always the stillness.

All this slipping between position and position has nothing to do with intellectual uncertainty or compromise. Parmenides and Zeno and Empedocles are not some philosophical fence-straddlers, trying to claim there could be a theoretical justification for adopting contradictory doctrines at the same time.

On the contrary: if you look closely at what they teach and at the way they teach it, slipping into and out of regions that to us are so familiar, you will realize their agility in shifting between one standpoint and another is just as significant as any of the standpoints themselves.

For to notice this subtle, persistent movement is to be watching their magic—is to see them casting their spell in a world of illusion, deceiving in a realm of deception.

The agility itself is what counts. And as Empedocles slides from this kind of statement into that, from what seems obvious to what lies behind, his teaching not only becomes more and more elusive.

It in fact undoes itself; unfolds; slowly unravels until nothing is left behind.

It can seem so solid, to begin with. Go on reasoning about it and you can be sure it will stay that way, because you are keeping it solid with your own thoughts. But live with it if you dare and after a while, when you try to touch it, it will have vanished.

He starts by bending towards us. This is for our benefit, though, not his.

His entire teaching is for our sake: an act of patient accommodation. If we are not careful we will think it simply represents his beliefs. And yet through what he says he is reaching out to our beliefs because he wants to draw us into something that, with our back-to-front ideas, we would find unbelievable if he tried to state it directly.

Here—in this process of first reaching out to us only to withdraw again, retreat, gradually disappear—is his magic charm for undoing the magic we are trapped by.

There used to be a clear awareness in Empedocles' time that ordinary human words are as weak and ineffective as humans themselves. But people also appreciated that there is another type of words: words whose origin is magical or divine.

And those words were understood as having a power all of their own, exactly like the potential of seeds. They are not just the simple bondings of sounds or letters they seem to be but natural realities in their own right that live, that have the magic ability to sprout and grow.

This is why any attempt to pin down Empedocles' teaching in terms of fixed principles, neatly to define it in terms of specific doctrines or dogmatic positions, is so futile. You can categorize a seed in any number of ways, even sterilize it with the help of modern technology if you want. But the mystery of a seed is that, left to itself, it will turn into something quite different from what it started out as—into a shoot, a stalk, a plant, a tree.

And as Empedocles' own teaching grows, and grows, it not only keeps being transformed into something subtler. It also leaves behind everything it was. A seed doesn't stay a seed, for our convenience, while it grows into a tree.

In the process of growth it will be destroyed.

This is why what he has to say is, really, not so much a teaching as the taking away of any teaching; the constant contradicting of what we thought was certain; the continuous undermining and destroying of whatever had come before; a completely natural process of unlearning all the things we believed we had learned until we are left with nothing but the naked reality of ourselves as we always have been, as we always will be.

And yet Empedocles' teaching grows into a tree unlike any tree you are familiar with. The larger it gets the less easily it can be seen, because it grows not in illusion but in reality.

In other words from our ordinary, mortal point of view it grows into nothing. It simply disappears.

So you can either walk away with the few pieces of fruit you came for, wondering what on earth all the fuss has been about. Or, if you are very lucky, you can disappear with it.

Either way, you will not find it anywhere in this illusory world of constant change and deception. But, if you ever manage to look up and see what became of it, you may be able to catch sight of the universe hanging in its branches.

4

And there is something else that has to be said.

The line running from Parmenides' teaching through Empedocles' didn't stop there. In fact we are told how it was continued; through whom. But no one either cares, or dares, to uncover what this really implies.

Ancient writers quite often mention in passing that Empedocles had a successor. To quote the words of one author who neatly summed up the situation as a whole: "Parmenides was the teacher of Empedocles who was the teacher of Gorgias."

And such a statement, if anyone ever comes across it nowadays, will be politely smiled at; then put aside. For, if treated with the seriousness it deserves, it has the power to destroy everything we take most seriously.

Both Gorgias and Empedocles were from Sicily. Nothing could be easier than to understand how one could have come into contact with and been influenced by the other. But that's not the problem.

The trouble is there is no room for this little line in the world as we know it.

Even in our history books, our carefully scripted mythologies of rationality, no place has been left for it because it goes where on all accounts nothing should. This one single line cuts a swathe right through the middle of what have become the most deeply entrenched assumptions.

That it should run from Parmenides, a "Monist," to the "Pluralist" Empedocles is bad enough; but that it should run from them to Gorgias is far worse. At least Parmenides and Empedocles were both philosophers. And yet Gorgias has come to be considered something very different from any philosopher.

He used to be known as a sophist. In fact he was sometimes even referred to as the father of sophists. And however much individual scholars might try to shift or redefine the dividing line between sophists and philosophers, the division still stands.

Philosophy is supposed always to have been a very solemn occupation. The sophists, on the other hand, have become famous for their verbal trickeries; for their "playful intellectual diversions" which seemed to make a mockery of every serious philosopher.

Of course to maintain this basic distinction means having to claim that Parmenides in particular, the father of logical philosophy, was the perfect antithesis of playfulness—is to have to stay oblivious to the goddess' constant joking, her endless amusement in making fun of humans.

And what makes the situation with Parmenides funnier still is that we are so self-righteous we never manage to hear her delightful laughter, never even notice her mocking jokes.

Philosophy is traditionally held to be a matter of careful reasoning and responsible argument. The sophists, on the other hand, have become notorious for appealing not to the force of reasoned argument but to something quite different: the sheer, emotional power of persuasion.

And yet to maintain this particular distinction means having to ignore the fact that Parmenides' goddess tells us in advance she will be following the path of persuasion to carry us to reality—and then goes on to demonstrate with overwhelming clarity just what she means when she starts persuading us, through her extraordinary logic, to accept conclusions which from every reasonable point of view could hardly be more absurd.

The danger is that any line running from Parmenides through to some sophist, not to mention someone who could be called the father of sophists, threatens to expose what a total illusion our fixed concepts of philosophy and rationality really are.

Gorgias, player of games, expert in persuasion, is said to have lived well past the hundred-year mark. Even so, his senses and alertness are described as staying perfectly fresh until the day he died. One story goes that, when asked how he lived so long with all his faculties intact, he explained this was because he never accepted invitations to dinner or got caught up in the round of social conventions.

It would be hard to imagine a more austerely straight-forward human being.

And yet to follow the line leading from Parmenides and Empedocles to such an apparently simple man is to discover the links holding together what for ages has been forced apart; to enter a place of total freedom where every sane consideration is thrown to the winds as the links that hold together our elaborate world of illusion fall apart.

For everything in this tradition is craziness. As Aristotle noted, Parmenides' account of reality is "close to madness"; and what the goddess then goes on to say about this world of deception only takes us closer. Empedocles talked, in a way no sensible person would even be aware of, about the need to follow mad Strife. Centuries later Arabs perceived him, with clear insight, as a madman making the craziest of announcements at the top of his voice.

And in a sense Gorgias is perhaps even crazier than either of them. For he, too, belongs to this line of impeccable madness at the roots of western culture which our sanity tries so hard to make us forget.

But the one regret, the lingering pain and sadness, is that due to force of circumstances this tradition with its freedom and joy should have been kept hidden from people in the West for so long.

5

Gorgias went to Athens and took the city by storm.

The Athenians were great lovers of words, clever talk. He gave them what they wanted. But they had never heard anything like this.

He made a point of appearing in front of audiences without preparing any set talk or topic. Instead, he would let the audience itself dictate the subjects he would discuss. As for himself, he simply trusted in the situation. He "surrendered to the moment."

"The moment," or *kairos* as it used to be called in Greek, was something very dear to his heart. He is said to have been the first person who ever wrote about it as a subject in its own right—even though, quite characteristically, he never attempted to define it.

And he taught nothing.

He laughed at anyone who tried to imply that he or anyone else had anything particular to teach to anyone. He himself had no definable wisdom to offer; no body of knowledge; nothing specific or precise. And as for why he adopted such a position of no position, the reasons he gave are still very clear.

He explained that people as a rule live in a world totally dominated by deception: *apatê*. They have no real desire for truth and, even if they did, would never be able to tell it apart from pure fiction. So that leaves only one way to influence or affect them.

This is not by trying to teach them some truth but by knowing how to persuade. For Gorgias explained how the spoken word, *logos*, is a magical power—a power of sheer deception that can make anything, however illusory, seem true. And the job of any speaker, any teacher, is to use that magic; is to trick and deceive.

Philosophers from Plato down to the present day have listened to these statements with a mixture of horror and disbelief. They point out, time and time again, that in describing words as a power of deception Gorgias appears to have missed something absolutely fundamental.

He has left out the crucial role played by *logos* in reasoned argument and discussion: its ability to carry us beyond the realms of mere persuasiveness into a world of certain, fixed, undeceptive reality.

But Gorgias has missed nothing out at all. For our rationality, our proud belief in the ability to argue our way to the truth, is an essential part of the deception.

Apart from a fictional dialogue that Plato wrote about Parmenides, known as the *Parmenides*, he also wrote one called *Gorgias*. Or to be more precise, these works of his were not so much dialogues as meticulously crafted mimes: deft caricatures of the characters involved that made them little more than puppets in Plato's hands. But, as fictions, they proved so persuasive and deceptively effective that along with Aristotle's writings they helped create the basis for our present intellectual order.

And this was just what was needed, is exactly what during the past two thousand years has been called for, to help give people's growing minds something solid and tangible to hold on to. The trouble is that we have no idea any more of how much heartache it has caused.

Plato was quite right when he implied through his fictitious mimes that there is some reality beyond the deception all around us. In fact to impress the existence of such a reality on people's minds was a part of his job. And yet the mistake he made, the necessary mistake, was to suggest that we can think our way towards it; can find it through argument and reason.

For we never can, because reality is hidden at any moment in the recesses of illusion—waiting everywhere to jump out at us as everything, far too subtle to be fixed or weighed or defined through any reasoning.

There used to be a story about Gorgias. Perhaps it's absolutely true or maybe it's not. It tells how he eventually read Plato's *Gorgias* for himself but, instead of getting angry or being upset, just said to the people around him: "What a fine satirist Plato is!"

After all, this kind of thing is only to be expected in a world of deception.

6

Aristotle provided a convenient definition of the sophists.

He called them speakers whose wisdom, unlike the wisdom of philosophers, is apparent rather than real—although there is a little uncertainty as to whether Aristotle was someone who would really have known how to tell the difference.

But, even so, what he said is helpful in drawing attention to how well at home sophists seemed to be in this world of appearances.

While most philosophers were tiring their brains out trying to quantify and define, working out theoretical reasons and justifications for everything as life slipped them by, someone like Gorgias was far more firmly rooted in the practicalities of everyday existence. And the importance he attached to *kairos* or "the moment" already says a great deal about what kind of man he was.

The quality of attentiveness that leads to trusting in the moment, being sensitive to it, alert to its needs, so focused in the present one knows without any hesitation what attitude is appropriate at any instant: this respect for *kairos* was, to Greeks, the trademark of someone who is an expert in *mêtis*.

A very closely related aspect of *mêtis* was the ability to keep adapting to different people or surroundings, keep adopting new faces in a world of endless deception, changing in harmony with the rhythms of constant change. In fact a beautiful little passage written by someone who had known Gorgias very well just so happens to present, as the archetype of the wise speaker, Homer's hero Odysseus—the master of *mêtis* and cunning "who knew how to be together with people in many different ways."

And this is the one side to the behavior of sophists Plato was most disturbed by. It was what lay behind something that to him seemed beneath contempt: their practice of pretending to teach while really doing little more than reflecting people's own moral values and ignorance back to them.

Time and time again he would attack them for their utter spinelessness, their only too obvious lack of any true ethics, in acting as mirrors to publicly held opinions and then having the nerve to call that wisdom.

Nobody could read the points he makes without being fully persuaded that Plato has every legitimate reason, every conceivable philosophical and moral justification, for what he says. You would have to be out of your mind even to suspect that something has been left out of the picture; that perhaps there is a little more to the situation than meets the eye.

Very eloquently Plato compares sophists to someone who starts studying the habits of a great beast, learning what it likes and what makes it angry, gentle or wild, how to approach it, how to touch it, "all the various sounds it tends to produce in reaction to different kinds of stimulus." Then the sophist goes on to turn the knowledge gained through careful study of that animal called public opinion into a systematic teaching and—instead of describing what genuinely is right as right or good as good or whatever is bad as bad—"uses all these terms in exact conformity with the beliefs of the great beast, describing as 'good' what makes the beast feel happy and calling 'evil' whatever makes it sad."

And the rightness of Plato's comparison, the perfect appropriateness of his attack on those who mimic such an ignorant creature, is crystal clear.

Or at least it is until you remember Empedocles. For there is an uncanny resemblance between Plato's vivid image of the great beast and Empedocles' quite conscious decision to imitate the beliefs of people in general, conform to their values, call what they like good and whatever upsets them evil.

There are sure to be those who will say that of course no real connection exists between what Empedocles did and things done by someone like Gorgias, his supposed disciple and successor; who will insist on it being pure coincidence that ancient tradition traced the origins of rhetoric, or the art of effective speaking cultivated by the sophists, back not only to Sicily but to Empedocles in particular. And, of course, they would be fully justified in doing so.

But the trouble is that we left every "of course" behind a long while ago. Our proud "of courses" are just what ensured that Empedocles, through his supremely simple act of mirroring, would trick us all. They are what made even the brightest of philosophers fall straight into his trap.

One thing we can be certain of, though, is that Empedocles' imitation of the great beast was infinitely more meaningful than anything Plato suggests or allows for. And there is also something else we can be sure of.

This is that *kairos*, the art of yielding to the needs of the present moment, involved far more for Gorgias himself than simply adapting to the level of the people he was addressing; mirroring their expectations; reflecting their crudities back to them. In fact he had a perfect reason for refusing to define *kairos*, which is that it's far too elusive ever to be defined.

Anything you think it is, it may well be in the moment you are thinking. But it won't be in the next. This is the kind of reality we are dealing with. And if *kairos* for Gorgias meant adapting to people, going along with them, it could also mean the exact opposite when the time demanded.

Essentially the situation was much the same for him as it was for Empedocles, whose real knowledge lay in the ability to use both Love and Strife when needed at the appropriate moment. During the twelfth century a Persian writer from Khorasan in Central Asia noted, with a strange accuracy no one would expect to find, that Empedocles could only do the work he had to do because he knew how to apply either or both of his two principles at precisely the right time. For everything has its place, serves its purpose; and sometimes people can only be taught with the help of love, kindness, gentle words.

But sometimes, as this Persian writer went on to explain how Empedocles worked, the teacher has to be ruthless and cut like a sword.

You will find no such statement about Empedocles or his teaching anywhere in the entire Greek philosophical tradition. This is not too surprising because Persian mystics, in their appreciation for the ever-changing subtleties of the moment, were a great deal closer to the sophists than most philosophers ever have been.

And, just like Empedocles, Gorgias knew that there are times when one has no choice but to cut and destroy.

By Gorgias' time people were already ruining Parmenides' teaching with their minds.

Parmenides himself had made the situation as plain as he could. His poem was a sacred text; a path to the stillness that lies beyond the grasp of our restless, wandering minds. But the trouble is that these minds are so deceptive they will do whatever they can to prevent anyone accepting a gift from the gods.

He had offered a chariot for travelling into another world. The response of philosophers has been to dismantle it and smash it, jealous that anyone would want to get away.

What they did was to begin reasoning with Parmenides, trying to improve what he said, criticizing him for not making better sense; adjusting his logic to make it more palatable, more pleasing, more persuasive. Rather than allow it to perform its real purpose, which is to initiate the devastating process of changing us, they took the other route of changing it. In other words they did what always happens when the mind gets hold of something. They brought it down to their level: made it their own.

And Gorgias had already had enough.

A master of concealing wisdom behind what seems like tedious nonsense, he was fed up with so much tedious nonsense masquerading as wisdom. And in this line, so infinitely mysterious no one nowadays would even want to allow such a tradition could exist, he did something that for a long time people have realized he was doing—although without understanding why on earth he did it.

He took Parmenides' teaching and totally destroyed it.

Parmenides had argued that everything is, and that whatever you perceive or recognize or talk about has to exist simply because you perceive or recognize or discuss it. Gorgias argued, following the same logical principles, that nothing exists and that even if something did exist no one would be able to perceive or recognize it; and that even if it did exist and could be perceived or recognized, nobody would be able to say a word about it to anyone else.

Through his own words he was communicating the impossibility of communicating anything. And, in doing so, he turned the whole of Parmenides' teaching upside down.

That teaching had led to absolute fullness. Gorgias' led to absolute emptiness. He took away the everything offered by Parmenides only to replace it with sheer nothingness.

And the most important aspect of all this, which it can be so easy to miss, is that Gorgias makes no attempt whatsoever to refine or correct Parmenides' logic by producing something more reasonable. He is not trying to be realistically modest or cautious; to act as a mediator on behalf of common sense. On the contrary, he is being just as radical as Parmenides himself—and he reaches the same ultimate conclusion that our complicated world of existence and non-existence, of change and movement, is utterly illogical and completely unreal.

His reply to Parmenides is so clean it leaves nothing behind: no residue, no trace of any sticky compromise. He is so effective in undermining his position that, in the last resort, Parmenides' position and his own become the same. In either case the world as we know it is demolished and whatever we cling to so desperately, whatever we identify with so intelligently, is destroyed.

The paradox is that, by cancelling out Parmenides' teaching with such rigorous thoroughness, he ended up staying perfectly true to it.

And this is a very real paradox. For even though Parmenides was the father of western logic, what he himself taught had to be destroyed. Because he allowed no room for our wandering minds to operate, it was far too real; far too still. Westerners had a great adventure ahead of them that required they forget all about stillness—for a while.

But Gorgias' act of destruction was altogether different from Plato's murder of Parmenides. Both were needed, although for quite separate reasons.

Plato had to destroy the purity of Parmenides' teaching so as to keep this world of compromise intact. Gorgias had to keep the purity of the teaching intact by destroying the compromises. Plato's action was essential from the point of view of this world we live in but relatively unimportant from the perspective of the tradition Parmenides belonged to. Gorgias' action was essential from the point of view of the tradition, but relatively unimportant from the point of view of the world we live in.

And this is why scholars have made so little real effort to understand it. Inevitably they fall back on asking if Gorgias was being serious or playful with his strange display of logical virtuosity, without realizing how feeble such a question is.

For Gorgias came from a tradition of jokers. And yet the humor of Parmenides, or Empedocles, is far more than just playful.

Their laughter is more serious than all our trivial solemnities put together. Their jokes are only a reflection of what to them is the joke of the human condition; and the aim of their humor is to demolish our imaginary seriousnesses until a much greater seriousness is left.

As to Gorgias himself, any doubt about whether he is being serious or not appears more than a little naive when we consider a certain statement he is said to have made.

Destroy seriousness with laughter, laughter with seriousness.

The point he is making is very simple.

Just like Empedocles with his twin principles of Love and Strife, we have to be able to master laughter as well as seriousness while not identifying with either. And to do this is to be free—not only from taking anything seriously but even from not taking it seriously.

Then playfulness is no longer just playfulness, or seriousness only a matter of being serious. Instead, they are being used alike in the service of that indefinable something which lies behind them both.

8

Gorgias was not given to making sweeping statements outside of some quite specific context.

His style was more subtle and deceptively light-hearted than that. He would tend to address an individual topic that presented itself in the moment and make comments that corresponded to the situation, sliding into and out of focusing on particular issues with the same agility used by Parmenides or Zeno or Empedocles in sliding into and out of movement.

It was left to the listener to take such passing comments and apply them to the next moment—or the next.

One of them has been recorded as an observation he happened to make on the process of producing, and watching, a Greek tragedy. It reads like this:

Whoever deceives is more just than whoever does not deceive and whoever is deceived is wiser than whoever is not deceived.

Adding anything to such a perfectly rounded statement can seem pointless. And yet the situation calls for a few words.

Scholars have often tried to treat this remark by Gorgias as only having a bearing on the power of ancient drama: nothing else. But to isolate and insulate it like that is to show no appreciation for his method of communicating, his elusiveness, his disciplined open-endedness.

Even more, though, it means having to avoid the unavoidable fact that his statement here about deception is inseparable from what he says about deception elsewhere—portraying it as an absolutely fundamental principle which affects every aspect of human speech and thought and understanding, as the power responsible in one way or another for bewitching us all.

Then there is the matter of his exact wording when he refers to whoever deceives as "more just." Interpreters have done what they could to make it fit the immediate context; to twist and squeeze it until it applies to the theater and nothing else. But nothing works.

They mistranslate "more just" as "more articulate" or "more highly skilled at playing the literary game," as "more normal" or "more justly appreciated." And yet this is just nonsense and games-playing. For behind Gorgias' statement lies much more than art theory or literary criticism.

In fact he is touching on two issues that, to any reasonably sophisticated Greek, had the most profound and far-reaching significance. One is practical intelligence or wisdom. The other is the question of justice or rightness. And through this statement he is offering what could almost be described as a working definition of them both—in terms of that single principle, so fundamental for Gorgias, called deception or *apatê*.

But you can see at once how deceptive his words are. For in spite of their apparent preciseness they are so slippery and paradoxical, so much the reverse of what one would expect, that they offer the very opposite of a definition.

Instead, they are a riddle to ponder and keep pondering. Far from fixing or tying anything down, they open everything up. And what they point to is unlimited freedom.

Simply to be taken in by deception is ignorance. But to search for some reality behind deception and try leaving the deception behind: this is ignorance, too. It's also a violation of rightness, a perversion of justice.

And here, picked up by Gorgias so elegantly, presented by him so discreetly, is the thread that runs all the way through Parmenides' and Empedocles' teaching. From the moment when the Daughters of the Sun who are guiding Parmenides use deceptive words to trick their way past Justice, through the time when the great goddess who is teaching Parmenides tells him she is about to talk deceptively, to the point where Empedocles announces he is going to communicate with humans using the language which is right for them even though this will mean having to deceive them, the line Gorgias belongs to is one continuous affair of outright deception intertwining with rightness and justice.

Deception, to these people, is wisdom's ornament and truth's halo. Nobody, however foolish or wise, has the slightest chance of escaping it. For according to this tradition there is no ascending to the truth. There is only a descending, a constant bending to embrace illusion as well as truth through learning the justice of deceiving and—behind even that—the wisdom of being deceived.

From any ordinary point of view, to be deceived seems stupid. But even this is an illusion, because something exquisitely valuable lies hidden in the process of deception that has to be experienced to be believed.

The point behind what these people are saying and demonstrating with such persistence, in such infinitely subtle ways, is that illusion is ingrained in reality. This is why, for Parmenides, existence is in bonds; is why the goddess adds a second half to his poem. It's why Empedocles, as a god, adapts himself to humans and automatically deceives everybody without even having to deceive.

Everything, in this tradition, is a part of that one single pattern. And when we see the pattern, give way to the deception, we are free. For all that really binds us is our illusory ideas of what it is to be free.

To see the pattern means, to be sure, not just being taken in by the deception any more. Nothing could be more crucial. But it also means not having to struggle towards some imaginary reality apart from the deception, because to try not to be deceived is far more foolish than to be deceived.

Talk about truth and you lose sight of it. Understand illusion and you will find the truth right in the middle of it. Create great philosophical schemes about reality and you fall straight into deception. Appreciate the power of deception and you come face to face with reality. Run away from deception, try to avoid it, and you are deceived.

But embrace it and you have reality itself. For, ultimately, the only protection against deception is to surrender to it.

By wholeheartedly allowing ourselves to be deceived we are no longer deceived. And then we are just like actors.

All we have to remember is that life, real life, expects us to act very well.

The thread of *apatê*, and *apatê*, and *apatê* running right through this tradition is so continuous that it seems impossible anyone would fail to notice it.

But because it's as deceptive as deception itself, as subtle as the gentlest laughter, nobody does. The first step in understanding anything at all is not to underestimate it. And the fact is that there can be no tying down such a line of tricksters and deceivers.

Because they are tricksters, their involvement with deception is not going to be neatly confined to any specific comments about deception they might choose to make. On the contrary: they are always playing with our deepest assumptions regardless of what they say, running rings around them, doing what we least expect. And of course we do the best we can not to watch them do it.

But although there is no tying down this line of deception, there is no way to escape being tied down by it.

So thin it can hardly be seen, so important no one has wanted to see it, we are all held in its invisible grip. Its invisibility has been the cause of its power just as its power has been the cause of its invisibility. And yet the more we go on ignoring it, the tighter its grip will become—like a noose around our dancing minds.

This thread stretches back to the origins of the world as we know it, is what wraps our future and past together, is what happened to give rise in its invisible ways to our familiar forms of thinking. And now we need to adjust our eyes so we can make it visible again.

For our restless minds have had their fun. They have gone through their curve of learning. The next dance will be for those who are willing to discover what it means to move in total stillness.

We can look to the East if we want for the sense of meaning and direction lost in the West. But to find freedom there from the turmoil of the West, its intelligent chaos, is ultimately only to end up more bound.

Trying to escape from our own civilization can offer no real solution. What now is needed more than anything else is to penetrate to the roots of this western world and release the wisdom that has been waiting there for so long.

Gorgias was not just playing some lighthearted game when he turned Parmenides' logic back on itself and unsaid everything the goddess had said about reality. That was only the most visible part of what he did: was no more than symbolic of the fact that he had to destroy this tradition, and all it represented, with what can seem a brutal finality.

He swept up each trace of the meticulous work and effort that had gone into creating it and threw everything away. To us, even the idea of performing such an action can sound mad. But, to be quite honest, up until then the tradition had not exactly been a model of conventional sobriety.

And Gorgias had the most perfect reason for doing what he did.

There are traditions that visibly maintain a presence in this world of illusion. Inherited by successor after successor, passed down from one generation to another, they are constantly available. But apart from their major virtues of accessibility and continuity, they also have a tendency to run into trouble. The more visible they are, the more tired they can sometimes become: rusted, corrupted, weighed down by the burden of their own past.

And the extraordinary thing is we really believe these visible traditions are the only ones that exist. For we base everything so much on illusion, on all the shifting mirages in this world of change, that we don't realize reality is never bound by what we assume we see or know.

There are visible lines and invisible ones. Some traditions have the function of rooting themselves in this familiar world and providing a certain continuity and guidance. But there are others that always stay completely rooted in another world.

They lack the visibility of a continuous tradition. And yet they have another type of continuity, another kind of power altogether different from anything we are used to. They appear, then disappear. They manifest in periods and in places where a particular understanding of timelessness is called for; where a certain quality of need, of deep dissatisfaction, means a time for renewal has come.

And because they are not burdened by any visible past they stay pure in a way our minds can never appreciate. As they weave their way freely into and out of this existence they operate on a level beyond both time and the reach of our senses where everything, including East and West and all illusory traditions, is one.

When Gorgias destroyed the line he belonged to, he really destroyed nothing except for an illusion. And he destroyed it in such a conscious way that he made sure it would always be available to come back, as paradoxical as ever, when needed: timely and yet timeless, visible but also invisible, ordinary as well as utterly extraordinary.

First it seeds itself and then grows—only to destroy itself in harmony with the seasons and the cycles of time. But, just as with nature, the very fact that it destroys itself means there will never be a time when it is not about to return to bring a new sense of life back again.

ELEVEN

See: out went the sower to sow

<small>GOSPEL OF MATTHEW</small>

We have talked about this tradition and around it: said what had to be said. And now there is nothing left to do except to give it.

It will make you a god—which is not too surprising considering how, regardless of our beliefs, we are gods already. Even so, that may be just a little more than you expected. We are all very happy receiving a pearl or two of wisdom, but not the treasury. We tend to love being presented with fascinating new ideas but not with something that takes every idea away only to present us, in exchange, with our immortal selves as they always have been; always will be.

And so I have left this strange gift of what has no place, no time, no beginning or end, until last.

But before it can change hands there is one thing we need to do. We have to go back right to the start of Empedocles' esoteric poem—back all the way to that initial point where he has just faced Pausanias with the full horror and impotence of the human condition.

Here is where the real mystery in his teaching, the mystery underlying all the other mysteries, begins. But the beauty of the teaching is that unless you have the humility to recognize yourself from his portrait as being one of those appallingly helpless human beings, living a life which is no life, without the slightest shred of any true *mêtis* or genuine awareness, with all your "palms" of perception closed up, you will not even be humble enough to notice what is being given.

And neither will you ever grasp the significance of the fact that here Empedocles appeals to a goddess to help him.

You may remember how he explains to Pausanias that the unconsciousness of ordinary human existence is so total most people will never be able to

see or
hear or consciously grasp the things I have to teach.
But as for you:
because you have come aside here, you will learn.

And then comes the point where, to initiate his disciple's learning process, Empedocles does something that was far too important for me just to mention it casually in passing. He invokes the help of a Muse.

That he, a god, should need assistance may seem strange. One thing we have to understand, though, is that in this world of illusion gods need help as much as anyone.

For a god to be free, divinely mad, is easy. But to act appropriately and responsibly in a world of apparent sanity: that requires a particular kind of help.

And so he calls the Muse to him. He asks her to speak fittingly and properly on his behalf, to start by saying the kind of things that mortals are used to hearing—but, far from stopping there or holding back, to keep on going and take the human listener who follows what she says all the way to the furthest reaches of wisdom.

Then, once he has outlined to her in his inimitably enigmatic style just how he would like her to cooperate, he can stand back and allow her to take over.

The first half of his plan is complete.

2

Empedocles' preparatory work for his great poem of initiation falls into two halves that perfectly balance each other; are quite symmetrical. The first involves explaining to his divine helper, the Muse, exactly what he needs from her in the way of co-operation.

The second involves explaining to Pausanias precisely what he needs in the way of cooperation from him, his human disciple. And this is what he says.

> *Come now: watch with every palm how*
> *each single thing becomes apparent. Don't hold*
> *anything you see as any more of an assurance*
> *than whatever you hear, or give those loud*
> *sounds you happen to be hearing preference*
> *over the sharp tastes on your tongue. And don't*
> *reject the assurance provided by any other limb*
> *that offers some passage for perception, but*
> *perceive how each single thing becomes apparent.*

You are likely to listen to these words and say there is no mystery here, not even the shadow of one. On the contrary: Empedocles has come out at last into the clear light of day and is talking about what you or I or anyone else happens to be utterly familiar with, our very ordinary world of the senses.

And yet there is nothing ordinary here at all.

Historians of philosophy have always been insistent that the only thing he is expecting Pausanias to do here is to trust and accept the evidence of his own senses; nothing more. And certainly it's quite true that the question of whether we can trust what our senses tell us was to become a favorite topic for debate among intellectuals during the centuries after Empedocles.

But we should try to bear in mind that to Empedocles himself, for whom the whole of reality is riddled with deceptiveness through and through, such a theoretical question as whether or not we can believe the things we perceive would have appeared more than a little naive. And soon we will start to see what he really does mean when he tells Pausanias to accept the assurances offered by his senses.

First, though, there is something particular we need to notice about his language in these lines.

Twice he comments on the ability of Pausanias' senses to provide some form of "assurance." The Greek word he uses here is *pistis*, which would come to mean different things to different people—trust to philosophers, faith to Christians. And yet we can't afford to forget that, in Empedocles' own time, it still had some very strong and specific connotations.

It referred then, above all, to the particular kind of pact or agreement entered into by two parties who need to establish a sense of mutual cooperation and trust. There was nothing unusual about one of the parties being a divinity while the other was a human. And, in such a context of shared trust and cooperation, the word *pistis* played an important role.

Most often it tended to be used for indicating the type of assurances exchanged or offered, the various pledges and tokens of good faith. To receive *pistis* meant to accept an assurance or a pledge; to reject *pistis* meant to refuse a guarantee, a tangible symbol of commitment. And Empedocles' own use of the word in formulating these instructions for Pausanias suggests he is not simply telling him to believe the different kinds of evidence provided by his various "palms" or "limbs."

He is urging him to accept them as pledges of good faith; is warning him not to reject the assurances and guarantees they will be providing.

And this could hardly be more relevant to the situation Empedocles has been working to bring about.

His purpose in first addressing the Muse and then turning to address Pausanias has been to establish a functional relationship between them: to act as an intermediary who with all the persuasiveness at his disposal calls the two parties together only to encourage them both not to hold back. The Muse's role is to be the teacher and guide. Pausanias' job is to learn and follow. And in such a situation—where Pausanias is being expected to surrender without reserve, to obey implicitly and absolutely regardless of what he is told—nothing could be more natural than for the Muse to have to provide him with some assurance of her trustworthiness.

In other words, through his opening instructions Empedocles is already offering the subtlest of hints that whatever Pausanias happens to see or hear or taste or feel will be an assurance of this teaching's reliability.

All his sense perceptions will be pledges from the Muse.

That could sound rather strange. But the simple fact is that everything Empedocles has to say, regardless of how familiar it might seem at first sight, is going to be strange for us.

And in time its meaning will become clear.

3

There is one crucial point to note about Empedocles' instructions for Pausanias. This is that the things he tells him to do are things we never do ourselves.

As a matter of fact, they are altogether beyond our experience.

People can live what to any external observer would seem the fullest of lives without touching, even once, the state Empedocles is pointing to. And this is because we spend all our lives fast asleep in a dream.

His first instruction to Pausanias is not to perceive but to perceive that he is perceiving—to watch the perceptive process itself. In other words he is telling him not just to look or touch or hear but to look and touch while fully conscious of looking and touching, to hear with the awareness that he is hearing.

And anyone who starts to do this seriously will begin to become aware that what passes for ordinary human existence is nothing but a dream.

You may find it easy, right now, to notice for a split second the objects in front of your eyes while also noticing that you are noticing them; to become aware for the briefest moment of all the sounds or silence in the background. Probably it will seem so easy you will wander away, quite contented because now you know there is no mystery here for you.

And you will be back again in the dream.

This state of awareness is the trickiest of things because it never extends beyond the present moment. The reason why Empedocles instructs his disciple about it, presents it to him as such a very specific practice, is because it doesn't do itself. It isn't automatic but only lasts for as long as you stay conscious.

The moment you become fascinated by something you perceive, you will be dragged off by your nose into a seemingly external world of spiralling shapes and colors. The moment you wander off after some fascinating thought inside your head you will be left with unseeing eyes, staring blankly into space all over again, deaf to the gentle sounds around you. And this is how we pass our lives, silently tugged backwards and forwards from one state to the other: always lost, except perhaps in the most fleeting moment, to ourselves.

For Empedocles, exactly as for Parmenides, one of the most extraordinary facts about human existence is that people appear to be such creatures of the senses and yet never use their senses at all.

They are just used by them—bashed around by them, buffeted here and there. And the worst aspect of this situation is the way we manage to believe, like blind people so blind they think they are not blind, that we can see the whole.

But so far we have hardly even touched the surface of what Empedocles in these few words is telling Pausanias to do.

If he were instructing him not only to look but to become aware at the same time of looking, that would be important enough. He is not, though. He is explaining to him that as well as being aware of whatever he is seeing he also has to be aware of every single thing he is hearing; touching; tasting; feeling.

Nothing is to be left out. Not the slightest preference is to be shown to one sense as opposed to any other. And this choiceless, all-embracing awareness can only happen in one particular moment: right now. For if you miss anything now you are missing everything. You are asleep again.

Even to think about what you are doing is to lose that awareness, because in the moment of thinking you have already left the present moment.

The demand for such complete, uncompromising attention is so unreasonable that it seems only sensible to tone down what Empedocles is saying; to want to make him demand less than he really is demanding.

But Empedocles is, to say the least, not the most reasonable of teachers. And while the practice he has just outlined is far more strenuous than our wandering minds can ever manage, there is that other faculty he has already mentioned by name which at any or every moment is perfectly up to the task—the sleepless alertness, always present by its very nature, called *mêtis*.

Few things could seem to demand more effort than the process of getting used to this awareness. But nothing is more effortless than the awareness itself. And what had looked impossible to begin with becomes easier with time because even though each moment of awareness is only an awareness in the one moment, *mêtis* is like an organism that actually nourishes itself. Or, as Empedocles explains in a single line quoted from his poetry by later philosophers who sensed it must mean something but were rather too busy thinking to see what:

For humans, mêtis *grows in relation to what is present.*

This phrase of his, "in relation to what is present," happened to be a common one. It was used very often for describing how somebody acquainted with the ins and outs of *kairos*, with the art of responding effectively to the needs of the present moment, would plan and act. And that, of course, is essential to what *mêtis* is.

But here is where we find ourselves being brought right back to the heart of that tradition which Empedocles, along with Parmenides, belonged to.

For both of them, accumulating enough *mêtis* to become an effective human being was no more than the smallest of beginnings. Any *mêtis* that comes to an end when the ship arrives in port or a chariot race is won hardly deserves the name at all. To them, its value lay not in helping them live human life to the maximum. Instead, what made it crucial was its capacity to carry them beyond human existence altogether.

Nothing could be more paradoxical than this tradition they both belonged to. It taught that, to become free from illusion, all we need to do is accept illusion wholeheartedly. To find what lies behind movement all we have to do is embrace it completely.

And, in just the same way, to go beyond this world of the senses all we have to do is use our senses to the full. For to open up our "palms," those instruments of *mêtis*, and perceive everything with total alertness right now is to open the way to a world of stillness quite unknown to our restless minds—is to become aware of the common factor linking each sense together, motionless, featureless, placeless and timeless, which is the consciousness we are.

4

Everything has its own appropriate name. And there is one expression that fits, to perfection, this extraordinary state of awareness Empedocles has in mind.

I am talking about common sense.

So casual, so deceptively familiar, this innocent little formula has the most ancient and respectable of pedigrees. *Sensus communis* in Latin, *koinê aisthêsis* in Greek, it stretches back more than two thousand years into our past.

And to tell its story in full, as it deserves to be told, could take almost as long all over again. For the history of this one single expression contains in miniature the entire history of the western world.

All our learning is here, all our knowledge. And so is all our foolishness.

For Empedocles the discovery of common sense—of that consciousness which is able to hear and see and touch and feel and taste at the same time—was a matter of direct experience. And to experience it was to start waking up from the chaotic dream of human existence into another state of awareness.

But this awareness was and still is so rare, so utterly demanding of everything we are, so incomprehensible to people in general because so far beyond the reach of our wandering minds, that the only way to have access to it is through the guidance of a teacher who has left the human condition behind.

The human mind is a wonderful instrument, designed to help us operate in a world of total deception. But that also means its power to deceive has no bounds, and one thing it will never do is leave alone what lies outside its domain.

Instead, it will automatically distort any reality it touches; convert it into something else. And this is just what happened with common sense.

To Aristotle, around a hundred years after Empedocles, the question of what it is that coordinates our senses had become an intriguing theoretical problem: one he honestly thought he could answer by thinking it through with his rational mind. But the crucial point he failed to grasp is that the faculty of reasoning he placed his trust in, that he personally did so much to develop and cultivate, is a power of infinite trickery.

And his greatest self-deception was to convince himself that what he didn't possess was already his.

For Empedocles, the training in how to perceive oneself perceiving was provided as part of an esoteric transmission from teacher to disciple. But to Aristotle any such instruction was unnecessary for a very simple reason. He confidently assumed this awareness is something we humans already have.

To quote the words he himself liked to use: "Whoever sees perceives that he sees and whoever hears is aware that he is hearing and whoever walks is aware that he walks. And similarly with whatever else we do, there is something that perceives us functioning. So whenever we perceive, we perceive that we are perceiving; and whenever we think we are aware of thinking."

Few things could sound more reasonable—and, factually, be more untrue. For, apart perhaps from in the briefest of moments which comes and goes as fast as lightning, we may be aware of what we are thinking or perceiving but never of the act of thinking or perceiving.

We only think we are. All we do is let our minds create the elaborate fiction that we are; and then this reassuring illusion helps to immerse us for a little while longer in our dream.

So the awareness of a common sense was suddenly not special any more. It was nothing to strive for because everyone supposedly already had it even though nobody did. And after Aristotle the rest of the process was as inevitable as the course of a ball bouncing step after step down a set of stairs.

Soon the expression "common sense" no longer even had any recognizable philosophical meaning. It drifted, instead, into becoming the commonest of trivialities like a scrap of paper pirouetting in the wind.

What had once been an extraordinary meditation technique was now something perfectly ordinary: so much so that every reasonable person possesses it without, of course, being able to tell quite what it is.

One more gateway to the divine had been blocked off and made into yet another dead end. A device that had been designed to wake people up had become converted into an instrument for sending them even deeper asleep.

And so you may be able to glimpse what no amount of words could do enough to convey—that everything in this world of humans has been stolen from the gods.

Just as Parmenides' divine logic was corrupted by being turned into reason, Empedocles' common sense was corrupted from the rarest experience of divine awareness and turned into something so familiar we no longer even care what it is.

If the original power and magical reality of what had been stolen were kept intact, that would not be so bad. But they never are. Everything is turned inside out and upside down, hollowed out and emptied of its meaning.

All we are left with are substitutes, and then substitutes of substitutes, which become the only substance we end up being able to live off.

We are like queens and kings who have to beg for our food only to find ourselves eventually eating nothing but paper. No one can go on surviving like this for long, though, however hard we all try to dull the pain of knowing inside ourselves that something is missing and however well we manage to reason with the humiliation of having to live without it.

But that's not the end of the story. For the avenues to re-discovering what has been forgotten, what has gone missing, are always open.

Strangely enough it never is too late to retrace our way back again, through the ruins of our own past, into the timeless present.

5

There can be no real question as to how the practice in awareness outlined by Empedocles ought to be done. The only way
to do it is to do it.

Any queries or answers are nothing but an obstacle, a way
to avoid doing it right now.

And yet there is one important question that has to be
asked about it, sooner or later. This is the question of how it
relates to Empedocles' teaching as a whole. For if his only aim
had been to make Pausanias become aware of everything he
is experiencing through his senses, he might just as well have
given those opening instructions and then ended the poem right
there—where it began.

But he doesn't. And to discover why he doesn't is what we
now need to do.

As for how we should do so, nothing could be simpler. We
just have to keep patiently watching and attentively waiting; to
put aside all our doubts and inner questions for the time being
and do the modest little things we are asked to do, step by step,
instead. For this teaching takes shape, as we have already seen
clearly enough, according to its own strange rules and rhythm.

It manifests in its own good time: will work its way inside
us and finally show itself not when we think we are ready, but
when it knows we are.

As the first step in this mysterious process, there is one
particular passage we have to look at and begin to understand.
In fact it contains a basic map of Empedocles' teaching; a plainly
annotated diagram of how it works. But the intelligence of

most people in the West has become so dulled by centuries of abstract thinking that they look at it nowadays and see nothing, recognize nothing, feel nothing.

The passage consists of lines from his poetry that were only made public for the first time in 1851. Before then they had been hidden away in the manuscript copy of an ancient Christian text that was kept on the holy mountain of Mount Athos—until a Greek who happened to be visiting the mountain came across the manuscript and carried it off to France.

And yet, for all the good these lines have done since then in helping scholars appreciate the true nature of Empedocles' teaching, that Greek might just as well have left the manuscript inside the monastery where he found it.

This extraordinary passage offers specific instructions to Pausanias on how to receive Empedocles' words: on what he has to do to make the teaching they contain effective. And here is what Empedocles says about his own words.

If you press them down
underneath your dense-packed diaphragm
and oversee them with good will and with
pure attention to the work, they will all
without the slightest exception stay with you
for as long as you live. And, from them,
you will come to possess many other things.
For they grow, each according to its
own inner disposition, in whatever way their
nature dictates.
But if you reach out instead after
other kinds of things—after the ten thousand
worthless things that exist among humans,

blunting their cares—then you can be sure
they will only too gladly leave you with the
circling of time, longing to return to their
own dear kind. For you need to know that
everything has intelligence and a share
of awareness.

If you catch the meaning of these words you will never be able to hear or read anything again in the same way as before. The situation is as simple, and as real, as that. For to understand them is to enter a world where words are no longer simply words; where teachings either blossom into life or, as a direct result of your attitude, fade away and vanish; and where you can never hope to learn anything unless what you want to learn decides to teach itself to you.

They are confronting us at last with the magic that pervades every line of Empedocles' poetry, every breath of his work— the magic of words themselves which have an intelligent life all of their own and the natural capacity, if treated rightly, to grow.

But before we start to follow where these statements of his about the power of the word are leading us, one rather elementary observation needs to be made.

This is that when Empedocles describes his own words as having to be treated with considerable care by whoever receives them, and as being able in certain favorable circumstances to grow, he is referring to what would soon become a very ordinary and quite trivial theme among the Greeks: the theme of words as seeds and of education as a kind of agriculture involving both teacher and learner alike.

As we have already started to discover, though, there happens to be a reality behind this formal equation of word with seed which is far removed from anything that could even remotely be considered commonplace or trivial.

And as for the particular process Empedocles is drawing attention to through these words of his, nothing could be more out of the ordinary.

6

To Empedocles there is just one alternative to magic. That alternative is magic.

Any distinction between some extraordinary magical realm and our ordinary, mundane, conventional world is purely illusory. For apart from the kind of magic, so very rare, that can free us and give us back the purity of consciousness which is rightfully ours there is another kind as well.

This is the magic that throws its spell into each and every corner of existence and through its bewitching power turns what happens to be utterly extraordinary into something just as utterly banal.

That initial piece of guidance offered by Empedocles on how to receive his words—"If you press them down underneath your dense-packed diaphragm"—could hardly be more specific, or practical. But you are not very likely to find it translated the same way anywhere else.

What you will find are versions that are far less out of the ordinary. In fact the most popular translation nowadays is "If you push them deep down in your crowded thinking organs." And this, of course, is all that most of us are familiar with: crowded thoughts along with the futile prospect of a few more short years devoted to making them even more crowded.

But it has nothing to do with what Empedocles is saying.

He is pointing to the exact opposite, which is the extraordinary process of leaving all those thoughts about ten thousand things behind. And although the ancient Greek language is beautifully flexible, it can only be bent so far. The modern ways of translating these particular words are linguistic impossibilities; the clumsiest transformations of something special into something banal.

What Pausanias is being told is to press down the words he hears below, underneath, his *prapides*. This word *prapides* was used to describe the area of the human body corresponding to what, in our language, is called the diaphragm and lungs. It could also be used for referring to a certain quality of intelligence or awareness which was viewed as being centered there: in the breathing apparatus. And so when Empedocles insists that his words need to be pushed down "underneath" the *prapides*, he plainly has a very physical location in mind.

Pausanias has to press the words he hears down below the compact muscle of the diaphragm—deep inside his abdomen.

And if he follows these instructions he will find himself in a rather interesting dual situation. Outwardly he needs to watch and listen and use all his senses at once with the maximum of alertness. Inwardly he needs to breathe in the words of his teacher and bury them deep inside his own entrails like seeds.

But of course the thing about seeds once they have been buried is that, to begin with, they are quite invisible. You are not even able to know they are there.

In other words there is nothing except for the sense world outside and the invisible germs within.

Nothing, though, is as miraculous as the power of a seed to grow. And we have to understand that Empedocles' teaching can never be a question of quantity, of trying to cram more and more words inside ourselves. On the contrary, to concern yourself with getting more than you have and to worry about what you imagine might be missing is futile; is to end up reaching out in insecurity like almost everyone else for the ten thousand worthless things.

These words of his are extremely powerful. And you have more than you could ever need. Out of a tiny seed something huge can grow. Out of a single phrase if treated well can come a plant, a whole tree. But one of the greatest mysteries here—inside this supreme mystery Empedocles is gradually allowing to take shape—is the unbelievable difficulty we can experience in doing something as simple as taking possession of what we have been given.

For we are so used to things coming and going that we always want more: are always reaching out to snatch at something else.

The one thing we need to grasp now, to try to learn, is that there is nothing left to grasp or learn. All we need has already been given and lies quietly inside us. This particular gift is the gift of a lifetime. And there will be no separation, no loss, unless you are careless enough to let it go.

It will never leave you if you want it. It will stay. But one point Empedocles makes absolutely clear is that we have to look after it, tend it. As a matter of fact we need to attend to it all the time, not just in bursts or episodes.

And even the smallest details of the language he uses reveal, if you care to pay attention to them, the kind of tending which is needed.

His choice of word when telling Pausanias to "oversee" his teachings once he has pressed them down under his own diaphragm happens to be a term only ever used by the great early poets such as Homer, or Hesiod, for describing one very specific process: the activity of overseeing the planting of seeds and the tending of crops. And again the single word he uses, *melete*, when instructing him to give his purest "attention to the work" was a term traditionally associated with the constant attention devoted by farmers to their work.

In short, the activity of pressing down Empedocles' words underneath the diaphragm corresponds to the action of a planter pressing down seeds underneath the surface of the earth. To do what he says is to become farmers of his teaching inside ourselves.

When the sun comes up, regardless of however fair or bad the weather, of whatever we have to do in the ever-shifting world of our senses, all the time we do this invisible work inside ourselves.

When the stars come out, the work goes on. For all our cares are focused on whether this quiet work is going well; on whether everything is being done that ought to be done without leaving out even the smallest detail.

And we have no conscious understanding of what we are doing because this work goes on below the level of our consciousness, where we labor in silence without any hands or legs or even any thoughts to help us.

The seeds need watering, but with a different type of water. They need sun, but a different kind of sun. And yet this work is carried out not in some supercelestial, ideal realm but in a place invisible to us only because we have lost the humility needed to stoop down low enough to reach it—a place that happens to be the origin of our existence, the source of all our experiencing and feeling as human beings, the roots of our entire sense-perceived world.

7

There is no end to the things that could be said about Empedocles' words about his own words. And yet there are only a few that should be said.

As for the rest: you will be able to discover them, by yourself, in your own good time.

Regarding those things that should be said, one has to do with the other great poet—apart from Homer—who influenced Empedocles' style and use of language more than anyone else.

His name was Hesiod. And commentators are very familiar nowadays with the fondness shown by Empedocles for deliberately evoking Hesiod's words; for imitating them and echoing them as a subtle way of adding extra levels of meaning to the things he said.

Mysteriously enough, though, there is one dimension to this influence which has been missed.

Hesiod wrote a famous poem about farming. And one of its most constant themes is that to work the earth is sacred, is a deeply religious activity. Above all it happens to be sacred to Zeus, father of the gods; it has to be done in complete obedience to Zeus' laws.

This has more than a little significance as far as Empedocles is concerned. For not only in those few lines where he explains how his words need to be received but also throughout his instructions to Pausanias he keeps echoing particular expressions and turns of phrase from Hesiod's agricultural poem. In fact the echoes are so persistent one could easily suppose he is preparing his disciple for life as a farmer.

But there is more to the matter than that. For we can now start to see why, in this particular passage about how to look after Empedocles' words, references to Zeus keep cropping up with extraordinary frequency. Empedocles assures Pausanias that if he does the work outlined for him he will come to possess, *ktêseai*, many other things in good time. He promises him that his words have the power to give increase and growth, *auxei*. One of Zeus' ritual titles was *Ktêsios*. Another was *Auxêtês*, "Giver of growth."

He was also known as *Plousios*, "Giver of wealth"; as *Geôrgos* and *Karpodotês*, "Farmer" and "Giver of Fruits." And just as significant is Empedocles' way of telling Pausanias to oversee, *epopteuein*, the planting of his words with pure, *katharos*, attention to the work. For two other titles of Zeus were *Epoptês* or *Epopsios*, "Overseer," and *Katharsios*: "Purifier."

There is nothing coincidental about this cluster of hinting references. To Empedocles, Zeus was a uniquely important god. When he identifies each of his four primordial "roots" or elements with a divinity, Zeus is the one he allows to represent *aithêr*—the element of our own immortality and pure divinity, the substance of our soul.

And this will help you understand something essential about the nature, the magic, of Empedocles' words.

All words have a magical power of their own. But the nature of their magic varies, because they carry the quality of consciousness of whoever uses them. The millions of spoken or written words released aimlessly and unconsciously into the atmosphere at every moment are a massive tidal wave sweeping through the collective awareness of humanity, devastating everything in its path, wiping away any glimpse of reality, destroying the germs of true understanding before they even have the chance to take root and grow.

And yet there are some words that act in a very different way because the substance they are made of is completely pure. Of course this sounds sheer nonsense to us. All we are used to understanding is what words refer to, not what they are. And in just the same way that we are always chasing off after some meaning outside of ourselves, our words are as lost as we are— wandering around in search of something to refer to, looking for something they can mean.

But even though the words spoken by certain people may appear to refer to this or that, like any other words, really they refer to nothing.

In fact they will have a far greater depth of meaning than other people's words. But even that meaning is an illusion because, in essence, these particular words are far too simple and powerful to mean anything. They need no reference outside of themselves. They mean what they are; are what they mean.

And the only way to receive such words is just as Empedocles describes. If they are not welcomed and treated properly they will shake the dust off their feet and leave. Try to rationalize or explain them away and you have already lost them. Try to argue with them and they will disappear. Even try to think about them and that means you have not breathed them deep enough inside yourself.

For the only place to work with these words, which are made from the substance of pure divinity and are messengers from our own true home, is at the borderline where consciousness meets unconsciousness deep inside ourselves. There is simply no other place they are able to grow except down there, in what seems to us to be sheer darkness.

And as Empedocles hints in his usual subtle way, by caring for these words we are doing something extraordinarily significant. We are becoming the farmers of our immortality.

8

To follow Empedocles' instructions means not to run off any more after other things but just to keep on doing this invisible, silent, humble work. And nothing could be more important because, as becomes clearer with time, to do it is in fact to be nurturing the origins not only of our own but of all existence.

The nature of the work is so humble we are left without even any eyes, let alone feet or fingers, to help us. And it's so invisible even the most learned scholars have never noticed any of Empedocles' subtle references to farming or seeds— which are like clusters of stars that go unseen in the light of day only to shine everywhere when the sun has set.

But they have noticed something else.

This is that in the passage where Empedocles talks about how to receive his words he is very deliberately invoking the language of initiation. Repeatedly they point out that his use of the word "oversee," right alongside his insistence on Pausanias' attention to the work being "pure," can be no coincidence because both these words used to be key terms in the ancient mysteries.

And this is perfectly true. Purification or *katharmos* was the traditional first stage in the mysteries, followed by *paradosis* or transmission of the mystery teaching itself. Only then, after the transmission had taken place, came the stage of *epopteia*: of overseeing. And although the different stages could be elaborated in greater detail so as to include a final one, "sharing the company of the gods," the crucial one around which everything else revolves was *epopteia*.

Purification was the very earliest phase; the stage of preparing the ground. Without pure hands and intentions no one can even start to receive what is pure. It means getting oneself ready, not only clearing out impurities and the results of wrong living in the past but also realizing that there is more to come: that one has hardly even begun to discover what life in all its fullness is.

Then comes transmission of the initiatory teaching. But the fact is that this is no more an end in itself than the preliminary, purificatory stage. And here is the reason why that teaching transmitted by Empedocles to Pausanias in the form of a poem includes, tucked away inside it, detailed instructions on how to use it; on what to do with it. For the real purpose of being given an initiatory teaching was to be brought by it to the stage of overseeing where, as we are told by ancient authors in no uncertain terms, "there is nothing left to learn."

And there is nothing left to learn not because you know everything but, on the contrary, because you can at last afford to relax and know nothing—in the quiet knowledge that whatever needs to be known will make itself known to you at the appropriate moment. There is nothing left to learn, nothing else to go after any more, because the mind goes quite silent and still in the awe of realizing it will never be able to understand even the tiniest fraction of what has just been given.

In short: scholars have noted something of infinite significance by pointing out that through his choice of words Empedocles is establishing a close connection between his teaching for Pausanias and the teachings of the mysteries.

But here, too, they have overlooked one fundamental detail. For long before Christianity, with its parables, the most important symbols in the ancient mysteries had to do with the growth of seeds and grain.

And it just so happens that this symbolism of nature and growth came most dramatically into play at the very same stage of initiation to which Empedocles is now bringing Pausanias: the stage of "overseeing" or *epopteia*.

It can be a bewildering experience—to lack nothing, to contain everything you will ever need inside yourself. And, because you are not able to see yet what has been given, it can be only too easy to fall back into the same old patterns of reaching out for more and more. But this is the whole point behind Empedocles' warnings to Pausanias. He is telling him that all he has to be careful of is not to become like some foolish farmer who wastes valuable time fantasizing about what doesn't concern him, envying other people for their possessions, hankering after the property of his neighbors.

And all he has to do is focus on the work already cut out for him.

He appears to be surrounded by a world of the senses that most people imagine they are at home in even though they drift around in it quite unconsciously. And he has to do what, from any ordinary human point of view, is impossible: to become aware with all his senses simultaneously, constantly, consciously.

He holds, inside himself, the germs of a teaching that most people have not even the slightest desire or use for. And he has to do what from any normal human point of view is absurd: to care for things he is unable to see or hear or touch.

In every possible direction he is being pushed to, then beyond, the limits of human experience. And in the face of these absurdly impossible demands it could seem he is being expected to make a superhuman effort.

But what's so strange about the entire process is that, as Empedocles himself so clearly hints, it looks after itself. And all the time that we think we are having to look after it, it's actually looking after us.

This is what it means to work with nature. It means participating in a process beyond human understanding that, even so, requires our human cooperation. And in spite of the silence, the quietness, nothing could be more dynamic.

There are sense impressions coming in from all around us. Those are the pledges from the Muse. There are the invisible seeds inside us. These are Empedocles' words—his spoken teaching, his *logos*—buried deep in our entrails. All the ground has been prepared.

And if you are even only slightly sensitive to the potential, the dynamism, in such a situation you are bound to realize that something extraordinary is about to happen. It's just a matter of going on doing what has to be done while waiting for the mysteriously inevitable.

As for Empedocles' own words, the outer form taken by his teaching: they are not important in themselves. In fact nothing at all is important except what happens to them— their metamorphosis, when everything is left behind.

TWELVE

The seed it grows from is the unseen.
Awareness is its trunk.
Its inner hollows are the senses.
Its branches are the great elements.
The objects of sense perception are its buds.

THE MAHABHARATA

And all that remains, now, is to go straight through to the end.

The next step brings us to one other mystery. For there is a certain passage in Empedocles' poetry which touches on just the theme that happens to concern us—the question of how exactly his own words are related to the task he has given Pausanias of staying alert with all his senses.

But although the general meaning of the passage is clear enough, one particular expression in it could hardly be more obscure.

Empedocles has been talking about how the cosmos began, weaving backwards and forwards with his story about its comings and goings, unions and separations, describing how the world as we know it is created and then destroyed.

All of a sudden he is shaking Pausanias to attention.

> Come now: if these words I spoke
> a moment ago appear at all lacking in wood,
> then look clearly at the witnesses to what
> I have just been saying.

And as witnesses Empedocles solemnly calls on everything Pausanias can see in the world around him—brilliant sun, luminous heavens, gloomy rain, solid earth. But he is also careful at the same time to remind Pausanias that he needs to feel the sun's warmth, the chill of the rain.

The humor, as always with Empedocles, is present right at the heart of the solemnity: just as delightful as ever. Sun and heavens and water and earth were traditionally called on to serve as witnesses to pledges and oaths. Here they are called on to witness a teaching being delivered in the form of a poem. And the sun was revered for its ability to look clearly at everything that happens. Here, though, the situation has been carefully reversed so that Pausanias is the one who is supposed to do all the looking.

Such cunning twists and inversions as these are only to be expected with a writer as subtle as Empedocles. And yet they do nothing at all to help us understand one supremely troubling word, *lipoxulos*, in the original Greek.

Its literal sense is unambiguous: "lacking in wood." But as for what it means here, no one has the slightest clue.

The first modern editors who tried coming to grips, two hundred years ago, with Empedocles' poetry were still refreshingly alert to the enigmas that it posed. *Lipoxulos* challenged them, provoked them. With the vividness of its imagery it seemed too strange a word even for a poet as strange as Empedocles to have used. But whatever solutions they attempted—doubting the correctness of the text, thinking up other words to replace it—nothing worked. Only too plainly he is evoking the image of a tree lacking substance or growth, of trunks missing branches or branches without a trunk.

As for why, though: people threw up their hands in despair.

And nothing much has changed since then—except that with the centuries perplexity has been transformed into quiet acceptance. Eventually even the strange becomes familiar. The real problems are magically forgotten as we learn how to focus on imaginary ones instead.

But, as always, the key to making sense of our lives lies in those details that seem most nonsensical. The small strangenesses surrounding us are our best possible clues to reality. They are the one thing we so badly need to help wake us up; and there are no mysteries we should let ourselves become too familiar with.

Empedocles' bizarre image of words "lacking in wood" is, through its strangeness, a sign that something is patiently waiting here to be understood. For we need to appreciate that, just as he compares his words to seeds, the imagery conjured up by those words of his is also seedlike.

It may not make much sense straightaway. But with time, in favorable circumstances, it will reveal exactly what it means.

2

Quotations from Empedocles' poetry come in all sorts of shapes and forms.

Some are long, some are short. And some are so short that the people responsible for quoting and preserving them never even felt the need to finish copying out a whole sentence:

> *If assurance about these things is, for you,*
> *at all lacking in wood—about how water*
> *and earth and* aithêr *and sun became mixed*
> *together to create all the shapes and colors*
> *of mortal beings that now exist, joined fast*
> *by Aphrodite, ...*

But in this particular case that hardly matters. The way Empedocles repeats his same concern with presenting guarantees and confirmations of what he is saying, repeats the same turns of phrase, even repeats the same strange word that means "lacking in wood," all goes to show he was just about to bring Pausanias back to his senses one more time and remind him to stay fully aware of the world everywhere around him.

This time, though, his focus is not so much on appealing to witnesses as on emphasizing Pausanias' basic need to be provided with "assurance": *pistis*. And that has a major significance. For it takes us right back to Empedocles' initial instructions about how we have to use our senses—and why.

As he has already indicated, the reason for becoming alert and staying alert is because every single sense provides some form of *pistis*. And it does this by offering assurances and confirmations, tangible pledges or guarantees, that the words spoken by Empedocles genuinely correspond to the way things are.

The real, underlying issue here is not whether the senses themselves can be trusted. It's whether they can help us trust his Muse. Our acts of conscious sense perception are not supposed to confirm their own validity. They are simply intended as confirmations of what she says. All the things we are able to see and hear and feel: these are the assurances she is offering.

For they are her tokens of good faith, her pledges.

But we, too, have our own part to play in this mysterious interaction. As a matter of fact every single moment that we consciously look at and listen to and experience whatever is happening around us, we ourselves are contributing something essential to the process.

We are making up for what Empedocles refers to as a lack of wood. We are slowly adding substance to those words germinating and transforming themselves deep inside our being.

And soon we will see how.

3

It's just another little fragment: a few words by Empedocles that you could hold in the palm of your hand and not even notice they are there.

But these are the words that turn all words into silence. For this little fragment is so dense in meaning, so deep in its significance, that it swallows up the whole universe and leaves just a ripple or two behind.

It begins sensibly enough.

Perverse people make a habit of
disobeying their superiors.

These words have all the typical appearance of a wise maxim—nothing too unusual to find in a poem claiming to offer helpful advice or instruction. But here, coming from Empedocles' mouth, they have a rather special importance.

In Greek, his word for "disobey" means quite literally "to break *pistis* with"; "to deny *pistis*." It could imply refusing to trust what someone says. It could even imply suspending belief in somebody's or something's existence. Later on it could mean to have no faith. And you could say there are tastes of all these meanings here.

But what Empedocles has in mind is also more specific than any of that. He is referring, above and beyond everything else, to the basic act of violating a relationship between inferiors and superiors founded on *pistis*: on mutual commitment and attentiveness, on cooperation and good will.

As a rule we have no idea of what such a relationship entails, of its infinite subtleties and rigors. We hardly even know who our true superiors are—let alone how to relate to them. For they are the powers that hold our destiny in the palm of their hand.

We tend to think very humanly that we have the power to act even when we don't, just as we prefer not to know that we know nothing. And the only way for us to start knowing or doing anything at all is with the help of these mysterious beings who know more about us than we understand about ourselves. This is the kernel of religion.

Nothing could be simpler, more natural, than to grow out of being human into becoming divine. Nothing could demand less in the way of effort while being so absolutely necessary. And in nothing are we helped so much.

But as for that perversity Empedocles refers to: it's to make a business of appearing to do everything possible while managing to avoid this one commitment, is to devote the greatest effort to neglecting it, to take endless care to forget it. Even then, though, we are never without superiors who quietly watch and wait.

And when we feel most alone is when they are closest to us, because they are not separate from our own selves.

Their existence is something so subtle that to relate to them may seem to demand nothing short of sheer faith. And yet the divine world is never limited by what seems to us to be the case. It always outstrips even our most refined and elevated notions of what subtlety is—which is why Empedocles takes the very crude step of rooting it, as firmly as he can, in this ordinary world of the senses.

Nothing could be more invisible than the link between the human and the divine. But with a sweep of his hand he takes that fragile thread of *pistis* and magically transforms it into its opposite: into the most visible and tangible object anyone could conceive of, which is the world around us.

All of a sudden everything visible has become quite transparent, a pointer to the invisible. Whatever we are able to see in whichever direction we look is a token, a pledge, from the unseen.

The habit has deeply ingrained itself in us, as solitary human beings, that we always have to choose between one thing and another. This apparent freedom of choice is what gives us our limited sense of existence, our illusory feelings of achievement; and it also makes us beggars because, by choosing one thing, we end up excluding everything else.

But nothing whatsoever, not a breath, not the tiniest object we are able to perceive, is excluded from the relationship of *pistis* between us humans and our superiors. For even though that relationship belongs to another world, it includes every single aspect of this.

And in the relationship itself, too, nothing goes unnoticed. Nothing is neglected or unreciprocated.

Every ounce of our attentiveness is demanded of us, but only so that we can discover how unbelievably attentive our superiors are to us. And the mystery behind their constant caring is that it can only ever start to bear any fruit through our constant attention to them—through our sensitivity and responsiveness to all their smallest hints, through our total obedience to whatever they command.

4

But then the fragment goes on.

Perverse people make a habit of
disobeying their superiors. You, though:
perceive just as the pledges from our Muse
command ...

And here you have come to the point of no return. Either you can break trust by going back again into the human world you are used to and doing your best, in the little time left to you, to make do. Or you can let it be transformed in front of your eyes into what it was always meant to be: eternity.

Empedocles is starting to spell out the nature of the divine command—or at least the first half of it. He is explaining where it comes from; how to obey; just what it involves. For we already know the identity of what he calls "the pledges from our Muse."

They are our sense perceptions.

They are everything we are able to see and hear, taste and feel. And these perceptions are inviting us, demanding of us, commanding us to do just what anyone would logically expect.

They are commanding us to perceive.

They are urging us to do the one thing that, by their very existence, they are bound to insist that we do. Perversity is when we fail as human beings to do that one thing by wandering off instead into thoughts and dreams.

They are commanding us, in this world of the senses, to stay present; to be aware.

This divine command is so simple in itself, is conveyed in a language so consistent with the guidance and instructions given by Empedocles elsewhere, that everything seems to add up quite perfectly. And it all does—except for one factor in the equation.

That factor is you. For these pledges, these assurances from the Muse, are not the type of reassurance you have been looking for.

They are not some kind of guarantee that life as you have known it is going to carry on. On the contrary, they are only assurances that this particular teaching will bring it to an end.

Everything Empedocles says does add up very nicely. The trouble is that he is a magician: not a mathematician. And behind the apparent logic and clarity of his words you will detect, if you are attentive enough, the unmistakable intonation of a sorcerer.

It can sound like nothing. But this is just the point. Nothing is more powerful than nothing when laced into the words of a sorcerer. It will make the ground disappear from under your feet; snatch away everything you believed in.

As for that expression, "the pledges from our Muse," it certainly sounds reassuring enough. There is a friendly quality of intimacy about it, a casualness and confident familiarity which are likely to set you at ease—and deceive you completely.

Up until a moment ago the world of the senses had been the whole field of your existence, the entire domain of your experience. It was what you thought you were born into, was where you imagined you would die and spend all your time until then. It was everything you lived for, wanted for its infinite charmingness and feared for its unfathomable grimness.

Now, suddenly, it consists of nothing but "pledges from our Muse." Good news, bad news, whatever gives you pleasure or hits you on the head: this is all just an assurance from the Muse. And now you may be able to grasp the real nature, to appreciate the true scope, of that agreement drawn up by Empedocles between his disciple and the Muse.

In this covenant between the human and the divine, mediated by someone both divine and human, the Muse is expected to offer a token of her sincerity. But her token turns out not to be some ordinary object.

Neither, for that matter, is it any extraordinary object. Even a rainbow in the sky would be far too modest.

With the most majestic of gestures Empedocles announces instead: as a pledge from our Muse take the world.

The sheer extravagance of such a gesture, its boundless humor and above all its uncontainable daring, are so stunning that the human mind can hardly even register what it means.

This is the doing of a man so crazy that, as we have already seen before, you need to be more than a little crazy if you are going to have any hope of understanding him.

It's the work of a sorcerer who is concerned not just with creating extra illusions to add to the one we happen to be immersed in, but whose greatest magic is to show that everything we think of as real is itself a trick.

And it's the teaching not of a human but of a divine being who is able to transform the whole of existence so that everything we are used to, or even not used to, is no longer just what it seems to be.

Instead, whatever you perceive and experience will be imprinted now with a divine signature—the signature of the goddess who is Empedocles' Muse.

There can be no such thing, any more, as an anonymous reality. Anonymity is the kind of brutal comfort you can no longer afford. On the contrary, every single thing you are able to perceive now exists for your sake and yours alone. Whatever happens to come to you through your senses is an intimate token for you, a gift to wake you up, and at the same time a sacred memento: a reminder of the work you have to do.

5

And then, with the end of the sentence, comes the rest of the instruction.

> *Perverse people make a habit of*
> *disobeying their superiors. You, though:*
> *perceive just as the pledges from our Muse*
> *command after splitting what I am saying*
> *in your entrails.*

The idea of "splitting what I am saying" is more than a little unusual. Quite literally Empedocles' language here means that his *logos*—his teaching as expressed in words—is something needing to be split.

And no one has the faintest notion of what this implies.

People nowadays try to find comfort in the explanation that he means we need to analyze the words of his teaching very carefully and divide them, then subdivide them, into different classes of logical statements. But we are not dealing here with Plato, or Aristotle.

Although the fact can be difficult to keep in mind, we are dealing with a magician.

There are others who have preferred, instead, to look for safety in the refuge of altering the Greek text: of doing what they can to make Empedocles say something slightly more familiar, a bit less out of the ordinary. Even that doesn't work, though. And it fails not just because no truly attractive alternatives exist, but for a more fundamental reason as well.

The text here, with its seemingly nonsensical mention of the need for splitting Empedocles' *logos* or words, is known to us thanks to a single author who quoted it in a work of his—only to refer back to it again a little later on in the same work. And, this second time that he happens to refer to it, he does so in the specific context of discussing what it means to "split" someone's teaching.

There is no point in even thinking of trying to change anything. The writer whom we have to thank for preserving this fragment of Empedocles' poetry is indicating, with all the clarity we could hope for, that the utterly strange idea of having to split "what I am saying" is authentic and correct.

But this is not quite the end of the matter.

The writer who quotes these words from Empedocles was called Clement of Alexandria. He is about the closest that ancient Christianity ever allowed itself to come to embracing and integrating Gnostic teachings. With the extraordinary subtlety of his mind, not to mention the direct access he had to esoteric traditions in his time, he was no fool. And here, where this particular passage is concerned, the greatest joke is not that he confirms with such simple elegance the accuracy of a text doubted and disbelieved by many of the most famous modern scholars.

It's that he explains, unnoticed by anyone, just how it needs to be understood.

The second time he refers to these words from Empedocles is in the middle of a passage where he has turned to look at different ways of grafting new growth onto trees—and at their symbolic meaning from a religious point of view. One type involves sliding the new shoot in between the wood and the bark of the existing tree, but is not the only method:

"Another type involves splitting the wood and inserting the cultivated shoot inside it. This is just what happens in the case of people who have devoted themselves to philosophy. For after their teachings have been split, then the recognition of truth takes place."

The reference here to Empedocles' own words is transparent. And of course it was natural Clement would want to interpret them as implying that the teachings of pagan philosophers, incomplete in themselves, can only bear fruit once the direct perception of Christian truth has been grafted onto them. But this does nothing to change the fact that he has grasped what no one for almost two thousand years has appreciated: in giving the instruction to split his teaching, Empedocles is using an image taken straight from the world of agriculture.

We already know just what his teaching happens to be doing where he says it is—"in your entrails." This is where it has been breathed in, pressed down firmly underneath the diaphragm.

And there, as seeds, his words will grow if tended well enough.

But this is only one single aspect of the process Empedocles is conjuring up. For now we are also able to understand his repeated concern about a "lack of wood." To be more precise, we can understand why he keeps on stating that the way to make up for any such lack is through sense perception.

If he were describing his teaching as some form of dead growth, the command to split it could simply suggest it will make good firewood. But he is not. His teaching is alive: first as seeds, then as what those seeds will grow into. And to split live wood implied something very specific for ancient Greeks.

To be more exact, it implied a process deliberately designed to add to the bulk and size of the wood itself. For to split living wood meant preparing it to be grafted with shoots that, once implanted, will give it extra growth and new life.

There is a tree that thanks to Empedocles' teaching is growing inside us, provided we have the humility and patience to look after it. His teaching is the tree. But however much attention we give it in the darkest places of ourselves, it still is not complete by itself.

It needs something else to help it grow. That something has to do with our senses. And this is why, in these few lines presenting the divine command that has to be obeyed, not one but two activities are mentioned side by side.

One is to split the teaching inside. The other is to perceive outside.

The whole point of Empedocles' repeated emphasis on the importance of staying alert to everything around us is not because he wants us to perform some exercise in awareness for its own sake. The purpose of perceiving consciously is so that all the perceptions provided by each single one of our senses can be implanted, like grafted branches, onto the tree growing up inside us.

And if you cooperate with this process you will soon make an extraordinary discovery—that the source not only of your own existence but of absolutely everything else's existence as well now lies inside yourself.

6

Grafting is a very particular and delicate affair.

What it means is that the shoots being transplanted need now to find their nourishment, their new source of life, somewhere else. And, not to put too fine a point on the matter, unless you are prepared for your whole life to be transplanted into a completely different mode of being you will never be able to discover the purpose of Empedocles' teaching.

None of the teachings offered by this tradition he belonged to are just some philosophy: more words to add to all the other words that people either leave to dry up in old books or try to dissect and crush with their minds.

They are what those words grow into—something so powerful that it will allow you, quite literally, to make sense of whatever you perceive for the first time.

There is a strange story we are told and, as well as being told, are expected to live. This is the myth of human existence. According to it we are born into a world of the senses so we can wander senselessly around in it for a short while. Then we die inside it while it goes on without us.

All our existence is based on the assumption that we are little selves in the middle of everything we perceive, surrounded by a vast cosmos which is separate and independent from us: the outside world, the world at large.

And when we carry out the divine command, when we actually do what Empedocles says needs to be done, the story is over. Not only is the structure of our entire life reversed; inverted; transposed. Even what had been turned upside down before is turned upside down, for good measure, one more time.

All of a sudden we become aware that, instead of our being born into the world, this world has simply been born in us. Wherever we look we are seeing not what we depend on for our survival but what now depends on us in order to survive. For through our divine awareness we are the source and creator and maintainer of the universe just as a tree sustains its branches and shoots.

To plant our perceptions in ourselves, to become the trunk and stock they all take their life from: this is not insanity, although it will certainly seem so from the human point of view.

On the contrary, it's only the ancient practice of common sense.

It's the action that has to be taken by humans who are ready to obey their superiors. And as a result of this one action, infinitely more real than any other decisions you imagine you have ever made, you will discover that nothing exists apart from you. There is nothing outside you any more: nothing out there at all. You are everybody, everywhere.

Everything is inside you now, rooted deep into your being. And with the entire universe inside of you, where in reality it always has been, you can sense for the first time how much power you hold in the palm of your hand. For the whole world— whatever you experience or perceive—is just buds on the tree that you are.

7

And so we are coming to the end of this book.

The book is yours—no one else's. For everything is your book. Even you are your own book as you write yourself in the depths of your being so you can read it in each episode of the life you seem to live. And every word ever written or spoken is spoken and written by you, for yourself.

But in this book that happens to be yours there is just one thing still left to say.

When Empedocles introduces his four primordial elements that become tangled and mixed to create our familiar world of illusion, he does so in a very particular way. He calls them the "roots" of all existence. And his deliberate use of imagery belonging to the realm of natural growth, of plants and trees, should be perfectly clear.

Perhaps you might think there is no real connection here with whatever he says about growth and trees elsewhere. For these roots refer to the world at large while his images of seeds and grafting and lack of wood all have to do with the world of the individual, with you in your private capacity either to neglect or to nurture Empedocles' words.

But, if so, you would be missing something quite crucial. For the whole purpose of this language about growth and grafting and the need for extra wood has been to bring you to the point of realizing that you are the world at large.

You, the apparently small individual, are so vast nothing exists apart from you.

There have been plenty of intelligent discussions about how people not only in ancient times but also right through to the Middle Ages and beyond often viewed existence rather differently from us. They tended to understand it in terms of detailed similarities, parallels, analogies between macrocosm and microcosm: between the great world which is the universe and the little world of the individual woman or man.

And yet all this talk about analogies or parallels is sheer confusion. For the individual human being is not just similar to the cosmos. In reality they are identical, one and the same.

When everything you perceive has been grafted onto you so that the entire world is your buds and branches and you are its trunk, then the roots of this cosmic tree plunge down into the nothingness inside you: beyond anything that exists, far beyond where the senses can reach. And it might seem pointless to ask in what such a tree could be rooted.

But in Empedocles' time there was one, very particular answer to that question about where the roots of all existence lie. They lie in Tartarus.

Tartarus is beyond everything that exists. And yet this is not to say it can just be described as non-existent. Non-existence normally means the denial of existence; Tartarus, though, is something altogether different. Far vaster than space, which is a part of existence, it's the power of sheer nothingness beyond this world of the senses that makes everything possible but in which only nothing can survive.

And to connect this sense-perceived world to that vastness by rooting everything in nothing is automatically to leave everything behind without having to do anything. There is no need at all to deny the existence created by your senses; to ignore it; to try rejecting or climbing out of it. On the contrary,

simply by sinking down right to its roots you are drawn without any effort into the reality that lies beyond.

You will already be rather familiar with that place. For it just so happens to be where this whole book started.

Here are the furthest limits and boundaries of existence where the cosmos comes to an end—past even the land of the Hyperboreans and the mythical world of Apollo.

Here is where Parmenides came to meet the goddess. Here is the source of an understanding, more logical than reason, more commonsensical than anything conceived of as common sense, more down-to-earth than this earth itself, which is so radical it quietly dismantles every notion and leaves nothing.

There is nowhere left to go and no need to go anywhere once you are here, because everything is inside you now. And everything is so small. However huge any scientists choose to make the age of the cosmos, you are more ancient. However far into the distances of outer space they claim it reaches, you reach further.

And you are fresher than time: the indescribable treasure that was never lost and that no one exists to find. For in the whole universe of shifting shapes and forms you are completely alone.

But, once you have realized this, you might just happen to throw a glance over your shoulder for the briefest moment and catch a glimpse of those who are like you—your true companions.

NOTES

ABBREVIATIONS

AP   P. Kingsley, *Ancient philosophy, mystery and magic* (Oxford 1995)

CQ   *Classical Quarterly* (Oxford)

D.L.   Diogenes Laertius, *Lives of the philosophers*

DP   P. Kingsley, *In the dark places of wisdom* (Inverness, CA 1999; London 2001)

DV   M. Detienne & J.-P. Vernant, *Les ruses de l'intelligence* (Paris 1974)

fr(s).   fragment(s). The fragments of Empedocles, Gorgias, Heraclitus, Parmenides are all cited according to the numbering in H. Diels & W. Kranz, *Die Fragmente der Vorsokratiker* (6th ed., Berlin 1951–2)

Il.   Homer, *Iliad*

LS   W. Burkert, *Lore and science in ancient Pythagoreanism* (Cambridge, MA 1972)

MV   M. Detienne, *Les maîtres de vérité dans la Grèce archaïque* (Paris 1967)

NM   P. Kingsley, 'Empedocles for the new millennium,' *Ancient Philosophy* 22/2 (Pittsburgh 2002) 333–413

Od.   Homer, *Odyssey*

PP   *La Parola del Passato* (Naples)

Th.   Hesiod, *Theogony*

WD   Hesiod, *Works and days*

SECTION ONE

"I will make ...": Isaiah 43:19.

Full references for this section can be found in *DP*. "*The mares* ... ": Parmenides fr. 1; cf. also *NM* § 8. J. Frère, *Les Grecs et le désir de l'être* (Paris 1981) 45 has a few perceptive comments on *thumos* at the start of Parmenides' poem. Repetition and incantation: *DP* 116–29, 246; *NM* § 8 with n. 111. For the Central Asiatic origins of the important Iatromantis figure called Abaris, see now W. Pohl, *Die Awaren* (Munich 1988) 31, 38–9. Parmenides' successors and magical incantations: S. Musitelli, *Da Parmenide a Galeno* (Rome 1985) 231, 266; *Magna Grecia*, ed. G. Pugliese Carratelli (Milan 1988) 234. Chariot of the sun, Daughters of the Sun, Apollo and the depths of night: *Tragicorum Graecorum fragmenta*, ed. S. Radt, iii (Göttingen 1985) 185–9 and iv (1977) 595 (F956); A. Dieterich, *Nekyia* (Leipzig 1893) 21; A. H. Krappe, *Classical Philology* 37 (1942) 353–70 and *Speculum* 18 (1943) 303–22; F. M. Ahl, *American Journal of Philology* 103 (1982) 373–411; A. Ballabriga, *Le Soleil et le Tartare* (Paris 1986) 242–4; also *DP* 87–92. "During deep meditation ...": A. Delatte, *La Vie de Pythagore de Diogène Laërce* (Brussels 1922) 224; *DP* 180–1 (cf. *AP* 284–8 with n. 25).

SECTION TWO

"Once you have touched it ...": *Theosophorum Graecorum fragmenta*, ed. H. Erbse (Stuttgart 1995) 8.102–4; *NM* n. 83.

Komizein and *komizesthai* mean to look after or tend to the needs of (never to "attend to" in the sense of learning from), or to carry away. But to explain what the goddess says as meaning Parmenides is simply to carry her message around from place to place in this world of ours would be to overlook his present, highly dramatic situation—in another world, faced with the return to this one. On bringing back a message from the underworld cf. Plato, *Republic* 614d and 619b; *Ardâ Vîrâz Nâmag* (ed. P. Gignoux, Paris 1984) 1.20, 3.5–7 and 14, 4.1–3, 101.2–7 (where the message brought back by Arda Viraz of one true path as opposed to other "non-paths" is already described as "the teaching of the ancients": on the *Ardâ Vîrâz* itself see P. Kingsley, *Studia Iranica* 23, 1994, 193 n. 25); and note also J. D. P. Bolton, *Aristeas of Proconnesus* (Oxford 1962) 121 (*adnuntiare*), 128 (*angeilanta*), 148 (*apêngeilen*). The frequent claim (so e.g. C. J. de Vogel, *Philosophia* i, Assen 1970, 103) that there can be no talk of any genuine shamanism in ancient Greece because people there only made journeys into another world for their own benefit, not as messengers for the sake of others, is based on the most acute disregard for the facts. Preserving revealed laws unchanged: Plato, *Laws* 738c–d; Plutarch, *Moral essays* 543a; *DP* 209–10. "*I*

Notes to Section Two

will do the talking ...": Parmenides fr. 2. Correction of *age tôn* to *ag' egôn* in 1 is easy and necessary; for the *egô/su* contrast cf. *Il.* 9.60, 262, etc. J. H. Lesher (*Oxford Studies in Ancient Philosophy* 2, 1984, 14 n., followed by P. Curd, *The legacy of Parmenides*, Princeton 1998, 24, 29, 56) has seriously claimed that the subject of *opêdei* in 4 is *keleuthos* instead of *Peithô*. But this is to forget both that *opêdein* is what one does along a path (cf. e.g. *Homeric hymn to Hermes* 200–9, Aeschylus, *Agamemnon* 426), not what a path does, and that Persuasion's routine role in art and literature was to serve as an attendant or companion for other goddesses (*MV* 64–6; this last point is also missed by D. Sider, *Hermes* 113, 1985, 363).

Philosophers who begin with riddles: *NM* §§ 7–8. Epimenides and riddles: H. Demoulin, *Épiménide de Crète* (Brussels 1901) 103. Parmenides as an initiate: *DP*; *NM* § 8. Initiation and riddles: *AP* 360–3. "No news returns": A. P. D. Mourelatos, *The route of Parmenides* (New Haven 1970) 21–4. For "not to be" as meaning death see e.g. Euripides, *Alcestis* 519–28 (where the language is significantly characterized as *asêmos*, "riddling": cf. Aeschylus, *Prometheus bound* 662, Herodotus 5.92b); W. Burkert, *Phronesis* 14 (1969) 29. On forking of roads and decisions in the underworld see esp. Plato, *Gorgias* 524a (*trihodos* and *krisis*); A. Dieterich, *Nekyia* (Leipzig 1893) 191–2; E. Rohde, *Psyche* (London 1925) 449–50; G. Zuntz, *Persephone* (Oxford 1971) 368; D. L. Blank, *Classical Antiquity* 1 (1982) 175–6; M. M. Sassi, *PP* 43 (1988) 390–5; A. V. Lebedev, *Philologus* 138 (1994) 25 n. 6. "With darkness and night": Demetrius, *On style* 100–1; R. Seaford, *CQ* 31 (1981) 254–5. "*For what exists ...*": Parmenides fr. 3. The Heideggerian silliness, which by now has slipped into mainstream scholarship, of translating this famous fragment as "For thinking and being are the same" and then claiming that it really means thinking and being are not the same is a game already parodied by Parmenides himself ("the same and not the same," fr. 6.8–9); cf. also S.-T. Teodorsson, *Classical Review* 50 (2000) 482. Thinking and making real in the realm of the gods: *MV* 51–61.

"*See how it is ...*": Parmenides fr. 4.1–2 ("however much you want to" helps make explicit the full force of the second-person middle *apotmêxei*; to take it, coming so soon after *leusse*, as third-person active could hardly be more unnatural or contorted. For the sense compare Chuang Tzu's rhetorical question "How can one get Tao so as to have it for oneself?"). The "Parmenidean way of life" and Zeno's death: *DP* 223–6. "*What exists ...*": Parmenides fr. 6. Those responsible for the earth-shattering recent announcement that the "true" reading of the Simplicius manuscripts at fr. 6.1 is *to noein* rather than *te noein* have been a little over-zealous in stating the facts: what they fail to mention is that DEW all read *to legein to noein to on* (F alone reads *teon*), which one hopes nobody would even try to defend. Karsten and Brandis had every justification for correcting the text—simultaneously and independently in 1835—to *to legein te noein t' eon*. As for fr. 6.3, some scholars

564

now prefer to replace Diels' supplement *eirgô* or "I hold back" (a form of *eirgein* had already been adopted by all editors since 1526 on the basis of fr. 7.2) with a form of the verb *archein*. But from the linguistic point of view this is extremely unlikely (cf. D. O'Brien's comments in *Études sur Parménide*, ed. P. Aubenque, Paris 1987, i 225 n.); to make Parmenides say "I will begin ... and then I will begin ..." is (in spite of N.-L. Cordero's desperate attempt to justify it, *Les deux chemins de Parménide*, 2nd ed., Paris 1997, 10–11) nothing if not implausible; and the aim of these scholars, to make Parmenides present only two different ways and not three by equating the second with the third, is totally misguided. The second, unspeakable and unthinkable way of utter non-existence (fr. 2.6–8) is a world apart from the contradictory third way that we humans constantly speak and think about—where existent things are denied existence and supposedly non-existent things are given it (frs. 6.4–9, 7.1). The reason why the goddess introduces only two paths in fr. 2 is not just for ease of presentation but because the third path that she will go on to describe in fr. 6 is, to her, no more than a bizarre invention of humans who are not able to help confusing and messing everything up: is our own, completely illogical fabrication. In fact the main meaning of the verb at fr. 6.5 is certainly "they fabricate," "they invent for themselves," even though there is just as certainly a very deliberate play of sound and sense between *plattontai/plassontai* and the following *plakton/plankton* (for such conscious ambiguity see NM § 8). As for the extraordinary difficulties often encountered in understanding how, at fr. 6.3, Parmenides could be held back from pursuing "this route" even though the two preceding lines have been summarizing the principles of reality quite correctly: they stem from the failure to realize that fr. 6.1–2 is, itself, designed as a refutation of the second route which leads to non-being. The goddess is not now rejecting that refutation, but simply confirming her rejection of what she has already been refuting. In fr. 6.9, *pantôn* is masculine and refers back to *brotoi* just as clearly as *autôn*, *hoi* and *hois* all do in 5–8.

"You ponder that!" (... *phrazesthai* ...) and riddles: U. Hölscher in *The Presocratics*, ed. A. P. D. Mourelatos (Princeton 1993) 230, citing e.g. Herodotus 5.92b (*phrazesthe*, in an oracle just referred to as *asêmos* or riddling). "All who are unacquainted ... but cannot see through them": W. J. Verdenius, *Parmenides* (Groningen 1942) 56. For a good introduction to *mêtis* see DV. *Mêtis* and "signs": DV 30 n. 67, 141–64, 214–15, 270–2. And *amêchania*: DV 27, 39, 53, 140, 268, 276–8, 287; L. Kahn, *Hermès passe* (Paris 1978) 78–113, 126–9. And "steering" (*ithunein*): *Il.* 23.316–17; DV 159, 215, 228, 240 n. "'Twin-heads' ...": Hesychius s.v. *dikranous*. For the configuration of ancient Greek "three-ways" cf. L. J. D. Richardson, *Euphrosyne* 1 (1967) 137–46; for their links with confusion, ghosts and the dead, S. I. Johnston, *Zeitschrift für Papyrologie und Epigraphik* 88 (1991) 217–24. Those who say we are already dead: *AP* 101–9.

SECTION THREE

"Think of nothing ...": *Selected poems from the Dîvâni Shamsi Tabrîz*, ed. R. A. Nicholson (Cambridge 1898) 168–9.

"*From this path* ...": Parmenides fr. 7.2–5. For the blatant self-contradiction in Parmenides' "much-experienced habit," *ethos polupeiron*, see e.g. Plato, *Laws* 951a–b (... *apeiros* ... *monon ethesin*). "The autonomy and superiority of the human reason ...": R. Tarnas, *The passion of the Western mind* (New York 1991) 21.

That *logos* could not possibly have meant "reason" in Parmenides' time has been pointed out e.g. by H. Gomperz, *Wiener Studien* 43 (1923) 125; M. Untersteiner, *Parmenide* (Florence 1958) cxxxii with n. 63; W. J. Verdenius, *Phronesis* 11 (1966) 81 and 12 (1967) 99–100; J. H. Lesher, *Oxford Studies in Ancient Philosophy* 12 (1994) 24; cf. also E. L. Minar, *Classical Philology* 34 (1939) 328–30 and P. Curd, *The legacy of Parmenides* (Princeton 1998) 63. On the evolution of the word *logos* in Plato's writings out of the basic sense of "talking," "discussion," see R. Robinson's essential comments, *Plato's earlier dialectic* (2nd ed., Oxford 1953) 83. It will be noted that, even in Plato's final work, this same sense of "through talking" is still very present and transparent in his use of the expression *logôi*. Cf. e.g. *Laws* 638c2 with Verdenius, *Phronesis* 11 (1966) 81 n.3; 966b6 with G. R. Morrow, *Plato's Cretan city* (Princeton 1960) 505–6 and n. 12; and note, also, the careful ordering of cumulative adjectives in *Sophist* 238c (*adianoêton te kai arrêton kai aphthenkton kai alogon*). Modern interpretations and translations of *logos* as used before Plato's time are still grotesquely over-rationalized. The expression *ho logos hairei* in Herodotus is often translated as "reasoning convinces" or "it stands to reason," but it only means that the story Herodotus is relying on strikes him as convincing: cf. 2.33 (*ho men dê tou Ammôniou Etearchou logos ... ephaske ... kai dê kai ho logos houtô haireei*), 3.45 (*legousi ... legontes emoi dokeein ouk orthôs ... oude logos haireei*), 6.121–4 (*ouk endekomai ton logon ... houtô oude logos haireei*); also Plato's *Crito* 48b–c (*houtos te ho logos hon dielêluthamen* ...), *Laws* 663d (*kata ge ton nun logon* ...) plus the shorthand uses of this expression that remained unique to it alone (Herodotus 1.132, 4.127, 7.41). Curd (63 n.) has recently tried, without troubling to read the context, to force the meaning of "thought" or "reasoning" onto *logou toude* in Aeschylus, *Persians* 170-1 (but cf. 161–2 *erô muthon*, 173–4 *phrasai ... epos*, 180 *lexô de soi*, 211 *humin d' akouein*, 215 *logois*), onto *Choephoroi* 521 (where *hôd' echei logos* means "so the saying goes"), and onto *logôi* in *Eumenides* 227 (for the verbal jousting involved here cf. 198 *antakouson*, 201 *logou*, 215 *logôi*, 221 *phêm'*). For the main sense of the word in Heraclitus see J. Burnet, *Early Greek philosophy* (4th ed., London 1930) 133 n. 1; K. von Fritz, *Classical Philology* 40 (1945) 235; H. W. J. Surig, *De betekenis van logos bij Herakleitos* (Nijmegen 1951); M. L. West, *Early Greek philosophy and the Orient* (Oxford 1971) 113–15, 124–9; J. Mansfeld, *Bulletin of the Institute of Classical Studies* 40 (1995) 225

nn. 2 and 5, 227–8. Heraclitus' statement in fr. 50, "Listen not to me but to the *logos*," has often been seen as a crucial proof that *logos* for him cannot possibly mean the words coming out of his mouth because "such a contrast between a speaker and his discourse is too bizarre" (M. Marcovich, *Gnomon* 47, 1975, 327). But this is to misunderstand the essential fact that he is doing just that: distinguishing between himself as speaker and the words coming through him. Cf. esp. West 115, 124–7; Robinson 8 (Socrates "even denies that it is Socrates who is doing the refuting. He speaks as if the logos were a person over whom he had no control ..."); C. H. Dodd, *The interpretation of the fourth gospel* (Cambridge 1953) 264 (the "habitual tendency of thought to attribute to the spoken word an existence and activity of its own"); H. Munn in *Hallucinogens and shamanism*, ed. M. J. Harner (New York 1973) 88–9 (referring to Heraclitus) with n. 2 ("... it is as if existence were uttering itself through him ... 'the man who in truth speaks, does not say anything that is his: from his mouth speaks language' ..."); Søren Kierkegaard's "Oh, that the talk might repel the listeners from the speaker" (*Purity of heart is to will one thing*, New York 1948, 69); and J. McDonald, *The message of a master* (San Francisco 1929) 32 ("Don't let my presence, or your impression of me, influence you in any way in your studies. Learn from my words only, not from me"). As for *logos*' specific early sense of "proportion," see *LS* 438–40.

The goddess' "trustworthy" *logos*: Parmenides fr. 8.50 with H. Boeder's comments, *Archiv für Begriffsgeschichte* 4 (1959) 104 and n. 158. For the deceptive connotations of *logos* in early Greek literature cf. W. K. C. Guthrie, *A history of Greek philosophy* i (Cambridge 1962) 421; M. L. West, *Hesiod: Theogony* (Oxford 1966) 231; MV 62–79; J. de Romilly, *Magic and rhetoric in ancient Greece* (Cambridge, MA 1975) 5, 25. For magic, deception, *mêtis*, and the Daughters of the Sun who "cunningly persuaded" Justice "with soft seductive words" (Parmenides fr. 1.15–16) see e.g. *Od.* 1.56–7 (... *thelgei*); Gorgias fr. 11 §§ 8–14 (... *ethelxe kai epeise ... goêteiai ...*); and MV 31 n. 6 (*parphasis*), 63 n. 83, 64 n. 88, 65, 67–8 with nn. 109–10, 142 n. 133. For the connotation of trickery in Parmenides' *epiphradeôs* note e.g. *Th.* 494 (*poluphradeessi dolôtheis*), with Hesychius s.v. *epiphradmôn* (*pseudologos*); and on the fundamental links between persuasion and magic see also A. Cameron, *Harvard Theological Review* 32 (1939) 9; C. Segal, *Harvard Studies in Classical Philology* 66 (1962) 146 n. 73 and *Arethusa* 7 (1974) 139; de Romilly 4; *AP* 91 n. 11, 220, 248 and n. 53, 306. A. P. D. Mourelatos' idea (*The route of Parmenides*, New Haven 1970, 146–7) that the Daughters of the Sun here in fr. 1.15–16 are establishing a formal relationship of trust and fidelity with Justice is quaint but, considering Parmenides' own choice of words indicative of cunning and deception, a little naive.

For *logos* and "talking to oneself" cf. Herodotus 1.34 (*heôutôi logon edôke*); 1.209 (*heôutôi*); 6.86 (*emeôutôi*); Euripides, *Medea* 872 (*emautêi*); Plato, *Republic* 534b (*hautôi te kai allôi*). People have often argued, or just assumed, that because

Parmenides repeatedly mentions "thinking" (*noein*) and "talking" (*legein*) together he must have considered them equivalent and interchangeable; but this is scholarship at its sloppiest. Thinking and talking were often mentioned together by Greeks for the simple reason that thinking was viewed as an internal process and talking as its exact equivalent, spoken out loud (cf. e.g. Plato, *Sophist* 263e; *Theaetetus* 189e, 206d; *Corpus Hermeticum* 9.1). As for Parmenides' "talking," it always means very clearly talking out loud: with his *logos* at fr. 8.50 and *legein* at fr. 6.1 compare esp. *phasthai* and *phaton* at fr. 8.8 (also fr. 2.6–8 and fr. 8.17).

   Kekritai d' oun: fr. 8.16. For the force of *d' oun* see *NM* n. 65. Scholars have often noticed the contrast between *akrita* in fr. 6.7 and *krinai* in fr. 7.5, but without seeing how closely both terms are linked with *kekritai* here.

   "Accommodation": P. Kingsley, *Phronesis* 39 (1994) 252; *AP* 17–18, 47–8. For the deliberate alteration by Greeks and Romans of words they found in older texts see e.g. J. Whittaker, *Phoenix* 23 (1969) 181–5 and 27 (1973) 387–91, plus his article in *Editing Greek and Latin texts*, ed. J. N. Grant (New York 1989) 63–95; J. Dillon, *American Journal of Philology* 110 (1989) 50–72; P. Kingsley, *Journal of the Royal Asiatic Society* 5 (1995) 178–81; also *AP* 24–7. For doctrinal alteration of Parmenides' text in particular, cf. Whittaker in *Editing Greek and Latin texts* 70; D. O'Brien in *Études sur Parménide*, ed. P. Aubenque (Paris 1987) ii 314–18, 334–9.

   The only two surviving quotations of Parmenides fr. 7.3–6 are Sextus Empiricus, *Against the mathematicians* 7.111–114 and D.L. 9.22 (*kritêrion de ton logon eipe, tas te aisthêseis mê akribeis huparchein* ...). For the Posidonian origin of the passage in Sextus see I. Heinemann, *Poseidonios' metaphysische Schriften* (Breslau 1921–8) i 203–18, ii 453–62; A. E. Taylor, *A commentary on Plato's Timaeus* (Oxford 1928) 35 n.; *LS* 54–6; A. A. Long and D. N. Sedley, *The Hellenistic philosophers* (Cambridge 1987) ii 243 with Sedley, *Elenchos* 13 (1992) 21–56; and note, too, that Posidonius' remarkable fascination with the role of light in his comments on the *Timaeus* (Sextus 7.93) recurs unmistakably in the comments on Parmenides' journey at Sextus 7.113. For the Posidonian origin of D.L. 9.22, see D.L. 7.54 with Sextus 7.93 (... *ho kritês tôn pantôn logos* ...: on the connection between these two passages cf. already J. Bake, *Posidonii Rhodii reliquiae doctrinae*, Leiden 1810, 231); also Sextus 7.89–91, 109–111, 122, 126–7, 131, 134, 139. All of these passages are concerned, precisely, with the issue of "judging by reason" (*krinein logôi*): for Posidonius' use of the terms *krinein* and *krisis* in this specific sense see Heinemann i 204, ii 459–64. It will be noted that Posidonius' projection of the senses–*logos* dichotomy onto Parmenides goes back already to Aristotle. Cf. *On generation and corruption* 325a13–14 and *Metaphysics* 986b18–20, 31–3, where Aristotle's expressions are an intrinsic part of his own vocabulary (as in *Metaphysics* 1025b27–8, 1035b13–15) and derive not from Parmenides but from Plato (e.g. *Phaedo* 99e–100a). Naturally this means that, ever since the time of Aristotle, the pressure to change the original text in Parmenides fr. 7.5 was enormous.

For alteration in our manuscripts of *logou* to *logôi* see e.g. Empedocles fr. 35.2 with *NM* § 9 and n. 152. For *logou*, alone in the genitive, preceding the accusative that governs it cf. Empedocles fr. 17.26; and for an exact parallel to *logou elenchon*, meaning "the demonstration contained in what has been said," see Demosthenes 59.115 (*ton elenchon ton tôn eirêmenôn*). The wording *logou ... ex emethen rhêthenta*, far from being redundant or repetitive, is pointedly emphatic (" ... as spoken *by me*"). And besides, this kind of duplication might seem redundant to us but was standard early-epic style when describing acts of speech (cf. e.g. Parmenides fr. 1.23). For *krinein* meaning "choose," "select," "judge in favor of" see V. Ehrenberg, *Die Rechtsidee im frühen Griechentum* (Leipzig 1921) 97 with e.g. Aeschylus, *Agamemnon* 471, *Eumenides* 487, *Supplices* 396 (where *sebas to pros theôn* is carefully echoed by 755's *theôn sebê*: note also the strong partiality implicit in 395's *xummachon d' helomenos Dikan*), Pindar, *Nemean* 7.7–8, Herodotus 5.5. Of course the fact that this relatively early sense of the word soon faded out of normal use will have made the need for a defining *logôi*, "by reason," even more pressing with the passing of time—and corruption of the text even more inevitable.

On the reading "heart of persuasive Truth" in Parmenides fr. 1.29 see G. Jameson, *Phronesis* 3 (1958) 21–6; O'Brien 315–18. Persuasion and force: *MV* 60–8, 73 n. 133, 78–9, 102 n. 87, 113 n. 32; P. Laín Entralgo, *The therapy of the word in classical antiquity* (New Haven 1970) 62–71, 88–100, 119–20; C. A. Faraone, *Classical Journal* 89 (1993) 9 n. 25, 19 n. 65; *AP* 306; and cf. also D. L. Blank, *Classical Antiquity* 1 (1982) 174. The bond between Parmenides and the Daughters of the Sun: *DP* 75.

A few aspects of the legal terminology in Parmenides' poem have already been noted by W. A. Heidel, *Proceedings of the American Academy of Arts and Sciences* 48 (1913) 718; J. Mansfeld, *Die Offenbarung des Parmenides und die menschliche Welt* (Assen 1964) 49, 104–5, 270–1. Mourelatos (150) and Lesher (*Oxford Studies in Ancient Philosophy* 2, 1984, 17 n. 19) have denied that it contains any references to legal procedure; but, even in fr. 7.5 alone, the direct combination of the words *krinai* and *elenchon* points clearly to legal practice. For mention of *krinein* or *krisis* together with *elenchos* cf. e.g. Gorgias fr. 11a § 34; Thucydides 1.131.2, 3.61.1; Lysias 19.6; Aristophanes, *Frogs* 785–6; Isocrates, *Speeches* 15.32; Aeschines, *Speeches* 1.85; Demosthenes 4.15 (*to de pragm' êdê ton elenchon dôsei, kritai d' humeis esesthe*), 18.15 and 226, 23.36, 25.37; Demades, *On the twelve years* 1.5; Platonic *Letters* 3, 319d; John 16:8–11; 2 Timothy 4:1–2; Jude 1:15; Josephus, *Jewish antiquities* 4.216. Underworld judgement at the fork in the road: cf. esp. Plato, *Gorgias* 524a (*... en têi trihodôi ... krinei ... epidiakrinein ... hina hôs dikaiotatê hê krisis êi peri tês poreias tois anthrôpois*) and *Republic* 614c–d (where, after Er has been faced with the judgement scene, he is told "he has to become a messenger to human beings" about what he saw and heard there), with *AP* 79–171. Incubation, descent to the underworld, Justice, laws and lawgiving: *DP* 204–19 with (on the Greek god *Nomos*) O. Kern's

comments, *Orpheus* (Berlin 1920) 32, 49–50. Parmenides as lawgiver: *DP* 204–5, 252–3; and note, in this connection, the evidence for very ancient links between lawgiving and the use of incantatory verse (cf. G. Camassa in *Les savoirs de l'écriture: en Grèce ancienne*, ed. M. Detienne, Lille 1988, 144–6). Connections between ancient Greece and prophets in the Near East: W. Burkert in *Apocalypticism in the Mediterranean world and the Near East*, ed. D. Hellholm (Tübingen 1983) 235–54 and *Wiener Studien* 107–108 (1994/95) 179–86; P. Kingsley, *Journal of the Royal Asiatic Society* 5 (1995) 185–91, 195–208; *AP* 236 n. 14, 383; *DP* 111–15; *NM* § 3. Islamic writers on early Greek philosophers as prophets and revealers of divine law: P. Lory, *L'élaboration de l'élixir suprême* (Damascus 1988) 14–18; *AP* 371–91, 395; *DP* 217–19. From southern Italy to Egypt: *AP*; *DP* 129–32, 145–6, 206, 218; *Lapis* 10 (1999) 63–8.

Lesher (*Oxf. Stud. in Anc. Phil.* 2, 1984, 1–30) and D. Furley (*Cosmic problems*, Cambridge 1989, 33–46) have argued at length over whether the word *elenchos* means "testing" or "refutation," but the passages they cite plainly show they have both missed the point. With regard to its basic sense of revealing, or exposing, the truth about something—often in the face of contradictory or fraudulent claims and sometimes with the natural implication of exposing so as to find defective—see also the straightforward definition at Demosthenes 22.22 ("an *elenchos* is when someone demonstrates the truth of what he says") which is then followed by the phrase *elenchos tês alêtheias*, "demonstration of the truth."

Socrates: J. Bussanich in *Traditions of Platonism*, ed. J. J. Cleary (Aldershot 1999) 29–51; P. Kingsley in *From Poimandres to Jacob Böhme*, ed. R. van den Broek and C. van Heertum (Amsterdam 2000) 29–31. Hermetic texts and incubation: ibid. 55–6, 63–4. The practice of *elenchos* in Hermetic groups: ibid. 26–31.

"There is only one tale … incomplete": fr. 8.1–4. At the end of 4 the reading *êd' ateleston* is impossible (it corresponds to *ouk ateleutêton* at 32, and to read *êd' ateleston oude pot' ên* … as a single unit here would not only disrupt the rhythm but also make nonsense of the whole argument in 4–6). Brandis' old but faultless correction, *oud' ateleston*, is supported by the fact that *atelestos* in Homer is more often than not preceded by a negative—and by the further fact that the one occurrence in Homer of *oud' atelestos* could not conceivably be more relevant to Parmenides' context, or more appropriate for him to evoke at this particular point ("Your path will not be in vain or incomplete," *Od.* 2.273). The resulting double negative at the end of fr. 8.4 is a perfect way of giving added weight to this final, and crucial, attribute of being. For the hymnic and religious effect created by Parmenides' accumulation of negatives, as well as for the significance of his emphasis on reality's "completeness," see H. Pfeiffer, *Die Stellung des parmenideischen Lehrgedichtes in der epischen Tradition* (Bonn 1975) 178–88.

"It never was … ": fr. 8.5–21. Although at the start of fr. 8.6 Parmenides very emphatically describes what he is talking about as "one," the fashionable theory

nowadays (e.g. Curd 64–97) is that instead of referring to one single one he is really talking about many "ones" all existing together. But this only goes to show that there is no limit to the ingenuity of the human mind in inventing what doesn't exist. For a clear ancient discussion of the one and only "now," "not existing in time," "unchanging and timeless" (*akinêton kai achronon*), see Plutarch, *Moral essays* 393a–b. J. Barnes (*The Presocratic philosophers*, 2nd edition, London 1982, 193) carelessly and quite illogically cites this Plutarch passage as stating that the eternal "now" exists in time, endures through time, contains all time—then goes on to dismiss the idea as "hopelessly confused" and adds "I am loth to ascribe such a vile thought to Parmenides." Of course the hopeless confusion, as well as the vile thoughts, are Barnes' own. At fr. 8.14 *pedêsin* needs retaining (on Parmenides' fondness for nouns ending in *–sis* see Mourelatos 5, with P. Kingsley, *Journal of the Royal Asiatic Society* 5, 1995, 190 and n. 112), as does the verb *pelein* at 19. For *apustos olethros* at 21, cf. *Od.* 1.241–2 and 3.88. The power of the divine word to make things happen: *MV* 51–64.

"*And also: there is no dividing ...*": fr. 8.22–33. *En tautôi menein* (29) is an idiomatic expression that means much more than "to stay in the same place," and was often used to characterize the unalterable state denied to human existence: cf. Epicharmus fr. 276.9 (Kassel–Austin), Herodotus 1.5, Euripides, *Ion* 969. There is no sound reason whatever for altering the manuscripts' *epidees mê* (see *CQ* 18, 1968, 72–3) at 33. For absence of need or lack as divine cf. e.g. Xenophon, *Memorabilia* 1.6.10; Bussanich 45. Religious language in Fragment Eight: E. Norden, *Agnostos theos* (Leipzig 1913) 248 n. 2; K. Deichgräber, *Philologus* 88 (1933) 349–50 and *Parmenides' Auffahrt zur Göttin des Rechts* (Wiesbaden 1958) 50; Pfeiffer 178–88; Blank 167–8; B. Feyerabend, *Rheinisches Museum* 127 (1984) 8 n. 34, 17 n. 58; and note also, for the religious use made of Parmenides' language, Plutarch, *Moral essays* 393a–b; J. Helderman, *Die Anapausis im Evangelium Veritatis* (Leiden 1984) 59–60; Norden 248 with C. Viano in *Alchimie: art, histoire et mythes*, ed. D. Kahn and S. Matton (Paris 1995) 115, 125, 138–43, 147.

"Parmenides clearly has in mind an action at law": Heidel 718. In fact, just as decisively as the juxtaposing of *krinai* and *elenchon* at fr. 7.5, Parmenides' double use of *pistis* (fr. 8.12 and 28; cf. fr. 1.30) alongside the words *elenchos* (fr. 7.5), *sêmata* (fr. 8.2), *ischus* (12), *dikê* (14), *krisis* (15–16), *anankê* (16, 30) and *alêthês* (28) points to the specific language of legal procedure. For *pistis* in the sense of "persuasive evidence" or "persuasive proof" cf. e.g. Antiphon, *Speeches* 5.84 (*dikastai ... ischurotatois ... pistin ... sêmeia ... alêthê*) and 6.27–8 (*elenchon ... dikaion ... ischurotatois ... pistin ... alêthê*); Isocrates 3.7–8 (*exelenchomen ... sêmeion ... alêthês ... dikaios ... pistesin*); Demosthenes 22.22 (*aitia men gar estin hotan tis psilôi chrêsamenos logôi mê paraschêtai pistin hôn legei, elenchos de hotan hôn an eipêi tis kai t' alêthes homou deixêi. esti toinun anankê ...*); Aristotle, *Rhetoric* 1355a1–1356a1 (*pistis ... alêthês ... dikaia ... kriseis ... anankê ... peithein*), 1377b18–22

(*pisteis ... krinousi ... dikê ... krisis*), 1417b21–6 and 1418b1–8 (*pisteis ... krisei ... dikaiôs ... elenchon ... dikêi ... pisteis*), and *Rhetoric for Alexander* 1428a16–23 (*sêmeia ... elenchoi ... pisteis*) with Plato, *Phaedrus* 266e. For the legal use of the word *ephêsei* in Parmenides' *ephêsei pistios ischus* (fr. 8.12) see e.g. M. Wurm, *Apokeryxis, Abdicatio und Exheredatio* (Munich 1972) 45–6.

Hymnic use of "for": Norden 157. On *apokêruxis*, the best general introductions are J. W. Jones, *The law and legal theory of the Greeks* (Oxford 1956) 288–90 and Wurm—although Wurm's idea that the legal adjudication of disinheritance proceedings was a relatively late and "evolutionary" development is contradicted by the Near-Eastern evidence (E. Cuq, *Mémoires de l'Académie des Inscriptions et Belles-Lettres* 39, 1913, 236–9; P. Pieler, *Gnomon* 48, 1976, 170–1) and involves a simplistic misunderstanding of the surviving evidence in Greek (see already S. Luria's fundamental comments, *Aegyptus* 7, 1926, 245–6). *Apokêruxis* and adoption: Jones 288; Wurm 5–6; also Cuq 185–91, 196–7. For the banishment involved, see Luria 246–7; and note M. van den Bruwaene's remarks, *L'Antiquité classique* 42 (1973) 704, on the force of the initial *apo-*. Disinheritance as *apôthein*: Jones 290 n. 1, Wurm 85–6 (and cf. ibid. 41, 45, for *exôthein*). On the use of persuasion and rhetoric for influencing the outcome, which eventually became such a striking characteristic of *apokêruxis* proceedings, see e.g. Wurm 23–45 plus H. I. Bell's observations, *Journal of Egyptian Archaeology* 5 (1918) 70–2. Taking away the name, cancelling the ceremony of birth: cf. esp. Demosthenes 39.39; Cuq 211–12; Jones 288; Wurm 3–4, 9–11, 16, 93 (§ 2). *Anônumos*: Parmenides fr. 8.17 (cf. *Od.* 8.550–4).

"*Because there is ...*": fr. 8.42–4. "*And what exists ... bright color*": fr. 8.34–41. 34 is sometimes taken to mean that "thinking is the same as the thought that *is*"; but this is wrong for several reasons. First, it involves ignoring the goddess' perfectly consistent indications (fr. 2.2; 3; 6.1) that by *noein esti* she means not "thinking is" but "exists for thinking." Second, to make *houneken* at this point mean "that" instead of giving it its causative sense is totally implausible (cf. *tou heineken*, fr. 8.13; *houneken* just before, at 32; U. Hölscher, *Anfängliches Fragen*, Göttingen 1968, 92). And, third, it makes no genuine sense whatsoever of the immediately following *gar* in 35. With regard to the exact meaning of *houneken* at 34, there are clear signs that some later philosophers took it as indicating a "final" cause in the Platonic or Aristotelian sense: "the ultimate purpose of thought" (Simplicius, *Physics* 87.17–18 Diels). But as far as Parmenides is concerned, this is a pure anachronism. Apart from its simplified sense of "that," *houneken* in early Greek poetry was always concerned with the fundamental fact of causation—regardless of whether it meant "owing to the fact that," "owing to which fact," or "that owing to which." And when we look at the various early uses of *heneka*, we see that it covered without distinction the whole spectrum of causality: cf. e.g. the continuous gradations in meaning from *Il.* 1.152–3 through 14.309–10, 22.235–7, 24.500–1 to 5.640. Also the same

fundamental problem remains that even if it were possible to understand *houneken* here as indicating a final cause, still no real sense could be made of the *gar* at 35.

As for the words *en hôi pephatismenon estin* in 35, they can only mean one thing: "in which it has been uttered." Commentators have been bothered by what they consider "a difficulty, namely, how can thought be expressed in Being" (L. Tarán, *Parmenides*, Princeton 1965, 123; cf. Mourelatos 171, "it is not at all clear ..."), and take the usual escape route of twisting what Parmenides says. But the ludicrous manipulations of these words that pass nowadays for translations— "to which it stands committed," "on which it depends for its expression," "that [i.e. thought] in which it [i.e. being] is expressed," "in that which has been expressed," "in what has been said [i.e. in the earlier part of Parmenides' poem]," "when one thing has been said of another"—are simply a vivid testimonial to how insane, in the fullest sense of the word, modern scholarship has allowed itself to become. "In Him we live ...": *Acts* 17:28. For Greek "in" as indicating dependence cf. Norden 19–23, 240–2; and for the "striking correlation" in later Greek philosophy between *en* and *hupo*, "in" and "caused by," see esp. R. Arnou, *Le désir de Dieu dans la philosophie de Plotin* (2nd ed., Rome 1967) 167–72. On the circle as uniting beginning and end cf. e.g. Heraclitus fr. 103; Hippocratic *Regimen* 1.19. *Mêtis*, circles and encircling: DV 37, 51, 55–6, 110–12, 269, 275–85, 290–2; L. Kahn, *Hermès passe* (Paris 1978) 92–3.

For the perfectly obvious meaning of *tôi pant' onom' estai* compare esp. *Homeric hymn to Aphrodite* 198 (*tôi de kai Aineias onom' essetai*: spoken by a goddess); *Od.* 19.409 (*tôi d' Oduseus onom' estô epônumon*); Plato, *Cratylus* 385d (... *tôi onoma einai ... estai ...*); also *Od.* 9.366, 24.306, *Hom. hymn to Demeter* 122, Aristophanes, *Birds* 277 and 644, *Wasps* 133–4, Demosthenes 43.73, 48.14, etc. Not only is this the completely natural explanation of Parmenides' words, but there is not a single valid alternative. For hundreds of years they have been interpreted as meaning "Therefore all things will be a mere name," but this is impossible. There is no way that *onoma* could mean "mere name" here without the addition either of a clearly contrasted term, or of a qualifying adjective such as "only." And any conceivable doubt should be removed by the verb *katethento* in the next line: *onoma katatithenai* was a well-recognized formula (so Parmenides himself, fr. 19.3 and fr. 8.53) that meant to establish a name, not to establish a mere name. But even that is not all. To take *tôi* at this particular point as "therefore" instead of as a demonstrative pronoun is extremely implausible (cf. *en hôi*, 35, and *to ge*, 37; Mourelatos 182); and the formal parallel between *tôi onom'* here and *tois onom'* at fr. 19.3 is definitely no accident.

The situation has been complicated by the manuscript variant *tôi pant' onomastai*, which L. Woodbury promoted as the correct reading in a sadly influential paper (reprinted with additions in *Essays in ancient Greek philosophy*, ed.

J. P. Anton and G. L. Kustas, Albany, NY 1971, 145–62). As far as textual matters are concerned: in Simplicius, *Physics* 87.1 (Diels) the manuscripts are divided with *onom' estai* the reading of F, *ounom' estai* of D, and *onomastai* of E and W (on which see L. Tarán in *Simplicius, sa vie, son œuvre, sa survie*, ed. I. Hadot, Berlin 1987, 261–2). Woodbury felt he could reject the reading of F as "inferior," but this is wrong for a number of reasons. First, D is a manuscript of exceptional value (H. Diels, *Commentaria in Aristotelem Graeca* ix, Berlin 1882, vi–vii) and it clearly supports the reading of F. *Ounoma* is such a common manuscript variant for *onoma* that editors of Greek poetry tend to refuse even to mention it when, as here, it occurs in violation of the meter; and in this specific case, where D offers *holon ... ounoma* instead of *oulon ... onoma*, we probably have a classic example of the phonetic metathesis or unconscious transposition of sounds so often produced by copyists. Second, far from F being "inferior" to D and E in particular, the opposite is often true. So for example, in the very next quotation from Parmenides on the very same page (87.15), DE give *pephôtismenon* where F offers the correct reading *pephatismenon*. A. H. Coxon (*CQ* 18, 1968, 74 n. 2; cf. n. 3 for Empedocles) has cited, from his own fresh collations of DEF and not from Diels' inaccurate apparatus, 20 examples of F alone preserving Simplicius' original text in those places where he happens to quote Parmenides; one could easily add more (e.g. *mounogenes* 30.2, *d' ekrinanto* 30.25 and 39.3, *tantia* 31.2 and 39.7, *kat' auto* 39.6, *pauô* 38.30 and 41.8, *tôi* 86.22 and 87.23, *pephatismenon* 87.15, *êd'* 120.23). It will be noted that these cases are all of precisely the relevant type—minor differences in word division or vowels where F has preserved the true reading but DE have not.

Third, there is the version of a line from Parmenides badly preserved in Plato's *Theaetetus* as *hoion akinêton telethei tôi panti onom' einai* (180e). Woodbury was obliged to deny that this is an inaccurate paraphrase of fr. 8.38 and claim it as an independent fragment from somewhere else in Parmenides' poem, because if it were just a paraphrase then Plato's *onom' einai* would plainly support the reading *onom' estai*. (In denying this Mourelatos, 187–8, forgets that the issue here is one of paraphrase and not paleography.) But in the debates and arguments over whether or not the solitary line in the *Theaetetus* is a paraphrase of fr. 8.38, hardly any attention has been paid to the actual details of Plato's known habits when quoting lines of poetry: to his patterns of inaccuracy, to the reasons for his inaccuracies, or to the exact nature of those inaccuracies. And here it just so happens that we can cite parallels and explanations for every significant difference between the text of fr. 8.38 and the line as quoted in the *Theaetetus*—parallels which show that Plato's line is indeed nothing but his own, characteristically loose, paraphrase of fr. 8.38. As for *einai* instead of *estai*: of all the changes that Plato used to inflict on the wording of his quotations so as to bring them into harmony with his own text, none was more common where verbs were concerned than turning an original indicative into an infinitive. So, just

a little further on in the same dialogue, he will replace an original *essi* with his own *einai* when quoting from Homer (*Theaet.* 183e; *Il.* 3.172). And in *Phaedrus* 260a he creates another *einai* out of Homer's *essetai* (*Il.* 2.361), which is an even closer parallel to the variation here between Plato's *einai* and Parmenides' *estai.* Cf. J. Labarbe, *L'Homère de Platon* (Liège 1949) 264–5, 329–30. As for *telethei* instead of Parmenides' *t' emenai*, compare *Republic* 468e where Plato has clumsily substituted *telethousin* for Hesiod's original *eisi* (see M. L. West, *Hesiod: Works and days*, Oxford 1978, 181–3; also Coxon, *The fragments of Parmenides*, Assen 1986, 3 n. 1). And as for *oion*, "alone" (not *hoion*; cf. Woodbury 148 with n. 10), instead of *oulon*, "whole": aloneness and wholeness are two divine attributes that were very closely linked in Plato's mind, as they also were for Parmenides. But while Plato cared a great deal about aloneness, he cared very little for wholeness. So, in the *Timaeus*, he mentions both aloneness and wholeness as attributes of the divine universe—but whereas he spares only one single word for its wholeness (*holon*, 34b) he dedicates a veritable panegyric to its aloneness (*hina oun ... estai*, 31b; *ouranon hena ... hautôi*, 34b). With regard to the specific word *oios*, we have to bear in mind Plato's well-documented habit of creating patchwork quotations by piecing them together from different sources. In fact several times elsewhere he quotes lines from Homer that begin with exactly the same word, *oios* (cf. esp. *Meno* 100a, also *Cratylus* 392e, *Republic* 386d); and, with his preference for aloneness over wholeness, he no doubt unconsciously allowed his memory here to embroider what Parmenides had said. For Plato's very pronounced tendency in his quotations to conflate words from quite different passages, often written by different authors, on a purely associative basis see *AP* 129–30 n. 57 with further references. And for a basic introduction to Plato's deliberate as well as unconscious habits of inaccuracy when quoting from earlier poets—modifying verses to fit his prose, preserving a few original words but altering others—see ibid. 126–30 plus J. Whittaker's invaluable comments in *Editing Greek and Latin texts*, ed. J. N. Grant (New York 1989) 63–95, esp. 66–7 and 94–5; also B. M. Perry, *Archiv für Geschichte der Philosophie* 71 (1989) 3–4 with n. 5.

Taken together, these considerations are already enough to rule out the reading *onomastai* on textual grounds alone. But that leaves the issue of grammar; and to take *tôi* as dependent on *onomastai*, "With reference to it all names have been given," is simply out of the question. Not one single example of such a construction exists in the whole of Greek literature (cf. e.g. M. C. Nussbaum, *Harvard Studies in Classical Philology* 83, 1979, 75 n. 37: "entirely unparalleled")—for the very basic reason that to take the dative *tôi* in this sense would be impossible without a governing *onoma* or *epi*. In the absence of either of these words, *tôi onomastai* could only mean "has been named by it" (so Empedocles B8.4; Euripides fr. 877.2). There are just three details that need some comment in this respect. (1) Woodbury (159 n. 14a) cites Pollux 10.137, *ônomastai de tôi kibôtiôi paraplêsion ti skeuos*

kandutalis, as a possible example of *onomazein* with a straight dative. What he seems not to have realized is that, if *ônomastai* is read (in which case there is no reason at all to reject the words *paraplêsion ti skeuos* as a gloss: Bethe only suggested this because he preferred to read *hômoiôtai* instead of *ônomastai*), then the dative will depend on *paraplêsion*. (2) He also claimed (159 n. 15) to find two examples of *onomainein* plus dative in Hesiod fr. 235.2 (Merkelbach–West) and *Od.* 24.341–2. But in the Hesiod fragment the dative *hoi* is dependent on the crucial *onom' emmenai*— just as in the standard expression *tôi onom' einai*. And as for the passage from the *Odyssey*, the *moi* is dependent not on *onomênas* but on *dôsein*: if this is not immediately obvious compare the *moi ... edôkas* at 337, *moi dôkas* at 340, and the identical use of *ônomasas* at 339. (3) In Athenagoras 6.252b = Theopompus F124 (Jacoby), *trapezan paretithei chôris onomazôn tôi daimoni* is sometimes construed as if *paretithei* goes with *chôris* and *onomazôn* with *tôi daimoni*. But *paratithenai* means "to set before," and must be taken here with *tôi daimoni* (cf. e.g. *Il.* 18.408, 23.810). This leaves the words *chôris onomazôn*, which together form a unit and are best translated as "expressly." Compare the common phrase *chôris tithenai* (Thucydides 2.24, etc.) and, for the strong sense of separation already inherent in the act of naming itself, Parmenides fr. 8.53–6 (... *onomazein* ... *chôris* ...).

Finally, a new fashion has been set by M. Burnyeat's idea (*Philosophical Review* 91, 1982, 19 n. 22) of reading *tôi pant' onomastai* and taking *tôi* to mean "therefore": the resulting translation is "Therefore it has been named all things." But this is to pick the worst of all possible scenarios. Once again, nothing could be less likely—just after both *en hôi* at the same position in 35 and the emphatic *to ge* in 37—than for *tôi* here to mean "therefore." And, even more absurdly (as Woodbury already warned, 149), this "therefore" would make Parmenides reason that the motionlessness and wholeness of being provide the explanation for why people describe it as moving and fragmented. One would have hoped no scholar would be willing to consider him quite so illogical. In short, *tôi pant' onomastai* is the ultimately useless phenomenon: a reading that from the textual point of view is unjustifiable and at the same time fails even to make any sense.

"Has no name, and all names refer to it": *A Coptic Gnostic treatise contained in the Codex Brucianus*, ed. C. A. Baynes (Cambridge 1933) IX.21–3. Cf. *Corpus Hermeticum* 5.10; the Hermetic *Asclepius* 20, with A. Henrichs' comments (*Illinois Classical Studies* 19, 1994, 50 and n. 110) on the tension produced by a divine being both having many names and having none; A. E. Affifi, *Bulletin of the School of Oriental and African Studies* 13 (1951) 850; W. C. Chittick, *The Sufi path of knowledge* (Albany, NY 1989) 41–4, 94–6.

SECTION FOUR

"As one coming suddenly ...": Lu K'uan Yü, *Practical Buddhism* (London 1971) 77.
"And from this point on ...": fr. 8.51–2. For the pointless modern attempts to
emasculate Parmenides' reference to the "deceptiveness" of the goddess cf. V. Hösle,
Gnomon 72 (2000) 4. On the deliberate ambiguity of the word *kosmos* here see
C. H. Kahn, *Anaximander and the origins of Greek cosmology* (New York 1960)
227; and for the very natural link between a "deceptive *kosmos*," a woman's jewelry,
and Aphrodite's charms in particular, *WD* 72–8 (*kosmêse ... kosmon ... pseudea
th' haimulious te logous ...*) with M. L. West's commentary on 73–5, *MV* 65–6 and
C. Calame, *The poetics of Eros in ancient Greece* (Princeton 1999) 44–6. *Mêtis* as
the power both to deceive and to tell the truth: *MV* 72–7. "Close to madness":
Aristotle, *On generation and corruption* 325a19; cf. *Metaphysics* 986b27–34. For
the play of opposites in Parmenides' account of our world see esp. A. P. D. Mourelatos,
The route of Parmenides (New Haven 1970) 222–53; *LS* 284 with n. 34 (on the
opposites of life and death). *"Nightbright ..."*: fr. 14; Mourelatos 224–5 (and note
the additional echo in the words *gaian ... allotrion* of the common phrase *gaiês
allotriês*, *Od.* 14.85–6, etc.). The Greek words for "light" and "human being": *NM*
n. 118.

Aphrodite in Parmenides' poem: Plutarch, *Moral essays* 756e–f and 926f–927a;
W. K. C. Guthrie, *A history of Greek philosophy* ii (Cambridge 1965) 61; G. Cerri,
Parmenide di Elea: Poema sulla natura (Milan 1999) 267–8, 273; *NM* nn. 136, 140;
and cf. H. Gomperz, *Psychologische Beobachtungen an griechischen Philosophen*
(Leipzig 1924) 20; G. di Santillana, *Reflections on men and ideas* (Cambridge, MA
1968) 106–14; H. Martin, *American Journal of Philology* 90 (1969) 190, 196, 199;
A. Capizzi, *Parmenide* (2nd ed., Rome 1986) 78; A. H. Coxon, *The fragments of
Parmenides* (Assen 1986) 243. It also is worth adding that specific analogies have
been noted between Parmenides' goddess in the world of illusion and standard
images of the Anatolian Great Mother: cf. esp. E. Pfeiffer, *Studien zum antiken
Sternglauben* (Leipzig 1916) 119–26, who compares Parmenides fr. 12.3–6 with
Orphic Hymn 27.4–7. This is hardly insignificant considering that the clearest
and most explicit testimony of all to the natural identification of Aphrodite with
the Great Mother comes from someone who, just like Parmenides, was a Phocaean
(Charon of Lampsacus, F5 Jacoby. Cf. W. Burkert, *Structure and history in
Greek mythology and ritual*, Berkeley 1979, 103 with n. 8 and *Greek religion*, Oxford
1985, 154, 178; also, for the Phocaean connection, L. Antonelli, *I Greci oltre
Gibilterra*, Rome 1997, 143). On the Great Mother at Velia see E. Langlotz, *Die
kulturelle und künstlerische Hellenisierung der Küsten des Mittelmeers durch die
Stadt Phokaia* (Cologne 1966) 30–2, 37–8; M. Guarducci, *Klio* 52 (1970) 136–7;
F. Graf, *Nordionische Kulte* (Rome 1985) 419–20; and add the *Suda*, s.v. *Orpheus*

(*Thronismous mêtrôious ... Nikiou tou Eleatou*), cited by W. Quandt, *Orphei hymni* (Berlin 1955) 22 as a parallel to Orphic Hymn 27.4–7 which happens to be the identical passage cited by Pfeiffer for its relevance to Parmenides' own poem. On Aphrodite and the Great Mother cf. also A. Dieterich, *Kleine Schriften* (Leipzig 1911) 135, 503; Graf 389 n. 51; G. Camassa in *Magna Grecia e Oriente mediterraneo* (Atti del trentanovesimo convegno di studi sulla Magna Grecia, Taranto 2000) 353–6.

Aphrodite and deception: *NM* § 9 with n. 142. For her magical powers of charming and binding cf. *NM* § 6 and n. 56. Aphrodite and *amêchania*: R. Pfeiffer, *Philologus* 84 (1929) 145–51; DV 267–8, 278 (and note also Pausanias 8.31.6 on Aphrodite Machanitis: cf. *MV* 66 n. 102); L. Kahn, *Hermès passe* (Paris 1978) 141–5. As navigator: Parmenides fr. 12.3; DV 142; P. Kingsley, *Classical Review* 44 (1994) 295 with n. 2. "Through *mêtis*" (*mêtisato*): fr. 13; DV 142; and for Aphrodite's notorious expertise in *mêtis* cf. e.g. *Il.* 3.416, *Hom. hymn to Aphrodite* 249, Aeschylus, *Suppliant maidens* 1037, *MV* 64, DV 267–8, *NM* nn. 67 and 142.

Persephone in Parmenides' poem: *DP*; *NM* § 8. The similarity in his language when referring to the two goddesses: ibid. with n. 107. For the Persephone–Aphrodite polarity cf. e.g. Burkert, *Greek religion* 177; M. Torelli in *Locri Epizefirii* (Atti del sedicesimo convegno di studi sulla Magna Grecia, Naples 1977) 175–9; Hippolytus, *Refutation of all heresies* 5.8.43 with A. Dieterich, *Nekyia* (Leipzig 1893) 191–2, O. Gilbert, *Archiv für Geschichte der Philosophie* 20 (1907) 37–8 and A. Lebedev, *Philologus* 138 (1994) 24–31. Regarding the trio Persephone–Aphrodite–Eros at Locri in southern Italy, see G. Zuntz, *Persephone* (Oxford 1971) 158–78. It also is important in this connection to note how the major role ascribed by Parmenides to Eros, alongside Aphrodite (fr. 13), now takes on an entirely different light thanks to the recent discoveries that show Eros playing a major role in the religious life of Velia: archaeologists, unlike historians of philosophy, are well aware of the link between these discoveries and Parmenides' poem (B. Neutsch in *Miscellanea di studi classici in onore di Eugenio Manni* v, Rome 1980, 1615–20; B. Otto in *Akten des XIII. Internationalen Kongresses für Klassische Archäologie*, Mainz am Rhein 1990, 400; *Supplementum epigraphicum Graecum* 40, 1990, § 904). On the merging of Persephone and Aphrodite in the Greek West cf. Zuntz 162–78; F. Costabile, *I Ninfei di Locri Epizefiri* (Catanzaro 1991) 125–42 (esp. 137: "... we are forced to think of a syncretistic divinity, a Persephone–Aphrodite ...."); D. Wortmann, *Bonner Jahrbücher* 168 (1968) 62.72 = D. R. Jordan, *Zeitschrift für Papyrologie und Epigraphik* 72 (1988) 251.72 (*Aphroditê Persephoniê*); ibid. 257 J = R. W. Daniel and F. Maltomini, *Supplementum magicum* i (Opladen 1990) 204.10 (*Aphroditê Persephoneiê*); AP 270–1.

"*So that nobody ...*": fr. 8.61. Coxon's arguments (225–6) for reading *gnômêi* rather than *gnômê* have a minimal effect on the overall sense, but are perfectly justified;

compare also the structure of *Il.* 23.345, an obvious model for Parmenides' line. The Homeric chariot race: *Il.* 23.262–652 (*mêtisasthai* 312, *mêtin* 313, *mêti* 315 and 316, *ithunei* 317, *mêti* 318, *parexelasêistha* 344, *parelass'* 382, *parelasseis* 427, *parelass'* 527, *mêtis* 590, *parêlasan* 638); DV 17–31; NM § 7 with nn. 73–4. For *Outis, ou tis, mê tis* and *mêtis* see *Od.* 9.364–535 (*Outis* 366, *Outin* 366 and 369, *mê tis* 405 and 406, *Outis* 408, *mê tis* 410, *mêtis* 414, *mêtin* 422, *ou ti* 448, *Outis* 455 and 460, *outidanos* 460 and 515; and cf. *Od.* 20.20 *mêtis*) with A. J. Podlecki's fine commentary, *Phoenix* 15 (1961) 125–33. For the importance of the passage see also G. Calmann, *Journal of the Warburg & Courtauld Institutes* 23 (1960) 60, 77, 81; D. Gallop, *Parmenides of Elea* (Toronto 1984) 24–5; M. Casevitz, *Études homériques* (Lyons 1989) 55–8; T. M. S. Baxter, *The Cratylus* (Leiden 1992) 113–14. "My dear heart ...": *Od.* 9.413–14.

Plato and the spherical earth: *Phaedo* 97d–e and 108c–110b; *AP* 88–95. For Pythagoreans before Plato's time as already holding the same idea see *AP* 89 and 172–94 (Philolaus' idea of the earth as an orbiting planet presupposes the earth is a sphere); also P. Kingsley, *CQ* 44 (1994) 317. On the inaccurate attribution of the idea to "Pythagoras" (D.L. 8.48) see *LS* 303–8 with 325, 409–12, and C. A. Huffman in *The Cambridge companion to early Greek philosophy*, ed. A. A. Long (Cambridge 1999) 67–9. Parmenides: D.L. 8.48 and 9.21 (Theophrastus § 227 E/D Fortenbaugh–Huby–Sharples–Gutas); P. Friedländer, *Plato* i (New York 1958) 386; M. Untersteiner, *Parmenide* (Florence 1958) 92–3; Kahn, *Anaximander* 115–18 and in *Journal of Hellenic Studies* 90 (1970) 109; L. Tarán, *Parmenides* (Princeton 1965) 296–8; *LS* 303–5; Coxon 236; I. G. Kidd, *Posidonius* ii/1 (Cambridge 1988) 223–4; Cerri 53–4. "A stange freak of history ...": Guthrie ii 65 n. 1.

Parmenides' terrestrial zones: Posidonius F49.10–14 and F209 (Edelstein–Kidd); H. Berger, *Berichte über die Verhandlungen der Königlich Sächsischen Gesellschaft der Wissenschaften zu Leipzig, Philologisch-historische Klasse* 47 (1895) 57–108; A. Fresa, *Atti dell'Accademia Pontaniana* 12 (1962–63) 265–6; *LS* 305–6; K. Abel in *Paulys Realencyclopädie der classischen Altertumswissenschaft*, Supplementband xiv (1974) 999–1000; Kidd ii/1 222–5. The once-common idea of Posidonius simply projecting the theory of zones back on to Parmenides is refuted by the fact that, far from wanting to agree with him or find support in him for his own views, Posidonius cites the measurements Parmenides had given for the relative dimensions of the zones only to criticize him for making the equatorial region too large. Also significant is the fact that he immediately goes on to discuss, in much the same kind of way, the views held by Aristotle on the same theme; for here we are a little luckier than with Parmenides because we are able to check what Posidonius says against Aristotle's own surviving words. He is accurate in every point of detail (Kidd ii/1 225). The connection between zones and a spherical earth: E. Honigmann, *Die sieben Klimata* (Heidelberg 1929) 25–6; Kidd ii/1 221–4. For the theory of zones as a result of travel

north and south see esp. Berger 98–101, 108. Knowledge of the earth as a sphere, and travel north and south: Aristotle, *On the heavens* 297b–298a; Cleomedes, *Caelestia* 1.5 (28.44–56, 30.104–113 Todd); William of Conches, *Dragmaticon philosophiae* 6.2.6; Copernicus, *De revolutionibus orbium caelestium* 1.2 (ed. A. Koyré, Turin 1975, 36); G. Vlastos, *Plato's universe* (Seattle 1975) 39; D. Fehling, *Rheinisches Museum* 128 (1985) 201; C. H. Roseman, *Pytheas of Massalia: On the ocean* (Chicago 1994) 80, 141.

The ocean beyond Gibraltar as another world: F. M. Ahl, *American Journal of Philology* 103 (1982) 401; Antonelli 65–71, 100–1, 151–8; R. Kotansky in *Ancient and modern perspectives on the Bible and culture*, ed. A. Y. Collins (Atlanta 1998) 160–95. The idea that Greeks were prevented from sailing out into the Atlantic by a Carthaginian blockade is just a modern myth: the real factors that held them back were quite different (Antonelli 98–9, 144–6; A. T. Hodge, *Ancient Greek France*, London 1998, 29–31; S. Bianchetti, *Pitea di Massalia: L'oceano*, Pisa 1998, 27, 52–4). The songbird: Pindar, *Olympian odes* 3.43–5 (also *Isthmian* 4.11–14, *Nemean* 3.20–3 and 4.69–70); J. S. Romm, *The edges of the earth in ancient thought* (Princeton 1992) 16–19. Phocaeans, harsh places and privacy: J.-P. Morel, *PP* 37 (1982) 484, 489–91, 496 (H. Tréziny), 499–500; *DP* 199–200 with refs. City of Seals: E. Akurgal, *Anatolia* 1 (1956) 10 n. 14; *DP* 12. Seals: R. Goossens in *Mélanges Franz Cumont* (Brussels 1936) ii 715–22; DV 111 n. 17, 161 n. 134, 242–58. *Mêtis* and seals: DV 111 n. 17, 242–58. Phocaeans as tricksters: *DP* 20 (escaping the Persians); DV 282–3 (use of Carian naval tactics); Hodge 3, 94 (Massalians at Athens); F. W. Walbank, *Polybius* (Berkeley 1972) 127 and *A historical commentary on Polybius* iii (Oxford 1979) 612 (feigning ignorance: cf. *Il.* 3.200–24 with DV 30–1).

Euthymenes: C. Müller, *Fragmenta historicorum Graecorum* iv (Paris 1885) 408–9; H. Diels, *Kleine Schriften zur Geschichte der antiken Philosophie* (Hildesheim 1969) 66, 391; W. Aly, *Hermes* 62 (1927) 305–12; P. Fabre in *Actes du 107ᵉ Congrès national des Sociétés savantes, Brest 1982, Section d'archéologie et d'histoire de l'art* (Paris 1984) 28–30; G. Camassa in *Idea e realtà del viaggio*, ed. Camassa and S. Fasce (Genoa 1991) 7, with refs. Not brave but mad: Fabre, *Les études classiques* 43 (1975) 29. Phocaean journeys up the coast of Spain: R. Wenskus in *Untersuchungen zu Handel und Verkehr der vor- und frühgeschichtlichen Zeit in Mittel- und Nordeuropa* i, ed. K. Düwel et al. (Göttingen 1985) 94; Camassa 8; Antonelli 68, 70, 96–105. Albion and Hierne: Avienus, *Ora maritima* 108–12; A. Schulten in *Cambridge ancient history* vii (2nd ed., Cambridge 1954) 771; Fabre, *Revue des études anciennes* 94 (1992) 15; Roseman 88. The "solid sea": H. J. Mette, *Pytheas von Massalia* (Berlin 1952) 1–6; R. Carpenter, *Beyond the Pillars of Hercules* (London 1973) 174–9; Ahl 397–9; Roseman 83, 92–5, 100, 120–1, 135; B. Cunliffe, *The extraordinary voyage of Pytheas the Greek* (London 2001) 126. Ancient Phocaean literature: Aly 300–8. Regarding when Pytheas lived: although it has become traditional to date him

and his travels to around 320 BC, recent scholars have come to realize that the arguments for such a late dating are quite worthless (Fabre, *Les études classiques* 43, 1975, 32–3; Roseman 52, 155 n.; Bianchetti 28–9). And yet so, too, is the argument that he must have lived after Eudoxus. For all we are told by Hipparchus (*Commentary on Aratus* 1.4.1) is that Pytheas was more accurate than Eudoxus in his astronomical observations; and, as the case of Pytheas himself so abundantly proves, in the history of science better knowledge is no sign whatsoever of lateness (cf. also D. R. Dicks, *The geographical fragments of Hipparchus*, London 1970, 152; *LS* 303). As for the extensive evidence that Pytheas' account of his journey shaped and influenced the Pythagorean myth reproduced by Plato at the end of his *Phaedo*—which means Pytheas lived and wrote in the 6th or 5th centuries BC, not the 4th (*AP* 143–60)—I leave this to perceptive readers to discover for themselves.

The tides: Roseman 60–2, 73, 80–2, 102–4. Foreign words: C. F. C. Hawkes, *Pytheas* (Oxford 1977) 38. Pytheas' measurements and the astronomers: Dicks 179–91; G. Aujac, *Revue des études anciennes* 74 (1972) 78 n. 2; Hawkes 7–8; Roseman 8–9, 30–61, 69, 117–26. Pytheas and the spherical earth: Abel 1030; Aujac 83–5; J. Herrmann, *Griechische und lateinische Quellen zur Frühgeschichte Mitteleuropas* i (Berlin 1988) 433–4; Roseman 34, 79–80, 145; Bianchetti, *Sileno* 19 (1993) 23 and *Pitea* 46.

For Pytheas, Euthymenes and the theory of zones cf. Strabo, *Geography* 2.3.3 with Aujac 74–5; also Berger 91, 98–101, 107–8, Aujac 77–80, Abel 1002–3, 1031. Phocaean cohesiveness: J.-P. Morel, *PP* 21 (1966) 404–5, *Bulletin de correspondance hellénique* 99 (1975) 895, *PP* 37 (1982) 492; Hodge 9, 18, 96 with n. 9. Massalia and Velia: Fabre, *Les études classiques* 43 (1975) 149, 156–7 and *Revue des études anciennes* 94 (1992) 13, 16; E. Lepore, *PP* 25 (1970) 53–4; Morel, *PP* 37 (1982) 492–3; G. Manganaro, *Chiron* 22 (1992) 392; also Hodge 28, 125, 263 n. 56; and cf. D. Musti, *PP* 21 (1966) 322 with Langlotz 16 n. 18. The "riddle" of Parmenides and the Phocaeans: ibid. 87–8 (for Odysseus cf. also Aujac 78, 82–5); *DP* 160. Phocaeans as exiles: Morel, *PP* 37 (1982) 491–2, 500.

Denunciation of Euthymenes: Romm 200–1. Dicaearchus: fr. 111 (Wehrli). Eratosthenes: Strabo 2.4.2 (... *diaporêsanta* ...); also Aujac 85 n. 2. *Aporia*: DV 25, 110–11, 139–63, 210. Strabo: *Geography* 1.4.3–5, 2.3.5, 2.4.1–2, 2.5.8, 3.2.11, 3.4.4, 4.2.1, 4.5.5, 7.3.1; Roseman 24–38, 46–53, 60–73, 125–35. For the spherical earth in Plato's *Phaedo* as strictly mythical (and the attempts that have been made to avoid this) see *AP* 90 with n. 11.

SECTION FIVE

"The deluded ...": H. V. Guenther, *The royal song of Saraha* (Berkeley 1973) 68–9 (quotation courtesy of Herbert Guenther).

Pytheas travelling by land as well as sea: Strabo 2.4.1–2. Phocaeans, their journeys, heroes and Heracles: *DP* 21–3, 28–30, 73. Parmenides and his teacher as heroes: *DP* 61–74, 139–49, 160–2, 173–87. Heracles searching out the waters and making the land known: Pindar, *Nemean* 3.21–6, *Isthmian* 4.55–7. The imitation of Heracles: *AP* 250–77, 297 n. 27; *DP* 29–30. For Pytheas, amber, the land of Apollo and the Daughters of the Sun cf. esp. A. H. Krappe, *Classical Philology* 37 (1942) 359, 365 and *Speculum* 18 (1943) 303–22; also F. M. Ahl, *American Journal of Philology* 103 (1982) 394–404. Considering how important Apollo was not just for the Phocaeans in general (*DP* 58) but at Massalia in particular (cf. A. T. Hodge, *Ancient Greek France*, London 1998, 79, 91, 125, 217 and, for the evidence of theophoric names, *PP* 37, 1982, 362; *Journal des Savants* 1988, 176–7, 181; Hodge 103–4), it is worth noting that even the name "Pytheas" itself was sacred to Apollo: for Pythian Apollo and Hyperborean Apollo see J. Burnet on Plato's *Phaedo* 60d2.

Amber and the route of Apollo: G. B. Biancucci, *Rivista di filologia e di instruzione classica* 101 (1973) 207–20. Pytheas and Hyperborea: Strabo 7.3.1 (for the combination here of "myth-telling" and "lying" cf. ibid. 4.2.1); H. J. Mette, *Pytheas von Massalia* (Berlin 1952) 2–3 n. 9, 4 n. 2; S. Bianchetti, *Sileno* 19 (1993) 22–3; also Krappe, *Class. Phil.* 37 (1942) 359, 365; C. F. C. Hawkes, *Pytheas* (Oxford 1977) 38–9. Apollo and the sun: Ahl 373–411; *DP* 89–90, 243. Pytheas and Avalon: Pliny, *Natural history* 37.35 (Abalum) with Krappe, *Class. Phil.* 37 (1942) 365 and *Speculum* 18 (1943) 303–22; also Hawkes 9 and Bianchetti, *Pitea di Massalia: L'oceano* (Pisa 1998) 196. For some basic comments on links between Pytheas' land of amber and Plato's Atlantis see R. Wenskus in *Untersuchungen zu Handel und Verkehr der vor- und frühgeschichtlichen Zeit in Mittel- und Nordeuropa* i, ed. K. Düwel et al. (Göttingen 1985) 99; and, in general, L. Antonelli, *I Greci oltre Gibilterra* (Rome 1997) 193–8. On amber, *glez*, and the transfer of Avalon to Glastonbury see Krappe, *Speculum* 18 (1943) 303–22 with Ahl 398, 402–8; and, from the British point of view, G. Ashe, *King Arthur's Avalon* (2nd ed., London 1973) 18–20, 93–6, 101, 181–3.

Where the sun goes to sleep: Pytheas fr. 9 (Mette) = fr. 13 (Bianchetti); cf. e.g. Stesichorus S17 (Davies). Daughters of the Sun, land of Apollo and the realms of Night: see the notes to Section One. Where the opposites merge: A. Ballabriga, *Le Soleil et le Tartare* (Paris 1986) 50, 77–81, 242–3; *DP* 70–1, 75. The lung of the sea: Strabo 2.4.1; F. Nansen, *In northern mists* i (London 1911) 66–8 with V. Stefansson, *Ultima Thule* (New York 1940) 94–8. Pytheas' famous "lung" has nothing to do with sea creatures but with the idea, common down to the times of Leonardo da Vinci

and Kepler, that the swells and tides of the ocean are the planet's breathing: F. Kähler, *Forschungen zu Pytheas' Nordlandreisen* (Halle 1903) 140–3; K. Reinhardt, *Kosmos und Sympathie* (Munich 1926) 58–60; C. H. Roseman, *Pytheas of Massalia: On the ocean* (Chicago 1994) 62, 115; R. Kotansky in *Ancient and modern perspectives on the Bible and culture*, ed. A. Y. Collins (Atlanta 1998) 202–3. For the meaning of the word *aiôreisthai* both here (Strabo 2.4.1) and at the parallel passage—also describing the point of access to Tartarus—in Plato's *Phaedo* myth (111e–112b) see Kähler 115 n. 1, 129, 147–8; *AP* 141–2, 148 n., 159 n. 41. "Neither walkable nor sailable": Strabo 2.4.1; cf. e.g. Pindar, *Pythian* 10.29–30, *Nemean* 4.69; O. Neugebauer, *Astronomy and history* (New York 1983) 372–8 (*aplôton*). H. Fränkel, *Early Greek poetry and philosophy* (Oxford 1975) 106 n. 24 notes the cosmological implications here but overlooks the eschatological, and is badly confused in stating that while Pytheas saw the "lung" with his own eyes he only heard about the cosmic "bond" or "fetter": Strabo makes it quite clear that what Pytheas described as a lung and as a fetter is one and the same. (On the genuineness of Pytheas' eye-witness accounts cf. e.g. Stefansson 96–7; Roseman 43 n. 29.) Pytheas at the edge of the cosmos: Strabo 2.4.1–2 (*desmon tôn holôn ... mechri tôn tou kosmou peratôn*); cf. esp. *Th.* 736–45, *Il.* 8.478–81; G. Cerri, *PP* 50 (1995) 439–56; Antonelli 33–9. It will be noted that Pytheas' arrival at the boundaries of Tartarus on his journey to the far north was all the more natural because Tartarus and the underworld were viewed by Greeks as lying not just to the west but also towards the far north where east and west merge into one (cf. Cerri 443–4 with n. 28, 456 n. 72; P. Fabre, *Revue des études anciennes* 94, 1992, 11–12; J. R. Russell, *Revue des études arméniennes* 18, 1984, 481–2). For the greatest heroes making their way to the limits of the cosmos see Ballabriga 130–1 (although his statement that Homer's Odysseus was "the last of these traveller-heroes" could hardly be more wrong). "They are beyond man's ken": M. L. West, *Hesiod: Theogony* (Oxford 1966) 339.

"Illuminating thoughts ... understanding": Fränkel 481 n. "Here in the allegory ...": H. Diels, *Parmenides: Lehrgedicht* (Berlin 1897) 50. For a far wiser approach to Parmenides' Daughters of the Sun see K. Kerényi, *Töchter der Sonne* (Zurich 1944) 66; W. Burkert, *Phronesis* 14 (1969) 6–9. Sound of piping, land of amber: see W. Fauth, *Hermes* 106 (1978) 237–8 with (for the link between poplars and amber) Krappe, *Class. Phil.* 37 (1942) 354, 369–70, *Speculum* 18 (1943) 309. On inner and outer journeys cf. Ahl 402 and esp. Burkert, *Gnomon* 35 (1963) 237–40.

"*What's needed ... all there is*": Parmenides fr. 1.28–32. The word *dokounta* in 31 meant either "appearances" or "opinions," "beliefs"; but of course for Parmenides there is no difference, because our opinions are what makes things appear to us the way they do (cf. esp. fr. 19.1). Here, *ta dokounta* clearly resumes the *doxas* of 30 and means in the first instance our own beliefs: for this sense of the word cf. e.g. Plato, *Timaeus* 48c; H. Bonitz's *Index Aristotelicus* s.v. *dokein*;

W. Kranz, *Studien zur antiken Literatur und ihrem Nachwirken* (Heidelberg 1967) 137–8; F. Trabattoni, *Hyperboreus* 4 (1998) 8, 10–12. For the sense of *dia pantos* in 32 compare D.L. 1.35. As to the alternative manuscript readings in 32, *perônta* and *per' onta*: first, the archaic verb *perônta* is far more likely to have been corrupted into *per' onta* than the other way around. This is nowhere truer than here, where our only source for the quotation is a lengthy passage in Simplicius that interminably discusses the nature of *ta onta* (*On the heavens* 556.4–560.6 Heiberg; for this type of corruption, due to the quoter's context, cf. *CQ* 45, 1995, 27). And second, *per' onta* completely fails to offer any acceptable meaning in spite of all the far-fetched attempts that keep being made to explain it: see L. Tarán, *Parmenides* (Princeton 1965) 214 n. 32; R. Brague in *Études sur Parménide*, ed. P. Aubenque (Paris 1987) ii 50–1; and cf. also A. A. Long, *Phronesis* 8 (1963) 93 n. 2. As for the frequent claim that *per' onta* has better manuscript support than *perônta*, this is the type of vague generalization that could hardly be more misleading. In fact the one and only manuscript of Simplicius to offer *perônta* here (558.2 Heiberg) also happens to be the one that, repeatedly when Simplicius is quoting from early poets such as Parmenides, stands alone in preserving rare and difficult words: cf. e.g. 559.17 (*apustos*), 377.18 (*allêxai, ampsuxai*), 530.7 (*thoôi*), 591.5 (*moniêi*). And this is not even to mention the important fact that William of Moerbeke's Latin translation of Simplicius unambiguously corroborates the reading *perônta*: J. Mansfeld, *Bulletin of the Institute of Classical Studies* 40 (1995) 230 n. 32, 231 n. 33. "The most controversial text": G. E. L. Owen, *CQ* 10 (1960) 84.

    Perân, peirata, and travelling to the furthest limits of the cosmos: *Od.* 10. 508–12 (... *perêseis ... alsea Persephoneiês ...*) with Cerri 441–2, Antonelli 33–4; Stesichorus S17 Davies (of the sun) with J. S. Morrison, *Journal of Hellenic Studies* 75 (1955) 60, Burkert, *Phronesis* 14 (1969) 9, DV 142–3 and n. 55 (comparing a fragment from Aeschylus' *Daughters of the Sun*), Ballabriga 78–9; Pindar, *Nemean* 3.19–26 (... *abatan hala kionôn huper Hêrakleos perân ...*) and *Pythian* 10.27–30 (*perainei*); Apollodorus, *Library* 2.5.10 (*dieperase*, of Heracles and the sun); Antonelli 38 n. 19; Kotansky 170–3, 182, 209 n. 135. For the notorious unbelievableness of opinions about the furthest boundaries of the cosmos note e.g. the responses to Pytheas' own journey as listed in Strabo 2.4.1–2 ("unbelievable," *apiston*; "totally at a loss as to whether he should believe"; "no one would believe Hermes himself if he were to say he had done it"; "not even he believed"), and compare the title *Apista* or "Unbelievable things" given to mythological novels written under the direct influence of Pytheas—romances in which we are presented, as we are by Parmenides, with the blatant paradox of true deceptions (S. A. Stephens and J. J. Winkler, *Ancient Greek novels*, Princeton 1995, 103, 107; cf. also Bianchetti, *Pitea* 72–3, 77). *Perân*, signs and *mêtis*: DV 143 with n. 55, 269–73.

Bonds, fetters and *amêchania*: *Homeric hymn to Hermes* 157, 257–8; Theognis 1078; Aeschylus, *Prometheus bound* 52–9; Apollonius Rhodius 4.880; Oppian, *Halieutica* 2.72, 77–8; DV 53, 63, 267–8, 276–8 with n. 75, 287; L. Kahn, *Hermès passe* (Paris 1978) 78–113. "The bonds of helplessness ...": Theognis 140–2. *Mêtis* and bonds: DV, esp. 23 n. 23 and 29 n. 62, 49–51, 85–96, 109–14, 261–92; Kahn 76–164. For binding and deceiving cf. e.g. *Il.* 23.585 (*dolôi pedêsai*), *Od.* 8.274–317; Sophocles, *Women of Trachis* 1050–7; DV 23 n. 23, 29 with n. 62, 93, 124, 261–90. "Fetters of deception": Timon fr. 48.3 (Di Marco) = *Supplementum Hellenisticum* § 822.3. Binding as magic: *Il.* 13.434–5, 14.73; *Od.* 5.383, 10.19–24; S. Eitrem, *Opferritus und Voropfer* (Christiania 1915), index s.v. Binden and *Symbolae Osloenses* 21 (1941) 50–60; R. B. Onians, *The origins of European thought* (2nd ed., Cambridge 1954) 352–75; P. Moraux, *Une défixion judiciaire au Musée d'Istanbul* (Brussels 1960) 53; M. Eliade, *Images and symbols* (London 1961) 92–124 (note esp. the intrinsic connection in India between cosmic bonds and *mâyâ*, the divine power of magic or illusion); P. Laín Entralgo, *The therapy of the word in classical antiquity* (New Haven 1970) 21–2; DV 85–6, 90, 94, 266; Kahn 110–12; J. G. Gager, *Curse tablets and binding spells from the ancient world* (New York 1992); R. Kotansky, *Greek magical amulets* i (Opladen 1994) 284; NM § 6 with n. 56, § 9 with n. 150. Incantations and binding: Eliade 109; J. de Romilly, *Magic and rhetoric in ancient Greece* (Cambridge, MA 1975) 12–13 with n. 32; C. A. Faraone, *Journal of Hellenic Studies* 105 (1985) 150 and *Transactions of the American Philological Association* 119 (1989) 156; Kotansky in *Magica hiera*, ed. Faraone and D. Obbink (New York 1991) 108–10; NM § 9 with n. 150. For *apatê* and magic cf. NM n. 142. *Amêchania*, trickery and deception: *Th.* 589, *WD* 83, *Il.* 15.14–33 (*amêchane ... dolos ... apataôn ... apatêsas*), DV 140, 267–8, 278. *Amêchania* and magic: *Il.* 14.215 with 15.14; Callimachus, *Hymns* 5.84 with Sappho fr. 130 (Voigt) and Theocritus 14.52; DV 267–8; Kahn 110–12.

Parmenides, Zeno and adoption: *DP* 150–7, 249. Parmenides, Zeno and Indian logic: J. A. Taber, *Indo-Iranian Journal* 41 (1998) 226–38. *Mêtis* of the slower and the faster: DV 56, 267. Lipara, Velia and Zeno: D.L. 9.26; L. Bernabò Brea, *PP* 37 (1982) 371–3; G. Manganaro, *Chiron* 22 (1992) 390–4; *DP* 225–6. (For Velia and Lipara cf. also M. Gras, *Dialogues d'histoire ancienne* 13, 1987, 170 with n. 30, and note as well the interest shown in Lipara by Pytheas of Massalia: Bianchetti, *Pitea* 104–7, 206–8). Lipara and the *Phaedo* myth: *AP* 76, 86, 100. Oulis: Manganaro 386 n. 5; *DP* 56–9. "A Parmenidean way of life": *Cebes' tablet* 2; *DP* 223–4. Deception, opinions, "wander around ...": *Cebes' tablet* 5–6. "Not all at once ...": ibid. 3. Zeno, Lipara and Athens: E. Lepore, *PP* 21 (1966) 270–8; V. Panebianco, *PP* 25 (1970) 62–3; *DP* 197–203, 224–6. Plato, Zeno, Parmenides: *DP*. "In one sense": Plato, *Sophist* 241d. "By a truly creative act ...": E. R. Dodds, *The Greeks and the irrational* (Berkeley 1951) 209.

SECTION SIX

"I know ...": Empedocles fr. 114.1–3.
For detailed references see *AP*; *NM*. "*Palms ...*": fr. 2; *NM* § 7.

SECTION SEVEN

"The helplessness ...": *Collection des anciens alchimistes grecs*, ed. M. Berthelot and C.-É. Ruelle (Paris 1887–8) ii 86.3–4.
"*I will tell ... and yearn for each other*": Empedocles fr. 17.1–2 and 6–8, fr. 21.7–8; *NM* nn. 126–7. "Logical": W. K. C. Guthrie, *A history of Greek philosophy* ii (Cambridge 1965) 168. *Aithêr*: *AP* 15–50; *NM* nn. 115–16. "*On came ...*": fr. 35.12–17; *NM* nn. 142 (*thauma*), 158. "*Made to wander away from their own ...*": fr. 22.3. "*There were so many ...*": fr. 61.1–3. "Has been brought under," "is firmly fixed ...," "harmony": frs. 26.7, 27.3; *NM* n. 159. Love and blood: M. R. Wright, *Empedocles: the extant fragments* (New Haven 1981) 237–8. "Wanting to reach ...," "whole-natured," "young night-time shoots ...": fr. 62.1–6; *AP* 51–3 and 78 with, on the movement of like to like, *NM* § 9 (at fr. 22); and for the "whole-naturedness" see M. Delcourt, *Hermaphrodite* (Paris 1958) 104–29 or L. Brisson, *Le sexe incertain* (Paris 1997) 67–102. "*Not yet ...*": fr. 62.7.
"*Won't you stop ...*": fr. 136. "*Father raises ...*": fr. 137.1–2; cf. G. C. C. Chang, *The hundred thousand songs of Milarepa* (New York 1962) 566–7 = *Sixty songs of Milarepa* (Kandy 1966) 43–4 ("How can one but feel sorrow for these sinful men. How foolish and sad it is to indulge in killing ... How sad it is to do an act that in the end will hurt oneself. How sad it is to build a sinful wall of meat made of one's dying parents' flesh. How sad it is to see meat eaten and blood flowing. How sad it is to know confusions and delusions fill the minds of men ..."), with ibid. 43 n. 1, 64 n. 3. "Spring up from there ...": fr. 146.3; *NM* nn. 33, 37. "*Whenever ...*": fr. 115.3 and 5. Note that in fr. 115.3 the correction of *phobôi* to *phonôi* is essential (cf. both J. Mansfeld, *Heresiography in context*, Leiden 1992, 293 and M. L. Gemelli Marciano, *Gnomon* 72, 2000, 399); also that, for Empedocles himself, *phonos* need only mean blood rather than bloodshed or murder (B100.4). For the mockery of a line often reproduced as fr. 115.4, which is an obvious intrusion into Empedocles' poetry stylistically as well as both linguistically and sensewise, see G. Zuntz, *Persephone* (Oxford 1971) 194–6; W. Burkert, *Gnomon* 46 (1974) 325. Regarding Empedocles' specification in 5 that the *daimôn* is "long-lived," most scholars' insistence nowadays on interpreting this as meaning the *daimones* are not immortal is a fine example of misplaced logic. It is no coincidence that "long-lived" was a standard epithet of the gods in ancient Vedic tradition, where the intended contrast is not with

some eternal life or immortality but with the "short-lived" existence of humans
(cf. Empedocles B2.4); see also Sophocles, *Antigone* 987, *Oedipus the king* 1099.
"Limbs": frs. 27.1, 134.1. *"Made to wander away from the blessed ..."*: fr. 115.6–8.
"Unfamiliar place": fr. 118. "Covered-over cave," "through the darkness": frs. 120,
121.4 (cf. *AP* 36–9; *NM* n. 159). Zuntz (204) raised an objection to placing fr. 121
after fr. 120 on the grounds of "the very obvious fact" that a cave is not a field
and a field, however dark, does not belong in a cave. But while his argument is
appropriate for this world, it has no bearing on the next: cf. Virgil, *Aeneid* 6.237,
262–3 (entry into cave) followed by 441 (arrival at the dark fields) with Zuntz's
own comments (201) on the relevance to Empedocles of *Aeneid* 6. *"For them ..."*:
fr. 128.1–3. For the significance of the offerings to Aphrodite as described in this
fragment cf. Burkert, *Greek religion* (Oxford 1985) 62 with J.-P. Vernant in
M. Detienne, *Les jardins d'Adonis* (Paris 1972) xiii (incense, Aphrodite, and the
power of illusion); H. von Fritze, *De libatione veterum Graecorum* (Berlin 1893)
36–7 (pouring of libations on the earth as offerings to underworld divinities); and for
Aphrodite herself as an underworld goddess see *NM* n. 159 with A. Delivorrias'
comments, *Lexicon iconographicum mythologiae classicae* ii/1 (Zurich 1984) 131
§ 1377. "The greatest abomination ...": fr. 128.9; Zuntz 207. The double fall in
Christianity: E. Smith, *Some versions of the Fall* (London 1973) 69–91, 211–15;
R. M. Schwartz, *Remembering and repeating* (Cambridge 1988) 91–110; and for
the ancient Near-Eastern background to Milton's *Paradise lost* in particular cf. e.g.
G. McColley, *Harvard Theological Review* 31 (1938) 21–39. For the paradoxical
but very common idea that, although man's fall from innocence is a tragedy which
has led to unbelievable suffering, it ultimately paves the way to attaining a far higher
state see esp. Theophilus, *To Autolycus* 2.24 ("God transferred him from the earth
that had given birth to him into paradise and induced him to advance himself so that
by growing and becoming perfect, and even being declared a god, he could ascend
to heaven"); A. O. Lovejoy, *ELH* 4 (1937) 161–79; and cf. also P. Vidal-Naquet
in *Langue, discours, société: Pour Émile Benveniste* (Paris 1975) 374–90. *"The
might ..."*: fr. 115.9–12.

SECTION EIGHT

"It's Aphrodite ...": *Exegesis of the soul*, Nag Hammadi Codex II.6, 137.2–3; *NM*
n. 159. "Already my heart ...": *Od.* 4.260–2.
    "The love and the desire ... most cautious and wise": *Il.* 14.198–9 and 216–17;
NM n. 55, § 9 with n. 142. *"Watch her ..."*: Empedocles fr. 17.21–6 with *NM*
§ 9. "Arouses ... our souls": Proclus, *Hymns* 2.9; Julian, *Orations* 4.33. *"Just like
when ..."*: fr. 23; *NM* nn. 45–6, 67, 80, 142. "Stunned and senseless": Plutarch,

Moral essays 139a; *NM* § 9 with nn. 143–4. *"Those that are resistant ..."*: fr. 22.4–5 with *NM* n. 147. *"Everything comes together ..."*: fr. 35.5–6; *NM* § 9 with nn. 155–61. *"In the oceans ..."*: fr. 105.1–3; *NM* n. 80. "I reckon ...": F. W. Sturz, *Empedocles Agrigentinus* (Leipzig 1805) 292. "His hope ...": ibid. 541. The soul as *aithêr*: *NM* n. 116. For a classic statement of the Greek view that only what is pure will be allowed into the company of what is pure see Plato, *Phaedo* 67b (*mê katharôi gar katharou ephaptesthai mê ou themiton êi*). *"No one ..."*: fr. 15; *AP* 366 n. 21. For the words "prophesy in his chest" (*phresi manteusaito*) see *Il.* 1.107 (*phresi manteuesthai*, of Calchas); for prophecy in the *phrenes* or chest, R. B. Onians, *The origins of European thought* (2nd ed., Cambridge 1954) 60 n. 2, 66 (cf. *NM* n. 164); and with the language used in fr. 15.4 compare e.g. Plato, *Phaedrus* 246c (*psuchê kai sôma pagen*) and *Phaedo* 67c–d (the soul finds purification *ekluomenên hôsper ek desmôn ek tou sômatos ... lusis kai chôrismos psuchês apo sômatos*), together with J.-P. Mahé's comments, *Hermès en Haute-Égypte* ii (Quebec 1982) 253–4. For the direct link between prophetic insight itself and the state of "release," or separation, see E. R. Dodds, *The Greeks and the irrational* (Berkeley 1951) 157 n. 3; M. Detienne, *La notion de daïmôn dans le pythagorisme ancien* (Paris 1963) 69–85.

SECTION NINE

"A disciple ...": M. Asín Palacios, *Abenmasarra y su escuela* (Madrid 1914) 44, 146 = *The mystical philosophy of Ibn Masarra and his followers* (Leiden 1978) 47, 162; D. De Smet, *Empedocles Arabus* (Brussels 1998) 174, 206.

"Anyone who follows ...": Aristotle, *Metaphysics* 985a4–7. "Love is the name ... evil": Plutarch, *Moral essays* 370d–e. "Outwardly ...": St. Gregory, *Moralia* 3.28.55 (reading *in facto rem*). For the same principle cf. F. Buffière, *Les mythes d'Homère et la pensée grecque* (Paris 1956) 35–6, 56 n. 45, 460, 477–8; H. Jonas, *The Gnostic religion* (Boston 1958) 92–6 with G. A. G. Stroumsa, *Another seed* (Leiden 1984) 82–8; E. Wind, *Pagan mysteries in the Renaissance* (2nd ed., London 1968) 27 n.; J. Z. Smith, *Map is not territory* (Leiden 1978) 151–71; also *AP* 237 with n. 16. *"For all mortal beings ..."*: Empedocles fr. 8.1–4 (where the words "there is no end in death" also mean, with pointed ambiguity, "there is no end to death"). *"When light ..."*: fr. 9; *NM* § 9. *"The might ... mad Strife"*: fr. 115.9–14. On the text, far superior in every way, offered by Plutarch for fr. 115.13 cf. U. von Wilamowitz–Moellendorff, *Kleine Schriften* i (Berlin 1935) 481–5; G. Zuntz, *Persephone* (Oxford 1971) 198. For examples (particularly relevant to the clearly authentic verb *ienai* as preserved by Plutarch) of *pisunos* being used to describe what one trusts in so as to get out of a difficult situation see *Il.* 5.204–5 (*eilêloutha ... pisunos*), 24.295 (*pisunos ... iêis*) and 313 (*pisunos ... iô*); for an exact parallel to Empedocles, as an "exile"

from the gods, placing all his "trust" in Strife (*phugas* ... *pisunos*) to get him safely home cf. Aeschylus, *Suppliant maidens* 350–2 (*phugada* ... *alkâi pisunos*); and note the play on *Il.* 9.238 (*mainetai* ... *pisunos*) in his *mainomenôi pisunos*. "They see ... understanding": Matthew 13:13 (cf. *NM* § 4 with n. 31; § 9 on B110). For *mêtis* as the act of trusting in something dangerous, see *Th.* 506 (*pisunos*) with DV 83–90. Plotinus on mad Strife: *Enneads* 4.8.1. Plato on madness: *Phaedrus* 244a–245b, 265a–b; W. J. Verdenius, *Archiv für Geschichte der Philosophie* 44 (1962) 145 and n. 62; W. K. C. Guthrie, *A history of Greek philosophy* ii (Cambridge 1965) 227. "One kind is caused ...": Caelius Aurelianus, *Chronic diseases* 1.5 (cf. B. Inwood, *The poem of Empedocles*, 2nd ed., Toronto 2001, 207 n. 80). Dismemberment as initiation: *AP* 291 with n. 6 (see also J. R. Russell, *International Journal of Ancient Iranian Studies* 1, 2001, 50). "When he came down ...": *Theology of Aristotle* 1.31; *AP* 57 n. 21, 380–4 (and for the same paradoxical scenario, of the misunderstanding of a misunderstanding leading to the right interpretation, cf. *AP* 195–213). Empedocles in the Arab and Persian world: *AP* 375–90. The sorcery of love and strife, and Empedocles' use of binding magic: *NM* §§ 6, 9. For the body as a ship crossing the ocean of life cf. fr. 98.3 (with D. Sider, *Mnemosyne* 37, 1984, 24 n. 39) and fr. 20.5; also A. E. Taylor, *A commentary on Plato's Timaeus* (Oxford 1928) 264–7 (on a passage very dense with echoes of Empedocles).

Honesty and lies in Empedocles' time: *DP.* "I will say the truth ...": *Homeric hymn to Hermes* 368–9 (and cf. 389–90 for Zeus' laughter). In much the same way Gorgias starts one of his pieces by insisting that he will tell the truth, then goes on to describe how utterly deceptive words are, and ends by calling everything he has said "a game" (fr. 11 §§ 2, 8–14, 21; Verdenius in *The sophists and their legacy*, ed. G. B. Kerferd, Wiesbaden 1981, 125). For the "rhetoric of trickery," or the deceptive art of being undeceptive, cf. already *Il.* 3.200–24 with DV 30–1 (Odysseus' *mêtis*); and e.g. Chaucer's *Franklin's prologue* with A. C. Spearing, *The franklin's prologue and tale* (Cambridge 1966) 17–19.

SECTION TEN

"And the bones ...": R. M. Pirsig, *Zen and the art of motorcycle maintenance* (New York 1975) 345.

"*They keep changing ...*": fr. 17.6–13 (cf. fr. 26.5–12; the term *akinêtos* here certainly includes the idea of changelessness but, just as definitely, has the basic sense of motionlessness). Divine words as seeds: *AP* 229–31, 299, 362–3. "Parmenides was ...": Olympiodorus, *Gorgias* 8.8–10 (Westerink). Gorgias and Empedocles: *NM* n. 122. "Playful intellectual diversions": *LS* 425. "Surrendered to the moment": Philostratus, *Lives of the sophists* 1.1; and for *kairos* cf. Gorgias fr. 13. "What a fine

satirist ...": Athenaeus 505d. *Kairos* and *mêtis*: DV 22–3, 28, 32, 185 n. 49, 195, 199, 210–13, 297–8; and for *mêtis* and the present moment cf. also DV 21, 37–8. Odysseus "who knew ...": Antisthenes fr. 51 (Caizzi); *NM* nn. 29, 122. Plato on the great beast: *Republic* 493a–c. Empedocles as father of rhetoric: *NM* n. 122. The Persian from Khorasan: Shahrastani, *Al-milal wa-'l-nihal* ii 71.1–10 (Kilani); C. Baffioni, *Elenchos* 3 (1982) 99; D. De Smet, *Empedocles arabus* (Brussels 1998) 143–4, 170. The same tradition also occurs, significantly, at the culminating point in Suhrawardi's *Hikmat al-ishrâq* (§ 275 = *The philosophy of illumination*, ed. J. Walbridge and H. Ziai, Provo 1999, 161): for the background to this tradition see S. Sviri, *Jerusalem Studies in Arabic and Islam* 9 (1987) 316–49 and, on Suhrawardi and Empedocles, *AP* 381–90. For "the moment" in Persian Sufism, and its relation both to the image of the cutting sword and to *qahr* (Suhrawardi's equivalent to Empedocles' Strife), see G. Böwering, *Iran* 30 (1992) 80 (*waqt* as translation of *kairos*) and 83. "*Destroy seriousness* ...": Gorgias fr. 12 (the context of Aristotle's quotation clearly indicates that the words *tôn enantiôn* have been imported by Aristotle himself). "*Whoever deceives* ...": fr. 23. It will be noted that elsewhere (fr. 11 § 18) Gorgias cites painting for its deceptiveness and that the closely related *Dissoi logoi* (3.10) mentions painting, together with tragedy, as prime examples of deception: cf. Empedocles fr. 23.

SECTION ELEVEN

"See ...": Matthew 13:3 (cf. Mark 4:3).

"*Come now* ...": Empedocles fr. 3.9–13 (note in Empedocles' *guiôn pistis*, "the assurance provided by" Pausanias' "limbs," the delightful play on the expression *cheiros pistis*, "assurance of a hand" or "pledge of a handshake": cf. L. Gernet, *Revue des études grecques* 30, 1917, 370–2 and also A. P. D. Mourelatos, *The route of Parmenides*, New Haven 1970, 141, 147). "*For humans* ...": fr. 106; for *pros pareon* here cf. e.g. Herodotus 1.20, Thucydides 3.40, Isocrates, *Archidamus* 34 and (for the connection with *kairos*) Sophocles, *Philoctetes* 149–51, Arrian, *Anabasis* 5.22.5. "Whoever sees ...": Aristotle, *Nicomachean ethics* 1170a29–32. "*If you press* ...": Hippolytus, *Refutation of all heresies* 7.29.26 = Empedocles fr. 110; for commentary cf. *NM* § 9. Degrees of initiation: *AP* 230–1, 299, 367–8; *NM* §§ 4, 9.

SECTION TWELVE

"The seed ...": *Ashvamedha Parva* 47.12–13 (cf. *Bhagavad Gita* 15.1–2).
"*Come now ...*": Empedocles fr. 21.1–2 (reading *tônde* with the manuscripts).
"*If assurance ...*": fr. 71. "*Perverse people ... entrails*": fr. 4; *NM* nn. 165, 169.
"Another type involves ...": Clement of Alexandria, *Stromateis* 6.119.2. Cf. Columella,
On trees 26.1–9 and *On agriculture* 5.11.1–11, *Geoponica* 10.75–7, Petrus
Crescentiensis 2.22 (... *secundus est, cum surculus scisso infigatur ligno* ...); this type
is *enkentrismos* or "grafting" proper (*Geoponica* 10.75.1 and 5). It will be noted
how closely Empedocles' tone of instruction (*keletai*, fr. 4.2) corresponds to the
traditional language of guidance in agricultural procedures: *WD* 298, 316, 623;
Theophrastus, *Researches into plants* 2.2.5 (... *auxêtheisan enkentrizein keleuousin*
...); Pliny, *Natural history* 17.115 (... *praesectam findi iubet per medullam* ...). On
Clement's "recognition of truth," *epignôsis tês alêtheias*, cf. e.g. M. Dibelius,
Neutestamentliche Studien Georg Heinrici ... dargebracht (Leipzig 1914) 176–89;
as for Empedocles' own *gnôthi* (fr. 4.3), there is not the slightest good reason to doubt
that it has the standard early meaning of "perceive." For Tartarus, cosmic tree and
elemental roots see *Th.* 727–8 with H. S. Schibli, *Pherekydes of Syros* (Oxford 1990)
70–1; Virgil, *Georgics* 2.291–2 with U. Holmberg, *Der Baum des Lebens* (Helsinki
1922) 53.

"This book is a journey back to the source—not only of western civilization but, more importantly, to the source within you. Read it! To understand it is to be transformed."

ECKHART TOLLE
author of *The Power of Now*

"Stunningly original, *Reality* is momentous in its implications. This book is aimed at one of the highest ends I can imagine—to restore to us the understanding that the original purpose of Greek philosophy was to launch the Western mind on a profoundly spiritual course. It shows, in a way which to my eyes is completely convincing, that the founders of philosophy were not just proto-physicists whose ingenious conjectures have long been shelved. They were spiritual giants whose understandings have not been surpassed and may never be surpassed."

HUSTON SMITH
author of *The World's Religions*
and *Forgotten Truth*

"*Reality* contains the purest and most powerful writing I have ever read."

MICHAEL BAIGENT
author of *Ancient Traces*
and *The Holy Blood and the Holy Grail*

"There are few writers today you must read. Peter Kingsley is one of them. With absolute clarity he writes about the most challenging issues, and at the same time is inspiring in the most ancient sense: filling us with spirit and hope. His words will change the way you imagine your life."

THOMAS MOORE
author of *Care of the Soul*
and *Dark Nights of the Soul*

"Peter Kingsley is a successor to Carl Jung and Joseph Campbell. His lectures and writings—especially his latest book, *Reality*—reveal hidden dimensions of consciousness and how it manifests in the world. His message conveys hope and meaning, and reveals majestic qualities of the mind we have forgotten and which have been ignored by Western 'authorities' for centuries. Peter Kingsley is a transformative and life-changing force in our world. Never have we needed such a message as now."

LARRY DOSSEY, M.D.
author of *Healing Beyond the Body,*
Reinventing Medicine, and *Healing Words*

"Dr. Kingsley's remarkable new book, *Reality*, is extraordinarily valuable. It would be difficult not to conclude that, through his research into our past, he has found the key to the modern world impasse."

ROBERT A. JOHNSON
author of *He, She, Inner Work,*
and *Balancing Heaven and Earth*

"This epochal work is not only a seminal study of the origins of Western thought. It also is a guide for the rediscovery of truths which lie hidden in the souls and minds of men and women today—and which urgently need to be brought to light in a world groping in so much spiritual and intellectual darkness. It seeks nothing less than to reveal the original nature of Western philosophy in its true, but long forgotten, sense. And through doing so it forces contemporary human beings to reexamine what it means to be human."

SEYYED HOSSEIN NASR
author of *Knowledge and the Sacred*
and *Religion and the Order of Nature*

A Story Waiting to Pierce You:
Mongolia, Tibet and the Destiny of the Western World

(GOLDEN SUFI CENTER PUBLISHING, 2010)

"A true *encanto*, an incantation, this book is pure music. It sings to the reader. This is the real thing. In each paragraph of the book, the Spirit is there. This is what the native people of the Americas have been trying to say, but were never permitted to. This song is the song of wisdom that we native people have not been allowed to sing."

JOSEPH RAEL (BEAUTIFUL PAINTED ARROW), from the Foreword

"The rich and dense scholarship in this book is admirable, nay incredible, with worldwide scope. Scholarly discussion depends on evidence—of which *A Story Waiting to Pierce You* offers the most surprising riches combined with overwhelming expertise."

PROF. WALTER BURKERT, author of *Greek Religion* and *Babylon, Memphis, Persepolis*

"Let this book wake you up into new sunlight. It is not just a book, and so to be read with the mind. Peter Kingsley's voice is a friend, and also a way of seeing, of remembering essence, of walking in a great circle around an island you have always loved, but only rarely visited."

COLEMAN BARKS, translator of Rumi

"Peter Kingsley is more than a master storyteller. He is a magician who reveals the golden thread of truth which makes its way through time and space, secretly holding the fabric of our world together. *A Story Waiting to Pierce You* reveals the surprisingly mystical origins, and purpose, of western culture as well as what it means to participate in its eternal unfolding right now."

ADYASHANTI, author of *Emptiness Dancing* and *The End of Your World*

"In this profoundly erudite and eloquent book is a startling ancient secret that will forever alter the way we think about the origins of western civilization."

PIR ZIA INAYAT KHAN, spiritual leader of the Sufi Order International and founder of the Suluk Academy

"This is a book of miracles—deceptively simple, actively profound. It is a core story of human becoming, the secret history that holds the codes to what we were and what we yet may be."

JEAN HOUSTON, author of *A Mythic Life* and *The Hero and the Goddess*

"A blazingly alive work of scholarship and spiritual insight"

PROF. JACOB NEEDLEMAN, author of *What is God?* and *The Heart of Philosophy*

"This book, this amazing and empowering song, is a miraculous gift to the Mongolian people. In reading it I felt as if I was traveling through time to experience our source and listening once again to the songs of my ancestors."

ONO GANZORIG, Director of *Mongol Environmental Conservation*

"By challenging some of our most fundamental perceptions of early European history, Peter Kingsley pushes out the horizon of the modern world and opens a new chapter in our appreciation of European–Asian relations. His innovative research into the spiritual and intellectual debt of ancient Greece to Inner Asia not only broadens our understanding of the past, but also helps us to understand better who we are today."

PROF. JACK WEATHERFORD, author of *Genghis Khan and the Making of the Modern World*

"A work of great and courageous scholarship—a blockbuster to open the closed minds of those, East and West, who have chosen to ignore or denigrate the immense role played by shamanism in the spiritual and political origins of what we know today as Tibetan Buddhism. Peter Kingsley's endnotes alone justify purchasing the book."

MICHAEL HARNER, author of *The Way of the Shaman*

"*A Story Waiting to Pierce You* is, simply, piercing. Peter Kingsley is a master of adamantine prose and peerless scholarship. His work is truly worthy of that overworked term *wisdom*. And he is a master stylist: he turns you upside down and inside out without your knowing it is happening. This book will inspire, delight and enlighten many but will also challenge others because it is a mirror that reflects our most stubborn prejudices about the origins of our most sacrosanct cultural beliefs. And for that, Peter Kingsley deserves the highest praise."

LARRY DOSSEY, M.D., author of *Reinventing Medicine* and *The Power of Premonitions*

"This book is a game changer and truly timely. It makes whole a species foolishly fractured by racial, religious, ethnic, nationalistic divisions. It calls us to wake from our sleepfulness so the arrow of truth can pierce us and we can learn again who our ancestors really are. It calls us all to our common unity and ecstasy and future."

MATTHEW FOX, author of *Original Blessing* and *The Hidden Spirituality of Men*

"This is a small book. You can read it in an hour. I suggest that you read it several times and really get the golden idea at its core. Then bring that idea to everything you do—every decision, every choice, every plan, every interpretation. Live by an entirely different guidance. Walk like you've never walked before."

THOMAS MOORE, author of *Care of the Soul* and *The Re-enchantment of Everyday Life*

In the Dark Places of Wisdom

(Golden Sufi Center Publishing, 1999)

"This remarkable book speaks with equal power to the scholar and the seeker alike. To absorb what it says is to encounter a completely new vision of the ancient world that lies at the root of our own civilization. Right there, at our own feet, lies a forgotten tradition that has the power to transform all our views about our culture and our life."

Jacob Needleman, author of *Lost Christianity* and *The Heart of Philosophy*

"With its surprisingly fresh and original approach, *In the Dark Places of Wisdom* includes a wealth of suggestions and observations hardly ever made before ... The philosophical and mystical roots of Western civilization start to appear in a completely new light."

Walter Burkert, author of *Greek Religion* and *Ancient Mystery Cults*

"Peter Kingsley is a master excavator of lost and hidden meanings. He accomplishes nothing less than giving us a new pair of eyes by which to see the true philosophical and spiritual depth of the ancient world upon which our own civilization is built. In the beautiful and penetrating language of an accomplished storyteller, he shows the absolute relevance of history and wisdom to our own present life."

Georg Feuerstein, author of *The Yoga Tradition* and *Tantra, the Path of Ecstasy*

"Quite simply a masterpiece: a work of immaculate, luminous scholarship which recovers for Western civilization the treasures of wisdom discarded by Plato over 2000 years ago. No-one could fail to respond to this story or be moved by the poetic prose which takes us 'as far as longing can reach' and opens a door into depths which have never been recognized, let alone explored by our culture."

Anne Baring, co-author of *The Myth of the Goddess* and *The Mystic Vision*

"Compelling, fascinating, hard to put down. Told in a direct, lucid style the story reads like an intriguing detective novel. Each page reveals new depths of thought—revelations that can serve us today if we are to survive the contemporary illusions of reality that are poisoning our souls."

Rudolfo Anaya, author of *Bless Me, Ultima* and *Tortuga*

"This gives me great hope, the dawning of insight. It is a very important book that at last brings the past to life and true relevance again—a pioneering effort in recovering the origins of our humanity and uncovering the source from which each of us springs."

David Appelbaum, author of *Everyday Spirits* and former editor of *Parabola*

by Peter Kingsley

Ancient Philosophy, Mystery and Magic

(Oxford University Press, 1995)

"Every scholar dreams of writing a truly original book, but in reality hardly anyone ever does. A truly original book, one that can transform a whole discipline, appears at the most once in a generation. In the field of ancient philosophy, Peter Kingsley's *Ancient Philosophy, Mystery and Magic* is such a book."

Prof. A. A. Long, University of California at Berkeley

"A masterpiece, gripping, urgent and important: a unique pioneering work."

European Review of History (Oxford/Paris)

"The thesis is argued with immense learning ... courageous, original."

The Times (London)

"Provides a storehouse of new insights ... compelling."

Gnosis (San Francisco, CA)

"*Ancient Philosophy, Mystery and Magic* is very readable and its snappy, almost breathless pace conveys the excitement of the exploration of a newly opened tomb. I cannot recommend this book too highly; it sets the terms for future investigations of ancient esotericism."

Caduceus (Seattle, WA)

"A remarkable achievement: challenging, learned and at the same time enthralling to read."

Classical Review (Oxford)

"Bold and extremely significant ... Kingsley's book may well be the most important book about Presocratic philosophy in years, and it is certainly one of the most exciting, challenging, and stimulating."

American Historical Review (Washington, DC)

"Extremely rich ... deals with topics of the utmost interest for the comparative student of religious phenomena in ancient societies. Dr Kingsley has put us all very much in his debt."

Numen (Leiden)

"Of great interest to students of Islamic thought, while being of an even greater significance for the field of Greek and Western philosophy, since it challenges the commonly held view of the whole foundation of Western philosophical thought."

Journal of Islamic Studies (Oxford)

PETER KINGSLEY works with the sacred tradition that gave birth to the western world. His revolutionary understanding of the history as well as the destiny of western civilization has changed many people on the deepest level — transforming their awareness not only of who they are but also of their purpose in the modern world. Recognized internationally for his groundbreaking work, and the recipient of numerous academic awards and honors, he lives with his wife Maria in North Carolina.

For further information visit
www.peterkingsley.org